Pop Modernism

POP
MODERNISM

Noise and
the Reinvention
of the Everyday

JUAN A. SUÁREZ

University of Illinois Press   URBANA AND CHICAGO

Library of Congress Cataloging-in-Publication Data

Suarez, Juan Antonio.

Pop modernism : noise and the reinvention of the everyday /

Juan A. Suarez.

p.   cm.

Includes bibliographical references (p.   ) and index.

ISBN-13: 978-0-252-03150-2 (cloth : alk. paper)

ISBN-10: 0-252-03150-4 (cloth : alk. paper)

ISBN-13: 978-0-252-07392-2 (pbk. : alk. paper)

ISBN-10: 0-252-07392-4 (pbk. : alk. paper)

1. American literature—20th century—History and criticism.

2. Modernism (Literature)—English-speaking countries.

3. Postmodernism (Literature)—English-speaking countries.

4. English literature—20th century—History and criticism.

5. Arts and society—United States—History—20th century.

6. Arts and society—England—History—20th century.

7. Popular culture—English-speaking countries—History—20th century.

8. Avant-garde (Aesthetics)—English-speaking countries.

9. Kitsch—English-speaking countries.

I. Title.

PS228.M63S83   2007

820.9'113—dc22   2006100941

In memory of Fernando Suárez Sánchez

Contents

Acknowledgments

Research grants from the J. F. Kennedy Institut für Nordamerika Studien at the Freie Universität-Berlin and from the University of Murcia allowed me to start on this project. At different stages I was assisted by the staff at the Kennedy Institut, the Biblioteca Nebrija (University of Murcia), the Library of Congress, the Purdue University Library, the Museum of Modern Art Film Study Center, and Columbia University. I owe very special thanks to Charles Silver at the Museum of Modern Art Film Study Center, and at Columbia I had the invaluable aid of David Moore at the Inter-Library Loan Office, Trevor Dawes, the former head of access, Kristina Rose at the Media Center, and the librarian Karen Greene. Research for chapter 6 was underwritten by Project BFF2003–00655; my thanks to Angeles de la Concha, head of this research project.

At a more personal level, I have received encouragement from many individuals, near and far: Jim Naremore and Barb Klinger assured me the project was interesting and have written countless letters of recommendation over the years. Chris Straayer invited me to teach a class at New York University while I was still writing this book. Lise Mote and Mike Boeglin were wonderfully hospitable during one crucial summer. Douglas Crimp, Laurence Erussard, Clara Calvo, Mª Dolores Martínez Reventós, José Antonio

Orero, Pedro Férez, Hilaria Loyo, Constanza del Río, and David Vilaseca have been great friends, and so has been Celestino Deleyto, who invited me to teach a graduate seminar at the University of Zaragoza that eventually evolved into this book. The annual conference of the Spanish Association for Anglo-American Studies provided a friendly forum where many of these ideas were first tried out. Jesús Benito, Ana Manzanas, and Aitor Ibárrola were kind and receptive since the early stages of the project, and A. Robert Lee was helpful on T. S. Eliot's accent. For help with illustrations I thank Robert Haller and Wendy Dorset at Anthology Film Archives, Judy Kwon at the Menil Foundation, the wonderfully efficient Susana Barrio at VEGAP Madrid, and, above all, Cecile Starr, who graciously lent me some production stills from *In the Street*. The many students that, over the years, have taken my classes at the University of Murcia have been captive but generally interested listeners. At the University of Illinois Press, I am indebted to my editor, Joan Catapano, for lending this book a friendly ear, and to the press's anonymous readers, for extremely helpful suggestions on an early version of the manuscript that contributed decisively to its final form. My parents, Juan Antonio and Maruja, my sister, Rosaura, and my American family, John and Roz Moore, have always been near. And David Moore has seen me through it all as our lives changed fast and furiously; he has given constant support and love.

Some sections of the book have appeared, in substantially different versions, in *Österreichische Zeitschrift für Geschichtswissenschaften* (2004); the *Journal of American Studies* 36.1 (2002); *New Literary History* 32.3 (2001); and Ana Manzanas and Jesús Benito, eds., *Narratives of Resistance: Literature and Ethnicity in the United States and the Caribbean* (Ciudad Real: Ediciones de la Universidad de Castilla–La Mancha, 1999).

Pop Modernism

Introduction
Modernism,
Popular Practice,
Noise

One of the lasting benefits of the euphoric celebration of the postmodern that took place in the early 1980s was a renewal in our understanding of modernism. Identified with television, cybernetics, 1960s "surfiction," and pop art, postmodernism was initially theorized as modernism's democratic offspring. While modernism had allegedly been elitist and disconnected from the social and material life of modernity, postmodernism entailed the fusion of high and low and allowed the entrance of minority and subcultural concerns into the artwork. While modernism had labored toward preserving the traditional functions of art and enforcing discrimination, postmodernism, we were told, learned from Las Vegas and the contemporary mediascape, annulling in the process the great divide that, in the view of many, had split the culture of modernity into two irreconcilable realms—avant-garde and kitsch, highbrow and lowbrow.[1]

1

It was soon apparent, however, that this sharp distinction between modernism and postmodernism rested on a partial conception of modernism—a conception that reduced the experimental ferment of the beginning of the twentieth century to a small canon and privileged the most self-reflexive moments in modern art. Gone from the picture were the alternative perspectives of women, queers, and artists from the peripheries; the fascination with machinery, fashion, and cities; and the modernist immersion in the pop life of the times. This reductive account drove a wedge between an elitist high modernism and the promiscuous, pop-oriented avant-gardes and ignored the existence of many overlaps between the two,[2] but it also simplified work of the canonical figures—from Stéphane Mallarmé to T. S. Eliot and Ezra Pound, Gertrude Stein to James Joyce, or Vincent van Gogh to Jackson Pollock. Their connections to modernity's material, sexual, political, and popular cultures, where they found much of their inspiration, were regarded as anomalies or marginalia that had little bearing on aesthetics. As a result, modernism appeared strangely disembodied and sublimated, unhinged from some of its most vital contexts.

As a host of intellectual attitudes invested in hybridity, alterity, peripheral perspectives, and in the critical power of the popular, postmodern critique allowed scholars to reembody and materialize modernism. One could say that postmodernism authorized the recasting of modernism as a cultural moment that foreshadowed contemporary interests—and therefore purveyed a more "usable past"—and that was more nuanced and contextualized than earlier cultural histories had envisioned. As a result, the "new modernisms" that emerged from a considerable number of studies[3] since the mid-1980s have revealed that, as Peter Wollen once put it, postmodernism was not a radical departure but the return of a number of modernist traits that had been suppressed from retrospective accounts.[4]

Particularly important among these traits is the embeddedness of modernism in popular culture. Modernism and popular culture were, in Theodor Adorno's words, "twin halves" of the culture of industrial modernity. While the full-fledged forms of modernism and popular culture arose nearly simultaneously in the early years of the twentieth century, their antecedents date back to the 1850s and the protomodernist work of Edouard Manet, Charles Baudelaire, Gustave Flaubert, Herman Melville, and Walt Whitman, and to the early forms of consumer culture, such as dime novels, penny papers, daguerreotypes, prints, chromolithographs, panoramas, dioramas, the first World Exhibitions, and the original department stores.[5] The first outbreaks of modernism were French impressionism and the Viennese Secession, but most of its early landmarks, including futurism, cubism, imagism, dada, and expressionism, belong to the years preceding World War I. This was a time when industrialized entertainment, disseminated by new electronic technologies, experienced an unprecedented expansion; when the portable photographic camera and the phonograph became household items; when the periodical press became more image-based than before; when advertising became more aggressive and pervasive; and when the boom of the nickelodeon turned the cinema from a fairground sideshow and technological curiosity to the dominant popular entertainment.[6]

Largely because they originated around the same time and developed alongside each other, modernism and mass culture had many structural similarities. Both were products of the machine age—of streamlining, mass production, and speed—yet maintained an ambiguous relationship with technology. They seemed to oppose what early twentieth-century critics in the United States called the genteel tradition, partly because of their stylistic novelty and partly because, as new public spheres, they often disseminated working-class and ethnic sensibilities. They were eminently urban and reflected the rhythms and heterogeneity of metropolitan life. And, in different ways, they were centrally concerned with commodities and consumption. Modernism and mass culture shared iconography, themes, and stylistic devices. Montage, for example, was the eminent cinematic device and a staple of modern aesthetics. The stylistic heterogeneity, fragmentation, and multi-perspectivism of modernism had a popular counterpart, if not a predecessor, in the quick succession of performances, genres, and media packed into vaudeville and variety shows. And excess and sensationalism were as likely to be found in freak shows, crime papers, and Keystone comedies as in futurist soirées, dadaist exhibitions, or surrealist games. These examples indicate that, as a number of scholars have shown and this book will further demonstrate, avant-garde and modernist aesthetics often arose from a selective appropriation of popular expressive forms. And conversely, as Miriam Bratu Hansen suggests, popular culture in modernity was already a form of "vernacular modernism," since many of its products—such as fashion, music, cinema, and advertising—gave expression to distinctly contemporary forms of sensibility and embodiment.[7] Hence, in the era of the electronic media and mass consumption, distinctions between high and low, experimental and mainstream, avant-garde and kitsch designate temporary positions in the cultural feedback loop rather than actual substantive differences. The point, to put it crudely, is not only that modernism learned from Coney Island, which it did, but that it often aspired to being a delirious amusement park, while Coney Island was already a modernism of sorts.[8]

The tight interpenetration of modernism and the popular, which has been excavated by numerous scholars in the last decade and a half, is the point of departure for the present book, which seeks to fill in some important gaps in our knowledge of high/low relations in the history of American modernism and to defamiliarize somewhat our conception of the workings of popular culture. The chapters that follow articulate the evolution of a pop-oriented modernism in the United States from the beginning of the twentieth century to the eve of pop art. In the process, they rescue a number of relatively neglected figures (Vachel Lindsay, Charles Henri Ford, Parker Tyler, and Helen Levitt) and genres (the city film, the modernist ethnography), and re-interpret central texts and authors (T. S. Eliot, Joseph Cornell, Charles Sheeler, Paul Strand, John Dos Passos, Zora Neale Hurston, and James Agee) with the overall purpose of rescuing forgotten concerns, histories, and webs of connection and influence. What emerges from my diachronic look is the enormous variability of modernism's engagement with the popular. This engagement evolved in tune with the changing definition of modernism, from its emergence in the early years of the century as part of an anti-Victorian front of innovation and rebellion, to its consolidation in the 1920s, to its reformulation as a political aesthetic in the 1930s, to its further mutation in the 1940s as a synthesis of a shrinking cultural front and a slightly deracinated experimentalism. Through these stages, modernism engaged an evolving mass culture that changed from predominantly live to predominantly pre-recorded entertainment, from small- to large-scale production units, and from amusement to propaganda, as, during the 1930s, it was often put to the service of explicit political agendas on the right and on the left. If in the early decades of the century, mass culture was seen by modernists as part of a vital reaction to a bloodless high tradition that seemed to have run its course, in the mid- to late 1930s it began to be increasingly conceptualized as a bureaucratic, totalitarian development that had lost its connection with spontaneous artistry and that threatened to impoverish the mental life of its users. This was the picture drawn in the eve of World War II by a number of intellectuals, including Dwight Macdonald, Clement Greenberg, Joseph T. Farrell, and John Dos Passos, whose selective characterizations of the popular, shaped by the pressures of a particular historical moment, had long-lasting influence well into the 1960s.

A historical perspective like the one offered here also reveals that modernism and popular culture were not substantive but strategic concepts subject to considerable variation and shifts of emphasis. Hence, the modernism of the experimental New York journal *The Soil* and the first city films, for example, opposed Victorianism and aligned itself with technology and industrial culture, while that of other authors rejected machine art and streamlined design and turned to myth (Lindsay, Eliot), nineteenth-century interiors and domestic art (Cornell), narrative realism (Dos Passos), or to the rural and preindustrial (Hurston, Agee). A similar range of variation appeared in the modernists' view of popular art, which they characterized, at different times, as dissident *and* complicit; democratic *and* totalitarian; slick and streamlined *but also* rough-edged and unpolished; new *and* expressive of ancient myths and timeless forces; ethnically and subculturally inflected *and* standardized; feminine *and* masculine; queer *and* straight. The point of the following pages is not to adjudicate among these competing definitions—they are all "true"—but to explore the functions they served at particular junctures, the alignments and negotiations they entailed, and the images and concepts they generated.

A second, and perhaps more specific, goal of this book is to show not only what a pop-indebted modernism was like but to inquire into how it worked, because it was all a matter of work—of intervention and transformation. What drove modernism toward the popular was not merely the desire to question cultural hierarchies and divides; it was also the urgent aspiration to reinvent the practice of everyday life in modernity. I will show that modernism was an art of users confronted with a new, at times overwhelming, material environment—the second nature of industrial capitalism. The main components of this environment were images, (city) spaces, and things—the three guiding threads in this study—and modernism was a form of productive consumption of these. It was thus what Michel de Certeau calls an *art de faire:* a plurality of modes of rerouting what hegemonic culture, through the media and the productive apparatus, handed down to consumers.[9] If modernity was characterized, in George Simmel's classic formulation, by "hypertrophy of the material spirit"—of the material environment, the world of things—then modernism was a way of doing something with this abundance of means.[10] In the process, it exposed and critiqued the limitations of everyday life while it simultaneously sought to escape them.

This double orientation, toward the critique of the quotidian and the attempt to transcend its limits, is central to the authors I study here, from Lindsay and Eliot to Agee and Levitt. But in their perspective, limits and means of transcendence were often one and the same thing. The modernists often regarded metropolitan environments, the iconography of the media, and mass-produced commodities as agents of oppression, but used creatively, they could open up emancipating styles of being and doing. In this way, modernists insistently addressed one of the central contradictions of modernity: the fact that the mass-production of everyday life ended up generating a fragmentary, leaky reality that was as inescapable as it was uncontrollable, a reality endowed with vastly increased possibilities for micrological manipulation at the level of daily tactics—consumption, the reception of images and sounds, the engagement with objects, and the uses of space. Trying to envision what the cybernetic society of the future might be like, de Certeau speculated in the mid-1970s: "One would thus have a proliferation of aleatory and indeterminable manipulations within an immense framework of socioeconomic constraints and securities: myriads of almost invisible movements, playing on the more and more refined texture of a place that is even, continuous, and constitutes a proper place for all people. Is this already the present or the future of the great city?"[11] But is this not also the great city's past since at least the second Industrial Revolution? And, furthermore, are not the myriad movements—"Brownian movements of invisible and innumerable tactics," as de Certeau calls them elsewhere—that make up the tissue of everyday life in the metropolitan environment the basis for what we call modernism?

What I propose, then, is that modernism is a form of everyday practice parallel to that of anonymous consumers everywhere. My view dovetails with earlier descriptions of modernism as a "minor" aesthetic (as Gilles Deleuze and Félix Guattari suggest) or a form of "dialectal" usage (according to Michael North) that frays and derails other—"major"—languages.[12] To this I want to add that its raw materials are frequently not linguistic and emphatically nonaesthetic—they may consist of commonplace things, gestures, ways of traversing or inhabiting locations, arts of looking and making visible. These materials do not always come from up high—national-official culture, the great tradition—but from the anonymity of the streets, movie theaters, amusement parks, department stores, and dance halls. Saving the differences stemming from modernism's institutional affiliations, artistic credentials, and self-reflective stance, what modern artists did with the landscape of modernity was structurally analogous to what ordinary people did as they went about their daily rounds. Popular practice was one of modernism's structuring influences, and experimental artists frequently drew on, recycled, or simply captured and captioned ready-made users' tactics and languages. Examples to be examined in this book include the queer street styles refashioned in Parker Tyler and Charles Henri Ford's novel *The Young and Evil;* the (often sinister) folk and amateur art published in the surrealist magazine *View;* the aesthetics of poverty described in James Agee's and Zora Neale Hurston's unorthodox ethnographies; the children's games and graffiti reproduced in Helen Levitt's photographs and in her film *In the Street,* made in collaboration with Agee and Janice Loeb. Popular ways of doing also inform Charles Sheeler and Paul Strand's experimental film *Manhatta,* which can be read as a form of spatial practice such as taking a stroll through the city; Vachel Lindsay's film theory, which seeks to harness the energies latent in popular spectatorship to civic purpose; T. S. Eliot's *The Waste Land,* essentially a D.J. session that treats the literary tradition as a sound archive to be manipulated by means of gramophone technology; and John Dos Passos's *USA* trilogy, which reworks hegemonic media languages to highlight their mendacity and absurdity.

I will further show that these forms of modernist manipulation radically defamiliarized the quotidian. They showed that neither the available media languages nor the materials of daily life were totally pliable and transparent; on the contrary, they were pitted with opacities and resistances and dragged in unsuspected connections and secret histories that could not be easily managed. Part of this instability was located in objects—which in modernity means the mass-manufactured products that glutted the daily horizon—and arose from what Bill Brown has memorably called "the secret life of things."[13] Far from inert, things contain memories, incarnate desires, and exist in times and rhythms that are irreducible to those of humans. Lindsay discovered this strange animation of the inorganic in the film image and devoted much of his film writing to bringing this unsettling undertow under control. Other authors, like Ford and Tyler, Cornell, Hurston, Agee, and Levitt, were equally aware of the liveliness of things, but unlike Lindsay, they pursued the destabilizing pull of the object; in this way they redrew the contours of the quotidian and questioned the closed conceptual systems that constricted it.

The pulses of quotidian otherness were also perceptible in the kaleidoscopic nature of the urban spectacle and in the cacophony of the media. Both functioned like random text generators that endlessly purveyed sights, sounds, assemblages, and connections in an infinite combinatory operation that had neither center nor direction and whose basic principles were chance and montage (both were also central in experimental art). In addition, modern cities and media were inscription surfaces on which the random transits, connections, and disjunctions of people and objects left traces that were often unreadable and impregnated the everyday with mystery. In their different ways, Lindsay's film writings, Strand and Sheeler's *Manhatta,* Dos Passos's *USA* novels, and, to a lesser extent, Eliot's *The Waste Land* sought to structure this otherness of the quotidian, but in the process, they ended up mimicking its functioning—its randomness and combinatory force—and thus testified to its inescapable nature. Contrarily, Cornell, Ford and Tyler, Hurston, and Agee, Levitt, and Loeb pursued it and amplified this otherness in their work.

Noise, in the cybernetic sense of nonsignifying matter, is another name for the otherness that modernism, as an art of practice, discovered in the heart of the quotidian. Modernism and the everyday life of modernity were actually full of noise: not only the clang of machinery and the din of traffic ("the sound of horns and motors") but also occurrences and recesses that simply refused to yield sense. The material cause of this ever-present opaque component was the analog media—sound recording machines, film, and photography—that were the hardware of modernity and of modernism. As they provided direct transpositions of the real, the media exemplified modernity's exploratory drive; they were used to increase the range of perception, the thresholds of visibility and audibility. Because of this, Walter Benjamin compared the media-based exploration of the quotidian with psychoanalysis: By studying the debris of language and daily behavior, he proposed, Freud discovered a subjective unconscious that punctuated conscious behavior and thought. Likewise, by means of a comparable "deepening of apperception," the camera—and, one could add, the sound media—discovered an "unconscious" of everyday life.[14] In Benjamin's essay, "The Work of Art in the Age of Mechanical Reproduction," the idea of a perceptual unconscious has positivistic overtones, as he claims that the "new structural formations" perceptible through the camera lens "extend our comprehension of the necessities which rule our lives" (236). But, as is the case with the Freudian unconscious, the unconscious of the quotidian is not completely readable or knowable; it also contains an obdurate material residue impregnable to interpretation. In a seldom-cited footnote, Benjamin shifts the emphasis away from knowledge and points out that "film is the first art form capable of demonstrating how matter plays tricks on man" (247)—of demonstrating, that is, how matter escapes human attempts to fully understand and reduce it. This happens because through their nondiscriminatory receptivity, technologies of electronic reproduction register the automatism of the world. They capture sense and nonsense and mix signifying matter with opaque traces and textures—an involuntary gesture, the distracting fold of a fabric, the grain of the voice. In this manner they convey not only information but also the stochastic disorder of bodies and things. Media/ted representation thus reveals an uncanny double of the quotidian—a shadow realm of meaninglessness and contingency alongside the intelligible. Relayed by the camera or the microphone, "reality" becomes pregnant with secrets, and the known constantly slips into the unknown.

These ideas define modernism's media/ted exploration of the everyday—its depiction of daily life as a realm that is at once knowable and enigmatic, predictable and contingent. These ideas were also at the core of surrealism; hence, I will be looking at American modernism through the lenses provided by this avant-garde formation. One of the surrealists' main contentions was that rationalization and standardization were not the only by-product of modernity; technological modernity brought about (in Max Weber's famous term) disenchantment but also allowed for the reenchantment and reinvention of the quotidian. The surrealists' use of film and photography and their writings on these media radically questioned the idea that information, standardization, and regimentation directly emanate from the use of the media. Surrealism showed that mechanical reproduction does not always discipline and simplify perception; it also enables the emergence of chaos and magic in the midst of the everyday. This insight was most programmatically advanced by the surrealists, but it was also shared by the French theorists of *photogenie* in the 1910s and 1920s; by critics such as Béla Balázs, Siegfried Kracauer, and Walter Benjamin in Weimar Germany; and, more recently, by Roland Barthes, Friedrich Kittler, and Michael Taussig, among others.[15] Analogous views on the reenchanting effect of the media on everyday life were developed in the United States during the early decades of the twentieth century by a number of modernist critics of film and photography, including Robert Alden Sanborn, Kenneth Macgowan, R. J. Coady, Vachel Lindsay, Parker Tyler, and James Agee, and by writers and artists such as Joseph Cornell, Zora Neale Hurston, and Helen Levitt. In some cases (such as Coady, Sanborn, Tyler, Cornell, Levitt, and Agee) it is possible to spot a direct influence from the French avant-garde; in others (such as Linsdsay, Macgowan, and Hurston) the connections may be merely coincidental. In any case, the wide spread of these views suggests that the surrealists may simply have formalized a distinctly modernist way of understanding the effect of the media. Their perceptions were probably part of a larger modernist idiom and can therefore be extrapolated to the work of writers and media producers not directly linked with this movement, and this is one of the things I do here. I have sought to renew our perception of figures such as Lindsay, Sheeler, Strand, Eliot, Dos Passos, Hurston, and Agee by showing that their work can be profitably navigated by using a surrealist compass. And in the cases of Tyler and Ford, Cornell, and Levitt, whose work has already been associated with surrealism, I have nuanced or substantiated more fully this association. Overall, I have attempted to supplement existing historical characterizations and to flesh out connections between the body of work I study in these pages and a set of ideas that exerted considerable influence in their cultural moment.

The presence of noise in modern textuality—it got louder the more directly modernism tackled the everyday—confirms Friedrich Kittler's insight, developed at length in his *Discourse Networks, 1800/1900,* that the most distinctive feature of modern art may be the pervasiveness of the unsignifiable, not as the outside of sense but as its constitutive support and inevitable shadow. After the machine was there to register it, and after cultural production was done exclusively with or alongside machines, it was harder to keep out the racket. Deleuze and Guattari have pointed out the pervasiveness of noise in Franz Kafka's writing: "[U]nformed material of expression," intense, "monotone, and always nonsignifying."[16] Similar noise can be discerned through the texts I study, and this book is an attempt to pick up this pervasive vibration. If, as Bill Brown has suggested, modernism was a way of doing things with things, it was also a way of doing things with noise, of making noise with things.[17] Hence the radical break between previous artistic regimes and modernism might then be that modernism unfolded in the shadow of what Jacques Lacan calls the unsymbolizable real, or noise. And the real, once more, was registered by the media—automatic recorders-transmitters, external memory devices—that did not allow the world to stop writing itself and that put it all down and made it available for disconcerted perusal.[18]

Like the real, which in Lacan's famous formula always returns to its place—the real is, in fact, what returns—unformalizable "noise" insistently recurs in modernist text generation. It is always the background murmur that the more traditionalist modernists (Lindsay, Sheeler, Strand, Dos Passos) tried to subdue, while others gave it ample play. One way or another, it is always there, often in images of dissolution, of disorder, of an abyss that yawns behind identity and culture, those precariously pinned defenses. Take queerness in Tyler and Ford's novel *The Young and Evil;* or Haitian popular life and religion in Hurston's account; or children's street games in Levitt, Agee, and Loeb's *In the Street:* they all circle around a sublimity that acts as vanishing point and vortex; that simultaneously organizes and scrambles perspective. Most often the unsymbolizable takes the form of irreducible enigmas—"stains" in the picture—that solicit attention without yielding sense. This is what Eliot conveyed in his early poetry, full of fragments and unaccountable moments; what Cornell sought to produce in his objects, films, and assemblages; what Agee spotted in daily life and popular film; and what Levitt and Loeb captured in the teeming streets of working-class districts.

Yet noise is perceptible as well in the specters of madness and breakdown that weave their way through this book and haunt the artists and works I discuss. There is a touch of insanity in Lindsay's visions of "the prophets" hovering in the sky; in Eliot's early poetry, a product of shattered nerves and psychotherapy; in the voices, lights, and nineteenth-century ballerinas that populated Cornell's reveries; in the zombies and indefinable threats that Hurston confronted in her voodoo studies; and in the drink and depression that punctuated Agee's short, fractured life. After all, mental breakdown is the result of sensory overload, and madness is the perception-consciousness apparatus working on fast-forward, pursuing connections, chance, and inarticulate matter for their own sake, disregarding sense and the protocols of restraint that define the socialized subject. When this is not madness, it is modernism, but it is not easy to tell them apart. As Kittler reminds us, in the discourse network of 1900, pathology and (aesthetic) experiment become nearly indistinguishable, and text generation is "a simulacrum of madness," "delirium protected from the loss of the word."[19] (And how about delirium as a research method? One of the goals of Benjamin's *Arcades Project* was "to cultivate fields where, until now, only madness has reigned."[20])

Noise was not only an important component of the modern everyday but also of popular culture—whether rural folklore, children's street games, the practices of urban subcultures, or electronically relayed images and sounds. In all its modalities, the popular is traversed with contingency, and the modernist engagement with the popular consistently revolved around it. Modernism showed that popular practice does not only trade in meanings but also in intangibilities and opaque affect; it is not only message but (to resuscitate Marshall McLuhan's terminology), above all, massage. Its seductiveness lies only partly in (ideological) content. It is just as important to take into account the way the media and popular ways of doing and seeing move our bodies and stimulate our sensorium. As an example, Miriam Bratu Hansen attributes Hollywood's international spread to this mode of nonverbal stimulation, and she explicitly follows the clues scattered in the surrealist writings on film: "I take [the statements of surrealists describing the cinema's defamiliarization of everyday life] to suggest that the reflexive, modernist dimension of American cinema does not necessarily require that we demonstrate a cognitive, compensatory, or therapeutic function in relation to the experience of modernity but that, in a very basic sense, even the most ordinary commercial films were involved in producing a new sensory culture."[21] The new sensory culture contributed to reshape the physignomy of the quotidian. This, however, is not always a cartographable physiognomy; it contains obscurely intuited possibilities that are often more effectively utopian the more obscure they remain. It might be this opacity of popular artifacts that keeps us coming back for more. Take Elvis, for example: in Greil Marcus's account, much of what he did, especially in the early Sun Studio recordings, cannot be figured out; it shades off into "a cultural wilderness, unmapped and untamed. . . . Just what was it that he did? Where was the formula?"[22] Because we cannot answer with any certainty, we are still caught in the spell. But isn't this opacity the raw material of film and music cults, of cinephilia, of the plural—and often incommunicable—enthusiasms of the fan? At the center of all these pop infatuations, isn't there an obscure insistence that all the trivia knowledge in the world, all the critical study, all the traffic in memorabilia, and all the pilgrimages to the hallowed sites cannot contain? And if the secret could be cracked, a final meaning delivered, would we keep revolving around it?

And what to do with this knowledge? How can we put it to work? As a plea for mysticism and irrationality in cultural studies? In modernism studies? As another stand against interpretation? As I see it, the point is not to eschew critical discourse. There is a lot of it, and a lot of interpretation, in what follows because these opaque stains in the surface of modern textuality delineate a sort of unconscious that demands to be read, even as it hides its tracks. These stains are often markers of subterranean histories and knowledges that were not clearly articulated in the past but might be more readable from our present, as the dimly understood energies of an earlier era reemerge in more recognizable configurations. (A quotation compiled by Benjamin in the *Arcades Project*: "The past has left images of itself in literary texts, images comparable to those which are imprinted by light on a photo-sensitive plate. The future alone possesses developers active enough to scan such surfaces perfectly."[23]) From a different perspective, we could also regard these stains as akin to the absolute contingencies with which temporality, according to Benjamin, "sears" the photograph. These stains are marks of the historicity of the texts under study: moments that once made sense but no longer do; fossilized bits of lived life; messages whose code we have lost but may still retrieve (partially, gropingly) by means of archeological work. The point in this retrieval is to resuscitate the political promises these fragments once contained for the way in which they may illuminate our present—and signal ways out of it. But in addition, these opaque stains remain accretions of formless substance whose incommensurable affect should be allowed to resonate alongside (conventionally understood) cultural sense.

The goal, then, is to take critical and historical analyses as far as they can go, accompanying or supplementing them with what Michael Taussig, inspired by Benjamin and Adorno, calls a "sensuous knowledge," a knowledge that adheres to "the skin of things" and "disconcerts and entrances by spinning off into fantastic formations."[24] Taussig has suggested that the purpose of critical discourse should be to explain the object of study while preserving its "*graphicness*": "to penetrate the veil while retaining its hallucinatory quality."[25] This is partly an ethical decision, based on respect for the absolute particularity of the world and of others. The happiness of philosophy, Adorno proposes, resides in resisting the imperialism of instrumental reason, or refusing to annex what is alien by means of abstract thought. Thought should capture the object but also allow itself to be caught by it and yield to the concreteness of things. Such a mode of knowing is profoundly ethical, but it contains a political wager as well. Sensuous knowledge preserves the force of "the somatic moment" without reducing it to a fact of consciousness.[26] And the somatic, obdurate and inarticulate as it might be, provides significant leverage for transformation, as popular culture has always shown. Merely conceptual knowledge only goes so far. Reality might begin to transcend itself, in Benjamin's words, "only when in technology body and image so interpenetrate that all revolutionary tension becomes bodily collective innervation, and all the bodily innervations of the collective become revolutionary discharge."[27] By analogy, one could speculate that only when the critical-historical investigation of the past is stirred by somatic pulses and punctuated by affect might it liberate the energies needed to reinvent the present and, perhaps, emancipate the future.

■ ■ ■ ■ ■

The eight chapters that follow do not make up a linear, homogeneous history; they present the material in the form of constellations centered on a particular text or artistic formation. They are fairly self-contained and can be read in any order, but since their arrangement is roughly chronological, sequential reading may have the advantage of showing the transformation of given preoccupations and motifs through the diachronic evolution of modernism. They are grouped in three sections: the first, "Noise Abatement," studies authors who registered but tried to suppress the otherness of modern material culture and life. Chapter 1 discusses Vachel Lindsay's film criticism as an early attempt to manage the crisis in perception introduced by the cinema—in many ways the main embodiment of modern visual culture. While the cinema's fragmentariness, its enhancement of objects, and its association with speed furthered modern disintegration, the medium could also order the quotidian, as Lindsay recommends, by offering spectators legible, monumental spaces and modern mythologies. Chapter 2 studies Paul Strand and Charles Sheeler's film *Manhatta,* the first significant title in the history of American avant-garde cinema, and explores the film's ambiguous depiction of metropolitan street life: while it gestures toward the city's inapprehensible plurality, its dominant tendency is to reduce it to a series of linear patterns and shapes. Chapter 3 studies the portrayal of the media in John Dos Passos's trilogy *USA,* one of the summits of 1930s social realism. It analyzes Dos Passos's representation of the noise of the media and his attempts to suppress this noise by means of realistic narration, historical reference, and popular speech. The chapter contrasts Dos Passos's pessimistic characterization of the media with the more optimistic views of his leftist contemporaries.

Section II, "The Rustle of the Quotidian," studies two modernists who sought to dwell in the midst of modern noise, much as they often disliked it. Noise is understood as a literal aural assault in the case of T. S. Eliot, or, in a more figurative sense, as the enigmatic pulses of things in the case of Joseph Cornell. Questioning the centrality of the visual in discussions of modernity and modernism, chapter 4 explores the effect of the voice media on modernist writing and, more specifically, the influence of gramophone technology, noise, and popular music on Eliot's *The Waste Land.* Chapter 5 reads the work of the surrealist Joseph Cornell as an exploration of "object automatism"—the latencies and histories buried in objects and mass-cultural artifacts—by means of filmic and photographic processes such as framing and montage.

In section III, "The Murmur of Otherness," the estrangement of the everyday is brought about by the peripheral subjects present in queer modernism and in a number of modernist ethnographies. Chapter 6 analyzes the convergence of experimentalism, sexual dissidence, and street practice in Charles Demuth's and Paul Cadmus's paintings, in George Platt-Lynes's photographs, and, especially, in Charles Henri Ford and Parker Tyler's novel, *The Young and Evil*. Chapter 7 explores Zora Neale Hurston's study of Haitian popular life and religion, *Tell My Horse*, and shows that Hurston discovers a disturbing undertow of death and violence at the heart of everyday life. Her interest in these forces of cultural negativity translated into a distinctively modernist style of writing and filming ethnography—one that tried not only to explain the culture under study but also to convey its opacities and indeterminacies. Chapter 8 studies Helen Levitt, Janice Loeb, and James Agee's experimental film *In the Street* as a combination of 1930s documentarism and 1940s New York surrealism. In addition to being an exponent of Levitt's style and concerns, the film was shaped by the peculiar view of the popular advanced in Agee's film criticism and in the surrealist periodical *View*. *In the Street* locates in children's games and the life of city streets opacities similar to those Hurston detects in Haitian popular life. The film looks back to the surrealists' manner of inhabiting the city, but its valuation of street life also anticipates later experimental formations such as junk and installation art, minimalist dance, Beat literature, and the underground cinema.

Assemblage, pop, minimalism, and the underground are usually regarded as exponents of a new cultural logic that we have been calling postmodern for several decades. Yet modernism seems to have always been postmodern, and the postmodern seems to be the intensification of some formerly marginalized modernist traits rather than a substantially new logic. The difference between the two may be a matter of tempo and scale or degree of self-reflexivity rather than of quality. With this I do not intend to refute the existence of postmodernism, or to reject a term that still has heuristic value; I only want to stress the relevance of a number of modernisms that still have much to teach us about our present ecology of images, bodies, pleasures, and spaces.

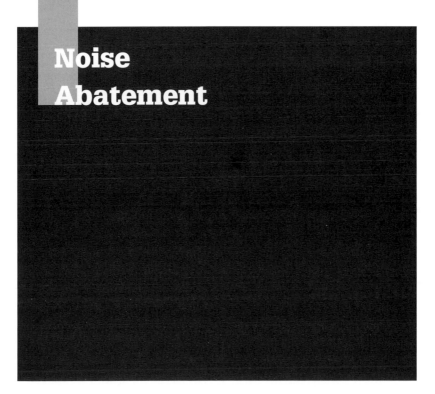

Noise
Abatement

1 Reading Modernity

Vachel Lindsay's
Theory of Film

Vachel Lindsay was one of the first modernists to grant popular culture serious consideration and to explore the way in which media images shaped the modern everyday. Born in Springfield, Illinois, in 1879, he trained as a painter in Chicago and New York before he turned to writing. He first gained fame as a representative of the "new poetry" with such pieces as "General William Booth Enters into Heaven" and "The Congo." He belongs to the renaissance of the early 1910s, the wave of cultural innovation and social radicalism that brought about the first experimental galleries and theater troupes, the "little magazines," Greenwich Village bohemia, the vogue of feminism and Wobbly anarchism, the Patterson Strike Pageant, and the Armory Show, which popularized European modernist art in the United States. These developments coincided with the onset of what Lindsay famously called a "hieroglyphic civilization," an environment completely dominated by the mass-reproduced image, disseminated through billboards, illustrated maga-zines, photographs, and films. Lindsay found much inspiration in this new environment. Rejecting the romantic view of the poet as an isolated indi-vidual who recollects emotion in tranquility, he immersed himself in city life and popular entertainment, and, as he once wrote to a friend, he composed most of his work "not by listening to the inner voice and following the gleam—but by pounding the table with a ruler and looking out at the elec-tric sign [and] going to Vaudeville."[1] His poetry paid homage to movie stars like John Bunny and Mae Marsh and to the spectacle of urban modernity; it was often modeled on the beat of popular tunes, written in the syncopated rhythms of ragtime and delivered, during his massively attended reading tours, in an emphatic style he liked to call "higher vaudeville." At the same time, his modern enthusiasms were tempered by his devotion to small-town values and midwestern agrarianism, his respect for religion, and his nostal-gia for the lost order of Victorian times.

This ambiguity affected Lindsay's view of film, the medium that, for him, best reflected the characteristics of modernity. His book *The Art of the Moving Picture* (1915) was the first extended treatment of cinema from an aesthetic perspective to be published in the United States. It made him a celebrated expert; his views were frequently solicited by some of the main journals of the day, such as the *New Republic,* and he was courted by D. W. Griffith and the stage designer Gordon Craig.[2] However, his success was short-lived. The book was revised and reissued in 1922, but Lindsay quickly fell out of favor with the public and the intellectuals. A lengthy follow-up project, tentatively titled "The Best Movies Now Running," was never pub-lished during his lifetime, victim to Lindsay's inability to interest editors in this work and to a deteriorating mental condition that made sustained intellectual effort difficult.[3]

As a consequence of this quick eclipse, Lindsay's idiosyncratic work re-mained ignored by subsequent generations of film critics and theorists. *The Art of the Moving Picture* predated the attempts of little magazines such as *The Soil, The Seven Arts, Broom, Contact,* or *The Dial* to establish a dialogue between modernism and popular culture, yet these publications did not pay Lindsay much attention. Lindsay's most felicitous coinage, the notion of mo-dernity as an eminently visual "hieroglyphic civilization," still has currency among cultural historians of early twentieth-century America, yet thorough discussion of his work is rare.[4] The neglect is, to an extent, understandable. Unlike such early theorists as Hugo Muensterberg, Siegfried Kracauer, or

Rudolf Arnheim, for example, he is a fairly unsystematic thinker whose ideas are formulated as loosely strung opinions in peculiar poetic language. And yet, there is a subterranean logic to his arguments, one he shares with a number of contemporaries who sought to clarify the specificity and effect of the new media.

In-depth discussion of Lindsay's film writing began in the early 1970s, when Glenn J. Wolfe and Myron Lounsbury provided detailed glosses of *The Art of the Moving Picture*. It has continued in more recent decades with analyses by Nick Browne, Laurence Goldstein, Rachel O. Moore, and Miriam Hansen.[5] Wolfe explores the parallels between Lindsay's characterization of film as a hieroglyphic language and Eisenstein's fascination with Chinese ideograms; Lounsbury frames Lindsay's theory within the revolt of Progressive-era intellectuals against Victorian gentility. In a book that analyzes the reactions of American poets to the movies, Goldstein focuses on Lindsay's idealization of female stars as icons of Madonna-like purity that would have an ordering effect on society.[6] Moore studies Lindsay's film work as an example of a widespread tendency among early film theorists to associate the cinema with magic, ritual, and premodern thought.[7] Browne and Hansen focus on the parallels between Lindsay's theory and the evolution of the commercial cinema of his time.[8] Browne sees Lindsay's resort to hieroglyphics as an example of orientalism and exposes how the industry used references to the Orient to underline the universal appeal of film just as film was being defended as a means to Americanize recent immigrants and therefore to monitor otherness. Hansen links Lindsay's views to contemporary characterizations of film as a universal figural language promising a post-print, post-Babel utopia and shows how this dream, shared by Lindsay and the industry alike, was being fulfilled around the time his study came out by the language of the classical narrative cinema.[9]

Cumulatively, these discussions build up a complex view of Lindsay's theory and its relationship with his times, yet they tend to remain confined to the realm of film. They fail to address the fact that his views of film do not simply obey the logic or history of the medium. A broader, more finely contextualized approach is needed to explore what is most distinctive about Lindsay's thought and also the continuities between his theories and those of contemporaries who shared many of his concerns. I will show in this chapter that Lindsay's ideas about the cinema stem directly from his conception of modernity as a milieu of perceptual scattering and shock, dominated by unanchored visual stimuli and floating signs and driven by unprecedented speed. It was also an environment in which objects became humanized and harbored unsuspected latencies. With its emphasis on visuality, its fragmentary form, its rapid pace, and its defamiliarization of the world of objects, the cinema replicated the experience of modernity in condensed form. Its intrinsic functioning tended to increase the strangeness of the material world and the speed of contemporary life, and therefore to add up to the confusion of a world without center, guarantees of order, or sense. Yet at the same time, the cinema could be used as an ordering agent that might provide readable visual symbols, clearly delineated spaces, and mythic narratives capable of harnessing communal aspirations and fantasies.

Seen within this wider conceptual matrix, Lindsay's defense of formal (and, as we will see, social) uniformity appears as an anxious response to what he saw as the incoherent modern milieu and the disintegrating potential of film. It was a response, however, that ended up confirming the strength of those forces he sought to neutralize. While his overt purpose was to distil civic qualities from the messy outgrowth of the popular and to recruit the cinema for the goals of traditional high culture, in the end, his analysis of the image speaks of hybridity, complexity, and promiscuity and re-creates the unmanageability of objects and the vectors of acceleration that inform commercial culture and everyday life. Despite his conservative agenda, many of his formulations resonate with the ideas of Siegfried Kracauer and Walter Benjamin, who also explained film as a reorientation of perception brought about by industrial technology, and he also coincided with some sectors of the interwar film avant-garde in placing at the center of the cinema the experiences of speed and disorientation before the world of things. Lindsay sought the eradication of these experiences, while avant-garde filmmakers and critics mined them to produce alternative figurations of desire, sociality, and subjectivity—to produce, in sum, a renewal of the quotidian. In any case, they all perceived a connection between the feeling of disorientation or mythic wholeness one experiences in front of the screen and the delineation of everyday life.

Taxonomy

Lindsay's interest in the cinema is an extension of his fine-arts education. Early in *The Art of the Moving Picture,* he states that "[t]he motion picture is a great high art, not a process of commercial manufacture," and it therefore needed what the established arts already had: a vocabulary, a set of concepts to evaluate individual works and the general progress of the medium, and "a policy."[10] This was all the more pressing since in modernity the image had displaced print as the main vehicle of communication. "A tribe that has thought in words since the days that it worshipped Thor and told legends of the cunning of the tongue of Loki, suddenly begins to think in pictures" (*A* 213). And elsewhere: "We think in pictures if we think at all" (*P* 242). Like many of his contemporaries, Lindsay considered Thomas Edison a contemporary Gutenberg, the artificer of a media revolution that called for new forms of literacy (*A* 252). Lindsay's film theory was an attempt to clarify modernity and its social languages. In this respect, it is related to such works as Walter Lippmann's *Public Opinion* (1922), Robert Park and Ernest Burgess's *Introduction to the Science of Sociology* (1921), or the collective volume *Civilization in the United States* (1923), edited by Harold Stearns, all of which appeared around the same time as the second edition of *The Art of the Moving Picture*.[11]

Lindsay starts his first film book with a taxonomy of film genres. He sidesteps the early nonnarrative cinema (panoramas and actualities) and applies himself to the output of the nickelodeon era, which he idiosyncratically divides into "photoplays of action," "intimate photoplays," and "photoplays of splendor." These categories are not mutually exclusive and often combine in individual titles. Action films are symptomatic of the accelerated tempo and mechanization of contemporary life (*A* 38). "Intimate photoplays" are devoted to psychological characterization and indoor drama—to "the half-relaxed or gently restrained moods of human creatures" (*A* 49). They usually take place indoors, and their main formal device is the close-up (*A* 47, 49). The picture of "splendor" is a less coherent category. It includes films where spectacle, or "attraction" (Tom Gunning's term), takes precedence over narrative or character development.[12] This category is subdivided into pictures of "fairy splendor," "crowd splendor," "patriotic splendor," and "religious splendor," depending on whether the spectacle stems from film tricks, mass scenes, or scenes of patriotic or religious exaltation. Based on the ability of trick photography to animate inanimate objects, the picture of fairy splendor also practices the close-range visual exploration typical of the "intimate photoplay." But while the "intimate" picture dwells on faces and gestures, the trick film explores the realm of objects. Both genres offer a surgical examination of everyday materiality that the German philosopher Ernst Bloch calls a "micrology of nearness" (*Mikrologie des Nebenbei*) and that Bloch's friend and contemporary Walter Benjamin relates to an "unconscious optics."[13] The focus on quotidian textures and the use of close-ups contrasts with the epic sweep and monumentality of the other pictures of "splendor," which depend for their effect on the long shot. Rather than dive into the concrete, they visualize concepts such as "nation" or "community" by means of mass scenes. The picture of religious splendor, in addition, may give sensual form to prophecies, trances, and spiritual forces ("the unseen powers of the air"), bringing them closer to the imagination of spectators. Lindsay further establishes a series of parallels between his film genres and traditional artistic media. He relates the action film to sculpture, the intimate film to painting, the trick film to the fairy tale, and the spectacle film to architecture.

For all the apparent offhandedness, there is an underlying logic in this sequence of genres. They go from concrete to abstract and from character- to community-centered. The arrangement also evinces a sense of teleology. While the earlier genres purvey mindless pleasures, films with patriotic and religious subjects best fulfill the social mission of the medium, as they provide images of cohesiveness that counter a scattered material horizon and a fragmented polity. This teleology may be folded into the historical evolution of the cinema. The chronologically earlier "chase films" and "trick films," with their looser, episodic narratives and their emphasis on spectacular display, evoke the aesthetics of early cinema and the historical connection between film and fairground attractions, while "films of splendor" are representative of the industry's attempt, starting in the early 1910s, to endow its output with cultural respectability. Hence another implicit axis in the sequence spans from least to most artistically reputable genres, or, what is the same for Lindsay, from residual preclassical to emergent classical narrative film.

Objects, Speed, Distraction

But these are our terms, not Lindsay's. The fundamental difference he establishes is between films that emphasize fragmentation and those that unify the disparate into new (mythic) wholes; or, to put it differently, between films that reflect and therefore abet modernity's disorder and films that seek to correct it. In any case, there was no doubt for him that modernity was a confusing environment, a scrambled inventory of images and objects—and of images as objects, since, thanks to mechanical reproduction, images are discrete, material, portable, and susceptible to combination and manipulation: "The cartoons of Darling, the advertisements in the back of the magazines and on the bill-boards and in the street-cars, the acres of photographies [*sic*] in the Sunday newspapers make us into a hieroglyphic civilization closer to Egypt than to England" (*A* 22). Film and photography certainly played an important part in the transformation of collective life into a hieroglyphic environment, but so did other developments, two of which are evoked in Lindsay's quotation: the chromolithograph and the illustrated magazines.

Chromolithographs were the immediate predecessors of billboards and posters. They were mass-produced, glossy color pictures that became immensely popular after the Civil War. Together with the dime novels and the penny papers, they constituted the main form of mass culture in the nineteenth century.[14] Many fell under Clement Greenberg's category of "kitsch"; others were reproductions of well-known museum pictures, which could now be enjoyed by a large sector of the public. They were first used as home decorations, yet in the late decades of the century, chromolithographs began to appear as large-scale advertising images, thus advancing the colonization of everyday life by the mechanically reproduced image and the consequent fragmentation of the visual continuum. In this they were aided by other forms of spectacle: the cinema, the World's Fairs, and the popular press.

The popular press became predominantly image-centered around the 1890s. New inks, paper types, and printing techniques (such as zinc etching, mentioned by Lindsay in his second film book [*P* 182]) allowed the cheap reproduction of black-and-white photographs and color illustrations and brought about the first generation of glossy magazines (*McClure's,* the *World's Work,* the *Saturday Evening Post,* and *Ladies' Home Journal*). Pictorialism and gloss came by the hand of a revolution in reading described by the historian Christopher Wilson as "the demise of the gentle reader" and the emergence of the consumption-driven page skimmer.[15] Magazines promoted this shift as they shortened their items, directed readers' attention more forcefully, simplified and sharpened their style, shifted their focus from literature to information, and interspersed regular writing and imaged-based advertisement. According to Lindsay, "*The Saturday Evening Post* is nothing but a condensed billboard, the stories and the editorials being about a third of the journal, and the rest advertising" (*P* 183). Traditionally a means of cultivation and contemplation, reading was refashioned by the glossies into an activity halfway between window shopping and a crash course on current issues. Reading became more product- than process-oriented, and product orientation was often clinched by images, functioning as visual anchors for a report, an article, or an advertisement. For the Chicago sociologist Robert Park a consequence of this was that people tended to think more and more in "concrete images, anecdotes, pictures, and parables." The main exponents of this leaning toward concrete images and objects were the Sunday papers, whose success contributed to the rise of the department store.[16] The newspaper was an advertisement vehicle for the commodities available at the stores, and both store and paper were exorbitant compendiums of the messy object world and sought to engage the desire of the viewer by means of enticing visual displays. In these respects, they anticipated the cinema. In Lindsay's second film book, *The Poetry and Progress of the Movies,* the department store, with its senseless accumulation, often appears as a metaphor for the bad film, the one that offers "heaped-up material merely bought and paid for, the loot of a robbed civilization" rather than "the well-organized splendor of a growing culture" (*P* 184). Yet, with typical ambiguity, the department store also has positive connotations as shorthand for the seductive lavishness of American cinema, as opposed to the "tightwad habits" and "economy" of European productions (*P* 138).

The cinema contributed greatly to the senseless heap of modernity. As Lindsay often pointed out, the distinctiveness of the medium lay in its ability to fragment the world into discrete images (which he often called hieroglyphs) and to recombine these at will. The problem was that the fragments served on screen were not always subordinate to a unitary design; they had a way of escaping the centripetal pull of the text and of increasing the disorder of a world in pieces. Film tended to dwarf or to objectify humans, turning them into "dolls" and automatons, and to humanize objects, granting them agency and personality (*A* 53, 161, 189–90). In addition, it often portrayed speedy motion, increasing the disconnected quality of modern experience and the fleetingness of its meanings.

These effects were most evident in what Lindsay labels action, intimate, and trick films. Based on chases, coincidences, and frantic transitions, action films revealed the connection between the cinema and the modern cult of speed. "The hurdle race," Lindsay states in *The Art of the Moving Picture,* "is the fundamental movie plot and all others derive from it" (*A* 36–44). And in his posthumously published book of the 1920s, he writes: "None of us has perhaps realized how closely akin is the motion picture to the all-conquering Ford car" (*P* 235). For Lindsay, as for a number of subsequent film theorists and historians, filmic pleasure derives to a great extent from the enjoyment of movement and, more concretely, from the bodily sensations and optical distortions afforded by mechanical transport—trains, cars, fairground rides, and elevators.[17] The idea makes perfect historical sense: the Lumière brothers had already paid homage to railway journeying, and one of the main prenickelodeon genres was the travel film, which showed panoramas taken from moving boats, balloons, and especially trains. The theater chain Hale's Tours made this genre its staple. To heighten the connection between spectatorship and travel, the interiors of Hale's theaters were built to resemble a train compartment, the ushers were dressed as conductors, and the screen stood for the view from the front of the engine or from the observation platform in the rear. The illusion was clinched with sound effects (whistles, hisses, and clatter) and with the swaying motion of the seats.[18] The connection between film watching and movement has survived in later narrative film, especially in action and adventure genres, as well as in other forms of popular culture. Speed, simulated or real, remains an important component of contemporary popular cinema as well as of video and computer games, skateboarding, risk sports, and dance—all of which have developed synergical connections with film. But the association between cinema and speed is not only a matter of historical antecedents or peripheral links. Film viewing always provides a form of virtual transit. It grants a symbolic triumph over matter in the weightlessness of the spectator, who is transported across vast distances by the image and spared dead, empty time by virtue of the editing and the fast-paced plot. Simultaneously, and here is where Lindsay disapproves, matter returns in the way displacement intensifies bodily sensation and attenuates reflective consciousness.[19]

The pleasure of movement arises from placelessness, dehumanization, and scattering.[20] Going beyond much contemporary theory, which has tended to locate cinematic pleasure in the way commercial cinema centers spectators ideologically and cements social identities, Lindsay shrewdly acknowledges another important source of enjoyment: the experience of destabilization attached to speed.[21] But for him, this type of amusement is unseemly, carnivalesque, attached to the bodily substratum. It is part of the medium's early history and occasionally erupts through the interstices of the more reputable films, threatening to dissolve their organic unity and to distract spectators from the purported message and aesthetic wholeness. When this happens, the consequent "jumping," "twitching," and "sharp edges" result in distorted and distorting texts—"galvanized and ogling corpses," "misplaced figures of the order Frankenstein"—that affront the spectators' morals and rack their nervous systems (*A* 41). The intoxicating enervation produced by the filmed image adds to that of factory work, mechanization, metropolitan life, and the increased tempo of existence.

In a way, Lindsay's dislike of speed was prefigured in the long walking journeys he undertook in 1906 and 1908, during which he avoided motorways and railroads and stuck instead to back roads and country lanes, but it was not fully articulated until the mid-1920s in his posthumously published film book.[22] In it he connects the success of the prewar action film to the reigning optimism about technological progress and to the fashionable advocacy of "the strenuous life." After World War I, however, it became harder to romanticize speed, energy, and their technological supports without recalling their destructive effect in the European battlefields. The main task after the catastrophe was "to rebuild the brain and fancy of mankind" from the ground up, starting with fairy tales: "Beginning again, we must begin as children" (*P* 174). This is precisely why *The Thief of Bagdad,* the Douglas Fairbanks's vehicle directed by Raoul Walsh in 1924, became one of Lindsay's fetish texts. Its lively pace and its adventure plot, set in a number of distant locations, maintained the excitement of the hurdle race, but at the same time, its orderly form and fantasy tempered the irrational pleasures of speed. These qualities made Fairbanks's movie an important corrective to much of 1920s popular culture, which was still caught up in a mindless cult of velocity. Contemporary films, in particular, often recalled the manic pace of the Sennett chase and turned the mind into "a circus gone wrong . . . not harmonized by a manager with a sense of color, or form, or reason" (*P* 183). When this happened, the cinema approximated jazz, which in Lindsay's second book condensed everything dissonant and destructive in contemporary culture: "the dirty dance" and "hysteria" (that is, uncontrolled female sexuality, the flapper [*P* 368]), surface, clock time, and "glaring light." Its antidotes were ordering female presences, hieroglyphics (whose tidy symbolism should promote spirituality), depth, "eternity" (as he calls the epiphanic perception of the past in the present), and "indirect lighting" (the "light of romance" that pervades fairy tales and reveals the true essences of things).[23]

If the photoplays of action revel in speed and bodily sensation, intimate photoplays and trick pictures portray the unruly complexity of the object world. These genres exploit the cinema's ability to give objects and body parts human qualities and to turn humans into things. "Now the mechanical or non-human object . . . is apt to be the hero in most any sort of photoplay while the producer remains utterly unconscious of the fact. Why not face this idiosyncrasy of the camera and make the non-human object the hero indeed?" (*A* 63). And later: "I have said that it is a quality, not a defect, of the photoplay that while the actors tend to become types and hieroglyphics and dolls, on the other hand, dolls and hieroglyphics and mechanisms tend to become human. By an extension of this principle, non-human tones, textures, lines, and spaces take on a vitality almost like that of flesh and blood" (*A* 161). The trick film literalizes this by making objects act like people. Lindsay's example is a Pathé film, *Moving Day,* in which furniture, clothes, tools, and a whole train of personal belongings follow a family in its relocation to a new home. A film such as this demonstrates the ability of the camera to re-enchant the daily life of modernity and to bring about a return to an earlier animistic stage. But at the same time, by representing a chiasmus according to which humans and objects exchange attributes and eventually occupy the same plane of existence, trick films are also symptomatic of a modern disorder, one to which Marx, no less than Lindsay, was quite alive.

Filmed objects are what objects always are in modern capitalism: commodities, or in Marx's famous wording, "very queer thing[s] abounding in metaphysical subtleties and theological niceties."[24] Their queerness stems in part from their value, which is a function of the amount of labor expended on their production. Labor, a social relation between producers and capital owners, solidifies in a commodity as value, and when this happens, the social character of value disappears and takes on the appearance of a natural quality of the object, an emanation of its very essence that market prices simply translate into the language of currency. In commodities, producers confront the result of their own activity in an alien form that acts independently of their will or intention: "[T]heir own social action [that is, their work] takes the form of the action of objects, which rule the producers instead of being ruled by them." This is partly why, in Marx's formulation, in commodity exchange social relations between people take "the fantastic form of a relation between things," and simultaneously, things become strangely possessed. A humble table that "steps forth" as a commodity becomes "something transcendental": "It not only stands with its feet on the ground, but, in relation to all other commodities, it stands on its head, and evolves out of its wooden brain grotesque ideas, far more wonderful than 'table-turning' ever was."[25]

The table behaves so giddily for other reasons as well. One of them is the manufacturing revolution that took place in the United States between the 1840s and the 1870s. Like its earlier analogs in Western Europe, it replaced artisan with industrial production. Household objects—clothes, implements, furniture, tools—once manufactured in the home or by local craftsworkers were increasingly produced in factories in distant locations. As a result, they cropped up magically, ready for use, in the public's experiential horizon like pictures on a movie screen. They appeared abstracted from the time and labor involved in their manufacture, trailing behind them hints of a secret history never witnessed by the buyer. For the German sociologist George Simmel, in this situation, the product acquires "objective independence." It becomes "an objective given entity which the consumer approaches externally and whose specific existence and quality are autonomous of him."[26]

The social life of commodities cannot be explained only by appealing to use- and exchange-values; there is an additional quality in things that emanates from their cultural value: their connotations and symbolic weight. These attributes circulate in consumption, a complex activity that involves much more than simple exchange of money for goods; it is also an important means for the articulation of social identities in modernity. As the contemporary sociologists Thornstein Veblen and Georg Simmel diagnosed, who one is *is* often a function of what one buys and wears, of the kind of persona one constructs through a selective appropriation of market goods. Or, inversely, the things one buys and wears endow one with specific roles and a sense of self. Just as in dreams, in consumer culture objects acquire peculiar latencies; they (dis)place and control subjects rather than being controlled by them. In Stuart Ewin and Elizabeth Ewin's words, "Within the logic of consumer imagery, the source of creative power is the object world, invested with the subjective power of 'personality.'"[27]

Yet it must be noted that use and display do not completely exhaust the life of things. After they become appropriated as markers of identity and personal circumstance, there remains in them an unaccountable density that eludes pricing and social meaning and has to do with their concrete immediacy—a quality that Michael Taussig has named their "particulate sensuosity" and that Jacques Lacan once described as a "gratuitous, proliferating, excessive, nearly absurd" trait in matter.[28] This excess is at the center of all the varied object tropisms; it is what consumption and desire try but constantly fail to bind, so they have to start again with something else, something new.

The haunted character of things became especially visible in the last decade of the nineteenth century in a number of cultural institutions such as department stores, illustrated magazines, Universal Exhibitions, museums, and the cinema.[29] In movies, Lindsay pointed out, "moving objects, not moving lips, make the words of the photoplay": "When two people talk to each other, it is by lifting and lowering objects rather than their voices. The collector presents a bill: the adventurer shows him the door. The boy plucks a rose: the girl accepts it" (*A* 189). Beyond the narrative functionality of things, the screen also showcased their sensuous power, and this was not always to the good. If allowed to radiate untrammeled, this power might derail the spectator's attention through gratuitous stimulation (*A* 142). To prevent this, things had to be endowed with spiritual signification. In a section of *The Art of the Moving Picture* titled "Furniture and Inventions," Lindsay discourages the trickery of a film like *Moving Day,* and to show how it might be done, he fantasizes about a possible good object: a film version of the story of Cinderella. The plot should naturally revolve around the shoe, whose material, glass, is "chosen to imply a sort of jeweled strangeness from the start." When Cinderella loses her shoe, "it should flee at once like a white mouse to hide under the sofa. It should be pictured there with special artifice, so that the sensuous little foot of every girl-child in the audience will tingle to wear it." As the plot develops, it should "move" and "peep" from its hideout until found by the prince, and at the scene of the coronation, it should be "more gazed at than the crown, and on as dazzling a cushion," aglow with "inner life" (*A* 143–44). Notice, however, that the "inner life" of the shoe cannot entirely reduce a plurality of corporeal tingles on the part of the audience and foot fixations on the part of the critic. Almost the contrary: the more exalted and spiritually coded the object, the stronger its corporeal appeals, as if the effort to eradicate the attractions of matter only made these attractions more intense. In passages like this, Lindsay re-creates something akin to what contemporary French critics were calling *photogénie:*[30] the defamiliarized perception of objects that the cinema, with its ability to reveal in extreme close-up the physiognomy of the material horizon, is uniquely capable of transmitting.[31] But he is also placing the connection between film viewing and the enticements of material in quite a different scene.

While early film theorists such as Hugo Muensterberg, Béla Bálazs, Jean Epstein, and Lindsay psychologized the material basis of cinema by identifying the apparatus with mental faculties, psychoanalysis materialized the psyche, demonstrating its connection to bodily and objectual supports. Lindsay's first film book came out around the time when Sigmund Freud was producing his first extended formulations of the psychoanalytic object (breast, phallus, feces) and its substitute, the fetish.[32] These concepts concretized fantasy and desire by attaching them to elusive object series, lures of a wholeness always at hand yet always irretrievable. The fetish, in particular, revealed the radical dis-organ-ization of desire, its independence from the organic body and its detours through the world of commodities and matter. The fetish is inevitably a commodity (an accessory, an item of clothing, a type of fabric, or a texture, like leather or fur) or a commodifiable item. It could be Cinderella's shoe or, let us say, hair: a body part that can be ornamented, trimmed, teased, curled, braided, or flipped after the dictates of the fashion system. But it is also something that desire raises to the status of an ideal object, a status that the fetish cannot always keep up, and consequently, it often ends up reverting to idiotic (no)thingness, to absurd material accretion. Lindsay's work helps us see that, like psychoanalysis, the cinema dwelled on the strange pulses of matter—its uncontrollable oscillation between animate and inanimate, oversignification and blankness, ideal object and excreta.

Many avant-garde filmmakers made the seeming autonomy of objects the basis of their aesthetic and critical programs. The 1920s films of Luis Buñuel, Hans Richter, Fernand Léger, René Clair and Francis Picabia, Dziga Vertov, or Sergei Eisenstein, to name a few, are full of intensely cathected things. At times, as in the work of Eisenstein, they are subordinated to wholistic symbolic ensembles; other times, in films by Buñuel, Richter, or Léger, things are used to displace humanistic complacencies and to create webs of association usually ignored by routine perception. This molecular, rather than molar, use of objects attempted to short-circuit the symbolic categories that governed their use and, by extension, sought to negate the social order where they were inserted. Richter defined his dada film *Vormittagsspuk* (1928) as "the rhythmical story of the rebellion of some objects against their routine."[33] The objects that fly through the air, topple, and crash in his film are often emblems of bourgeois respectability such as derby hats, porcelain coffee sets, ties, and bushy patriarchal beards. Here the ghostly in the object, which Lindsay wanted to bind to visions of wholeness, is let free to wreak havoc with habit and sense, and to increase the mess.

The distance between Lindsay's proposals and these avant-garde blueprints for dissolution can be gauged by contrasting his ideas with those of the critic Siegfried Kracauer, a contemporary Weimar thinker peripherally linked to the Frankfurt School. Like Lindsay, Kracauer located the cinema at the intersection of a host of modern phenomena: the haunted transactions between people and things, the mechanization of the human figure, the attenuation of subjectivity and psychology in sensation and speed, and the monstrous accretion of objects and images that is modernity. These phenomena conformed what Kracauer called a culture of "distraction," characterized by "pure externality," a "fragmented sequence of splendid sense impressions."[34] The newly fashionable film palaces of 1920s Berlin, with their streamlined architectural "*surface* splendor," were the apt setting for the "cult of distraction," which took place above all in programs combining film with vaudeville and variety acts, musical performances, pantomime, and ballet. Presented in quick succession in the course of an evening, this collage of attractions and media undercut the illusionism of the narrative feature and questioned its artistic aspirations. Best of all, it conveyed "the *disorder* of society" and "the uncontrolled anarchy of our world" (95). As Kracauer later elaborated in his writings of the 1940s, the cinema, especially the early narrative genres such as adventures and physical comedies, was the medium that best re-created the clutter of a world devoid of intention or meaning. It brought spectators face to face with a radically alien material horizon unassailable by consciousness, moving with its own independent momentum.[35]

Kracauer and Lindsay read the cinema as a reflection of modernity's untidiness and alienation, but while the materialist German thinker envisioned a demystifying political use for distraction, the idealist American sought to transcend it through myth. For Kracauer, distraction mimics the shock-driven tempo of metropolitan life and industrial work, and out of this symptom of dispossession rises a form of culture closer to the life of the masses—a culture that rejects bourgeois art and the categories on which it is based. Fragmentary mass culture refuses to postulate spurious harmonies that might occlude the reality of alienation (and the alienation of reality—its hijacking by an oppressive instrumental rationality). Its surface effects mirror the living conditions of the masses, their immersion in an inauthentic world over which they have little control. In this mirror image the masses may find the lineaments of their condition and perhaps the impulse to change their reality: "[W]ere this reality to remain hidden from the audience, they could neither attack nor change it; its disclosure in distraction is therefore of moral significance" (94). As it is, distraction may be the antechamber of the revolution; it "evokes and maintains the tension which must precede the inevitable and radical change" (95).

For Lindsay, however, distraction is artless evasion. He consequently rejects early cinema, along with its pleasures, and the type of media collage that enveloped it, because of their scattering effect. He discourages, for example, the combination of movies with vaudeville performances and circus acts and proposes making film the center of the spectacle without any added attractions. "Whenever the photoplay is mixed in the same program with vaudeville, the moving picture part of the show suffers. The film is rushed through, it is battered, it flickers more than commonly, it is a little out of focus. The house is not built for it. The owner of the place cannot manage an art gallery with a circus on its hands" (*A* 216). In addition to impoverishing the visual quality of the film, this mixture weakens its artistic integrity by bringing an artistic medium down to the level of a mindless street show. In another passage, he criticizes Biograph's sensationalistic advertisement of D. W. Griffith's *Judith of Bethulia* because it reduces the film to a succession of spectacular effects ("the death-defying chariot charges at break-neck speed"; "the dancing girls in their exhibition of the exquisite and peculiar dances of the period" [*A* 88]). Taking the film on these terms amounts to slipping into earlier spectatorial habits and, consequently, missing its artistic dimension. This accumulation of "attractions" must be relegated to a secondary plane. The "real plot" of the film, he claims, is the "balanced alternation" of four strands of action: Judith's story, the "gentle courtship" of Nathan and Naomi, crowd scenes, and battle scenes. The artistry of Griffith's film resides in its proportion, order, and rhythm (neither a "boresome self-conscious quietude" nor "the usual twitching" but a serene flow). In his later work, Lindsay praises Douglas Fairbanks and Raoul Walsh's *Thief of Bagdad* along similar lines. Like Griffith's *Judith,* its rhythm is "organic, flowery and human, not geometric and metallic." Its visual design and montage "bring order and vista into the cluttered lot of a world too rich" (*P* 184). These pictures merit serious study, but their sensationalistic advertisement panders to the spectators' hunger for thrills and directs their attention to the peripheral, surface details of the text, not to its message or to its organic construction—the unity of effect brought about by the classical codes.

The classical style sought to "linearize" the visual signifiers on the screen. Editing, framing, and mise-en-scène were used to curtail the potential fragmentation and randomness of the photographic image and to produce maximally readable narratives driven by clearly visualized cause-and-effect relations.[36] At the time when Lindsay's book came out, this linearization still competed with the wider variety of appeals and attractions that the cinema had inherited from its nickelodeon and prenickelodeon days. Lindsay's discussion of *Judith of Bethulia,* in particular, reflects this transitional stage. Made shortly before *Birth of a Nation,* this title is one of Griffith's definite steps toward long narratives in the classical mode. The uncertainty of the industry concerning these still-unusual productions led to a certain hesitation in advertisement. This may be why the film's promotional description bows to a mode of spectatorship less receptive to well-wrought wholes than to scattered intensities—those disturbing elements that Lindsay's theory fully acknowledged yet simultaneously tried to reason out of existence.[37]

Hieroglyphics, the Mother

So how does one eliminate distraction? How can one reduce the cinema's all-enveloping sensuousness? How can the object be tamed and hieroglyphic modernity yield sense? Lindsay's answer was: through hieroglyphs. These were to be the basic building blocks in the construction of orderly films devoid of distraction. In *The Art of the Moving Picture,* Lindsay describes them as cinematic renderings of the ancient ideographs combining the photographic representation of "elementary and familiar things" with "a more abstract," or symbolic, meaning (*A* 200). Some of his examples are literally based on Egyptian script and run from the obvious to the wildly whimsical. The Egyptian ideograph "throne," for example, will have a photographic representation that will instantly telegraph to the audience that "you are dealing with royalty or its implications" (*A* 201). The ideograph "duck" will be translated into shots of the bird that will "suggest the finality of Arcadian peace" (*A* 202). In turn, the Egyptians' wavy line, which mutated into the *n* of the Latin alphabet, reappears in film in "the glittering water scenes"—"a dominant part of moving picture Esperanto"—and they refer to a restricted symbolic constellation: "[T]he spiritual meaning of water will range from the metaphor of the purity of the dew to the sea as a sign of infinity" (*A* 205). The sign shaped like a lasso crops up in modern films as a literal lasso or a noose. Its symbolic value is "solemn judgment and the hangman" or "temptation." Lindsay connects it with the spider web, "representing the cruelty of evolution" (*A* 208). Lindsay's hieroglyphs were not always such close transpositions of Egyptian ideographs; in a broader sense, any visual image susceptible to symbolic interpretation became for him a hieroglyph. In his analysis of *The Thief of Bagdad,* the image of an all-curing magic apple is "a hieroglyphic of promise, of hope, and . . . healing" (*P* 176). The image of a scepter with a deadly serpent in its hollow combines "[t]he scepter, the hieroglyphic of authority, the serpent, of death—the two together have become the hieroglyphic of official death" (*P* 176–77). The meaning of these visual representations is not static; it may change from film to film, even within the same film, depending on its context. What is crucial for Lindsay is that spiritual principles should be made available through a tangible embodiment and that sensual stimulus be anchored on sense. Hence balancing the concrete and the abstract, matter and sense, film hieroglyphics could reduce the unmanageable world of things and therefore be used to articulate "a delineation of experience," "pictures with a soul" (*A* 200).[38]

Lindsay's attempt to create a universal visual language based on iconic representation is undercut by the slightly capricious nature of his hieroglyphs. If they must be interpreted—as he obsessively interprets them—it is because their meaning does not rest on direct metaphorical equivalences that bypass language and bring interpretive drift to a halt; instead, their meaning is a function of a system of differences, of the web of relations that they are a part of in any given text. Lindsay's hieroglyphs, which are intended as ultimate proof of the general accessibility of the visual, end up demonstrating the implication of all meaning in the scene of writing, that is, in a system of signification based on an irreducible play of difference and deferment—what Jacques Derrida famously called *differánce*.[39] In addition, the centrality of the hieroglyphic in film construction runs against Lindsay's investment in the classical continuity style. The discrete symbols on which films should be built draw the attention of the spectator and resist total absorption into the narrative flow. They turn the film into what Miriam Hansen has called, in relation to Griffith's *Intolerance,* "a reading space" ruled by analogies and correspondences rather than a transparent narrative to be unself-consciously consumed.[40]

While the earliest and most extensive formulation of the hieroglyphic appears in Lindsay's first film book, he later extended it to his poetry. In the 1925 edition of his *Complete Poems,* published six years before his death, he defined his poems as "hieroglyphics" and his readings as "hieroglyphic sermons." He points out in this way that his poetry is less lyrical than descriptive and "analytical," and because of this the French critic Marc Chénetier has called Lindsay a "semiotician" of modernity.[41] While they occasionally deal with subjective states, his poems most often provide symbolic readings of concrete objects, images, settings, or characters (historical or fictional) and, conversely, they embed abstractions in concrete form. In the process, quotidian realities would be mapped within larger signifying schemes. A poem to an electric advertising sign on Broadway ends with the proclamation: "The signs in the street and the signs in the skies / Shall make a new Zodiac, guiding the wise, / And Broadway make one with that marvelous stair / That is climbed by the rainbow-clad spirits of prayer."[42] Lindsay's hieroglyphs then bring together a number of opposites: the material and the spiritual; modern visuality and ancient notation systems; obscurity (far from self-evident, they seemed to require Lindsay's expert knowledge) and (presumed) readability; the mass-cultural present and past mythologies.

Lindsay's hieroglyphs inherit a nineteenth-century American fascination with these forms of writing prompted in part by Jean-François Champollion's decoding of the Rosetta Stone in 1822. This fascination left an important trace among the authors of the American Renaissance, to whom Lindsay had an important intellectual debt. In these writers, like in Lindsay, the fascination with hieroglyphics was reinforced by the influence of Emmanuel Swedenborg, the Swedish mystic whose doctrines were extraordinarily popular throughout the century. (The transcendentalist philosopher Ralph Waldo Emerson once called the mid-nineteenth century "the age of Swedenborg," and the literary historian F. O. Matthiessen toyed with the idea of giving this title to his classic study of 1850s U.S. literature.[43]) Swedenborg saw the physical world as a ciphered inventory of spiritual realities, a sensuous incarnation of metaphysical principles; his way of splitting matter from spirit and his disavowal of the crudities of the former in favor of spiritual sense can be discerned throughout Lindsay's film writings. During his youth, Lindsay was a member of Springfield's Swedenborgian circle and, by his own admission, faithfully attended their meetings (C xxi). But if his hieroglyphs look to the past, they also find their place in a wider modernist idiom. As they tried to communicate abstractions through the sensuous surfaces of everyday things and, conversely, to spiritualize the quotidian, and as they sought to highlight the mythic underpinnings of the commonplace, they were structurally analogous to the "mythic method" of William Butler Yeats, James Joyce, or T. S. Eliot; to Walter Benjamin's dialectical images; to Ezra Pound's "intellectual and emotional complexes"; to Sergei Eisenstein's montages; and to Georg Simmel's *Momentbilder*. All of them used the principle of assemblage (of concrete and abstract; present and past) to establish connections between seemingly distant realities and to open paths of sense through the visible.[44] In addition, Lindsay's hieroglyphic perception was also replicated in the writings of a number of contemporary modernists seeking to understand mass culture.

One example was the writing published in the New York little magazine *The Soil*, which appeared for a over a year between 1916 and 1917. The review was inspired by the enthusiastic "Americanism" of the photographer Alfred Stieglitz and the group of artists and intellectuals that clustered around him, and by the playful anti-art stance of the French avant-garde, which championed devalued cultural forms. Its editors and contributors praised machinery, skyscrapers, and hanging bridges as ultimate emblems of modernity, and they interpreted urban popular phenomena as contemporary avatars of ancient myths and timeless archetypes. They compared boxers in the ring to Greek statues ("Phidias might sign his name under that frieze of naked-ness") and mythological figures ("Jack Britton was the Theagenes . . . and Ted Lewis was Euthymus"), or invested them with allegorical value ("this is Skill against the Brute"). The head of the rhinoceros at the Bronx Zoo was to a commentator "more powerful than the Minotaur"—an example of "mythology in the flesh"—and magic acts at revues and cabarets seemed reincarnations of ancient religious rituals.[45]

Along similar lines, for the imagist poet H.D., the cinema unveiled "a classical vibration" in the everyday. She often saw film images as visual pa-limpsests; quotidian objects and landscapes evoked, in a sort of superimposi-tion, traditional artistic iconography and myth. She discovered in Kenneth Macpherson's experimental film *Borderline* (1930), in which she starred next to Paul Robeson, visual echoes of the art of Mena-period Egypt, Hokusai Japan, classical Athens, and quattrocento Florence. She praised the mythic overtones of G. W. Pabst's *Joyless Street:* one of its protagonists, Greta Garbo, seemed to H.D. a new Helen, and the film's urban setting resembled a mod-ern Troy or "a mournful and pitiful Babylon." And the excellence of Russian films lay for her in their "biblical" qualities; the ideas in them were "as great . . . as those carved in lightning on the rock of Sinai."[46] As is the case with Lindsay, these views express an antimodern modernism. If, in Baudelaire's fa-mous definition, the modern was "the transitory, the fugitive, the contingent" half of art,[47] H.D. and the writers of *The Soil* focused instead on the other half that is "the eternal and immutable," mythological resonance and "classical vi-brations." Through them, the dizzying heterogeneity of the present could be made to signify; its strangeness could be reduced and redeemed.

This way of reading replicates, perhaps unwittingly, the discourse of pop-ular culture, which abounded in hieroglyphic gestures at the time. The cen-tral motif of the 1893 Chicago World's Fair was the White City, a spectacular pastiche of ancient Roman architecture built out of staff around an artificial lagoon. Intended as the central display at the fair, it seemed a suitable sym-bol for the nation as a whole, as it clothed American imperialist ambitions and economic and technological prowess in the style of an earlier empire. Years later, visitors to the 1900 World's Exhibition in Paris were greeted by La Parisienne, a huge allegorical statue symbolizing the city, perched on a golden ball on the main entrance to the fairgrounds. In New York City, the famous Coney Island amusement parks, Luna Park and Steeplechase, were fantasy landscapes straight out of the *Arabian Nights*. They featured belly dancers, camel rides, and elephants, and their flashy architecture combined

Renaissance and Levantine elements with minarets, domes, and pagodas. The more delirious Dreamland, the last and most sophisticated of the Coney Island parks, contained two gigantic domes that offered tableaus portraying "Creation" and the "End of the World—According to the Dream of Dante." They were conceived as panoramas and involved extended human and animal casts and complex lighting and sound effects; and they were meant to be enjoyed from ornate boats that glided along water canals. Some of the most popular restaurants and cabarets in New York in the 1910s and 1920s followed suit, if not so spectacularly: Murray's Roman Gardens provided a panorama of antiquity that mixed Roman, Greek, and Egyptian styles, and Louis Martin's Restaurant boasted Assyrian columns and "Babylonian" balconies allegedly imitating the legendary hanging gardens.

Live entertainment often collapsed the "primitive" and the latest dance crazes: the 1920s performer Gilda Gray, who made her name with the shimmy, consolidated her career doing South Sea and Oriental dances in Ziegfield's Follies. The point of these orientalist and primitivist gestures was not to impose order on the new or to lend it the weight of tradition, as attempted by Lindsay, *The Soil,* or H.D. Rather, it was to separate fun from normality and to revive historical image repertoires as mere play of surfaces and masks. But as they did so, they transcended their immediate circumstances and gained a symbolic, archetypal dimension. These gestures may have also had a legitimating function. If popular entertainment embodied transhistorical impulses and mythic archetypes, attempts to police it, suppress it, or even to resist its lure would seem to contradict a timeless kernel in human nature.[48]

While part of a larger cultural idiom, Lindsay's fascination with the mythic potential of mass culture responded as well to a family history and a gender politics that deserve some commentary. In his autobiographical writings he recalls that one of his childhood treasures was Rawlinson's *History of Egypt*. This gift from his father probably started his lifelong devotion to hieroglyphs, which, as we have seen, gave him a vocabulary and a structure to interpret the surrounding culture. But it was his mother who "destined" him to be an artist. She taught painting and English at a Kentucky college, read papers on art history to the Illinois Art Association, and toured the Midwest delivering "spoken epics" to large audiences, "oratorical triumphs in imitation of her forensic and senatorial Kentucky and Virginia ancestors" (C 12–14). In addition, she wrote and staged two "miracle plays" during Lindsay's childhood. One of them, *Olympus,* had a mythological subject, and

Lindsay was cast as Cupid. He had to let his hair grow for the performance, defying his blind paternal grandfather's hatred of "effeminacy." In his early youth he decided to pursue his artistic calling against his maternal grandfather's contempt for poets and artists. He devoted himself to painting, the dominant vocation among "all the elegant young ladies in our family" (*C* 15). The cover of his first sketchbook was graced with Guido Reni's painting *Aurora,* loved by his mother and himself, in which the goddess dominates the composition and strews flowers in the path of the sun.

Art and myth are thus aligned with the mother, or at least with feminine figures, and, as Laurence Goldstein has pointed out, so are the dominant hieroglyphs in most of the films Lindsay valued.[49] As he defends the use of film to portray the unsung heroism of small-town life, he imagines a movie scenario set in his hometown. It would be presided by a golden Madonna-like statue ("Our Lady of Springfield") that unaccountably descends from the sky and becomes the center of the town's life and the visible incarnation of its spirit (*A* 175–78). And in his analysis of *The Thief of Bagdad,* he turns the princess (Julanne Johnston) into the moral and graphic center of the film. Her presence "transmutes the whole story" into "an inspirational flowering" (*P* 189). Her tall, slender shape is a hieroglyphic of spiritual aspiration ("things towering toward heaven") echoed throughout in visual motifs such as the minarets, the spears of guards and soldiers, the tall ceilings of the palace, and the flights of the protagonist on magic carpets and winged horses (*P* 190). Conversely, if Fairbanks's earlier *Robin Hood* was an artistic failure, it was largely because "there was no Maid Marian" substantial enough to hold the picture together. In thus fetishizing female presence, Lindsay may have been addressing something besides movies. The death of his mother in 1922 marked the beginning of his psychological decline, accentuated by the need to vacate and rent out the family home in Springfield, one of the few stable elements in his wandering life (*P* 75).

Lindsay's devotion to femininity is not particularly liberationist; it is symptomatic of an oppressive idealization of women common in Victorian society. In *The Thief of Bagdad,* the princess is a passive, ornamental figure confined to interiors and reified as object of exchange between her father the Sultan and her suitors. Even her presumed centrality in Lindsay's reading of the film is subordinate to male desires, since she is the fulcrum on which Lindsay's homosocial identification with Fairbanks-Ahmed turns. Myron Lounsbury shows that both Ahmed and Lindsay are outsiders trying to break into forbidden territory (*P* 135). Ahmed is a thief who, after breaking into the palace, becomes love-smitten at the sight of the princess and tries to pass as a prince to win her hand against a number of rather unsavory aristocratic suitors. Lindsay enjoyed an ephemeral celebrity in the mid-1910s, but in the following decade, when he wrote his analysis of *The Thief of Bagdad,* his star was fading fast. He was unsuccessfully romancing prominent figures in the Hollywood studios—Fairbanks was one of them—in an attempt to get hired by the industry as an aesthetic consultant. The fact that Ahmed is in full possession of his powers while Lindsay was not when he wrote on the film suggests a compensatory fantasy at the heart of Lindsay's identification.

Ordering principles—the hieroglyphic, myth, and art—are identifiable with a motherly presence; and they are, at the same time, imposed on a mass culture whose sensuous materiality and confusion Lindsay came to identify, in the 1920s, with what he saw as the shrill femininity of the flapper and with jazz, the "outrages of hysteria" (*P* 187) that he presumed to be the soundtrack to the flapper's life (*P* 301, 305, 313). In his commentary on the Valentino vehicle *Monsieur Beaucaire* he trusted that such stylish fare would contribute to abolish "the saxophone and the reign of the raw Jezebels"—two practically coextensive plights (*P* 311). The hieroglyphic character of popular culture can also be gendered as female. Unlike the images consciously crafted by a few visionaries like Griffith or Fairbanks, most often the random hieroglyphs of mass culture mystify and obscure, separating vision from understanding: "We want to know the meaning of those hieroglyphics that they are thrusting upon us, for the present as unsolved, in many phases, as the hieroglyphic ruins of pre-historic Mexico and South America. The American mind has become an overgrown forest of unorganized pictures" (*C* xxii). As enigmas, these disorienting hieroglyphs bring up the "'heads in hieroglyphic bonnets,'" the synecdoche of femininity that Freud tried to decode in a famous 1933 lecture.[50] Freud's question, "What does woman want?" slips easily into Lindsay's, "What do mass culture's hieroglyphics mean?" In his search for an answer, Lindsay opposed a maternal superego against the unruly, feminine materiality of the popular—or, in his own imagery, "Our Lady of Springfield" against the flapper.

Myth

Ultimately, the ordering potential of the cinema does not stem from isolated hieroglyphs but from their combination into "myths," or narratives capable of engaging the audience's longing for transcendence. "There is in this nation of movie-goers a hunger for tales of fundamental life that are not yet told. . . . This lantern of wizard-drama [the camera] is going to give us in time the visible things in the fullness of their primeval force" (*A* 290). Elsewhere, Lindsay writes: "Man's dreams are rearranged and glorified memories. How could these people reconstruct the torn carpets and tin cans and waste-paper of their lives into mythology?" (*A* 237). The cinema, a machine of vision, should become a visionary machine capable of restructuring private and public fantasy. At this point, Lindsay's ideas closely resemble those of the other pioneer film theorist in the United States, the German-born psychologist Hugo Muensterberg, whose book *The Photoplay: A Psychological Study,* came out in 1916, only a few months after Lindsay's *Art of the Moving Picture.* A professor at Harvard University, where he had been hired upon William James's recommendation, Muensterberg's film theory was inspired by his pioneering experiments on psychophysics and the physiology of perception. Lindsay's theory, in contrast, was an entirely intuitive affair with no claim to scientific legitimacy. They have therefore been seen as polar opposites in method and approach, and yet they do have points of convergence. They agree that the cinema imitates mental processes. For Muensterberg, it simulates the mechanisms of attention, imagination, memory, and emotion; for Lindsay, it replicates the workings of his sudden hallucinations.[51]

These hallucinations started in the summer of 1904 during one of his stays at the family home, and they accompanied him, on and off, for the rest of his life. They seem to have been especially abundant during his residency in New York City later that year, when they frequently assaulted him while lying in bed at night and while wandering around the city. (They were particularly vivid one day that he was in midtown, walking up and down Broadway handing out tickets for a YMCA function.) They cropped up so often that he eventually set aside a notebook to record "magic" and "spiritual adventures that approach the unseen."[52] He later wrote that the visions were assuredly "sent," "came in cataracts," and "painted themselves in the air," as befits the aspiring painter he was, or the film critic he would become.[53] In any event, and as is usually the case, his madness copied his media, projecting his desire through the technologies of representation most familiar to him. Determined not to be "conquered by pictures in the air," Lindsay articulated them into a cosmology. Its graphic version is the map of the universe that opens his *Collected Poems.* The written one was a book, later destroyed, with the title, "Where Is Aladdin's Lamp?" The interrogative inflection lets on a certain nostalgia for the periodic loss of the visions of "the Prophets" parading in "gorgeous apparel" on placid summer days through the family estate. It seems that Lindsay eventually found a replacement for the lamp he lost—at a theater near him, where other lamps, handled just right, could pour their share of specters. Perhaps his attempt to bind the film to a theory was determined, at some level, by his desire to make these visions yield meaning and to make them return at will.

Lindsay sought to give his private flirtations with ghosts a social resonance. Films could do for the collectivity what his hallucinations had done for him. They could supply the nation with "tales of fundamental life" and new mythologies. Their impact would depend especially on their form— more concretely, on their *architectural* form, which is especially noticeable in the large settings and mass scenes of the "pictures of crowd splendor." Lindsay thus anticipated an idea that later critics have theorized more fully: the cinema offers spaces for virtual habitation and transit,[54] and, furthermore, these spaces have a largely unconscious effect, since, according to Walter Benjamin, they are appropriated "in distraction" by "tactile" habituation, not by rapt concentration and engrossed study.[55]

The main influence on Lindsay's insights here is the "City Beautiful" ideal, in vogue at the time he wrote his first film book. Its main promoters were the art historian Charles Eliot Norton and the architect Daniel H. Burnham, the designer of the "White City" of the 1893 Universal Exposition in Chicago and of some early high-rises, such as the Flatiron Building in New York. The goal of the movement was to provide urban centers with a recognizable outline and aesthetic unity by means of monumental public spaces, open vistas, and civic monuments expressive of the city's history, self-image, and aspirations. Modeled after the World's Fairs, these environments would be globally planned. They would substitute "synthetic" for spontaneously lived space and would standardize the perception of the city, directing the free-floating gaze of the urban dweller to predetermined points of interest, to particular meanings and narratives. In this respect, their effect would be similar to that later promoted by the style of the classical Hollywood film, which also can be seen as a form of spatial regulation seeking to standardize and homogenize audience response. At bottom, the City Beautiful movement was a form of environmental behaviorism rooted in aestheticism: it attempted to fuse the disparate urban masses through unitary design and to attain social harmony through art while leaving untouched the structural causes of fragmentation and unrest.

Like new civic centers, Lindsay maintained, film sets should be designed with a view toward harmony and proportion. Spatial backgrounds should provide the main motifs, "moods," and "effects" of the plot; and, conversely, characters and events should embody the spirit of the film's spaces. These should not be treated as neutral backdrops but as actants in their own right, "backgrounds that clamor for utterance through the figures in front of them, as Athens finds her soul in Athena" (*A* 171). The desired goal was a tight matching between material space, character, and action, a matching that should be ideological and graphic, with the "definite system of space and texture relations retained throughout the set" acting as a conduit for edifying ideals (*A* 170). For Lindsay, one of the few films that lived up to these standards was James Cruze's epic of the 1840s westward migration, *The Covered Wagon.* He read it as a collection of graphic patterns and correspondences dominated by "the overarching cover of the end of the wagon," which frames the main actions of the film: under it the hero meets the heroine, and their love story gradually unfolds. In addition, this space is laden with symbolic and cultural resonances: "Every single covered wagon is a temple of domesticity, religion, and aspiration on lumbering west-going wheels. The arch of some of these covered wagon canopies is so perfectly curved it could be made the model of some gigantic dome, as beautiful a curve as the curve of the Taj Mahal, and it may yet possibly suggest some of the domes and minarets of the Northwest Pacific Coast" (*P* 274–75). The shape of the wagon's cover is echoed across the landscape in the curves of cliffs, rivers, and rolling hills and in the mass scenes: the Indian army is "a mass of moving architecture," and so are the wagons, especially when they close in a circle, forming an improvised fort.

These idealized architectural spaces should embody national character and community spirit, providing spectators with figurations of their collective identity. In them, Lindsay proposed, "America . . . must visualize itself again" (*A* 276). This may be the reason why the "crowd picture" is the favorite of the unstructured urban "mob," which gathers nightly in the theaters "to watch its natural face in the glass," presumably to find out what it is (*A* 234, 78, 93). A film like Cruze's, with its patriotic charge and harmonic visuals, might give the mob the self-image it needs; and in the process, it may help to appease many "spites, hates, and race rivalries," blending the different cultural strands of the nation into a unity. Even the obstreperous "alien" element will be integrated, and "immigration will be something else than tide upon tide of raw labor" (*A* 275).[56] This sounds like a blithe attempt to negotiate a shared culture but is actually an exclusionary statement. Immigration, which for Lindsay is a shapeless flow, will become structured by joining in on a postulated American tradition. And in the compact logic of the sentence, this tradition predates the alien flood; it can order and reduce it but remains a self-enclosed entity that does not engage in dialogue with it.

Dreams of cultural unity haunted many of Lindsay's contemporaries as well. Unity was a driving concern for the critics grouped around the progressive little magazine *The Seven Arts*—essayists such as Randolph Bourne, Van Wyck Brooks, Paul Rosenfeld, Waldo Frank, and James Oppenheim. Brooks's popular *America's Coming of Age* (1915) was a sort of manifesto among them. In one of the best-read sections of his book, Brooks decried the split between highbrow and lowbrow culture in the United States—between the "dessicated," ineffectual ideals of high culture and the "catchpenny realities" of business and industry—and the lack of breathing space in between. What was needed was a unifying middle ground blending "highbrow" aesthetic and intellectual concerns with "lowbrow" hands-on practicality.[57] Similar ideas crop up elsewhere in Brooks's circle. In the editorial of the first issue of *The Seven Arts* (November 1916), James Oppenheim proclaimed the need for an art that would bring together the varied strands of "the national life" and would give the United States "that national self-consciousness which is the beginning of greatness." In this same issue, Paul Rosenfeld, under the pseudonym Peter Minuit, reiterated in an article on Alfred Stieglitz's gallery, 291, that cultural self-consciousness was the country's main need, and art was the means to procure it. For Brooks, Rosenfeld, and Oppenheim, the model for this unifying new culture was the high tradition grounded in specific American conditions and epitomized, among others, by Walt Whitman.[58] Randolph Bourne advocated a cosmopolitan transnationalism that would integrate the preindustrial traditions imported by immigrants.[59] The writers of *The Soil* were more inclusive, extolling the expressive potential of industrial folklore and mass entertainment. The movies, the dances of the day, sports, vaudeville, jazz and ragtime, store-window displays, comic strips, amusement parks, the popular press, rodeos, skyscrapers, and dime novels were the materials to draw upon in the construction of a new culture. In this pursuit, unity was still the foremost imperative: "We need a welding factor. We will be a hyphenated nation until we have an art."[60]

For Lindsay, who stood halfway between the elitism of *The Seven Arts* and the unabashed populism of *The Soil*, film could be the main vehicle of unity and self-consciousness, yet only as long as it tempered its fragmenting effect by means of cohesive design and myth. "Because ten million people enter daily into the cave, something akin to Egyptian wizardry, national rituals will be born" (*A* 288). Unity was foreshadowed in one of the most apposite topics for the screen: the oceanic crowd, a uniform expanse that engulfs individual difference. "The sea of humanity is dramatically blood-brother to the Pacific, Atlantic, or Mediterranean," he states in his characterization of the crowd picture (*A* 67). And elsewhere, he frequently invokes scenes where crowds "move as oceans," "descend like cataracts," "flow like rivers," or toss like waves or "wheat-fields on the hill-sides" (*A* 58, 163–64). These emphatic images betray the rhetorical force needed to postulate the unity of what was in fact a diverse plurality. The crowd may have looked like a natural growth on the screen, but not in the theaters or in the streets of any large American city at the time, as Lindsay well knew. The nature metaphors smuggle into the representation of the crowd a homogeneity that can only be imagined in long shot but would dissolve at closer range; they also mystify as national fate the simple accident of the market, since what brings people together in modern industrialized societies in the first place are the imperatives of work, consumption, and survival. That Lindsay chooses films with historical subjects (such as *Judith of Bethulia* or *The Covered Wagon*) as examples of the unifying potential of the cinema shows nostalgia for premodern times, or perhaps a certain evasiveness. After all, organic commonality is more easily pictured the further one recedes from one's immediate surroundings.

Automatism

Lindsay's appeals to an organic polity are of a piece with his defenses of orderly film hieroglyphics and spaces and with his proposition that the cinema ought to supply the nation with "tales of fundamental life" and "national rituals." All of these are on the side of order, proportion, tradition, and what he called "human rhythm" and were intended to neutralize sensory overload, "distraction" (in Kracauer's sense of the term), the odd animism of the material world, and the mechanical quality of modernity. Another way of putting it is to say that the goal of Lindsay's theory was to bring under control the *automatism* of everyday life in the modern world. The word, borrowed from the surrealists' vocabulary, designates the uncontrollable nature of modernity, where things travel too fast, bodies are overstimulated and transported across landscapes blurred by speed, and thought keeps getting ahead of itself, generating connections beyond the thinker's control. Blame it on the machine: "The most inert soul in the world once learning to drive a car, even a Ford, is swept relentlessly past his own resolutions and convictions" (*P* 235). "The man in the street" appears "a mechanical toy, amused by clockwork. . . . All his thinking is done by telegraph. . . . Dominated by a switchboard civilization, he moves in grooves from one clock-splendor to another."[61] In a world propelled by the spasms of machinery, film acts as the *pharmakon* of modernity, the poison that cures. It is a mechanical device that, while capable of duplicating the dominant "speed-mania" of a machine-run environment, might still be able to slow things down to a more restful pace. While reproducing thought unbound—"thinking from picture to picture, leaping from vision to vision"—it could steer the perception-consciousness apparatus and set mental images in some sort of "reasoning succession" (P 183).

Lindsay's repulsion toward an automatic modernity was only matched by his ability to perceive and describe this automatism. One could argue that he feared it so much because it lay perilously close to home. His visions, with which he seemed to live comfortably through most of his life, were completely beyond his control. He did not call them automatic, but others did. When he was still unknown, he sent a fan letter with some of his poems and essays to William James, whose *Varieties of Religious Experience* he admired. In his reply, James thanked Lindsay for his inspired jottings, politely declined the young poet's offer to take to the road together, and praised his "semi-automatic inspirations" and his "free attitude" toward them.[62] Lindsay's amiable attitude toward his internal automatism was not to last. At the end of his life, exhausted by protracted reading tours that provided for his livelihood but left him enervated and prostrated, he complained of "flywheels" whirring in his head and of constantly hearing the clatter of trains, as if the machine connections he tried to conjure away had finally invaded his mind.

This was only the culmination of a tendency that had been there all along. His poetry and his film writing, where he tried to purvey some structure for a runaway world, also registered various forms of automatism. Intended as forms of symbolic ordering, his poems were celebrated by contemporaries for their noise, unusual rhythms, and sound effects. "The Congo," for example, is punctuated by the line "Boomlay, boomlay, boomlay, BOOM" and is full of intensely percussive passages. And "Santa Fe Trail," one of his best-liked pieces, imitates the sound of car horns and the drone of engines. His film writing often succumbs to the seduction of "splendid sense impressions," or machine-driven distraction. The coherence and order he advocated were completely entangled in the dispersal he sought to avoid. Like meaning *in* the movies, the meaning *of* the movies had to be laboriously pieced together from fragments and scattered traces, but it kept threatening to break out of continuity, to assert the blind automatism of the machine. As a result, his film criticism constantly oscillates between dispersion and unity, chaos and order, distraction and myth. Attempts to structure and systematize coexist with considerable conceptual dispersion. In his preface to the *Village Magazine,* a montage of prose, colorful sketches, poems, and miscellanea that he put out twice in his lifetime, he defended the fragmentary magazine format as an alternative to the pretended uniformity of the book. But his film books are anything but uniform. In book 3 of *The Art of the Moving Picture,* Lindsay claims to step down "from the oracular platform and go down through my own chosen underbrush for haphazard adventure" (*A* 216). What emerges from this excursion is a loose series of reflections on censorship, the nickelodeon and the saloon, California as a spiritual symbol, the use of sound, the possibility of government-sponsored films for information and propaganda, and technology and spirituality. Likewise, *The Poetry and Progress of the Movies* is more a collection of commentaries on individual films than a structured whole. Uneven and digressive, it works better as a string of insights than as a sustained argument. For all his desire to bind the image into stable meanings and mythic wholes, Lindsay's enterprise often slips into the kind of proliferating disorder he sought to eliminate. And this may be all to the good. His writing comes alive most often in its fragments and details, in the descriptions (reproductions?) of distraction—the "splendor" of particular hieroglyphics, of reenchanted objects, of breathtaking spaces—not in its turgid attempts at a (mythic) theoretical totality.

In many ways, Lindsay was a modernist in reverse. Early on, Ezra Pound had described him to Harriet Monroe as a futurist,[63] presumably because of his flirtations with the cinema, ragtime, and electric signs. And one could further connect him to the surrealists, who broke into public life as Lindsay was writing his second film book, for his perceptive awareness of the shadow life of things, his attention to the latencies of filmic space, and his skill in spotting enchantment in the midst of the everyday. Yet in the end, Lindsay recoiled from modernity. He discovered that everyday life in the modern world was pervaded by moments of automatism, opacity, and sensorial excess, but instead of exploiting their disruptive role, he sought to bring them in line with his traditionalist allegiances—with past mythology and fantasies of national unity. For all his antimodern modernism, however, he still located decisive pressure points that were worked over by later generations of experimental artists who, like him, were particularly responsive to the role of objects and spaces in film and daily life. As we will see in the chapters that follow, much experimental art in the first half of the century was primarily about spaces and things: city films, modernist poetry and narrative, surrealist assemblage, and avant-garde ethnographies brought readers and spectators up close against the material and the architectures of modernity. They tracked the unpredictable paths of things and explored (and resisted) existing spatial configurations. Many subsequent modernists, especially those aligned with peripheral cultures, changed the direction of Lindsay's intervention but largely maintained his focus of interest. And in this way, they confirmed Lindsay's valuable insight that in popular culture, like in everyday life, much of what matters takes place in our relations with things, with space, with mere matter.

Reading the Modern City
Paul Strand and
Charles Sheeler's *Manhatta*

Manhatta

In many ways, *Manhatta,* a modest city film made by the photographer Paul Strand and the painter-photographer Charles Sheeler in 1920, seems a direct illustration of Vachel Lindsay's ideas. It portrays the modern city as an idealized architectural space and a hieroglyph of modernity, and it appears to follow Lindsay's recommendation that the cinema be used to structure the contingency of modern life and to provide icons of unity in times of instability and dissolution. The main such icon in the film is the landscape of Lower Manhattan. This area of New York City was at the time the main showcase of skyscraper architecture in the world. With its influential stock exchange and corporate headquarters, it had become the center of international finance and commerce after World War I had devastated its European competitors.

Manhatta lacks a storyline; it depicts a day in the life of the city through a series of sequences that run from morning to evening. It begins with views of the southern tip of Manhattan at sunrise followed by images of commuters stepping off a ferry on their way to work, and it ends with the sun setting over the Hudson River. In between, there are shots of skyscrapers, street crowds and traffic, landmarks of old New York (Trinity Church and its graveyard), locomotives, construction sites, and boats in the harbor. The film's temporal frame stresses the repeatable nature of these slices of life and implies that one of the wonders of the city is that its movement and energy spontaneously recur as part of its routine. The visual material is interspersed with quotations from Walt Whitman that emphatically celebrate the city's grandeur and introduce the different sequences. The line, "When million-footed Manhattan, unpent, descends to its pavements," is spliced with shots of crowds. "[H]igh growths of iron, slender, strong, splendidly uprising toward clear skies!" introduces takes of building sites, and the verse, "Gorgeous clouds of the sunset! Drench with your splendor me, or the men and women generations after me!" leads into the final shots and suggests cyclical recurrence.[1] Whitman's words lift the film's ordinary street scenes into the realm of myth, and they also bind the present to the past, portraying everyday urban modernity as the fulfillment of Whitman's idealistic aspirations.

The film was shot over a period of several months in 1920, and it premiered on July 24, 1921, at the Rialto Theater, a mainstream commercial cinema in New York City. Grandiloquently titled *New York, the Magnificent*, it was featured as a "scenic" in a program together with an orchestral overture, a musical performance, a ballet, a comedy, and a feature film (the English production *The Mystery Road*).[2] Afterwards, it fitfully circulated in Europe as cult fare and was revived in the United States toward the mid-1920s by film societies and art theaters, called at the time "little cinemas." Despite its limited exposure, it had enormous resonance. It allegedly inaugurated the American experimental film tradition as well as one of its most prolific genres, the "city film" or "city symphony." Shortly after the premiere of the film, Paul Strand wrote to his mentor, the photographer Alfred Stieglitz, that "apparently everybody has been making a reel of New York."[3] If "everybody" made such reels, only a few remain on record—enough, however, to confirm the popularity of the genre. In the fifteen years after *Manhatta*'s first screening, a number of American filmmakers as different in interests and temperament as Robert Flaherty (*Twenty-Four Dollar Island*), Herman Weinberg (*City Symphony* and *Autumn Fire*), Jay Leyda (*A Bronx Morning*),

Irving Browning (*City of Contrasts*), and Robert Florey (*Skyscraper Simphonie*) tried their hand at the city film. The genre matured in Europe, where the best-known titles were produced: Walter Ruttmann's *Berlin*, Dziga Vertov's *Man with the Movie Camera*, Jean Vigo's *A Propos de Nice*, Alberto Cavalcanti's *Rien que les heures,* and Joris Ivens's *Rain.*

Manhatta transposes into the medium of film the kind of iconography that Strand and Sheeler had been exploring separately in their paintings and photographs. At the time of their collaboration, they were promising young artists in the New York scene. It seems that they became acquainted in the mid-1910s at 291, Alfred Stieglitz's gallery, the earliest outpost of modern art in New York City and the meeting place for an informal group of critics and artists that historians have called "the Stieglitz group." At the time, this included the critic Paul Rosenfeld, the painters Marsden Hartley, Arthur Dove, and John Marin, and the critic-cartoonist Marius de Zayas, among others. (Charles Demuth and Georgia O'Keeffe would enter the circle in later years.) Strand, who had been born in New York and studied photography with Lewis Hine at the Ethical Culture School, became a member of the group in the mid-1910s, when his original work earned him Stieglitz's friendship and support. Stieglitz gave him a solo show at 291 and published his photographs in the prestigious *Camera Work.* Sheeler was an occasional visitor at 291, but his social base was Walter Arensberg's circle, another intellectual cadre that met at the Arensbergs' salon and included William Carlos Williams and the French dadaists Francis Picabia and Marcel Duchamp. Sheeler was born in Philadelphia, where he studied at the Fine Arts School with William Merritt Chase. (Chase had been Vachel Lindsay's teacher at the New York School of Art in the early 1900s.) Sheeler's early painting, influenced primarily by Paul Cezanne, had been shown in the Armory Show in 1913. He was also known as a photographer. To supplement his income, he had been freelancing since the early 1910s, taking pictures of art works for a number of New York galleries and of buildings for architectural firms. In 1917, Marius de Zayas's Modern Gallery showed a selection of his photographs along with others by Strand and Sheeler's friend, the sculptor Morton Schamberg. Strand and Sheeler shared a detached, documentary style and an interest in abstraction and geometrical patterns that they carried into their film. Their early photographs anticipate some framings and motifs later used in *Manhatta,* as do some of Stieglitz's shots of New York made in the 1900s. And yet the genealogy of their film must be traced beyond their authors' individual careers to larger cultural developments.[4]

Manhatta and subsequent city films are driven by the exploration of the contemporary metropolitan landscape. This interest informs a variety of fields in the American 1910s and 1920s: from painting, photography, and literature to cultural criticism, social science, and the cinema. In painting, city scenes were a favorite subject of the realist Ashcan School painters, who portrayed the new metropolis with nearly photographic objectivity, and of experimental artists such as Frank Stella or John Marin, interested in the challenges that urban dynamism posed to traditional laws of perspective and composition. In photography, Strand's and Sheeler's urban views were indebted to those by the photo-secessionists Alvin Langdon Coburn, Edward Steichen, and Alfred Stieglitz. The modern city was also amply represented in literature. T. S. Eliot's *The Waste Land,* Ernest Hemingway's *The Sun Also Rises,* or John Dos Passos's *Manhattan Transfer,* to name some famous examples, prominently feature the city as (in Eliot's language) an objective correlative of a fallen, disenchanted world. In the social sciences, the late 1910s and 1920s saw the birth of modern urban sociology in the work of Robert E. Park, Louis Wirth, Lewis Mumford, and many others who were influenced by continental figures like the German philosopher Georg Simmel. Furthermore, the mid- and late-1910s witnessed the emergence of what some historians have called "the rise of city planning,"[5] prompted by the increasing complexity of cities and by the need to make the urban layout functional and expressive of the city's character, aspirations, and ideal images of itself. *Manhatta* shares the strategies and goals of many of these discourses. It is at once a documentary, a critical statement about modernity, a formalist exploration of patterns, movements, and rhythms, and a visual counterpart of the descriptions of the metropolitan experience produced by contemporary sociologists, architects, and planners. And it is, besides, a testimony to the connections between film and urban habitation.

The cinema had been joined to the city from birth. Before the film industry relocated to Hollywood, it thrived in large northern cities, where the anonymous urban crowds were the cinema's main audience. They were also one of the cinema's main topics, since the metropolis, its crowds, and its architecture were important purveyors of cinematographic spectacle, as witnessed by the popularity of an early genre, the "urban panorama." The cinema immediately appropriated the modern city in large part because the modern city was eminently cinematographic. Monumental and cyclopean in scale, it was often built to be looked at rather than lived in—just like a set. Yet the emphasis on visual accessibility was not merely a matter of aesthetics. Baron de Hausmann's reform of Paris during the Second Empire evidenced that the new urban spaces were often designed to enforce legibility and surveillance, and therefore to control the masses in an era racked by social unrest. The parallel between the modern city and the cinema makes sense not only in terms of global design but at the most intimate perceptual level as well. Walter Benjamin has influentially suggested that the sensorial experience of the industrialized city, a panorama of speedy transitions and ever-changing perspectives, offered a preview of film spectatorship, as the constant refocusing of attention demanded by the urban setting anticipated cinematic cuts and shifts in framing.[6] Extending this notion, one might say that the way one picks out points of reference and determines directions has a counterpart in Hollywood's analytical editing, which aims to keep the viewer oriented in space. Continuity editing, largely formalized by an artist of small-town origin, D. W. Griffith, might be read as an attempt to stabilize perspective and to provide clear visual vectors through the perceptual tangle of urban actuality. The difference between early cinema, with its looser spatial articulation, and classical cinema could be compared to the difference between submitting to the sensorial bombardment of the city and trying to regiment its plurality. *Manhatta* does both, yet in the end, a desire for regimentation prevails.

Despite its influence, *Manhatta* has received scant scholarly attention. The film is often mentioned in histories of avant-garde and documentary film, and in more recent years it has received some attention from scholars of early twentieth-century American art and culture, such as Dickran Tashjian, Karen Lucic, Miles Orvell, Celeste Connor, and Wanda Corn. While they all contribute interesting and well-informed insights, they tend to treat the film in passing, as a text that is adjacent to their main interests. Tashjian locates it within the evolution of American dadaism; Lucic and Orvell study it as an exponent of Sheeler's aesthetic treatment of industry and technology; Connor detects in it the anti-urban attitudes characteristic of the Stieglitz group in the 1920s; and Wanda Corn argues that it has many parallels in theme and construction with Joseph Stella's painting *Voice of the City*. Exceptions to such insightful but incidental treatment are Scott Hammen and, especially, Jan-Christopher Horak, whose excellent writing on the film provides a thorough and compelling interpretation.[7]

Horak reads the film as an ambiguous text that combines modernist and antimodernist traits. On the one hand, "*Manhatta* is central to film modernism's project of deconstructing Renaissance perspective in favor of multiple, reflexive points of view" (271). This is most apparent in the film's stress on abstract patterns and collapsed perspectives and in its refusal to center the spectator. On the other hand, such experimentalism is contradicted by the presence in the film of "antimodern" concerns and ideologies, such as "Whitmanesque romanticism" and the assimilation of the landscape of modernity to natural phenomena. These antimodern ideologies are evident in the film's structuring frame—the span from sunrise to sunset, a natural cycle binding the artificial metropolitan environment—and in its conclusion, which shows the reflection of the sun in the waters of the harbor and evokes the merging of nature and city into a harmonic unity. By attempting such a fusion the film further undercuts its own modernism; after all, Horak continues, closure and the reconciliation of contraries are strategies used by classical Hollywood cinema to solve ideological contradiction and to appease conceptual scandals. Horak traces the film's ambivalent modernism to the ideology of the Stieglitz group, whose members were equally committed to the machine aesthetic and to nature; to experimentation and to a romantic view of art and the artist.[8] This contextualization of the film is convincing and thoroughly researched but somewhat selective. Stieglitz is indeed a direct influence, yet others remain to be accounted for. A broader perspective is needed to explore developments outside the filmmakers' immediate orbit. Two of these are the discourse of the little magazine *The Soil* and the modernist reception of popular cinema. Both influenced decisively the way the film "practices" the city and formalizes urban space. *Manhatta* oscillates between giving in to the proliferating disorder of city life and imposing some order on it, even if it leans more toward order than dispersion. This oscillation allows us to see the film as a text at the crossroads not only of modernism and antimodernism but also of two different conceptions of modernism and two competing views of the urban everyday.

The Soil and Urban Collage

Manhatta's way of portraying the city has an important antecedent in *The Soil,* an influential but largely forgotten little magazine published in New York between December 1916 and April 1917. It was launched by Robert J. Coady, a Manhattan-born artist, critic, and art dealer. He studied painting in New York and Paris, where he frequented the American expatriate colony gathered around Gertrude Stein and became friends with a number of local artists, among them Henri Rousseau. When World War I broke out, he moved back to New York and soon after, in June 1914, opened the Washington Square Art Gallery in Greenwich Village and, later on, the Coady Gallery on Fifth Avenue. These galleries specialized in contemporary experimental art, which was suddenly in high demand after the success of the Armory Show in 1913. *The Soil* was started as an offshoot of Coady's activity as an exhibitor and dealer.[9] The original motivation for the journal was a 1916 exhibition at the Anderson Galleries curated by a forum directed by the art critic Willard Huntington Wright and including Alfred Stieglitz and Robert Henri among its members. The exhibition sought to promote a number of contemporary American modernists that, in the eyes of the forum members, had been neglected in the Armory Show. Coady disputed the forum's vision of American art in an open letter to the *New York Sun* in March 1916. He claimed that the chosen selection did not rest on a clear definition of American art; the show championed work that was simply imitative of European models, and, more importantly, the real native achievement was not to be found in the official art institutions but in the realms of popular culture, technology, and everyday life.

Coady's journal did not reject gallery art but placed it in dialogue with these other realms of creativity. Its pages offered an exuberant mixture of modernism, technology, and the popular arts. It combined reproductions of the work of Claude Lorraine, Vincent van Gogh, Pablo Picasso, and Henri Rousseau with photographs of locomotives, skyscrapers, steam hammers, and cranes and pictures of athletes, comedians (Bert Williams), singers, clowns ("Toto"), bullfighters (Joselito "el Gallo"; the picture was a gift from Gertrude Stein), and film stars (Charlie Chaplin, who also contributed an essay to the first issue; Annette Kellerman, of *Neptune's Daughter*; and J. P. McGowan, an actor in and director of adventure serials). The mixed quality of the magazine's visual style was also apparent in the writing. Pieces by Wallace Stevens, Maxwell Bodenheim, and Gertrude Stein competed for attention with decidedly lowbrow genres: the Nick Carter serial "The Pursuit of the Lucky Clew"; sports chronicles; and articles about magic, billiards, dressmaking, shop-window arrangements, or the dime novel as literature. A number of items were devoted to nonwestern art and cultures. The December 1916 issue, for example, contained a photographic spread on South Sea Island objects and an excerpt from Carl Lumholz's *Unknown Mexico* on the racing feats of the Tarahumara Indians, and the July 1917 issue featured a "Congo sculpture" on the cover. The April 1917 issue had a section on children's art, which Coady, following Stieglitz's example, had exhibited in his gallery. The show, incidentally, was not only an aesthetic statement; the artists were black children, and Coady's intention was to raise funds for the American Circle for Negro War Relief, an organization that aided the families of black servicemen.

The journal's way of combining "legitimate" modernism, technology, and popular expression implicitly stressed their common roots in metropolitan modernity. The easy passage between the popular and technology was based on their mutual implication, as most popular art was by this time mechanically reproduced and disseminated, and also on their anti-artistic nature. In the eyes of the editors of *The Soil,* both were forms of practice that owed little to the post-romantic notions of art upheld by the genteel tradition. While, according to these conceptions, art is born out of introspection and has little to do with utility, popular culture and technology spring from compulsion and need. Here lies their particular Americanness, modernity, and truth—three qualities that are interconnected in the philosophy of the journal. Art is "true," in the terms of *The Soil,* when it responds to "everyday demand"—when it stems from specific requirements and works to satisfy them. This hands-on quality is what makes it specifically American. In the words of a contributor, "What is called Americanism does not dwell in men's minds; it is a sort of compulsory service."[10] Born out of compulsion, for example, was the skyscraper, an innovation prompted by the increase in land values, congestion, and the necessity to build upward. "It was when architects began to conceive of a building based, decoratively, on its internal structure that they began to shake off the prestige of antiquity."[11] Sport and popular culture stem from analogous forms of compulsion. The movements of boxers and bronco riders respond to the need to beat their opponents and keep their balance. And the art of the moving picture, the comedian, the variety performer, and the cabaret singer arises from the need to hold the attention of the jaded urban spectators while depicting in sharp, recognizable outline aspects of these spectators' experiences. This celebration of art born under compulsion was not exclusive to *The Soil.* It was quite influential in this phase of American modernism, which, as Miles Orvell has shown, was driven by the desire for "authenticity," for an art that would be free of artifice and firmly planted in immediate reality.[12] Paul Strand was an exponent of these ideas. In a brief essay published in 1917, he rejected pictorialism and praised photographic objectivity because it developed "out of actual living" and of the limitations imposed by the apparatus.[13]

Because it demoted high art and celebrated machinery and the popular, *The Soil* can be aligned with a number of historical avant-garde formations.

In fact, as Judith Zilczer and Dickran Tashjian have pointed out, its irreverence and sense of humor were close to contemporary dadaism.[14] The ties between *The Soil* and dada were personal as well as ideological. Coady knew Duchamp, who, in turn, was highly appreciative of Coady and was delighted with his magazine. Yet *The Soil*'s main link with the movement was the notorious Arthur Cravan, a writer, boxer, sometime painter, and cultural agitator at large.[15] Cravan was born in Lausanne, went to school in France, and became active in the Paris art scene in the early 1910s. He combined a career in boxing with the publication of an art review of which he was the sole author, writing under a variety of pseudonyms. Cravan was especially known for his penchant for scandal and for savage reviews of the work of his contemporaries that often bordered on insult. In 1916, he migrated from Paris to New York via Barcelona, where a number of figures of the French avant-garde (Sonia Delaunay and Francis Picabia among them) converged during World War I. He stayed long enough to charm the local intelligentsia and to challenge the heavyweight champion Jack Johnson to a well-publicized fight, which Cravan lost, in the city's main bullfighting arena. In January 1917, he was a regular in the New York dada group led by Duchamp and Picabia and in the Arensberg circle. He eventually tired of New York and traveled to Newfoundland and then to Mexico, where he lived for a year with his partner at the time, the poet Mina Loy. He disappeared in Veracruz in December 1918, as he and Loy were waiting to board a ship for Buenos Aires, where part of the New York dada colony then was. Cravan contributed occasional poems and brief reflections to *The Soil* and was the instigator of the homage to his uncle, Oscar Wilde, in the last issue of the periodical. But in addition to Cravan's contributions, the journal's dada spirit also cropped up in jokes that took aim at artistic pretension. Images of riders at rodeos bore captions like: "Not among the art notes," and, "He doesn't need an -ism to guide him." A black smear on the page was titled, "Evening of the three hundred and sixty-sixth day of the year." And in a late issue a highly abstract canvas by Morgan Russell, titled "Cosmic Synchromy," was printed next to a picture of an egg, captioned "Invention—Nativity," by A. Chicken. Russell's solemn pronouncement on method and intention, printed at the bottom of the page, contrasted with A. Chicken's laconism: "Cluck, cluck."

Despite the agrarian resonances of its title, *The Soil* is best read as an example of an eminently modernist genre: the urban collage. It is made up of the juxtaposition of urban actualities: pictures of department-store windows, locomotives, and skyscrapers; articles on the New York harbor and the Bronx Zoo; reports on rodeos, circus shows, and boxing nights; records of conversations heard on the street and on the bus (accompanied by detailed transcriptions of background noise); and interviews with the stars of the day. Coady defended the artistic value of all these manifestations of city life in his two-part manifesto, "American Art," published in the first two issues of the magazine: "There is an American Art. Young, robust, energetic, naive, immature, daring, and big-spirited. Active in any conceivable field." And he proceeded to enumerate its achievements (I quote selectively, as the list goes on for a full page):

> The Panama Canal, the Sky-Scraper and Colonial architecture. The Tug Boat and the Steam Shovel. The Bridges, the Docks, the cutouts, the Viaducts, the "Matt M. Shay" and the "3000" [two locomotives photographed on the facing page]. Jack Johnson, Charlie Chaplin, Bert Williams. Ragtime, Syncopation, and the Cake-walk. The Window Dressers. Football. Coney Island, the Shooting Galleries, the Beaches, *The Police Gazette,* Krazy Kat, Nick Carter, Deadwood Dick, Walt Whitman and Poe, William Dean Howells, and Gertrude Stein. The Zoo. Staten Island Warehouses. Parkhurst Church and the Woolworth Building. The Movie Posters. The Jack Pot. Dialect and Slang. The Cranes, the Plows, the Drills, the Motors, Steam Rollers, Grain Elevators, Trench Excavators, Blast Furnaces—This is American Art . . . an expression of life—a complicated life—American life.[16]

Coady's manifesto, a Whitmanian catalog of personal raves, anticipates *Manhatta*'s collage structure and foreshadows a number of the film's visual motifs: the skyscrapers, the tug boats, the steam shovel seen in a construction site, the bridges (the Brooklyn Bridge appears in several shots), the docks, viaducts, locomotives, the Woolworth Building, cranes, plows and drills, and Walt Whitman, the source of the film's intertitles. Even Staten Island is at one point visible in the distance (though not its warehouses). Coady complains that this art is "as yet, outside of our art world."[17] Remedying this omission was the program of the journal and, apparently, also the goal of Strand and Sheeler's picture.

These visual motifs anticipated in *The Soil* were included in *Manhatta* because they were considered emblematic of New York City. And yet, as emblems, they are somewhat contradictory: some belong to the city's spectacular, official façade, and others to its unofficial existence. Such ambiguity is also present in *Manhatta*. The skyscrapers and bridges, the towering views they afford, and the architecture of the downtown corporate centers make up a grandiloquent spectacle expressive of the nation's industrial and financial power. At the same time, a number of homely signposts of daily life, such as the tugs, construction-site machinery, docks, ferries, anonymous pedestrians, an old cemetery (Trinity Church's), elevated trains, and the ever-present smoke, provide a backyard view of the city. The hesitation between these two types of icons can be attributed to differences in the filmmakers' sensibilities. Sheeler's urban photographs of the 1910s show a spectacle city of imposing skyscrapers and highlight geometry and mass. Strand was occasionally drawn to high-rise architecture, but he tended to favor views that lack spectacular value, and his work always retained some human interest. He pointed his camera toward homely side streets viewed from the platform of the elevated train, solitary passersby, yards in the backs of buildings, the casual mingling of pedestrians and traffic in nondescript intersections. Even when he showcased the stern gigantism of modern architecture, as in his most famous photograph of the period, "Wall Street," he still preserved some human reference in the figures of clerks hurrying to their desks in the early morning.

The affinities between *The Soil* and *Manhatta* go beyond distinct imagery and may be traced to a shared view of their role as cultural media. Coady's magazine operated, to a certain extent, as a recording mechanism. Acting as urban reporters of sorts, as camera-toting flaneurs, the journal's writers inventoried the sort of insignificant, largely unchronicled sights and practices present in Strand's early pictures or in many of *Manhatta's* scenes. They did so in short, nervous, descriptive pieces that were the equivalent of prose photographs. Their titles often have the abrupt quality of snapshots: "Tugs," "The Fight," "The Woolworth Building," "Prestidigitation," "To the Bronx Zoo," or "The Billiard Players." They convey the feel of reality surprised in flight by the camera. Once caught, these slices of the real were transposed to the pages of the journal, where their artistry and cultural significance were glossed. A typical example of this procedure is the article "Dressmaking," by F.M., which starts out with an elated sense of scoop: "There is a great deal more of art in the dressmaking shops than in the galleries. Particularly in most of those galleries which deal in so-called American art."[18] The body of the essay is an interview with a "dress specialist," Paul Louis de Giaferri, laced with emphatic proclamations on fashion as art. On occasion such scoops were illustrated with actual photographs. The April 1916 issue contained a two-page picture of the Monroe Clothes Shop on Broadway. Satirizing Joseph Stella's recent series of paintings, "Battle of the Lights, Coney Island, Mardi Gras," the caption quips: "Here is an exhibition of pictures

. . . in the midst of a real 'battle of the lights' at Broadway and Forty-Second Street. Daumier would have done it about the same way and . . . our modern genius could learn a lot from this remarkable example of solid common sense." Even when actual pictures were not used, the writing itself strives to convey photographic effects. Take, for example, the following description of two boxers in action by Robert Alden Sanborn, a regular contributor: "Art sits on the sidelines and wins bets from both of them. Phydias might sign his name under that frieze of nakedness, gliding through arenas of smoke in ten thousand instants of beauty."[19] The fragment moves nimbly from allegory to classical allusion to an invocation of the camera's ability to freeze the flow of action into discrete "instants."

This photographic mode seems particularly suited to *The Soil*'s tentative, fragmentary way of inhabiting the city, and it is also characteristic of city living at large. The brief, journalistic pieces, which were often accompanied by illustrations, allowed for surprising montage-like juxtapositions: machine art and movie-star interviews; shots of skyscrapers and children's art; the tugs in the harbor and the animals in the zoo. This kaleidoscopic variety is that of city life itself, and the magazine openly celebrated it, seldom attempting to reduce it to pattern or to curtail its play. *The Soil*'s abrupt jumps in topic, tone, and medium (from verse to prose to photography to painting) evoke the myriad shocklike sensations, perspectives, and transitions experienced by the metropolitan dweller in his or her excursions through the city. These traits of city life received wide attention in contemporary urban sociology. For Georg Simmel, the distinctive feature of modern metropolitan existence was an "intensification of nervous stimulation" caused by the relentless barrage of outer and inner stimuli to which the senses are subjected.[20] For Simmel's former student, the Chicago sociologist Robert Park, the city was "a mosaic of little worlds which touch but do not interpenetrate."[21] This gives city life a "superficial and adventitious character," introducing into it "an element of chance and adventure." In this heterogeneous environment, contacts, impressions, and information multiply, but their increase in number compels a decrease in depth. One comes into contact with many but really knows very few; sees more but understands less; has wider but shallower knowledge. The fleetingness of urban experience puts a premium on visual recognition. It favors a photographic rapport with one's environment—a rapport that another Chicago sociologist, Louis Wirth, described as "impersonal, superficial, transitory, and segmental" and, above all, based on what one sees, on surface appearance.[22]

This way of submitting to the city's insuppressible variety conditioned *The Soil*'s conception of art. The journal's snapshot approach entailed an additive, radically inclusive principle also at work in *Manhatta*. In practice, any object, scene, or facet of contemporary urban culture could be (and was) framed as art: a building site, barges and tugs, a crowd of passersby, an acrobat's routine, a boxing match, trains and horse-drawn carts, rodeos and circus shows, movie and sports personalities. Even the fish in the aquarium were reported by *The Soil* in the language of the art gallery: "Exhibition of the Freedom of Movement in Light and Space. Aquarium. Battery Park. New York City. Open Every Day 9:30 AM to 4:00 PM."[23] By choosing such artless subjects, *The Soil*, like *Manhatta*, captured and transfigured ordinary, ephemeral aspects of urban life. They did so by placing a frame around them—that is, by applying to them an intensified analytical attention; by re-creating them through the rhetoric of art and cultural criticism (with satirical intent at times). Such framing "elevated" the ordinary and exploited its visual and cultural potential. It also "lowered" art by bringing it into closer contact with life. Furthermore, this device displaced artistry from technique or subject matter to the act of pointing at, or choosing, a given particular from the countless possibilities of the actual. Evaluating Coady's conception of American art, Tashjian exposes its vagueness: its mixture of past and present, of canonical authors (Whitman, Poe) and pulp fiction heroes (Deadwood Dick), and of people, places, and things is too inclusive and nondiscriminatory to operate as a critical label. Yet this is exactly the point *The Soil* was trying to make: "American art" is not a canon of achievements but an attitude, the attitude that everything can be framed as art, that artistry is not an inherent quality but a function of context and discursive frames.

One of the main precursors of this view is Walt Whitman, perhaps the most generative model for American modernism, whose poetry treated everything from a pile of compost to "the scent of these armpits" as a worthy aesthetic subject.[24] In the early twentieth century, this ethos was pushed to its ultimate consequences by the dadaists. About a year before Coady launched *The Soil,* Marcel Duchamp started to produce his first ready-mades in New York, mass-produced commodities framed as art objects by the process of giving them a title, an authorial intention, and an exhibition context.[25] Well-known examples are the snow shovel titled "In Advance of the Broken Arm," the marble cubes in a birdcage, "Why Not Sneeze, Rrose Selavy?" and the notorious "Richard Mutt's Fountain," a porcelain wall urinal lying on its flat side that sent ripples of scandal across the art world. Duchamp also envisioned using the Woolworth Building as a ready-made and developed some notes to the purpose, but the project was never carried out . . . by him.[26] It was Sheeler and Strand who fulfilled Duchamp's design in *Manhatta* by slowly tilting their camera down the side of the building. Their ideology and spirit differ from Duchamp's, and yet at base they share with him a structural affinity: the framing of everyday particulars as (anti-)art.

It makes cultural sense that Arthur Cravan found in *The Soil* a fitting outlet for his cultural hooliganism, and that *Manhatta,* retitled *Fumées de New York,* was first shown in Paris at a dadaist event that also included a Man Ray film, readings of Guillaume Apollinaire's poems, and music by Erik Satie.[27] However, we should be careful to push beyond structural resemblances; *The Soil* and *Manhatta* practice a sportive, genial dadaism that never shares the aggressive despair of their European counterparts. They are Whitmanian celebrations of the common life and frequently conceive the modern material world as a hieroglyph of spiritual principles—American art and "Americanness." Notice, for example, the pantheistic note in Strand's conclusion to his essay "Photography": "Let us rather accept joyously and with gratitude everything through which the spirit of man seeks to an ever fuller and more intense self-realization."[28] In contrast, European dadaism, even when made in the United States by bon-vivant expatriates like Cravan, Picabia, or Duchamp, was less about self-realization than about self-dissolution. It intended to express the wholesale bankruptcy of continental culture, it was often shot through with sexual tension and bitter cynicism, and it jumbled the world's *disjecta membra* as fragments devoid of purpose or meaning, bits and pieces that do not add up.

City Films and Early Cinema

In addition to the ideology and the collage format of *The Soil, Manhatta* imitated the aesthetics of early cinema, more concretely, of the panorama films of the early 1900s. This attachment to an archaic form of filmmaking can be traced to the influence of 1910s and 1920s modernist film culture. At the time when the industry was acquiring its classical configuration with the feature film, the incipient star system, increasing production values, and the gentrification of the film product and the filmgoing experience, modernist critics and commentators rebuffed these developments and resolutely sided with preclassical genres—early shorts, actualities, serials, and physical comedies (like those by Chaplin or the Keystone Studios). For Robert Coady these rough, lively movies demonstrated the cinema's fullest potential: they accomplished "that for which it [the cinema] is constituted—visual motion."[29] Stripped to its essence, the cinema is a language of surface and speed, and these qualities, which for Vachel Lindsay were the blight of the new medium, made it, in Coady's mind, an apt vehicle for exploring and expressing modern life. The industry's recent emphasis on drama and narrative acted as a sort of censorship, curtailing the most distinct possibilities of the medium. Hence right around the time when the National Association of Motion Picture Producers was trying to forestall public censorship of its products, Coady polemically exclaimed: "Yet have not these organizers been censoring [the cinema] right along? Have they not been limiting its activity to 'the story,' the 'photoplay' and the 'photodrama,' limiting its scope in the field of visual motion?" (38). These ideas were articulated in Coady's essay "Censoring the Motion Picture," published in the December 1916 issue of *The Soil*. Coady spurned the trappings of respectability the cinema had acquired since the nickleodeon days—psychology, narrative, and, tied to both, illusionism. Film should not become a dramatic or narrative form: "To the moving picture, and to [film] acting, the story is merely a motive, a convenience or an excuse" (37). This is, ultimately, why stagy performers did not become part of *The Soil*'s pantheon; the magazine celebrated instead Annette Kellerman, a former swimming champion featured in aquatic spectacles that are the direct predecessors of Esther Williams's, and J. P. McGowan, who directed and acted in action serials. Both were athletic performers whose screen affect was tied to pure motion and acrobatics, not to their ability to convey subjective density.

Coady's views are echoed by other authors. One of them was Robert Alden Sanborn, a Harvard graduate on the edge of the Arensberg group who became a *Soil* contributor and a close associate of Coady. His essay "Motion Picture Dynamics," published in the itinerant journal *Broom,* another organ of American dadaism published in the early 1920s by Malcolm Cowley, Harold Loeb, and Matthew Josephson, also decried the literary baggage that frequently dragged down contemporary productions and celebrated the "boisterously young" early movies, rich in "quickness of movement" and visual contrasts. His paradigmatic example is the serial *The Girl and the Game,* released in 1915, directed by J. P. McGowan and starring Helen Holmes: "[O]ne of the best motion pictures ever produced from the standpoint of a critic of the art."[30] The statement is intentionally provocative: at the height of silent film splendor, when the lavish, meticulously produced blockbuster (such as *Robin Hood, The Thief of Bagdad,* and *Ben-Hur*) was in vogue, Sanborn picks as one of the pinnacles of film art a cheaply made old serial without any cultural credentials, one, moreover, that he has to watch at a neighborhood theater in Brooklyn, since it has long been banished from the first-run theaters on Broadway. But lack of pretension and physicality are what make the serial great. Its value lay primarily in the speed and excitement of the improbable narrative: "characters dashed out of places and in again, men grappled, tumbled off freight cars, and rolled down enbankments" (81). In the headlong plunge of the action, memorable cinematic moments pop up:

> In making a scene wherein a swift motor launch was to race in to a dock, barely slacken to allow some men to leap into the pit, and then, describing a beautiful arc, speed out to sea, McGowan timed the action to take place just the right moment previous to the expected entrance into the distance of a huge coastwise steamship. The result was pronounced and unforgettable. The swift arc cut by the launch was contrasted with the slowly-drawn direct line of motion of the larger boat. The arc completed, the smaller craft sped away, passing under the threatening bow of the great liner. Force was applied to force, two movements of contrasting beauty struck edges. Here was motion picture dynamics. (81)

This epiphanic moment condenses the essence of film: motion, graphic contrast, and speed devoid of psychological or narrative import. Sanborn's text is important because it exemplifies a form of spectatorship that helped configure an alternative cinema in the United States, and therefore provides a link between a style of film watching and certain types of filmmaking. It could be argued that an important sector of the early American avant-garde was based on a conception of the cinema akin to that articulated by Coady and Sanborn. Ralph Steiner's *H2O* and *Mechanical Principles,* Henwar Rodakciewicz's *Portrait of a Young Man,* and Mary Ellen Bute's abstractions implicitly rejected contemporary illusionism, dramatic incident, and "depth"; they treated the cinema as a medium for the display of motion and thus returned to early film's primal dynamism.

Like these films, *Manhatta* deflated dramatic and representational pretensions and highlighted the movement, surfaces, lines, and textures of the urban spectacle. In doing so, Strand and Sheeler drew on the urban panoramas: a discarded form at the time, yet one of the most popular film genres of the prenickleodeon era. The panoramas were one-take shorts depicting city scenes.[31] Some were random recordings of traffic and crowds; others photographed particular milestones (see, for example, *Panorama of the Flat-iron Building* from 1903, the year when the structure was finished and when Stieglitz took his first pictures of it). At times the camera was mounted on moving surfaces, such as trains, trams, ships, or even the subway. *Sky Scrapers of New York City from the North River* (1903) and *Washington Bridge and Speedway* (1903) provide views of the city from the decks of moving boats, a perspective echoed in several shots of *Manhatta,* and *Interior New York Subway* shows an underground train traveling from Union Square to Forty-Second Street. These films may have elicited the pleasure of familiarity, since they portrayed well-known sites; or they may have sought, as did *The Soil* and *Manhatta,* to transfigure the ordinary by means of its representation. They were a variety of what the film historian Tom Gunning has influentially called "the cinema of attractions": a type of cinema that solicits the spectator's attention not through narrative regulation but through the display of spectacle in the form of a unique view or event. In the case of the panoramas, the spectacle displayed is the dynamism of the city and also the camera's ability to signify it. By panning, tilting, or traveling, by opening a visual field and transforming perspective relations, by unfolding the entire height of a skyscraper, or by cutting into the crowds, these films display the camera's ability to "mobilize and explore space."[32] *Manhatta* is a throwback to the cinema of attractions and recalls the double spectacle of the panoramas. It offers striking views of city space and conveys a sense of wonder at the versatility of the instrument that articulates them.

At the same time, *Manhatta* is a panorama film with cubist self-consciousness. The early panoramas were characterized by a bid for completeness. *Panorama of the Flatiron Building,* for example, pans up and down the entire length of the structure. Other films provide 360–degree views from rooftops, observation points, or street corners (two examples are *Panorama from Times Building, New York,* and *Panorama from the Tower of the Brooklyn Bridge*), or travel slowly along the waterfront. Their symmetrical, deliberate camera movements usually attempt some closure; framings may be off-center, and beginnings and endings arbitrary, yet film panoramas often seek to produce a complete impression of the view at hand—whether a fish market downtown or a line of buildings on the Manhattan shore. *Manhatta,* however, foregoes such exhaustiveness. It reproduces the city as a fractured space. Shots of recognizable milestones appear truncated and asymmetrical: a shot of the Woolworth Building leaves the elegant top out of the frame, tilts down its side, and ends up lingering over the unremarkable constructions next to it. Balanced, well-composed takes alternate with others that refuse to pick a clear center of interest and merely open up a space for aimless drift. In the harbor sequence, for example, carefully composed views of cruise ships are spliced with erratic shots of scattered barges and tugs crossing the frame in different directions. Other times, barrier shots reproduce within a given frame the simultaneity and contrasts of perspective common in cubist painting. Two high-angle takes from the top of a skyscraper show distant ground-level activity through a thick stone balustrade close to the camera lens; and shots of the Brooklyn Bridge taken from the boardwalk show its gothic arches through the maze of cables that support the structure. (Wanda Corn points out that this view also fascinated the painter Joseph Stella, who reproduced it in one of the panels of *The Voice of the City of New York*.[33]) In addition, as Horak has noted in his landmark work on the film, *Manhatta*'s editing yields no clear spatial relations—only contrasts of mass, volume, and direction. The overall result is not a travelogue, an intelligible picture of the city, but a decomposition or dissemination of its landscape.

Such fragmentariness may originate in a modernist way of reading commercial films that consisted in dislodging discrete segments from the flow of the narrative. This is exactly what Sanborn does in the paragraph quoted above. The procedure appears in other contemporary modernist writings about the cinema. In an article published in the December 1916 issue of *The Seven Arts,* the drama critic (and future theatrical and film producer) Kenneth Macgowan proposed that the most significant moments in the cinema are the intermittent flashes of photographic beauty that appear in the crevices of the narrative. These moments of "visual distinction" are often involuntary and work against the general grain of the text: "Even the worst bungler gives once or twice—setting against it as his commercial creed may be—some new grasping at reality. It may be the rounding of a valley into view, the poise of a shoulder against a background, the proportions of a house to its frame of trees . . . the flare of shadow cast by a single point of light, or just the reflection and diffusion of a cross light under a summer pier."[34] If for Coady and Sanborn film's basic visuality demands a return to origins, for Macgowan it prompts a fragmentary reception, a sifting through the "flash and disjointed rush of mediocrity" for enlightened moments when "the director infuses life with the beauty of his pictorial art" (168–69). These ideas foreshadow those of the surrealists, also avid readers and debunkers of popular cinema, and equally fixated on fragmentary spectatorship. Compare, for example, Macgowan's statement with the surrealist procedure of watching films in bits and pieces, entering and leaving the theater arbitrarily, with complete disregard for the integrity of the plot. Or recall Man Ray's famous pronouncement: "The worst films I've ever seen, the ones that send me to sleep, contain ten or fifteen marvelous minutes."[35]

Following the clue provided by Macgowan's ideas, one can see *Manhatta* as a re-creation of the fragmenting, selective reading of a modernist spectator confronted with a standard commercial feature. One might also read it as an archive of memorable city views culled from narrative films; as establishment shots or montage sequences purged of the storylines that might have supported them. Seen in this fashion, the film pulsates with possibility: it anticipates a story without actually producing one. The ships and docks evoke departures and arrivals; the graveyard suggests bereavements; the crowd scenes, frantic searches for missing characters. One almost waits for the camera to light on a particular passerby and to follow her or him until a story ensues. The story, however, is always held at bay, constantly hinted at but constantly withdrawn. In this respect, *Manhatta* is a pre-story, an evocation of the milieu where narrative emerges, or else a sort of cinematic unconscious: the unruly profusion of objects, spaces, perspectives, and connections that the classical film has to repress or bind into a storyline to say what it says.

The Mass Ornament

This cinematic unconscious is coextensive with urban space: an endlessly connective surface where discrete elements are in constant motion, driven by an automatism that brings them together and pulls them apart in unpredictable and unrepeatable configurations. *Manhatta* records this anarchic proliferation, but at the same time, it imposes some order on it, reducing its contingency. This reduction takes place by eliding the complexity of the city's human landscape.

City space in *Manhatta* is abridged, syncopated in the manner typical of the city film. Lost in the abridgment is the individuality of the city dwellers, seen always at a distance as black dots scurrying along sun-drenched pavements or as a compact throng in ferries and thoroughfares. In an early scene, the commuters on a ferry boat appear as a faceless agglomeration on the front deck; as the boat enters the slip and the exit gates open, they pour onto the street as a liquid mass. They are filmed from behind in a high-angle shot that shows a sea of hats and makes them thinglike and unreadable. When readable at all, people are endowed with few marks of belonging or iden-

Manhatta. Frame enlargement.
Courtesy of Anthology Film Archives.

tity. The figures sitting and strolling in a park—probably City Hall Park—or among the tombstones in the Trinity Church cemetery, or ambling through the street seem uniformly middle class. They are serialized and streamlined, in part through the consistent use of extreme long shots and high angles; other times they are conflated with machinery and constructions. A worker in a ditch is barely distinguishable from the grey expanse of the dredge he seems to be operating. And other workers perched on the steel frame of a building are seen in silhouette, as extensions of the metal beams and cranes (this shot was the basis for Sheeler's later drawing, *Totems of Steel*). These examples indicate that the film turns city dwellers into abstractions and reduces them to pattern and movement. In fact, such reduction (or flattening, to recall Clement Greenberg's vocabulary) is central to the film's modernism. It recalls precisionist painting, a contemporary trend characterized by geometrical composition and rectilinear rendering whose main representatives were Charles Demuth and Sheeler himself. But it also recalls Strand's pathbreaking photographs of 1916 and 1917, in which, by shooting at extremely close range, he turned ordinary objects and settings such as bowls, chairs, a table top, and a porch railing into abstract studies of light, shadow, and plane. An analogous reduction of the city to a series of graphic patterns seems to have been the primary purpose of the film. As Strand wrote in an unpublished press release for *Manhatta:* "Restricting themselves to the towering geometry of lower Manhattan and its environs, the distinctive note, the photographers have tried to register directly the living forms in front of them and to reduce through the most rigid selection, volumes, lines and masses, to their intensest terms of expressiveness. Through these does the spirit manifest itself."[36]

The "spirit" is that of New York City, a synecdoche for American modernity and modernity at large. Its expression, Strand seems to suggest, somehow requires the erasure of the human landscape, or at least its complete equation with the material landscape. This erasure is frequent in Sheeler but stands in significant contrast with most of Paul Strand's early work. The last issue of *Camera Work* (published in 1917) featured six of Strand's portraits of anonymous street types: a blind woman, a sandwich man, a yawning street vendor, a burly gentleman in a derby hat, a wrinkled middle-aged lady, and a bleary-eyed fellow staring frontally at the camera in slightly soft focus. Produced at around the same time as his abstractions, their realism and direct social reference recalls the work of Strand's first mentor, Lewis Hine. Unlike Hine's, however, they were shot in candid fashion, using a prism lens that allowed Strand to photograph at an angle. Most were taken around the Lower East Side, several in Five Point Square. Captioned generically "Photograph, New York, 1917," they have subsequently become known by other titles. These pictures provide another view of the modern metropolitan milieu, this time indirectly shown through the beaten physiques of their subjects, whose faces and gestures individualize and translate into physiognomic terms the harrowing march of progress. (Strand stated toward the end of his life, "I felt they were all people whom life had battered into some sort of extraordinary interest and, in a way, nobility."[37]) In these snapshots, modernity is not a geometrical construct but an embattled, painfully negotiated process inflected by class position and cultural specificity. Neither class nor cultural identity are obviously stated but can be inferred. All of these characters seem working-class. One could easily read into them traces of the recent immigrant. Some of them stare warily, withdrawn, as if immersed in a cacophony of foreign voices they do not understand. Something of a rural (Eastern European?) manner clings to the style and demeanor of the sandwich man.[38]

This messiness of ascription and difference is lost in the towering perspectives and geometries of *Manhatta*. The "spirit" of modernity, *Manhatta*-style, demands the extreme long take, the establishment shot that blurs human details, or at least transposes them into what the Weimar theorist Siegfried Kracauer famously called the "mass ornament": the crowd transformed into spectacle in chorus lines, gymnastic demonstrations, stadiums, parades, or spontaneously in streets and public spaces.[39] These aggregates are "surface manifestations" of the historical process—emblems, in short, of modernity. Their underlying cause is the population increase in metropolitan centers. The effect of the mass ornament depends on the mediation of photography and film, since, like dancers in a Busby Berkeley ballet, the protagonists of these crowd scenes can not take in directly the show they are a part of; they have to see themselves reflected in a picture or on a screen. At bottom, the mass ornament signals for Kracauer the passing away of organic communities and the emergence in their place of the regimented, Taylorized mass. Lost in the mass ornament are the specificities of cultural and social difference, of locality and sedimented meanings—obstacles to the rationalization process that characterizes modernity: "Personality and national community [*Volksgemeinschaft*] perish when calculability is demanded" (69). And calculability *is* invariably demanded by the scientific management, profit maximization, and accumulation that characterize industrial capitalism. Because of this, Kracauer maintains that "the mass ornament is the aesthetic reflex of the rationality aspired to by the prevailing economic system" (70). From this standpoint, the faceless crowd in *Manhatta* becomes, with the rest of the film's iconography, an ambiguous hieroglyph for the two interrelated forces of "Americanness" and capitalist modernity.

As Kracauer points out, capitalist rationality obeys a truncated form of reason—"not reason itself, but obscured reason. . . . Rationality grown obdurate. Capitalism does not rationalize too much but *too little*" (72). Its particular rationality is characterized by "abstractness," an empty formalism endowed with nearly totemic powers that fails to address concrete life situations.[40] It does not take into account human beings in their concrete needs and particularities, and besides, it cannot determine its own limits. Its processes have become ends in themselves; its conceptual machinery has lost sight of goals and values beyond those that contribute to the endless growth of the system through relentless industrial expansion, ever-deeper cash flows, more thorough colonization of daily experience by commodities. As a self-propelled, unstoppable force, capitalist rationality turns full circle here. Born of the attempt to curtail nature as blind compulsion, it has become just another compulsive force, a perverse second nature. In Kracauer's words, "It is only a consequence of capitalism's unhampered expansion of power that the dark forces of nature continue to rise up threateningly, thereby preventing the emergence of a humanity whose essence is reason" (73).

The mass ornament partakes of this truncated rationality. With their abstraction and geometric splendor, the modern crowds replace earlier forms of community, often based on mystical appeals to the natural and the organic. Through abstraction and anonymity people might be able to loosen their ties to compulsive forms of community and to enter more open types of association based on elective affinities. However, under present conditions abstraction becomes an end in itself, not a platform for rewriting identity and remaking collective life. The gymnastics demonstration, the parade, or the chorus line hide, behind a pretence of order, the actual formlessness and dispossession of the crowd. These mass formations might also become renaturalized (as they did with the rise of Nazism) as new incarnations of the folk community and the "national spirit," expressions of a presumed "organic" bind. The abstract, geometrical mass then reverts to myth and nature.

This is indeed what happens in *Manhatta,* where the abstract crowds appear as organic accretions on the city's surface. Horak describes them as "ant-like," "insects crawling between skyscrapers."[41] Their biological regression is perfectly consonant with the film's eventual assimilation of the artificial modern environment onto nature—to the day cycle and the serenity of the sunset. And it is also of a piece with Vachel Lindsay's comparison of the crowd with "waves," "cataracts," "oceans," and "wheat fields." From the standpoint of Kracauer's ideas, the reassertion of nature would not be necessarily antimodern, as Horak proposed, but part and parcel of the film's ideological modernity and aesthetic modernism. Flattening and abstraction, the reduction of specificity and difference, and the volatilization of history produce a schematism that finds the natural back in the heart of the modern.

As a natural outgrowth, the crowd in *Manhatta* stands above local allegiances and particularities and might therefore be the image of a unified civilization. This dream of unity, which Vachel Lindsay sought to bring about through film, strongly appealed to a number of contemporary intellectuals, among them the editors and contributors to *The Seven Arts,* some of whom were close to the Stieglitz circle. The bid for unity may have seemed especially urgent in the United States in the early decades of the twentieth century, when the destruction of traditional rural societies, the relocation of large numbers of people into industrial belts, and foreign immigration (which peaked between 1880 and 1914) brought together vastly different population groups. The ensuing social and cultural heterogeneity was especially perceptible in cities. However, *Manhatta's* rendering of the contemporary urban milieu seems intent on exorcizing heterogeneity in favor of a uniformity reminiscent of the flatness of precisionist painting or the geometry of skyscraper architecture.

If flatness and schematism invoke harmony and integration—a cohesive polity without cracks—they also gloss over the complexity of cultural practice. Ethnic, class, and gender differences intervene in the practice of city life, yet these differences are at odds with, if not obliterated by, the film's formalism and its political agenda: unity, or the expression of "the spirit." In portraying the city, *Manhatta* stresses formal components (speed, flatness, movement, and line) and omits the multiplicity of the human landscape. As a result of this erasure, its streets appear remote and uninhabitable. While the film's exploration of the city is exhilarating for the way it contests traditional cultural hierarchies and gives shape to common, everyday experience, its inability to picture difference reflects an oppressive underside of modernism.

And yet it is possible that ideas that have an oppressive undertone today may have seemed utopian in the moment of their emergence. In particular, unity, which is often invoked to stomp down otherness, may have seemed a desirable objective when the film was made—but under what circumstances? *Manhatta* was filmed at a time of considerable strife, the immediate postwar years, marked by recession and unemployment as well as by racial tensions and labor agitation. Violent race riots flared up in the summer of 1919, first in Chicago and then in East St. Louis, Houston, Philadelphia, and Washington, D.C., among other cities. In November of the same year, the unrest among workers reached its peak; it has been calculated that about a million were officially on strike to protest low salaries and the skyrocketing cost of living, and possibly as many were engaged in unrecognized protest. Revolutionary labor organizations like the International Workers of the World were growing, especially through the Northwest, and membership in socialist and communist organizations was on the rise. Equally on the rise was the red scare, which eventually prompted the vicious repression of the Left led by the U.S. attorney general, A. Mitchell Palmer. What historians have called "the Palmer raids" progressively escalated to a pitch of hysteria comparable to that instigated by the House Un-American Activities Committee hearings in the aftermath of World War II. The result was a policy of deportations (the anarchist leaders Alexander Beckman and Emma Goldman, for example, were expelled from the country at this time), arbitrary arrests, the closing down of publications considered seditious, and blacklisting. The alibi for such measures was the presumed dimensions of the threat, hyped up by some sectors of the press and by particular political interests seeking to undermine the credibility of organized labor.

Unfortunately, the threat seemed real enough at the time due to a highly publicized string of terrorist attacks in 1919 and 1920. Explosive packets were sent through the mail to various government officials; only one went off, but the panic spread. A bomb did explode in front of Palmer's house in Washington, D.C., causing some material damage but no casualties. The most deadly attack took place on September 19, 1920, in what Frederick Lewis Allen, in his account of the event, called the financial center of the country: the intersection of Wall and Broad Streets in downtown Manhattan. Around this crossing stood the U.S. Assay Office, the Sub-Treasury Building, and the J. P. Morgan and Company headquarters, with the Stock Exchange only a few yards off around the corner. A charge of TNT hidden inside a horse-drawn wagon went off around noon, killing thirty-five people, injuring dozens more, wrecking the Morgan offices, and smashing all the windows in the area. The popular imagination attributed the atrocity to anarchists, but, even though the police followed every possible clue for

Manhatta. Frame enlargement.
Courtesy of Anthology Film Archives.

months, the identity of the perpetrators was never determined.[42] Did this take place before or after Strand and Sheeler had been filming on that exact spot? The austere façade of the House of Morgan appears in a shot that exactly replicates Strand's famous picture of Wall Street, taken from the steps of the Sub-Treasury Building several years before. Given the circumstances, it is possible that, at this particular historical conjuncture, the assertions of "the spirit" and the contemplation of serene geometries proposed by *Manhatta* may have been more soothing than the envisioning of a polity criss-crossed with difference. There is something reassuring in Euclidian absolutes. For the early twentieth-century art theorist Wilhelm Worringer, the reduction of the complexity of appearances to geometric shapes, which was as typical of contemporary modernism as of "primitive" art, obeyed the atavistic attempt to gain some control over an unpredictable environment and the vagaries of history. "In the necessity and irrefragability of geometric abstraction [one] could find repose," he claimed.[43]

Two Modernisms

Geometric abstraction drove one of the main genealogies of modern art, from Cezanne to 1960s minimalism and beyond. In architecture, this kind of formalism was associated with the functionalism most eminently practiced by the Bauhaus and Le Corbusier; when applied to urban space, functionalism gave rise to city planning. Planning sought to rationalize land use, to turn the city into a controllable mechanism where distinct areas were assigned particular uses and shapes and to superimpose linear designs on the unpredictable effervescence of quotidian practice. In many ways, *Manhatta* is decisively shaped by the formalist aspirations of modern architecture and by functionalist urban planning, as it reduces street life to its hardware—the narrow canyons between high-rises, the grid layout, and the communication routes.

   The tendency in recent cultural history has been to juxtapose the severity of modernism to the playfulness and the pop accents of the postmodern. While modernism is described as rational, geometric, and formalist, postmodern architecture is said to have learned from Las Vegas, the amusement park, and vernacular design. Opposing modernism and postmodernism in this fashion, however, we turn into successive cultural moments what was in fact a historical complex characterized by a diversity of modernisms unfolding simultaneously. Hence in *Manhatta,* for example, the bias toward the mass ornament and rational design combines with a tentative, street-level habitation of urban space that we have related to the antecedents of *The Soil,* the early urban actualities, and the popular narrative cinema. It is crucial to understand that these features are not only post- but also fully modern.

Manhatta brings together two different conceptions of modernity and modernism. One of them aspired to efficiency and streamlining. It was the kind of modernism that proclaimed that "less is more" and conceived modernity as a process of simplification and paring down, of increased control and management, or, in Walter Lippmann's famous (and revealing) formulation, of "mastery" as opposed to "drift." This modernism, with its mythic overtones and its absolutist ideology, has tended to obscure the existence of another, equally important, variety. This one is vaguely discernible in the bird's-eye views of *Manhatta;* it stirs in the shadow of the skyscrapers, on the edges of the financial districts, and on the main commercial avenues. Its main symbol—"stage," which connotes dynamism and performance, might be a better term—is metropolitan street life itself, with its ever-changing human landscape, its ethnic, cultural, and linguistic mix, its impossible geometry and difficult formalization. This is a modernism that forgoes abstraction. Rather than formalize, it seeks to trace (as the writer James Agee once put it) the "unimagined existence"—those parcels of social life not yet contained in discourse—and to do so without reducing them to pattern but respecting their opacities and irreducibilities. It conceives modernity as a period of increasing relativism and complexity where universals must be powerfully inflected and nuanced, where master narratives give way and social life takes on the character of a mosaic-like proliferation of what Jean-François Lyotard calls paralogisms—juxtaposed discursive fields not always commensurable or mutually translatable. If this modernism has a geometry, it is not Euclidian but fractal, one that dissolves straight lines and stable planes into nearly unaccountable profiles.

What I am saying is not new, of course. It has been intermittently discussed under different headings. It can be traced to the conflict between what Marshall Berman called "the modernism of the expressway," embodied by Robert Moses's brutal public projects of the 1960s, and "the modernism of the street," represented by some strands of 1960s experimental art such as junk installations and environments.[44] Berman's distinction was inspired by Jane Jacobs's indictment of modernist architecture and city planning, *The Death and Life of Great American Cities,* which differentiates between spaces regimented from above and the social and spatial practices sedimented through spontaneous collective use.[45] Jacobs's distinction is reworked in

Michel de Certeau's opposition between the cartographable city of buildings and traffic thoroughfares and the unmappable one of daily practice, lived and traversed by specific individuals.[46] (This opposition was suggested to him by the view from the observation platform in the south tower of the World Trade Center, looking over many of *Manhatta*'s original locations.) In a more abstract manner, all these oppositions can be subsumed under Gilles Deleuze and Felix Guattari's distinctions between segmentarity and micropolitics, the molar and the molecular, the striated and the smooth.[47] On one side of the divide, one finds abstraction, regulation, and reduction; on the other side, the free, unformalizable flow of practice and desire.

This distinction between two modernities and modernisms should not be used to impose a rigid conceptual symmetry on the modern but to discern that the two opposing tendencies combine in all its cultural expressions. *Manhatta* is a case in point, even if, in the end, the film appears more invested in molar accretions than in interstitial spatialities and ephemeral practice. By contrast, we could juxtapose *Manhatta* to a number of contemporary texts where the dominant drive is a molecular exploration of modern space and sociality. We have already mentioned Paul Strand's candid portraits of urban types and Lewis Hines's photographs. Within the tradition of the city film one could mention such titles as Jay Leyda's *A Bronx Morning* (1931), Joseph Cornell's and Rudy Burkhardt's *Aviary* or *Legend for Fountains,* or Helen Levitt, Janice Loeb, and James Agee's *In the Street* (1952). In all of these texts, the city is not a spectacle to be consumed in detachment or to be regulated from above but a porous terrain that offers multiple points of entry, modes of habitation, and trajectories. From the perspective of yet another "molecular" modernist, Roland Barthes, the city emerges in them as "a text of bliss": nonhierarchical play and dispersal, multiple languages and voices in suspension, and yet, "no sentence formed."[48]

Ultimately, distinguishing between these two modernisms—and two modes of inhabiting the city—is not simply a matter of academic discussion or of getting the record straight. It is also a question of rescuing modernism as a cartography for present practice, a set of instructions to maintain a modicum of critical consciousness today. To a great extent, the forms of architectural gigantism and the politics of administered space that *Manhatta* admiringly depicts are still very much with us, not only on film but, more trenchantly, in the ruthless advance of gentrification and urban reform—in the way our cities are sold out to planners, developers, and starchitects and our public spaces are hijacked by narratives and uses we democratically suffer but on which we have no say. *Manhatta*'s prelapsarian idealism recalls the promise that the modern city and its architecture once held, but also the fact that this promise has been seldom fulfilled. Rather than give it up for lost, we should maintain it as a legitimate demand on the horizon. At the same time, the film's combination of the macro- and micropolitical, of the elevated view of the planner and the close-up, tactile perspective of the daily user, suggests that no space is beyond appeal. There is always room for molecular practice, counterspectacle, and soft subversion—for strategies that may (or should) disrupt and reinvent the spaces (and the life) so brutally imposed upon us.

3

John Dos Passos's *USA*, the Popular Media, and Left Documentary Film in the 1930s

The Pop "Lost Generation"

After *Manhatta,* Charles Sheeler and Paul Strand parted ways. Sheeler's art did not change substantially; his paintings and photographs continued to portray modern machinery and architecture. Strand gradually dropped his early interest in technology and cityscapes—he would only return to them at the end of his career—to focus on nature, the human form, and preindustrial communities. He became gradually estranged from his mentor, Alfred Stieglitz, and from his early milieu, and around the mid-1930s he grew close to a number of Left artists and activists then working in New York, such as the stage director Harold Clurman and the committed filmmakers Leo Hurwitz and Ralph Steiner. At that point, his path crossed briefly with that of John Dos Passos, one of the most prominent modernist narrators, whose work, a mixture of urban document and modernist experimentation, has much in common with Strand's, and to a lesser extent with Sheeler's. Dos Passos's celebrated novel *Manhattan Transfer* (1925) reads as a companion text to *Manhatta,* as many of the novel's settings and chapter titles—"Ferryslip," "Metropolis," "Skyscraper," "Tracks"—seem drawn from the film. But there are also deeper ideological affinities: like Strand and Sheeler, Dos Passos found much inspiration in the urban everyday and in contemporary popular culture, but in the end, he also sought—in vain—to reduce them to pattern and muffle their noise. Finding out how and why he did so requires a tour through his aesthetics, his politics, and his contradictory fascination with documentary film and the popular media.

Born only a few weeks after the Lumière brothers held the first public film screening, Dos Passos belongs to the first generation to grow up in the era of Fordist accumulation, large-scale advertisement, cinema, and recorded sound. Like the other modernist fiction writers with whom he is commonly associated—F. Scott Fitzgerald, William Faulkner, and Ernest Hemingway—he came of age at a time when electronic communication had irreversibly transformed the social imaginary, reshaping the way images and stories were composed and disseminated. Perhaps because of this, the new media left important traces on these writers' work, and they themselves were, at different points in their careers and with varying fortune, involved in media production. It is well known that Faulkner, Fitzgerald, and, for a brief spell, Dos Passos were on the payroll of different Hollywood studios. Dos Passos was hired to work on the dialogue of Joseph von Sternberg's *The Devil Is a Woman,* one of Marlene Dietrich's vehicles, although little of his work was used in the final production. And like Hemingway, he wrote for the radio and for alternative film projects, such as the documentaries about the Spanish Civil War produced by a number of New York–based Left collectives in the mid-1930s. Hemingway, Faulkner, and Fitzgerald saw many of their works turned into films. This is hardly surprising, since film, like the other popular media, decisively influenced their writing. Hemingway was fond of describing his style as a form of "camera-eye" objectivity, a label Dos Passos also used, but with a very different purpose. Cinematographic devices are equally pervasive in Faulkner and Fitzgerald. Fitzgerald actually became a pop icon of sorts. His bestselling first novel, *This Side of Paradise* (1920), which appeared when he was still in his early twenties, and his subsequent short fiction turned him into a celebrity and one of the best-paid writers of his time. In fact, Fitzgerald, whom Dos Passos once described as "hopelessly good-looking," was perhaps the only modernist writer to become, at least for a few years, something like a star in an age when stardom was largely monopolized by stage and movie performers.

Among these writers, Dos Passos was particularly explicit in admitting his debt to popular culture. His writings of the 1920s and 1930s abound in fragments of song lyrics, allusions to jazz and Tin Pan Alley melodies, and references to the movies. *Manhattan Transfer,* for example, frequently quotes popular songs. They function as a sort of choral commentary and as a topical element intended to situate the action, which spans from the beginning of the century to the aftermath of World War I, by reference to the hits of the day. At the same time, the book's narrative technique, constantly cross-cutting among a number of characters and milieus, is eminently cinematic. In particular, its portrayal of urban space and its "collective protagonist" evoke the film actualities of the nickleodeon era but also the contemporary city film.

Dos Passos's theatrical work was similarly indebted to the popular arts. His play *The Garbage Man,* which premiered as *The Moon Is a Gong* at Harvard in 1923, featured a jazz orchestra performing on stage in full view of the audience. Imitating movie musical accompaniment, it cued the turns of the plot with snatches of popular songs and sound effects. The purpose was to promote an ironic Brecht-like "alienation-effect" and to re-create the vibrant atmosphere of the musical comedy, the revue, and the vaudeville, which were for Dos Passos the repositories of "the real American theater art."[1] His was not an isolated attempt. He may have been inspired by his friend John Howard Lawson's production *Processional,* which was set to blues and jazz rhythms and was, in Lawson's own words, "essentially vaudevillesque."[2] Years later, Lawson and Dos Passos joined forces with EmJo Basshe, Mike Gold, and Francis Faragoh to create the New Playwrights collective, which, under Gold's implicit direction, set out to combine revolutionary Marxism, European avant-garde experiments, and the American popular stage. The play that most clearly combined these influences was Gold's *Hoboken Blues* (1928), which incorporated (rather tactless) blackface minstrelsy, live jazz, revival meetings, and the cakewalk dances that had been popularized on Broadway by the black performer and comedian Bert Williams. Dos Passos provided the rationale for these experiments in a postmortem homage to the New Playwrights, where he stated that the only two possible avenues for theatrical innovation were "the breakdown of the pictureframe [*sic*] stage" and its illusionism, dated leftovers from bourgeois drama, and the use of "the tools that are being discarded by dying circuses and vaudeville shows"—the physicality, immediacy, and speed that the movies had also learned to purvey.[3]

These attitudes showed that Dos Passos, like the other members of the New Playwrights, was as responsive to American popular culture as to the Left European avant-garde, since sports, acrobatics, jazz, and circus acts were also part of the idiom of such Soviet and German experimenters as Erwin Piscator, Bertolt Brecht, Vsevolod Meyerhold, and the Moscow Proletcult Theater. This work was known to American artists either first-hand—Lawson, Gold, and Dos Passos visited the Soviet Union at different points in the 1920s—or through the published accounts of contemporary critics such as Kenneth Macgowan or Huntley Carter. Macgowan's *Continental Stagecraft* (1922), beautifully illustrated by the stage designer Robert Edmund Jones, was a survey of contemporary experimental tendencies in the European theater, the fruit of Macgowan's journeys in the continent. Macgowan, who had published essays on film in *The Seven Arts,* was a drama critic and would soon become a theatrical producer; with Jones and Eugene O'Neill, he took over the management of the Provincetown Players and produced several of O'Neill's works during the rest of the decade. In addition to surveying the theatrical avant-garde, *Continental Stagecraft* contained a discussion of the Parisian Cirque Medrano, a favorite attraction among Montmartre's artists, and of the possibilities of the circus as a performance space.[4] Huntley Carter, the drama critic for A. R. Orage's *New Age,* wrote two volumes, based on his own visits to the Soviet Union, which served as widely read introductions to the Soviet experimental stage: *The New Theater and Cinema of Soviet Russia* (1924) and *The New Spirit in the Russian Theater, 1917–1928* (1929).[5] They were mostly devoted to theater but contain extended treatments of film and radio as well. The European experiments were further popularized by the International Theater Exposition, organized by the *Little Review* co-editor jane heap and the architect Friedrich Kiesler and held in February and March 1926 in New York City. The *Little Review* devoted a special issue to the exposition later that year, featuring reports on the European avant-garde theater and a number of manifestoes by Luigi Russolo, Enrico Prampolini, Fernand Léger, Hans Richter, and Kiesler himself. It was illustrated with photographs and sketches of stage designs and contained some essays on film.[6] This number is yet another example of the fusion of avant-gardism, social radicalism, and pop leanings that characterized 1920s modernism in the United States, a fusion that was shared by the New Playwrights, the "lost generation" novelists, Harlem Renaissance writers, and contemporary cultural critics such as Gilbert Seldes and Edmund Wilson. Writing for *The Dial* in the early 1920s, Seldes and Wilson omnivorously covered the new writing by James Joyce, Marcel Proust, Jean Cocteau, and Gertrude Stein, Ziegfeld shows, burlesque, Charles Chaplin, Fanny Brice, Al Jolson, the Manhattan night life, and the jargon of the pervasive speakeasies.

Dos Passos's pop savvy, apparent in his wide-ranging knowledge and precise use of popular materials, was seldom combined with unqualified praise. Even in the 1920s, his view of the popular was never as celebratory as Wilson's or Seldes's; for him, the vitality and creativity of commercial culture were often tinged with impersonality and commercialism. And during the early 1930s, as the Depression deepened, his perception of what Seldes called "the lively arts" lost its dialectical quality. In the introduction to a collection of his plays published in 1934, the year of his Hollywood stint, he denounced that for all their technical proficiency, Broadway, the radio, or the screen sell "dreamworlds" that "dope the peoples of the world and keep them doped while the gentlemen on the inside are deftly going through their pockets."[7] These ideas reverberate throughout his fiction of the decade, which still abundantly references commercial culture, only this no longer connotes popular energy and inventiveness but appears instead as a symptom of modern ills: alienation, uprootedness, and mass deception. An example of this is the portrayal of film in his major achievement, the monumental *USA* trilogy.

The USA Trilogy

Dos Passos's *USA* (1938) gathered the previously published volumes *The 42nd Parallel* (1930), *1919* (1932), and *The Big Money* (1936). The author conceived this sequence as a wide-ranging panorama (he called it "a verbal photomontage") of America in the first quarter of the century. The novels revolve around twelve characters of different social and geographical extraction whose stories are told in a realistic manner. Interspersed with these personal narratives, some of which spill over more than one volume, are sixty-eight Newsreel and fifty-one Camera Eye sections, all of them written in an experimental style. The Newsreels are collages of found texts, including snatches of songs, journalistic prose, political speeches, headlines, and ticker-tape releases. The Camera Eye segments have been described as a "personal memory bank" (in Miles Orvell's phrase); they are extremely allusive autobiographical sketches whose full intelligibility often depends on a fairly intimate knowledge of Dos Passos's biography.[8] Thrown into the mix are twenty-seven condensed biographies of historical figures contemporary with the trilogy's fictional present. They are devoted to artists and creators like Isadora Duncan and Frank Lloyd Wright, inventors like Thomas Edison and Edward Steinmetz, politicians like Teddy Roosevelt and "Big" Bill Haywood, intellectuals like Thornstein Veblen, financers and industrialists like Henry Ford and J. P. Morgan, and there is one on a film star: Rudolph Valentino. They are written in a stylized, rhythmic prose that often approximates Walt Whitman's blank verse.

The idea that the trilogy internalizes cinematic devices has long been a constant in criticism. As with the earlier *Manhattan Transfer*, reviewers pointed out similarities between the novel's compositional strategies and the ability of the cinema to cross-cut between different locales and actions, to weave multiple storylines into an overall design, and to convey the abrupt jolts and transitions of modern life. In addition, film is explicitly alluded to in the very names of the Newsreel and Camera Eye segments. These cinematic references prompted the British novelist Compton Mackenzie to title his review of *1919*, "Film or Book?" And like him, commentators such as Malcolm Cowley, Edmund Wilson, and Mike Gold called attention, with varying degrees of sympathy or perplexity, to this amalgam of modes and media. In general, critics could not help pointing out that the Newsreels and Camera Eye interludes added a certain "strangeness" to the novel. They made the trilogy "kaleidoscopic," wrote Upton Sinclair; the Camera Eye sections seemed to him "queer glimpses of almost anything, having nothing to do with the story or stories," and the Newsreels were "'vaudeville material,' some of it interesting, some funny, some just plain puzzling."[9]

Pursuing the clues scattered in these early comments, scholars have subsequently attempted to specify further the relations between film and literature in Dos Passos's work. Inquiries have proceeded in two main (and mutually implicated) directions. Some have focused on narrative technique and have tried to ascertain to what extent the novel's descriptions, transitions, and focalizations mime mechanisms proper to film.[10] Others have sought to uncover specific sources and parallels in film and art history for Dos Passos's style, narrative patterns, and imagery. Critics have pointed out the novelist's debt to representations of urban scenes by the Italian futurist Umberto Boccioni, the German dadaist George Grosz, the French painter Fernand Léger, and the American avant-garde photographers Alfred Stieglitz and Paul Strand, among others.[11] In film, Dos Passos's main influences have been traced to the American director D. W. Griffith, who made parallel editing one of his narrative trademarks, and to the montage experiments of the Soviet director and theorist Sergei Eisenstein.[12]

Such a roster of influences and antecedents contains scant reference to two contemporary styles of documentary film that lend their names to sections of Dos Passos's trilogy: "workers' newsreels" and "kino-eye," or "camera eye," a term associated with the work of the Soviet filmmaker Dziga Vertov. The importance given to these sections in *USA* is consonant with the pervasiveness of documentary expression in 1930s culture. The desire to depict the contemporary scene informed established literary forms such as fiction or drama. One may think of the mixture of narrative and reportage in John Steinbeck's *Grapes of Wrath* or Josephine Herbst's trilogy, *Rope of Gold,* or of the factual approach of the Federal Theater Project's Living Newspapers. The interest in reporting also prompted the development of relatively new genres like the documentary book, a blend of sociology, journalism, and photography, some of whose best exponents include Erskine Caldwell and Margaret Bourke-White's *You Have Seen Their Faces* (1937), Dorothea Lange and Paul Schuster Taylor's *American Exodus* (1937), Richard Wright and Edwin Rosskam's *Twelve Million Black Voices* (1941), and, the strangest of them all, *Let Us Now Praise Famous Men* (1941), by James Agee and Walker Evans.[13] The cultural historian Warren Susman connects such documentary interest to the recent dominance of the new electronic media.[14] The 1930s saw the consolidation of the sound film, radio, and newsreels, which were becoming a staple ingredient in commercial film programs. It was also the time of the popularization of graphic journalism, prominently embodied in the United States by Henry Luce's *Life,* in Great Britain by *Picture Post,* and in France by *Vu;* all of these periodicals were based on photo-essays. Many of their strategies had been anticipated in the 1920s by the radical German magazine *AIZ* (*Arbeiter Illustrierte Zeitung*), for which John Heartfield produced some of his best-known photomontages. In view of these developments, one could say that the literature of the time attempted to assimilate the vividness of radio, photography, and film, which had displaced the printed word as the main channel of information.[15]

Alongside the growing prestige of the electronic media and particularly the cinema, documentary film gained increased attention as an instrument of Left political organization, education, and critique, not only in specialized journals such as *Workers' Theatre* (later renamed *The New Theatre*), *Experimental Cinema,* or *Film Front* but also in miscellaneous periodicals like the *New Masses* and the Communist Party organ the *Daily Worker.* Left documentary film evoked the possibility of mobilizing a popular medium in the struggle "against the interests," as Dos Passos's characters are fond of saying, and of fighting the media conglomerates of the time with their own weapons. As a temporary "fellow traveler" who was frequently involved in a number of causes and protests throughout the late 1920s and 1930s, Dos Passos was familiar with the range of Left contemporary documentary forms and the specific cultural politics they connoted. Exploring the significance of these modes in *USA* will expand our understanding of Dos Passos's major work. These documentary modes—workers' newsreel, Vertov's "camera eye"—are evoked by name yet appear, at the same time, highly contested. Their form and cultural politics are critiqued and eventually sidestepped. For this reason, they paradoxically figure in *USA* as an omission, a hole in the whole, and a highly significant one at that, since around this absence the cultural politics of the work take shape.

Reading Absences

This type of argument demands that we move beyond the positivistic bias common in historical analyses of influence and adopt an interpretive strategy that would endow with meaning not only what is actualized in the text but also the text's absences and omissions. At the root of this approach is the idea, first developed by the Swiss linguist Ferdinand de Saussure, that meaning is systemic and differential and must therefore be mapped within a network of relations of which discrete elements are a part and in relation to which they signify. What specific elements mean is not only a function of their presence in the communicative chain but also of those possibilities not actualized at a given time and in whose hollow a particular textual configuration emerges.

These ideas were imported into ideological criticism by the French philosopher Pierre Macherey in *A Theory of Literary Production,* which is largely devoted to questioning the protocols and ideologies of what he calls immanent, or text-centered, criticism. Such criticism seeks to expose the meaning or hidden structure of a text by working from a visible surface to a "deeper," invisible realm where "the truth" seemingly lurks. For Macherey such a procedure is founded on the unacknowledged conception of meaning as "a secret" embedded in the text yet inaccessible to the lay reader's gaze. The function of immanent criticism is largely tautological: to retell the text and, in the process, to expose its secret, "to free [its meaning] from all the impurities which alter and interrupt it, to ensure an essential adequation between the work and the reader."[16]

Opposing this procedure, Macherey advocates the expansion of the usual scope of critical discourse from the study of text as product to the exploration of the "determinate conditions" of meaning production (78). The emphasis on production connects the text to a material horizon outside itself; by virtue of this connection, textuality appears as the asymmetrical product of a negotiation with outside forces that are only retrievable as traces in the writing. Such a materialist perspective reveals signification not as a dispersed "wholeness" to be restored by criticism but as a conflicted plurality arising from the irresolvable tension between a number of discourses in mutual antagonism: "The book is not the extension of a meaning; it is generated from the incompatibility of several meanings, the strongest bond by which it is attached to reality, in a tense and ever-renewed confrontation" (80). In addition, Macherey's most radical proposal maintains that textual meaning is irremediably incomplete so long as it is always marked *and* enabled by certain gaps and silences that allow the text to say what it says: "The speech of the book comes from a certain silence, a matter which it endows with form, a ground on which it traces a figure. Thus the book is not self-sufficient; it is necessarily accompanied by a certain absence, without which it would not exist" (85).

This assumes that the work's form emerges through the selective realization of certain possibilities and that such realizations imply a number of avoidances, refusals, and gaps around what the text cannot, or will not, say. Since it is the mute gaps and absences that allow speech to emerge, we must, according to Macharey, "investigate the silence, for it is the silence that is doing the speaking" (86). The critical task is therefore double. First, criticism should try to retrieve the possibilities available in the cultural system. This procedure is akin to what the critic Hans Robert Jauss has named the "reconstruction" of the "horizon of expectations" of a given artistic form: the range of variation that readers can expect from a specific cultural artifact at a given time.[17] At a later moment, criticism should assess the meaning of the actualized utterance against the unrealized possibilities. In the caesura between the actualized and the unfulfilled possibilities takes shape the ideological work of the text, or its cultural meaning. In the following sections I will first reconstruct the range of practices and significations that the terms "camera eye" and "newsreel" connoted at the time *USA* was written and first published; and second, I will assess the trilogy's peculiar actualization of these terms. In the interval between absent potentialities and present realizations we will read the cultural politics of Dos Passos's text.

Radical Film Culture in the 1930s

At the time when Dos Passos was writing his trilogy, the cinema was being celebrated in Left circles for its capacity to expose the injustice of existing social relations and to mobilize the masses. An early exponent of these ideas was the journal *Experimental Cinema,* launched in Philadelphia in February 1930 by the aspiring filmmaker and Left sympathizer Lewis Jacobs. Jacobs's periodical sought to promote a type of art cinema that would function at once as a conduit of knowledge and a catalyst of worldwide solidarity. These ideals were forcefully expressed in the first issue by David Platt, one of the journal's contributors, in his position piece "The New Cinema." They were reiterated a few pages later by Seymour Stern, who compared the camera to the X-ray machine: both share the ability to "pierce through to the innermost" of reality and to deliver the truth about social relations. More explicit than *Experimental Cinema* in its commitment was the short-lived *The Left,* which was born and died in 1931. Its section on cinema opened with an epigraph from Lenin: "Among the instruments of art and education, the cinema can and must have the greatest significance. It is a powerful weapon of scientific knowledge and propaganda." Below Lenin's pronouncement, a piece also by Stern stated the need for a proletarian cinema "terrific as the sweep of a nation-wide demonstration—for food, for work, for the triumph of the working class." Such film would be an invaluable aid in bringing revolutionary consciousness to the masses.[18]

These ideas voiced the aspirations of Proletkult, the official postrevolutionary culture in the Soviet Union. The aim of Proletkult was to promote art that would express the experience of the working class and would advance its emancipation. In its early stages, Soviet officials encouraged the adoption of modernist aesthetics for their antitraditionalism and their antibourgeois connotations and the use of new media for their popular appeal. The constructivism of Popova, Tatlin, and El Lissitsky; the theatrical experiments of Vsevolod Meyerhold; and the early films of Dziga Vertov and Sergei Eisenstein (especially *Strike* and *Battleship Potemkin*) all belong to the early phase of Proletkult. The John Reed Clubs represent one American arm of Proletkult. The first of these was founded in New York City in 1929 by Mike Gold and Joseph Freeman, and shortly afterwards there were thirteen John Reed Clubs in operation in the main American cities. They were dedicated to promoting proletarian literature, which they did by organizing writing workshops, readings, lectures, debates, and encounters with writers and intellectuals and by publishing literary journals.[19] These journals included *The Anvil, Left Front, Left Review, Leftward, The Cauldron, Blast, Dynamo,* and the most enduring, the *Partisan Review,* which freed itself from Communist Party sponsorship to become a private enterprise driven by Trotskyist sympathies in the late 1930s. The activities of the New York John Reed Club included film screenings and discussions.

The Left idealization of the cinema rested largely on the achievements of Soviet directors, in particular on the worldwide success of Eisenstein's *Battleship Potemkin* (1926). Part of the reason for its success and that of later titles from the Soviet school lay in their appeal as art and as political films. When Lewis Jacobs declared in *Experimental Cinema* that it was "not until the projection of *Potemkin* that the cinema became aware of its individuality" and independence from the other arts, he praised the film on aesthetic grounds for its innovative form.[20] The London-based *Close-Up,* the modernist intelligentsia's film review, epitomized this formalist reception of Soviet film. In the opening issue, an editorial statement by Kenneth Macpherson described the Russian cinema as part of an international art-film front that also enlisted less explicitly political filmmakers. After Macpherson, many subsequent pieces confirmed this attitude. The American poet H.D.'s "Russian Films," for example, regarded the Soviet cinema as "biblical in spirit"—while it had an explicit political agenda, it rose far above it to universal mythic stature by teaching, in sum, "that life and the film must not be separated, people and things must pass across the screen naturally like shadows of trees on grass or passing reflections in a crowded city window." H.D.'s companion, Bryher—the pseudonym of Winifred Ellerman, whose fortune financed the publication of *Close-Up* and the activities of the affiliated filmmaking collective, Pool—was the author of a short book, *Film Problems of Soviet Russia.* In it she purported to deal with this body of work on aesthetic terms only, leaving aside distracting political issues that muddled aesthetic appreciation. This aestheticist attitude was continuous with the exhibition practices of the so-called little cinemas, the art houses of the time, and cinema clubs, which screened Soviet work back to back with *The Cabinet of Dr. Caligari, Un Chien Andalou,* or *Rain,* grouping these titles together on the basis of form and ignoring their widely divergent cultural politics.[21]

More committed reviewers, however, subordinated the artistry of Soviet films to their political radicalism and made their revolutionary form the outcome of revolutionary intent. An exponent of these ideas was Harry Alan Potamkin, a poet, the secretary of the New York John Reed Club, and perhaps the most influential film reviewer in the radical press of the time.

Writing in 1930 for *Experimental Cinema,* he stated that the "idea-dynamics of the Soviet film is dialectics," whose terms were: the thesis, the status quo; antithesis, the proletariat; and the synthesis, a new proletarian world order.[22] The politicized reception of Soviet films was furthered by the fact that they were frequently produced and distributed by the Workers' International Relief (WIR), a Comintern-controlled organization founded by the publicist Willi Münzenberg in 1929 in Berlin. Its goals ranged from providing aid in case of famine, war, or natural disaster to the promotion of proletarian culture throughout the world. To this effect, the WIR sponsored and financed workers' orchestras, dance and drama groups (like the Workers Laboratory Theatre and the German-speaking *Prolet-Bühne* in the United States), art and photography workshops, and film-related activities. Their main film production unit was in the Soviet Union and was responsible for, among other titles, Vsevelod Pudovkin's *Mother, The End of St. Petersburg,* and *Storm over Asia,* Dziga Vertov's *Three Songs about Lenin,* and Nicolai Ekk's *Road to Life* (the first Soviet sound film). Outside the USSR, the WIR sponsored workers' newsreel units and handled the distribution of Soviet films.[23] In the United States, the WIR affiliate, whose activities were reviewed by John Dos Passos in a 1930 article for the *New Republic,* handled the nontheatrical distribution of Soviet features to be used in rallies, membership drives, celebrations, and fund raisers.[24] On these occasions, they were often shown together with newsreels of strikes, breadlines, and Communist Party activities produced in Europe by workers' groups.[25] These exhibition contexts must have enhanced the revolutionary content of Soviet films and simultaneously reinforced the connection between their artistic quality and political engagement.

The alleged effectiveness of film in the social struggle prompted Left intellectuals to demand the production of revolutionary films in the United States. In the July 1930 *New Masses,* Potamkin, who had been running screenings and discussions in the John Reed Club rooms in New York, suggested organizing a group "for the study of the technique of picture-making and the education of workers in the cinema as an ideological and artistic medium." Concurrently, the *Daily Worker* published a piece by Sam Brody demanding a workers' film movement as it already existed in European countries. But if movie production was in order, what kinds of films should be made? Again, Brody and Potamkin came out in defense of newsreels.[26] The Soviet cinema's factual style and the Left conception of film as an agitprop tool made documentary the nearly inevitable choice.

There was, in addition, an urgent need to oppose the popular mainstream media. Decades later, the documentarist Leo Hurwitz reminisced that during the 1930s there was little in the popular Fox Movietone Newsreels or the Hearst-owned Metronome News that reflected the country's actual conditions: "Occasionally a newsreel shot of an unemployment demonstration of the Bonus March, always with a protective commentary to take the meaning out of the event."[27] This unofficial censorship was also noticed outside radical circles. Wilbur Needham, a *Close-Up* contributor, deplored in 1928 the extreme aesthetic and social conservatism of the American film industry, which limited severely what could appear on the screen: "Frank discussion of sex, the infrequent beauty of the human body (unless draped suggestively) and all hints at the radical in government or sociology disappeared long ago from the screens of America, impelled by the outraged toes of an emasculated minority. Not content with that, the movie monarchs descended another step from their thrones and voluntarily erased the Sacco-Vanzetti case from the screen, burning all news-reel shots of the murdered men."[28] The media historian Robert T. Elson confirms that in the 1930s, "[P]roducers and exhibitors alike were spineless when confronted with any protest by politicians, local censors, or patriotic groups." For example, due to German diplomatic pressure, by 1934 Adolf Hitler's regime had received scarce newsreel coverage, and when it did, its expansionist ambitions abroad and brutal repression of opposition forces at home were glossed over.[29] And in 1937, the *Esquire* reviewer Meyer Levin protested Paramount's suppression of newsreel coverage of the Memorial Day massacre, when police opened fire on unarmed strikers congregated outside the Republic Steel plant in East Chicago, killing ten of them.[30]

Reacting against this sort of evasiveness, Sam Brody proposed in the *Daily Worker* of May 20, 1930: "The newsfilm is the important thing: . . . the capitalist knows that there are certain things it cannot afford to have shown. He is afraid of some pictures." Potamkin, more restrained and betraying a residual aestheticism, also confirmed at about the same time the need for newsreels, but only as a start: "There is no need to begin big. Documentaries of workers' life. Breadlines and picketlines, demonstrations and police attacks. Outdoor films first. Then interiors. And eventually dramatic film of revolutionary content."[31] Additional advantages of documentary production were that it could harness the skill of the photographers already active in the Workers' Camera League, and it required a minimal crew and little postproduction.

The next step was not long in coming. In December 1930, Brody, Potamkin, and a few others established the Workers' Film and Photo League, a film production unit within the American section of the WIR. The philosophy and goals of the association were explained in Potamkin's "A Movie Call to Action" in the July 1931 *Workers' Theatre*. This agenda proposed, among other goals, "The encouragement, support and sustenance of the left critic and the left movie maker who is documenting dramatically and persuasively the disproportions in our present economy."[32] The Film and Photo League plunged into work with *Winter 1931*, documenting social unrest during that period. This was followed, between 1931 and 1935, by *Hunger March 1931, Hunger 1932, Bonus March,* and *Scottsboro Demonstration,* in addition to footage of the 1932 Footer Ford Communist Party election campaign, the coalminers' strike in Harlan County, Kentucky, May Day parades, demonstrations, rallies, and celebrations. These films were quickly shot and edited; their lack of production values was additional proof of earnest commitment. For the film historian Russell Campbell, "[R]ather than . . . of individual films, it is more correct to speak of 'footage'—news films processed and printed rapidly and then roughly edited for the quickest possible screening and maximum impact."[33] When the topical interest of a given title wore off, the footage was recycled in later productions.

But the activities of the Film and Photo League and its collaborators were not limited to film production. The league also ran film discussions and lectures and created a film school in its headquarters. Its newsletter, *Film Front,* reported on league functions, expressed members' opinions, and frequently translated and discussed the writings of Soviet filmmakers. This forum spread Dziga Vertov's theories on "kino-eye," a cinema devoid of fictional and dramatic elements, theories which were deployed in the United States in defense of newsreels. In his practice and writings, Vertov opposed the narrative strain of Eisenstein, Trauberg, and other members of the Soviet school. Like commercial filmmakers the world over, they traded, in Vertov's pugnacious metaphors, in "film-vodka" or "film cigarettes"—narcotics that distracted audiences from examining and understanding their immediate social reality: "Poisoned by film nicotine, the viewer [of plotted films] sticks like a leech to the screen that tickles his nerves."[34] Opposing this use of cinema, Vertov's manifesto-like writings of the mid- and late 1920s are impassioned calls for documenting the everyday reality of the new Soviet state: "[T]he movie camera was invented in order to penetrate deeper into the visible world, to explore and record visual phenomena, so that we do not forget what happens and what the future must take into account"

(69). Documentary cinema—*kinopravda,* or film-truth—was the mode best suited to this purpose, and kino-eye was the name Vertov gave to his own documentary formula: "Kino eye = kino-seeing (I see through the camera) + kino-writing (I write on film with the camera) + kino-organization (I edit). The kino-eye method is the scientifically experimental method of exploring the visible world."[35] This bid for actuality did not mean direct recording, in the manner of the 1960s cinema verité, but the presentation of "carefully selected, recorded, and organized facts (major or minor) from the lives of the workers themselves as well as from those of their class enemies" (66). Organization was essential to Vertov's films, which often present elaborate graphic and conceptual montage patterns. His skillful manipulation of trick cinematography—*Man with the Movie Camera*'s multiple exposures and split screens—and his sophisticated self-referentiality, perceptible in the foregrounding of the shooting and editing processes, were a far cry from the spare stylistic repertoire of the Film and Photo League's productions.

However, in the United States, camera eye was taken to mean direct cinema devoid of formal sophistication to be used for agitation and propaganda purposes. Speaking at the Film and Photo League's National Film Conference in late 1934, David Platt invoked Vertov's ideas in this connection: "'The Soviet film began with the Kino-Eye and grew organically from there on. The Film and Photo Leagues, rooted in the intellectual and social basis of the Soviet film, begin also with the simple newsreel document. . . . Aside from the tremendous historical and social value of the reels thus photographed, [newsreels] are also true beginnings of film art . . . the only films in America that breathe a spirit of art and life.'"[36] Such appeal to the Russian documentary legacy appeared increasingly necessary as league members and outside observers began to criticize the group's focus on newsreels and to demand more sophistication and broader range in production. Dissension would eventually lead to the split of the league into two factions: one was resolutely pro-documentary; the other, led by the filmmakers Ralph Steiner and Leo Hurwitz, appealed to the cultural authority of Eisenstein and Pudovkin and advocated a more dramatic, better-crafted cinema, since they believed that revolutionary films needed to be good art to reach the masses. They defended the production of character-centered narratives and highlighted the importance of actors, since they humanized the picture and provided points of identification for audiences.[37] This faction ended up divorcing itself from the league and creating another collective, New York Kino (Nykino), in the final months of 1934. The new group maintained its sympathies with the radical Left yet sought to distance itself from Communist Party directives. Nykino's attempt to influence a wider audience and to harness popular textuality for the spread of progressive ideas was somewhat prophetic. It anticipated the driving motivation behind the cultural projects of the Popular Front, launched in the Seventh Congress of the Third International, in July 1935.

This is the intellectual context in which newsreel, camera eye, social documentary, and the cinema as a tool for the exploration of reality accrued political momentum. It is important to point out that the influence of these debates spread beyond the immediate context of film production. The stage was one arena where the aims and philosophies of the documentary and newsreel movements had direct resonance. In the 1930s, there was a constant traffic of people and ideas between the film and theater milieus. Herbert Kline, the editor of *New Theatre,* was involved in the Film and Photo League and in Nykino. Ralph Steiner, a still photographer and league cameraman, shot *Café Universal* and *Pie in the Sky* with Group Theater actors.[38] The Living Newspapers, part of the Federal Theater Project, adopted cinematic montage strategies in their performances and occasionally used film clips and photographs as background, a technique imported from the German and Soviet stages.

As a close observer and participant in these developments, Dos Passos must have been well aware of league-related activities. He certainly must have bumped into league activists and cameramen in his visit to the Kentucky coalfields during the violent strikes of 1931 and 1932, events that supplied the subject matter for several league films and that are re-created in the last Camera Eye section of his trilogy. He was involved in the work of Nykino. With Leo Hurwitz, he wrote the English subtitles for the U.S. release of *The Wave,* a social melodrama shot in Mexico by a team headed by Paul Strand and Fred Zinnemann. In late 1936 and early 1937, when Nykino restructured and changed its name to Frontier Films, Dos Passos's name appeared in the news release with which the organization announced its existence. He is listed as an advisory-board member and consultant, along with Malcolm Cowley, Waldo Frank, Archibald MacLeish, Lillian Hellman, Clifford Odets, and many others. As a member of this group, he wrote the commentary for *Spain in Flames,* a hastily assembled newsreel film released early in 1937 to promote support for the Spanish republic, threatened by General Franco's right-wing coup. Shortly afterward, Dos Passos traveled to Spain to work as consultant and scriptwriter for a companion project: Joris

Ivens's *The Spanish Earth.* It was during the production of the film that he definitively broke with the official, pro-Stalinist Left.[39]

"The Speech of the People"

Neither the Newsreels nor the Camera Eye sections in *USA* replicate the form or the ideology of the contemporary workers' cinema. Workers' films and Dos Passos's Newsreels sought to link the individual and the public realms: proletarian newsreels did so to make audiences aware of the class dimension of their struggles, and Dos Passos's newsreels tried to evoke, in Edmund Wilson's words, the "public consciousness" contemporary with the private lives of the narratives. However, their respective strategies of presentation were quite different. Workers' newsreels were didactic attempts to instruct audiences by delivering unequivocal messages; Dos Passos's Newsreels, whose raw materials were the inexhaustible linguistic debris churned out by the media, are often pure delirium.

An early sequence of *Bonus March,* by the Workers' Film and Photo League, is a good example of the didacticism of Left newsreels. Shots of dead soldiers on the battlefield and of maimed and wheelchair-bound veterans are cut to takes of the U.S. flag, a priest, churches, a homeless man on a park bench, heroic statuary, and the eagle on the Bank of the United States Building.[40] The point—the devastating collusion of church, state, and financial interests in the war and its aftermath—is difficult to miss. A further example of this trait in workers' films was offered by Leo Hurwitz as he explained the unambiguous montage used in the league's film *America Today,* largely made up of recut fragments of commercial newsreels: "The newsreel shots are sure: President Roosevelt signing a state paper looking up at the camera with his inimitable self-satisfied smile, and a shot of fleet maneuvers. . . . By virtue of splicing the shot of the warships just after Roosevelt signs the paper . . . a new meaning is achieved—the meaning of the huge war preparation program of the demagogic Roosevelt government."[41] Yet "sureness" and the achievement of meaning are not exactly the goal of the kind of channel surfing that Dos Passos's Newsreels perform.

Dos Passos's Newsreels are extremely scrappy. The utterances they quote are abruptly cut, news items and advertisements start or end in midsentence, and the songs are scattered about, mixed in with bits of political speeches, headlines, and stock-market reports. At times the typography reflects this disconnectedness, but at other times unrelated texts are run together without visible breaks. The effect they convey is similar to that of speedily skimming a newspaper while a radio blares in the background and bits of print and snatches of song filter into consciousness. As an example, here is part of Newsreel 18:

Goodbye Picadilly, farewell Leicester Square
It's a long way to Tipperary
WOMAN TRAPS HUSBAND WITH GIRL IN HOTEL
    to such task we can dedicate our lives and our fortunes and everything that we have with the pride of those who know that the day has come when America is privileged to spend her blood and her might for the principles that gave her birth and happiness, and that she has treasured. God helping her she can do no other
It's a long way to Tipperary . . . (303)[42]

This assemblage is largely comic, due to the juxtaposition of the headline announcing family drama with the ensuing political statement and the eventual return to the song, which seems to have been droning on, indifferent to marital strife and international conflict. Because of the way the fragments are joined together, the antecedent of the solemn pronouncement "to such task we can dedicate our lives" appears to be the bathetic pursuit of philandering husbands.

Such cut-and-mix strategies evoke the camera's ability to juxtapose disparate fragments and to produce incongruous results. In this respect, the spirit of the Newsreels is closer to the zaniness of dada collages than to the earnest indoctrination of the Film and Photo League's productions, and their disorienting quality is also reminiscent of surrealist found objects. Modeled after the analog media, whose indiscriminate receptivity registers the infinite speech—and noise—of the world, they record sense and nonsense, signifying matter and semantic dross, and in the process they bear witness to the automatism of the public word, an "external" automatism independent from human consciousness or design. By contrast, Left film newsreels sought to suppress these very automatisms in the image and to convey straightforward messages.

This may have also been the purpose of Dos Passos's trilogy as a whole. One way to read the juxtaposition of modes and techniques in *USA* is to consider them as attempts to bring under control the disorder of the Newsreels. If the Newsreels sample, in Dos Passos's own words, "the clamor, the sound of daily life,"[43] the narratives, the biographies, and the Camera Eyes seek to make sense out of this clamor in different ways.[44]

One of these ways is by expanding and contextualizing the topical references fragmentarily rendered in the Newsreels, and this is done mostly in narratives and biographies. Hence, in *The 42nd Parallel,* the headlines and news reports about anarchist activity are fleshed out in the biography of Big Bill Haywood, the leader of the anarchist International Workers of the World (IWW), and in the narrative of Mac, the young typesetter who joins the IWW and helps to put out a radical newspaper during a miners' strike in Nevada. Similarly, in *1919* the absurdity of World War I, as described in songs and newspaper articles, is confirmed by the experiences of Dick Savage and his friends at the front; and the allusions to the repression of leftists and pacifists are corroborated in the narratives of Ben Compton and the biographies of Randolph Bourne, Wesley Everest, and Paxton Hibbens. The Newsreels in *The Big Money* dwell on the aftermath of the Armistice—economic slump followed by a reckless boom, labor unrest, and the brutality of the Palmer Raids—and, again, it is in the biographies and characters' stories that the obscure snippets of the Newsreels attain full sense.

The Newsreels do not always refer to newsworthy events, however; at times, they riff on themes and moods that recur through a particular character's story. Right before the first installment of Mary French's narrative in *The Big Money,* Newsreel 51 combines job advertisements offering "wellrecommended young girls and young women . . . good chance for advancement" (855) with a song about a certain Sally that went away. The job opportunities—"canvassers . . . caretakers . . . cashiers . . . chambermaids . . . waitresses . . . cleaners . . . file clerks . . . companions . . . comptometer operators . . . collection correspondents" (855)—belong in the clerical and service sectors, massively staffed by women since the turn of the century, and are concomitant with what historians have called the "incorporation of America." Thanks to this avenue for employment, Mary is able to become financially independent and to turn down her mother's money because "she said nobody had any right to money they hadn't earned" (863). In turn, the song—*"The sunshine drifted from our alley / Ever since the day / Sally went away"* (855)—foreshadows Mary's leaving the family home. But since Sally's departure is due to her death—*"Went down to St. James Infirmary / Saw my baby there / All stretched out on a table / So pale, so cold, so fair"* (855)—it also announces that Mary's subsequent story will be punctuated by bereavement. She quits college after the death of her father and becomes active in the labor struggle, but her career as an activist is overshadowed by the executions of Nicola Sacco and Bartolomeo Vanzetti and by the murder of Eddie Spellman, a young comrade killed by strikebreakers.

Part of the "noise" of the Newsreels stems from their contradictory nature, and, once more, narratives and biographies help to distinguish truth from falsehood in the chaotic mass of information. Newsreel 46, for example, in *The Big Money,* mixes headlines triumphantly announcing prosperity with others that report workers' riots and a song that muses about hard times.

> *The times are hard and the wages low*
> *Leave her Johnny leave her*
> *The bread is hard and the beef is salt*
> *It's time for us to leave her*
> BANKERS HAIL NEW ERA OF EXPANSION
> PROSPERITY FOR ALL SEEN ASSURED
> Find German Love of Caviar a Danger to Stable Money
> EX-SERVICE MEN DEMAND JOBS
>
> . . .
>
> JOBLESS RIOT AT AGENCY. (788)

The official pronouncements cannot drown the song's grim view of the way things stand or the headlines that report the desperate situation of the country after the war. Newsreel 47 continues in a similar mood: it announces, "CHANCE FOR ADVANCEMENT . . . Young Man Wanted . . . OPPORTUNITY . . . in bank that chooses its officers from the ranks . . . bronze fitter . . . letterer . . . patternmaker . . . carriage painter." Yet a song suggests that chances for advancement may take a long time to materialize: "*Oh tell me how long / I'll have to wait*" (790–91). Both Newsreels are in the middle of the narrative of the returning serviceman Charley Anderson and bracket his disastrous stint working for his brother in Minneapolis, an episode that demonstrates that "prosperity for all" was not "assured" and that former soldiers found serious difficulties reinserting themselves into civilian life. In another example, Newsreel 68 starts out with intimations of the impending stock-market crash of 1929—"WALL STREET STUNNED . . . Decline in Contracts"—followed by reassurances: "MARKET SURE TO RECOVER FROM SLUMP," "PRESIDENT SEES PROSPERITY NEAR." A few pages later, the biography of Samuel Insull—"Power Superpower"—shows that the market did not recover; its collapse brought down the numerous utility companies Insull controlled and, with them, his vast—and fraudulent—financial empire.

The recurrence of similar contradictions throughout the trilogy demonstrates the slippery character of truth in the public sphere. Still, sometimes contradiction might be better than certainty. Michael Staub and William Solomon have pointed out that contradiction undermines the truth claims of the media and prevents them from jelling into statements that, while coherent, may be partial and manipulative.[45] According to Staub and Solomon, the critical force of Dos Passos's Newsreels resides precisely in the way their fragmentariness and contradictions problematize the work of the media and render public discourse void.

Public discourse may be void and its claims to truth dubious, but, as Dos Passos's text shows, it has considerable performative force. In Newsreel 12, a headline announces: "Redhaired Youth Says Stories of Easy Money Led Him to Crime" (151). In *1919,* numerous Newsreels include songs that trivialize war—"*Oh Oh Oh, it's a lovely war / Oo wouldn't be a sodger ay / Oh it's a shame to take the pay*" (603)—and others cite misleading propaganda: "[T]he call for enlistments mentions a chance for gold service stripes, opportunities for big game hunting and thrilling watersports added to the general advantages of travel in foreign countries" (716). Did these misleading messages have any effect? Hibbens's biography, "A Hoosier Quixote," contrasts the "depths of vileness and hypocrisy" that "the war in New York" revealed with the idealism of the recruits—"the boys believed in a world safe for democracy" (514)—presumably imbued with the official line in army training camps. And in *The 42nd Parallel,* after watching Griffith's *Birth of a Nation,* Charley Anderson is ready to enlist, eager to be sent to Europe and experience first-hand the thrill of the battle scenes in the film. The irony is that, as Dos Passos, who served in the Ambulance Corps in World War I, knew all too well, and as numerous characters discover in due course, the war in Europe offered nothing like the romantic dash of Griffith's battle scenes or the "lovely" romps promised by patriotic songs and recruitment literature.

Narratives and biographies do their share in turning the media cacophony into a legible narrative, but they do not entirely succeed. There are numerous details and allusions that are not clarified by the other parts of the novel and therefore remain void of sense—pure noise. And the narratives themselves contain much that works against clarity and communicability, against the "assured meanings" that the Left media were aiming at.

Dos Passos envisioned his trilogy as a means to amplify the voices of those who are typically silenced and to revitalize the common language. This objective was articulated in his address to the first Writers' Congress (a Popular Front organization) in New York City in 1935, as he was finishing the last volume of the trilogy. The mission of the novelist, he claimed, is to elaborate a direct, precise language that will counter "the journalistic garbage of the day" and allow readers to map the social whole of which they are a part. The main source of this language is a sort of folk substratum: the everyday language of workers and ordinary citizens. The brief foreword to the 1938 edition of the three novels as a trilogy insists on this thesis and ends with the proposition that "*USA* is the speech of the people" (3). This speech is found in childhood memories and family talk and in the language of manual workers: "[I]n mother's words telling about longago, in father's telling about when I was a boy, in the kidding stories of uncles, in the lies kids told at school, the hired man's yarns" (2). Toward the end of *USA*, the simple language of home and work becomes charged with political potential; it is the means to oppose "the stronger . . . the rich," the ones who "hire and fire the newspaper editors the old judges" (1157), an idea echoed in the closing words of the last Camera Eye: "[W]e only have words against" (1210). It is also the last bond of solidarity in the bleak landscape of empty streets, indifferent crowds, and alienated individuals described in the foreword: in the midst of this desolation, "[o]nly the ears busy to catch the speech are not alone . . . it was the speech that clung to the ears, the link that tingled in the blood" (2).

In moments like these, Dos Passos's work comes close to the political project of 1930s Left documentary: using the cultural apparatus to amplify the whispers of the suppressed and to question the dominant noise that confuses and misleads. Yet at the same time, Dos Passos's text and the newsreel movement differ sharply in their respective attitudes towards the possibilities for such corrective work. For the newsreel movement, it was merely a matter of circumventing the unofficial censorship of the mainstream media and finding theatrical outlets. For Dos Passos, the difficulties were external—the noise of the media—as well "internal," resulting from a certain aporia built into the structure of the trilogy. Although *USA*'s main aim is restoring the speech of the people, it chronicles instead the instrumentalization of this speech and its remoteness from any realm of public effectiveness.

Rather than the biographies or the Camera Eye sections, the narratives might have been the main showcase for the speech of the people, as their language is powerfully colored by that of the characters whose adventures they tell. But who are the people in the novel? For their working-class background, Mac, the anarchist worker-printer, Joe Williams, Charley Anderson, before his meteoric rise as an aeronautical engineer, and Margo Dowling, before she makes it as a Hollywood star, might qualify, and so could a number of characters they meet along the way: Ike Hall, who travels with Mac through the Northwest; Anderson's mechanic, Bill Cermak; Margo's step-mother, Agnes; and the various sailors, vagrants, workers, and prostitutes with whom Williams becomes acquainted. The other characters rise into the middle or upper classes (like the public relations expert J. Ward Moore-house or the interior decorator Eleanor Stoddard), or are firmly ensconced in the middle class (Eveline Hutchins or Richard Ellsworth Savage), or else abandon it to embrace the workers' cause (Mary French and Ben Compton). The only characters with a political outlook compatible with Dos Passos's ostensive project are the activists Mary French and Ben Compton. What the others say or write can hardly be considered the speech of the people or any form of renewal of the public word. J. Ward Moorehouse adopts the language of producers—"chainlinks and anchors and ironcouplings and malleable elbows and unions and bushings and nipples and pipecaps would jostle in his head" (220)—but only to design publicity campaigns for various industrial concerns. Dick Savage abandons his early dream of writing "stirring poems to nerve [the people] for revolt against their cannibal governments" to write advertisement copy for Moorehouse. And Eleanor Stoddard sounds fastidiously status-conscious and precious throughout.

The working-class characters do not sound promising either. Initially, Charley Anderson is sympathetic to the IWW, attends union meetings, and ends up spending a night in jail for that, yet soon he begins to detach himself from the union. In one of the final scenes of *The 42nd Parallel*, Ben Compton, citing Eugene V. Debs's words, criticizes his desire to rise "from his class not with it." Charley counters: "Damn it, I don't want to spend all my life patching up tin lizzies at seventyfive a month" (353), and as the talk shifts to Debs's opposition to the war, he gives up the discussion—"It's too deep," he says (354)—and abandons the table to go on carousing. Joe Williams is vaguely sympathetic to radicalism but disavows organized politics, at times in shockingly nativist terms. When a factory hand he meets at a bar advises him "to join the I.W.W. and carry a red card and be a classconscious worker," he retorts that "that stuff was only for foreigners, but if somebody started a white man's party to fight the profiteers and the goddam bankers he'd be with 'em" (504).

Mac has an unsteady political consciousness; he alternates between periods of militancy and periods away from the struggle. After a spell of middle-class existence with his wife Maisie, his activism is reawakened on seeing a young protester who has chained himself to a lamppost. The protestor tries to read the Declaration of Independence but is silenced by the police:

"When in the course of human events . . . A cop came up and told him to move on . . . *inalienable right . . . life, liberty and the pursuit of happiness"* (105). Yet earlier on, at a miners' rally where the speaker, Big Bill Haywood, was clearly audible, Mac's mind wanders off halfway through the speech, and he ends up missing Haywood's message.

Mac's experience is representative, since the fate of all resonant social speech in the novel oscillates between suppression and neglect. It is a nearly sophistic dilemma: the speech of the people is either censored or disregarded by those who might stand to benefit from it. The exemplary stories in this regard are Ben Compton's and Mary French's. Compton becomes an underground agitator at the end of 1919. He is repeatedly beaten up, tried, and imprisoned for his organizing work and public appearances, yet he still becomes "quite a speechmaker": "He found out that when he got up on a soapbox to talk he could make people really listen to him . . . and get a laugh or a cheer out of the massed upturned faces" (727). His skill proves of little avail, though; he falls in disgrace and is eventually expelled from "the party" at the instances of Don Stevens, a jealous political rival. Apparently his speechmaking had become a little too good; as Stevens complains to Mary French, "A lot of those boys . . . think this is a debatingsociety. If they are not very careful indeed they'll find themselves out on their ear" (1218). Mary French's story in *The Big Money* is parallel to Compton's in more than one way, since in addition to following a similar trajectory, they are lovers for a time. Loosely inspired by the feminist reformer and activist Mary Heaton Vorse, French is the daughter of a doctor and an affluent lady with social pretensions. She is raised in a Colorado mining region, attends Vassar, and leaves without a degree to write journalistic exposés of living conditions and unfair labor practice in the Pittsburgh steel mills and the New York garment industry. At first, she cannot get her writing accepted for publication by Pittsburgh's conservative *Times-Sentinel.* When she finds an outlet in the workers' press, she fails to bring about much change, and as happens to Compton, her early enthusiasm is ground down by failure and by the party machinery. During a lovers' quarrel, Compton himself questions the value of her research, and later, while writing press releases for the Sacco and Vanzetti Defense Committee, she discovers that the words that had "made her veins tingle only a few weeks before" now leave her completely cold, "like the little cards you get from a onecent fortunetelling machine" (1150). Because of her committed reportage, French is the novel's closest counterpart of the contemporary film documentarists, and her inability to make herself heard—and if heard, understood—is a biting comment on the dubious efficacy of newsreel practice.

In part, the problem lies with the addressees of the revolutionary word: people like Mac, Charley Anderson, or Joe Williams. In addition to their waverings and inconsistencies, they are dominated by compulsions—sex and alcohol are the most frequent—that often take the upper hand over commitment. Charley Anderson's and Joe Williams's stories, sequences of drunken sprees and sexual escapades that culminate in self-destruction, are the most prototypical in this respect. The trilogy is rife with bodily excess reported with repulsed fascination, from the long lines of soldiers waiting for their turn with a prostitute (who is compared with a slot machine) in Camera Eye 33 (486) to the roaring benders and the "daily alcoholic haze" (1148) that, by the end, fill up most characters' lives. In these cases, it is the noise of the body and its demands that drowns the speech of the people.

The difficulty to hear this speech is further thematized by means of pervasive noise. Besides "a slice of a continent" or "a chronicle," USA is an extremely dense soundscape made up of conversations, songs, and, above all, the racket of daily life. Jarring and uncontrollable, everyday noise embodies the internal dissension, the opaque sublimity that prevents the work from fulfilling its avowed purpose of renewing language and making sense out of the quotidian cacophony. Particularly prominent are the ring of telephones, the jangle of office buzzers, the clatter of trains, the roar of engines, the wail of sirens, and, during the war, the blast of explosions. Before enlisting, Charley Anderson spends some time in New York, in an atmosphere "full of grinding gears and clanging cars and the roar of the 'L' and office boys crying extras" (350). As he leaves, the music of "the jazzband on the wharf" is still ringing in his ears (356). Dick Savage's arrival in Paris is preceded by an oddly harmonious train journey—"the little train jogged along in dactyls; everything seemed to fall into rhyme" (442)—but soon after arrival, his ears are also "ringing," first from an army talk about the dangers of venereal disease, and later from the sirens announcing an air raid (443), a sound that fills the wartime episodes in *1919*. When he becomes the boy wonder of the air industry, Anderson's life unfolds among the clang of the machines at the plant and the jingle of telephones that call him up to meetings, report his earnings in the stock market, or wake him up after one of his epic binges. Perhaps the pervasiveness of these invasive noises prompted Alfred Kazin to describe USA's style as "hard, lean, mocking," driven by "the rhythm of the machine."[46]

Noise also invades the Camera Eye episodes, which counterbalance the factual style of the main narrative with subjective, lyrical impressions seemingly written "from the inside."[47] Donald Pizer has called them a "symbolist autobiography" of the author, a repertoire of private memories influenced in technique, wording, and iconography by T. S. Eliot's early poetry.[48] At the same time, their elliptical, fragmentary style and idiosyncratic punctuation recall the Joycean interior monologue, and their reliance on rhythmic repetition brings to mind Gertrude Stein. In the same way that Dos Passos's Newsreels differ from the workers' newsreels, these episodes are remote from what Dziga Vertov's Camera Eye was taken to mean in America—a cinema of objectivity and direct testimony. They are actually much closer to the 1920s lyrical avant-garde, exemplified by Herman Weinberg's *Autumn Fire* or Henwar Rodakiewicz's *Portrait of a Young Man:* a cinema of fleeting impressions, formally sophisticated and detached from collective projects and public concerns.

But unlike the "film poems" of the 1920s, the lyricism of the Camera Eye sections is tinged with a political awareness that increases as the book advances. Taken as a whole, these sections make up a "novel of education" of sorts, describing their narrator's growth into social commitment. They run from childhood, when politics is a vaguely perceived realm full of mystery— as when during a Sunday-morning service, the narrator insistently wonders, "Who were the Molly Maguires?" (Camera Eye 11)—to participation in the war (most Camera Eyes in *1919*), to flirting with bohemia (Camera Eyes 29 and 45), to a period of self-doubt (Camera Eyes 46 and 47) that leads to engagement. Engagement is prompted by the Sacco and Vanzetti executions and by the miners' strikes in Pennsylvania and Kentucky (Camera Eyes 49, 50, and 51). While in the early Camera Eyes the narrator looks at politics with detachment, the impending execution of Sacco and Vanzetti near the end of the trilogy allows him no withdrawal and suggests the overarching project for the work: to "rebuild the words worn slimy in the mouths of lawyers districtattorneys collegepresidents judges" (1136).[49]

The growth into commitment is expressed in sonic as well as ideological terms. During his years at Harvard, the narrator feels like he is under a glass bell that keeps reality outside; only its noises intrude—the distant sounds of machinery ("streetcarwheels screech grinding in a rattle of loose trucks round Harvard Square and the trains crying across the saltmarshes" [263]), and the rumor of labor disputes that the protagonist has not yet learned to interpret ("millworkers marching with a red brass band through the streets of Lawrence Massachusetts" [263]). As he grows progressively responsive to social conflict, he comes to inhabit these noises. In Paris, right after he is discharged from the army, he takes part in the demonstrations of the General Strike of 1918 and recalls the antiwar chants ("Mort aux vaches . . . Vive les poilus") and scraps of the *Internationale* that fill the air (Camera Eye 40, 699). Back in the United States, he attends rallies, addresses crowds in Union Square, and walks the streets, where he absorbs the whistles and sirens at the harbor, overhears conversations, and catches glimpses of street protests quickly stamped out by police—"suddenly gaping back with yells at the thud of a blow a whistle scampering feet" (Camera Eye 47, 932).

Simply registering these sounds is not enough, however. They must be shaped into "a set of figures a formula . . . a speech urging action," and the narrator analyzes advertising billboards, "tatters of newsprint," and snatches of talk for clues as to how this might be done (892). The concise language of headlines and advertisements proves catchy with his listeners at a rally and grants him an "easy climb slogan by slogan to applause," but the simplicity of this language is also misleading, and in the middle of a public address "somebody" inside his head calls him "liar," and he falters. He ends up going home to read Martial's epigrams, ponder "the course of history," and lie in bed, "peeling the onion of doubt" (893). Later Camera Eyes suggest that politically effective language may arise less from the adoption of the media's shorthand languages—the "climb slogan by slogan"—than from historical awareness. History would provide answers to unanswered, perhaps long forgotten, questions—"Who were the Molly Maguires?"—and give some sense to what is, at the outset, only sound, a refrain in a boy's mind.

Who were the Molly Maguires? The shadow of the underground labor organization active in the Pennsylvania mining districts in the 1860s and 1870s hovers over the landscape of the final Camera Eye ("the valley hemmed by dark strike-silent hills" [1208]), which returns to the setting of one of the earliest ("the squirrels and minetipples in the middle of the blue Pennsylvania summer Sunday" [Camera Eye 11, 100]), and thus forms a loop linking beginning and end. More than half a century after the Maguires were disbanded and executed, exploitation is still the miners' lot, and the forces the Maguires were up against have only grown stronger: "[T]hey stand guard at the mines they blockade the miners' soupkitchens . . . the hiredmen with guns stand ready to shoot" (1209). Perhaps the "speech urging action" envisioned in Camera Eye 46 ought to show that the old conflicts keep coming back with renewed strength and that today's strikers are aligned with the rebels of another time. But to speak historically one needs to listen historically as well, to discern the echoes of "the old American speech of the haters of oppression" in the mouths of the miners and factory workers of today and in the statements of Sacco and Vanzetti protesting their innocence (1157–58): "[T]his fishpeddler you have in Charlestown Jail is one of your founders Massachusetts" (1136).

This way of speaking and hearing the past in the present remains a wish rather than an active principle. As is the case with the attempts at linguistic renewal through the speech of the people, this ideal informs the design *of* the book but is nowhere fulfilled *in* the book, where it is another missed chance. It remains an entirely private illumination, shared only by the narrator of the Camera Eyes and by the real-life journalist Paxton Hibbens. When Hibbens attended the 1912 Republican Convention at the Chicago Colosseum, the singing of "Onward Christian Soldiers," the convention's hymn, by the delegates merged in his mind with "the trample of the Russian *Marseillaise,* the sullen silence of Mexican peons, Columbian Indians waiting for a deliverer . . . the measured cadences of the Declaration of Independence" (513). Hibbens's sharp historical sense informed his journalism and his biography, *Henry Ward Beecher: An American Portrait,* which Dos Passos admired, but what difference did it make in the end? When he ran as a Progressive in Indiana he was not elected: "[T]he European war had taken people's minds off social justice" (513).

The historically informed "speech urging action" has to compete in the Camera Eyes with the same kind of cacophony that pervades other parts of the trilogy: "roaring avenues" full of traffic, the sirens, whistles, and trains, and, at the end of Camera Eye 47, the din of a Chinese opera at the Thalia—alien sounds that confirm the narrator's displacement: "the crash of alien gongs the chuckle of rattles the piping of incomprehensible flutes the swing and squawk of ununderstandable talk otherworldly music antics postures costumes" (932). And there is also the sound of the least historical of substances: money. "Make money in New York," advises an old gentleman in Camera Eye 46 "in whose voice boomed all the clergymen of childhood and shrilled the hosannahs of the offkey female choirs." As the narrator reflects on this recommendation, the clink of rolling cash reverberates through the city:

> winnings sing from every streetcorner
> crackle in the ignitions of the cars swish smooth in ballbearings
> sparkle in the lights going on in the showwindows croak in

the klaxons tootle in the horns of imported millionaire shining
towncars

. . .

make loud the girlandmusic show set off the laughing jag in the
cabaret swing in the shufflingshuffling orchestra click sharp in
the hatcheck girl's goodnight. (894)

This is an external racket, the murmur of modern life, but there is also
an internal source of noise: the constant repetitions that lower the semantic charge of language and turn it into a percussive instrument. Some examples, nearly at random: Camera Eye 15 repeats with mechanical regular-
ity the name "Mr. Pierce" together with phrases like "sound as a dollar,"
"smoked little brown cigarettes," "pulled at his dundrearies," "we played Fra
Diavolo on the phonograph," "and everybody was very jolly." Camera Eye
29 keeps returning to "the arbor" where the narrator sits "in the spring,"
to his "clipped skull," and to "swimming in the Marne"—a rare moment of
physical plenitude in the discomfort of the war. Camera Eye 46 insists on the
voice that "said liar to you" and on "peeling the onion of doubt," and Camera Eye 49 repeats "walking from Plymouth to North Plymouth," the setting
of the country's foundation—in the trilogy's Anglocentric terms—and of
Sacco and Vanzetti's tragedy.

In the end, the "clamor" of daily life represented in the Newsreels is not
entirely abated by the other parts of the novel; it echoes through them and
thwarts the attempts at making sense and recharging language with political
consequence. *USA* deflates the progressive potential attached to the ideologies and practice of newsreel and camera-eye aesthetics in 1930s Left media
culture. Rather than instruments of knowledge and agitation, the Newsreels
and Camera Eye fragments embody confusion, deceit, and noise. The uto-
pianism of the Left newsreel/camera-eye film tradition remains a road not
taken, a possibility of the cultural system alluded to but not actualized in
Dos Passos's trilogy.

Popular Culture on the Left

This possibility was being actualized elsewhere at the time. After the launch-
ing of the Popular Front in 1935, leftist critics and artists turned to the popular media and to entertainment to infuse into them some critical consciousness and to borrow from them imagery of widespread appeal. Symptomatic
in this regard is the presence of commercial writers in the Writers' Con-

gresses sponsored by the Popular Front. The Hollywood comedy writer Donald Ogden Stewart (blacklisted in the late 1940s following the HUAC investigations) gave a humorous address in the Second Writers' Congress in 1937, arguing that one could work in the mass media and still retain a radical political outlook. And in the 1938 Congress, the magazine writer Hope Hale encouraged writers to learn the commercial idiom of magazines like *True Story* or *Modern Romances* and to produce fiction that would be entertaining as well as critical of the status quo.[50]

Partly under the momentum of these ideas, the musical theater also became considerably politicized. Works by Marc Blitzstein (*The Cradle Will Rock* [1937], *I Got the Tune* [1938], and *No for an Answer* [1941]), George Kleinsinger (*Life in a Day of a Secretary* [1939]), and Aaron Copland (*The Second Hurricane* [1937]) conveyed social messages in an idiom steeped in blues, jazz, and the popular ballad. In New York, the Theater Arts Committee, one of the many radical theatrical groups of the time, founded in 1937 by members of the extinct Theater Union, put on Cabaret TAC, a very popular and very political act that was amply imitated across the nation. In Hollywood, the Motion Pictures Artists Committee followed suit with the revue "Sticks and Stones," and back in New York City, the Village Vanguard café housed another political cabaret called "The Revuers," also modeled after Cabaret TAC. Its performers, Judith Tuvim, Betty Comden, and Adolph Green, would eventually find their way to Hollywood, where they had long and successful careers. Judith Tuvim became the movie star Judy Holliday, and, as members of the Alan Freed Unit at MGM, Comden and Green wrote the music for such classics as *On the Town* and *Singin' in the Rain*. The slick *TAC Magazine* reported on politics and entertainment in a breezy style reminiscent of the popular gossip columnist Walter Winchell, but with a radical twist.[51]

Responding to this renewed interest in the popular media, the *Daily Worker* and the *New Masses* resumed their coverage of popular film, coverage that had been practically suspended during the high years of Proletkult, when commercial entertainment went unreviewed as it was presumed to be monolithically bourgeois and reactionary. Now, finely calibrated essays and reviews by Robert Stebbins (the pseudonym of the Camera League photographer and future filmmaker Sidney Meyers), David Platt, Robert Forsythe (the pseudonym of Kyle Crichton), and James Dugan assessed the progressive and the complicit in popular film.

There was much that was progressive in contemporary Hollywood. In fact, Hollywood's growing social awareness was one of the factors that prompted Hurwitz, Steiner, and others in the New York Film and Photo League to break with the Spartan documentarism of the league. Due to the pressure of contemporary conditions and to the increased realism allowed by sound, an important number of Hollywood productions in the early 1930s began to explore social problems and to portray contemporary society with gritty realism. Best known in this respect are the Warner Brothers and First National productions that, since the early 1930s, had been dealing with topical problems such as organized crime (*Little Ceasar, Public Enemy, Scarface*), miscarriages of justice (*I Am a Fugitive from the Chain Gang, 20,000 Years in Sing-Sing*), racial prejudice (*Massacre, Son of the Gods*), mob violence (*Bordertown*), and labor disputes (*Black Fury*). As an example, Mervin LeRoy's film for Warner Brothers, *I Am a Fugitive from the Chain Gang*, which was based on a journalistic exposé, was often singled out in the *National Board of Review Magazine* as an eloquent example of the social responsibility of the industry, proof that commercial film had finally become "a medium expressing the forces of social behavior and corrective social thought."[52]

These films were not exactly radical statements. They tended to individualize collective problems and to impose a spurious closure on the conflicts they raised, but their depictions of life in the United States were far from flattering, and Left commentators and reviewers took notice. James Dugan, writing for the *New Masses,* mused: "Were we asking for social content in the movies? Look who's giving it to us now. Republic Pictures has delivered a horse opry called *Under the Western Stars* [a Roy Rogers vehicle], which works up considerable excitement over the demands of dust bowl farmers for federal irrigation projects." In other reviews he praised Hitchcock's *The Lady Vanishes,* Frank Capra's *It Happened One Night,* and, perhaps more predictably, Michael Curtiz's *Robin Hood.* Dugan was not alone in this appreciation of commercial films. Also in the *New Masses,* Robert Forsythe celebrated the Mae West vehicles of the early 1930s, whose "Elizabethan rowdiness" signaled the death-toll of Puritan gentility. (He was a bit too optimistic: West's play *Sex* had been banished from the New York stage a few years earlier, and her films invariably raised waves of protest.) And Robert Stebbins (Sidney Meyers), from the pages of the *New Theater,* praised the Marx Brothers, Mae West, and *Mr. Deeds Goes to Town,* this last for its sympathetic portrayal of the working man.[53]

As Hollywood became radicalized, Soviet cinema increasingly imitated Hollywood. During the 1930s, it started to focus on the production of genre pictures and abandoned the montage styles of the earlier decade. If *Strike* and *Potemkin* had been the emblematic Soviet films of the 1920s, Sergei Vassiliev and Gregori Vassiliev's popular *Chapayev* (1934) would be the showpiece for the 1930s. Based on a popular novel, *Chapayev* was a melodramatic story shot and cut in a straightforward style, showcasing star performers, and centered on an individualized hero, a poor carpenter conscripted by force into the Soviet army, not on a collective protagonist as former films had done. The volume *Soviet Cinema,* a compilation of texts edited by Andrei Arossev in homage to the Vassilievs' film published in the United States in 1935, clearly spelled out the changes in orientation in the Soviet industry. Several statements proposed that the new Soviet style was "socialist realism": "the style of truthful portrayal of reality in its revolutionary development."[54] The new formula in Moscow was to create entertaining pictures with a message. The move was resisted in the United States by some diehard Proletkultists like Seymour Stern and modernists like Dwight Macdonald, both of whom deplored the new "theatrical" filmmaking brought about by sound and longed for the intensity of the old montage films. For Macdonald, a militant Trotskyist, the normalization of the Soviet film grammar and the cap on experimentation were of a piece with the authoritarianism of the Stalinist regime and the purges of dissidents; they demonstrated, for him, that political tyranny had its best ally in the standardized languages of mass culture, an idea he frequently invoked in his subsequent criticism and that is implicit as well in Dos Passos's *USA*.[55]

Read against these examples of the politicization of the popular and the popularization of political perspectives, Dos Passos's pessimistic characterization of the media appears somewhat shortsighted and untimely. It seems a phobic reaction rather than the result of reasoned political and aesthetic decisions. An irrational repulsion informs the Hollywood section of Margo Dowling's narrative and "Adagio Dancer," his portrait-biography of Rudolph Valentino, both in *The Big Money*. While in most other biographies the characters' trajectories are shaped by a combination of political and historical forces, Valentino's seems driven by pathology—by the (female) hysteria of movie audiences, described as a natural phenomenon outside historical determination, an epidemic that sweeps the nation and quickly subsides after his death. In life, Valentino is constantly mobbed by admirers who faint, scream, and try to tear up his clothes or break into his house. After he dies at the peak of his career, the funeral home where he lies in state is gutted by thousands of fans, fighting over "a flower, a piece of wallpaper, a piece of the broken plateglass window." Outside the parlor, the mourners overturn cars, smash shop windows, and block traffic and have to be eventually dispersed by mounted police. The instigator of this frenzy, Valentino, is described as a grotesque, an undecidable figure that combines what Dos Passos apparently regards as unreconcilable opposites. "The gigolo of every woman's dream" is athletic and muscular but also sexually ambiguous: called "a pink powderpuff" by the press, he writes "mushy" poetry, wears a slave's bracelet as token of submission, and apparently never consummated his first marriage. His external beauty hides internal decay. After he collapses in a hotel bedroom, doctors find his "wellmassaged," "elegantlymolded body" infected by acute peritonitis: "the abdominal cavity contained a large amount of fluid and food particles; the viscera were coated with a greenishgrey film; a round hole a centimeter in diameter was seen in the anterior wall of the stomach; the tissue of the stomach for one and onehalf centimeters immediately surrounding the perforation was necrotic" (927). At the core of the Hollywood fantasy is an excessive, indeterminate body blighted by disease.

Suggestions of organic disorder also pervade Margo Dowling's Hollywood narrative. The director Sam Margolis, who discovers Margo for the pictures, is a mercurial, effeminate anorexic on an exclusive diet of milk and cookies. Margo's co-star at Margolis's orders is Rodney Cathcart, an established actor with enormous appetite for food, drink, and sex who wastes no chance to grope her or to ingest yet another meal. When Margolis decides that he and Margo must get married as a publicity stunt, they fly off to Tucson for the ceremony with Agnes, Margo's stepmother, and Cathcart as witnesses; the bumpy return flight has them vomiting "frankly into their cardboard containers" (1125). The social world of Hollywood is split between the glamor of the movie industry's success stories and a squalid underworld of failed stars, fake royalty, addicts, blackmailers, and criminals. Margo's ex-husband, Tony, a "hop-head" and queer, provides a peek into the milieu of those who do not quite make it. He repeatedly tries to extort money from Margo and ends up murdered at a party, allegedly by his lover, Max Hirsch, who claims to be an Austrian count, but Margo describes him as a "bird with a face like a state's prison" (1109). Hardly a haven from this madness, the movie industry is run on the whims and hunches of cranks like Margolis himself; it is an incongruity and an unwholesome emanation of the disorderly—if attractive—bodies of those who work in it and of the hysteria of audiences.

Dos Passos's phobia toward the culture industry may be connected to his ambiguous identification with working-class culture. Michael Denning has attributed this ambiguity to the "proletarian sublime": a mixture of attraction and repulsion aroused by an emergent class of "despised laborers, of social Others," who lurk in the background of the narrative.[56] This new class could no longer be conceived by the 1930s in economic terms alone; it had to be categorized by appealing to ethnic and cultural difference as well. Its members were the protagonists of the second wave of immigration; they were the blacks, Asians, Latin Americans, Southern and Eastern Europeans (the feared "bohunk and polack kids" of Mac's childhood and of an early Camera Eye) that, since the turn of the century, joined in great numbers the workforce in the northern industrial belts. These "others" are a class the narrative courts but ultimately avoids; their sensibilities and perspectives remain secondary, rendered through the eyes of Anglo characters that view them from across an implicit racial and cultural divide. Barbara Foley has noted the novel's "white chauvinism"—a trait shared by other examples of proletarian fiction—and Michael Denning points out that "the racial landscape of *USA* is less a 'slice of a continent' than an ordinary Hollywood production."[57] None of the twelve character narratives tells a story of race or of immigrants, and the "colored people" who occasionally crop up make up a supporting cast of voiceless servants and exotic others. Mac's devoted Mexican wife; Joe Williams's "very dark" girlfriend Della; Eveline Hutchin's Mexican-Irish lover, the painter José O'Reilly; Charley Anderson's Japanese servant Taki ("they are a clever little people," says Charley [957]); Margo Dowling's Cuban husband Tony—all of them tend to evoke a mixture of fascination and disgust in the main characters, but also in the narrative, which holds them at a certain remove, as if it could not quite figure out how to integrate them into the proceedings.

Mass-produced popular culture was the culture of this class and, increasingly, the culture made by this class, especially as the children of the turn-of-the-century immigrants obtained a public education and gained a foothold in the booming field of publishing and media production during the 1920s and 1930s. The figure of Sam Margolis, a New York Jew who started out as a fashion photographer and ended up a popular Hollywood director, is an example of this. The culture he and others like him made—contemporary commercial culture—evoked in Dos Passos a form of sublimity analogous to that raised by their existence as a social group.

Something that may have further determined this perception is the association of commercial culture with industry and technology, always dehumanizing forces in Dos Passos's world. His early novels, *Three Soldiers* and

Manhattan Transfer, align machinery with the oppression of vital impulses in the name of industrial efficiency or profit. *Facing the Chair* contrasted the warm, accented speech of Sacco and Vanzetti with the mechanical language of prosecutors and judges and described legal procedure as a "'superhuman, stealthy, soulless mechanism.'"[58] He commemorated the executions of Sacco and Vanzetti in a poem for the *New Masses,* "The Black Automatons Have Won." And a few years later, in his 1935 Writers' Congress address, he proposed that one of the difficulties in the present was that "machinery and institutions have . . . outgrown the ability of the mind to dominate them." It seems these were not simply literary attitudes. Dos Passos's biographer, Townsend Ludington, has reported that when the writer moved into a room at the painter Elaine Orr's studio on Washington Square Park in the early 1920s, he ripped the telephone off its moorings as a form of revolt against "the system."[59] Hence the effect of the proletariat and the pop sublime are compounded, in Dos Passos's eyes, by a technological sublime. Mediated through industrial technology, popular culture is always on the side of "the interests," "the big concerns" that own it and use it for their purposes, and is thus automatically assigned a politics and a side in the struggle. For Dos Passos, the machine delivers an unconscious of the quotidian, as it does for the other artists and writers discussed in this book; only, in his case, this unconscious has a distinct political content that unequivocally remits to the dispossession of the masses.

The failure to provide a more nuanced view of mass culture limits somewhat the currency of Dos Passos's work. He did not see that activism must engage the commercial media, noise and all. As his contemporary Kenneth Burke polemically proposed in his speech to the First Writers' Congress, politics must rest on widely shared, affect-laden iconography if it is to have any reach.[60] And this iconography will inevitably have to stem from the entertainment industry, the last provenance of a common culture in industrial societies. After all, as a long line of thinkers from Antonio Gramsci to Stuart Hall have reminded us, popular culture often contains a promise of utopia, a glimpse of the good life, not only in the more or less explicit messages it communicates but also in its nondiscursive traits: its sensuous surfaces, sleek styles, and its way of acting on the body and the nerves of audiences. These nonverbal elements can lend politics something it often lacks: libidinal appeal.

Dos Passos was too invested in traditionally conceived art to discern such possibilities in mass culture. However, time showed that the real cultural momentum lay in the forms and media he had dismissed in his trilogy. The very culture he spurned, the classes he could not map in his writing, won out an equivocal, subterranean victory. While many of their specific political claims were rolled back and defeated in the backlash of the cold war and the McCarthy era, many of their rebellious sensibilities lived on beyond the radar of official culture. They impregnated popular music (bebop jazz, folk, rhythm and blues, doo-wop, rock 'n' roll), Hollywood film, cartoons, comic books, youth style, and even sports and later exploded, during the 1960s, in a panoply of fashions, musical modes, aesthetics, and social experiments. At that point it had become clear that the noise of popular culture is the vehicle of the really vital political messages, those too unconventional, too radical, or too inchoate to enter the official political game and its channels of representation.

Unable to fathom the possibilities of media activism and the importance of the popular, all Dos Passos had to go on, after finishing the trilogy, was a lingering resentment toward his former political allies, whose options would soon be exhausted anyway, and a retreat to the past and the soil. He devoted much of his later career to settling accounts with the Stalinist Left in another extensive novel trilogy, *District of Columbia*, and to the excavation, in a variety of history projects, of a storybook republic that—in a phrase included in the first edition of *The 42nd Parallel* but later excised—"had never existed" in the first place (1278). And he withdrew, at the same time, into a Jeffersonian existence, living as a farmer and man of letters on his family estate on the Virginia coast.

This kind of withdrawal puts Dos Passos in the company of Lindsay, Strand, and Sheeler, modernists who explored but ultimately recoiled from the noise of the quotidian. As we will see, others lent a friendlier ear to the rustle of modernity. The rumble of the media was one of the sources of T. S. Eliot's *The Waste Land*—and of much of modern writing, including Dos Passos—and the proliferation of objects that Lindsay regarded with apprehension was productively inhabited by Joseph Cornell's art. In addition, the "social others" that are elided in the aerial views of *Manhatta* or kept at a distance in *USA* reappear at the center of queer modernism and of the modernist ethnographies by Zora Neale Hurston, Helen Levitt, James Agee, and Janice Loeb. These "others" do not provide stable platforms of revolt or models of authenticity; they appear unsettling and disorienting, the bearers of secret histories and latencies that disrupt, in a variety of ways, the narratives of modernity and the linear trajectories of modernism.

The Rustle
of the Quotidian

The Art of Noise

The Gramophone, T. S. Eliot's
The Waste Land, and
the Modernist Discourse Network

Sonic Modernity

There seems to be universal agreement on the notion that modernity was, above all, a visual culture. "We are sweeping into new times," Vachel Lindsay diagnosed, "in which the eye is invading the province of the ear, and in which pictures are crowding all literature to the wall."[1] For Lindsay and many of his contemporaries, evidence of this new state of things was everywhere apparent in the profusion of posters, photographs, illustrated magazines, and films that crowded the perceptual horizon. The pervasiveness of these new images, together with the development of the technologies that brought them into being, have prompted critics and historians to favor visually oriented concepts—such as "hieroglyphic" writing, panoramic perception, the spectacle, or the simulacrum—in their attempts to define and assess modern experience. However, their near exclusive attention to the eye has tended to downplay the fact that in addition to a new visuality, modernity ushered in a radically new sound environment as well. Urban agglomeration and widespread mechanization resulted in significantly increased noise levels and in the introduction of unprecedented pitches, timbres, and rhythms—from the ring of the telephone to the roar of the combustion engine—into the quotidian soundscape. Simultaneously, the new "hieroglyphic civilization" of the turn of the century was accompanied by the popularization of a host of sound media such as the telephone and the phonograph. These prosthetic ears and mouths were first developed in the 1870s but did not become widely available until the 1890s, the decade that also saw the boom of the glossies and the portable Kodak camera and the beginnings of the cinema. Their influence was in many respects as generative and transforming as that of the image media, and yet we still lack a set of critical concepts to evaluate it.

In part, this may be due to the dominance of the scopic drive in western culture, where knowing has been traditionally associated with seeing much more than hearing, and seeing, in turn, has functioned as a way of ordering of the world around the consciousness of the perceiving individual. Ocularcentrism may have been further abetted by the physical properties of the image. Images are often tangible in a way that sound is not. They unfold sequentially, or discretely, and are easier to analyze into their components or to bring into focus; sound remains an (ordinarily) invisible, if pervasive, continuum—a pulsing not easily amenable to framing, perspective, or freezing. Still, the impact of aurality is far from untraceable; it can be perceived in the way that sound, reorganized and rerouted through new technologies, radically transformed daily life and cultural production around the turn of the century.[2]

Just as the image media, the sound media contributed to the concussive flow of stimuli and the multiplication of shocks that, according to Georg Simmel, Siegfried Kracauer, and Walter Benjamin, characterized modern life. Like the camera did in the realm of vision, telephones, phonographs, and radios detached sound from its original context and relocated it anew, and in this way they furthered the fragmentariness of the experiential horizon. Phonographs were capable of turning the flow of experience into an objectified remain—a recording. Music thus became a thing, and so did people: performers were reduced to a set of grooves on a surface.[3] At the same time, sound machines contributed to humanizing the world of things;

as telephones and radio relayed personality through disembodied vibration, they became bearers of human presence. In this manner, the sound media were also implicated in the extension of agency to inert matter and the turning of humans into objects that, according to Lindsay, were also effects of the cinema. The voice media were widely used in indexing the world, one of the earliest applications of the analog media. They fixed evidence and stored traces, but they were also sources of disorder that revealed the inexhaustibility of the quotidian. It is well known that machine vision revealed perspectives unavailable to the naked eye, enlarging the threshold of the visible and discovering an optical unconscious. By analogy, the aural media expanded the scope of the audible and revealed a parallel "aural unconscious." However, the scope of the unconscious, whether optical or aural, is not coextensive with the scope of the intelligible. Like the film or photographic camera, the sound media revealed (in Béla Balázs's term) the readable "microphysiognomy" of reality,[4] but they also tapped into the vast desert of the real on the edges of culture and bore witness to the constant ambient hum and the multiple reverberations of matter. This backdrop of noise—in its acoustical and informational senses—may have always been there, but for the first time it could be heard and stored. It enveloped daily life in a layer of tactile incommunicability that was part of modernity's distinctive vibration and generated strange frequencies that, in many cases, we have yet to respond to. In the previous chapter, I began to explore their effect in Dos Passos's *USA*. I would like to tune into them once more through the (perhaps unlikely) medium of T. S. Eliot's *The Waste Land*. I will try to show that these frequencies modified everyday perceptions and jammed the literature switchboard, powerfully reshaping conceptions of writing, subjectivity, discourse, and cultural hierarchy.

Here's a well-kept secret about modernism: during the composition of *The Waste Land,* throughout 1921 and early 1922, T. S. Eliot was attached to his gramophone much in the same way as Andy Warhol was later "married" to his movie camera, Polaroid, and tape recorder. Both artists, representatives of very different cultural moments and vastly separate in ideology, social and cultural positioning, self-understanding, and public personae, were nonetheless equally dependent on the technological continuum for the production of their work. While Warhol flaunted this dependence and a sense of kinship with the machine ("I've always wanted to be a machine"),[5] Eliot concealed it, recoiling into interiority, religion, myth, and tradition. But for a brief moment, Eliot's writing, like Warhol's multimedia projects, was uneasily entangled in gadgets, circuits, media networks, and technologies of textual production and reproduction. If Warhol mimed the workings of his gadgets, so did Eliot; if Warhol was a recorder-camera-xerox machine, Eliot was a gramophone. But the point here is not to pursue the (certainly contrived) parallel between these two wildly divergent figures. It is to rescue the technological dependency of one of the gray eminences of modernism and to resituate *The Waste Land*, an "apotheosis of modernity"[6] and mainstay of the twentieth-century canon, within the discourse networks of its time.

The term "discourse network" (an English translation of *Aufschreibesystem*) was coined by the German historian and theorist Friedrich A. Kittler to designate the material and ideological substratum of discourse and textuality—the web of "technologies and institutions that allow a given culture to select, store, and produce relevant data."[7] A discourse network is a sort of unconscious, or *impensé,* of signification. In a way, the term combines Michel Foucault's concept of the "archive," which had been applied mostly to print culture, with Marshall McLuhan's insights on the influence of media technologies on thought and cultural processes. In Kittler's work the term has a materialistic thrust. It seeks to deflect the interiorizing, psychologizing tendency of traditional literary hermeneutics by exploring how the material support, or hardware, of signification shapes textuality. This hardware connects abstract meanings to real, tangible bodies, and bodies to regimes of power, information channels, and institutions. Discourse and information hardware filter out some signals as "noise" and process others as meaning. At the same time, conceptions of "noise" and "meaning" are never sanctioned within a single discursive realm or medium. They are promoted and circulated by partially connected notation and information protocols. Hence in his description of "the discourse network of 1900" (where "1900" stands for the period stretching from the 1870s media revolution to the 1920s) to which modernism belongs, Kittler traces the traffic of ideologies, forms of discourse, and inscription mechanisms through the fields of psychophysics, psychoanalysis, the electronic recording media, and literature. Kittler's proposals stem largely from his analysis of German literature and culture. In applying them to T. S. Eliot and Anglo-American modernism, we will have to adapt them somewhat to preserve their validity. In much of what follows, I will seek to situate *The Waste Land* within a discourse network that brings together the electronic media, language automatism, psychotherapy and the discourse of the unconscious, and the idiom of popular culture.

This approach entails a shift in the customary parameters of discussion of

Eliot's most influential piece. Rather than an expansion of the usual hermeneutic debates on *The Waste Land*'s formal-conceptual unity (or lack of it), symbolism, sources, and meaning, what will be performed here is a surface exploration of its textual mechanics. The point is not to discover *what* but *how* the poem signifies. At the end of this investigation lie no further interpretations of the text but the unveiling of modes of inscription on which its meaning depends. These modes fragment the "organic" utterance, replay and recontextualize prerecorded voices, and turn language into a tactile stimulus at the expense of its communicative potential. We will also see modernism rendered other, traversed by a plurality of discourses (medical, technological, and popular) that have often been elided from the official histories of the modern. But this is at the end; at the beginning . . . the scratchy sound of the gramophone.

A Record on the Gramophone

The gramophone is heard in a prominent, if squalid, segment of *The Waste Land*. It appears in part 3 ("The Fire Sermon"), in one of the emblematic moments of modern degradation that the poem seeks at once to portray and to overcome. This is the sexual encounter between a jaded typist and a "young man carbuncular"—"A small house agent's clerk . . . on whom assurance sits / As a silk hat on a Bradford millionaire."[8] Their tryst is prefaced by elliptical views of the city (the polluted Thames and its banks; the bustle of traffic), invocations of death and decay, and by a brief passage, "under the brown fog of a winter noon," in which the ever-mutating first-person narrator receives an ambiguous invitation from a Mr. Eugenides, "the Smyrna merchant": "Asked me in demotic French / to luncheon at the Canon Street Hotel" (*CPP* 42–43).[9] These contemporary scenes are haunted by gadgets, mass-produced objects, and industrial landscapes that render the present mechanical, jarring, lifeless, and disenchanted. Take, for example, "the sound of horns and motors" in city streets; the "empty bottles, sandwich papers, / silk handkerchiefs, cardboard boxes, cigarette ends / or other testimony of summer nights" on the river banks; the "gashouse" by "the dull canal," where the rats scurry over moldy bones; or the customs forms that fill Mr. Eugenides's pockets.

As one more vignette of present-day decadence, the exhausted rendezvous between the typist and her suitor also unfolds under emblems of industrial modernity. It takes place in the early evening, after work, when "the human engine waits / Like a taxi throbbing, waiting." Home from the office, the typist lights up her stove, tidies up, and "lays out food in tins." Her guest arrives "with one bold stare." Once dinner is over, he makes his advance, which meets with neither resistance nor encouragement. The encounter is unspirited; the insistently mechanical rhythm of the lines underlines its somnambulistic quality. After he leaves, she remains prey to automatism and machine conditioning:

> She turns and looks a moment in the glass,
> Hardly aware of her departed lover:
> Her brain allows one half-formed thought to pass . . .
> paces about her room again, alone,
> she smoothes her hair with automatic hand,
> and puts a record on the gramophone. (*CPP* 44)

The music of the gramophone highlights the squalor of the scene and comes to stand for the vulgarity and disenchantment of contemporary existence. Similar connotations accrue around this device in other parts of Eliot's corpus. In the short story "Eeldrop and Appleplex," for example, gramophones provide a soundtrack for the dismal suburban setting: "[T]he gardens of the small houses to left and right were rank with ivy and tall grass and lilac bushes; the tropical South London verdure was dusty above and mouldy below; the tepid air swarmed with flies. Eeldrop, at the window, welcomed the smoky smell of lilac, the gramaphones [*sic*], the choir of the Baptist chapel, and the sight of three small girls playing cards on the steps of the police station."[10] In a very different piece, Eliot's homage to the British music-hall artist Mary Lloyd, the gramophone, along with the cinema and the radio, are blamed for replacing the "organic," participatory popular arts with the standardized, lifeless output of the culture industry.[11] And in "Portrait of a Lady," the stale pretentiousness of the lady's manners and quarters (which have "[a]n atmosphere of Juliet's tomb") is underlined by the music streaming from—where else?—a gramophone: "And so the conversation slips / Among velleities and carefully caught regrets / Through attenuated tones of violins / Mingled with remote cornets / And begins" (*CPP* 8). Later on in the poem, canned music is aligned once more with lackluster existence; its sound unnerves the hypersensitive first-person "narrator," the lady's interlocutor:

> I remain self-possessed
> Except when a street piano, mechanical and tired

Reiterates some worn-out common song
With the smell of hyacinths across the garden
Recalling things that other people have desired. (*CPP* 10)

But to return to *The Waste Land,* the gramophone's sound closes the poem's bleak, necromantic first half. Shortly afterward begin the intimations of rebirth and redemption. The next stanza evokes "the pleasant whining of a mandolin," heard in a pub on Lower Thames Street, and the neoclassical splendor of the Church of Magnus Martyr, by Christopher Wren (*CPP* 45). The folk performance and the "Ionian white and gold" of the monument offset debased modern existence and its accoutrements. The following section, "Death by Water," contains a poignant memento mori; and in the closing fragment, "What the Thunder Said," the scorched, rocky earth breaks into new life. The oppressive present is obscurely redeemed. Modern city scenes are replaced by timeless landscapes, while the shrill sounds of contemporary life are displaced by the rumble of thunder, mythic invocations drawn from the *Upanishads,* and literary allusions ranging from antiquity to the Renaissance. In the end, the choral voice of tradition drowns the artificial sounds of modernity—among them, the mechanical grinding of the gramophone—and restores to life a hard-won, new organicity. And yet if one listens closely, it becomes apparent that the sounds of tradition are played back by a gramophone. The organic, mystic unity with which, it is generally agreed, the poem ends, is entirely dependent on it. Its prerecorded sound is the condition of possibility for the entire work. In his attempt to modernize the idiom of modern poetry, Eliot was shaping an old medium in the image of a new one.[12]

Modernism and Language Machines

Modernism's mediality has not gone unnoticed. The critic Clement Greenberg located in it the emergence of modern aesthetics: "This is the genesis of the 'abstract.' In turning his attention away from subject-matter or common experience, the poet or artist turns it in upon the medium of his own craft."[13] As art turns self-reflexive and withdraws from external particulars, the medium becomes the message. So we are told that literature, for example, delves into the materiality of the word, music into pure sound, and painting into shapes, lines, and masses of color. While this is true, it is also a somewhat confining account of modernist aesthetics. Greenberg restricts modernist media-awareness to the traditional materials (or media) of artistic expression.

Yet there is another way in which modern artists turn to the media, and that is to the new media of mass communication: the telegraph, the radio, film, photography, the telephone, the typewriter, and the gramophone.

With the exception of photography and film, all these media focus on language. They amplify it, project it through space, dissect it into its basic components, and store it with the intention of playing it back. In all cases, language became unhinged from its print support, which was progressively displaced as the eminent linguistic medium. As it was newly encoded, channeled, inscribed, canned, and broadcast through a variety of media, language acquired new material embodiments as well as an unprecedented malleability. It could be manipulated in ways that had simply been impossible while it was borne by print and the spoken word.

The new media dissociated language from human corporeality. The typewriter, for example, interposed a mechanical contraption between hand and text and did away with the personal distinctiveness of handwriting. Other devices detached oral language from the physical presence of the speakers and reattached it to inanimate objects. The voice was then disembodied and, therefore, dis-organ-ized. The gramophone in particular broke up the continuum of spoken communication into its component parts. It scattered, in time and space, the sender of the message; her or his portable, reproducible sound; and the message's addressee (the audience).[14] The organic unity of a live musical performance or an oral exchange was dissolved and subjected to the detours of mechanic ensembles and electronic circuits. As we have already seen, there is a value judgement attached to that in *The Waste Land*. The typist's turning on the gramophone after mechanical sex denotes her immersion in an inauthentic world. Hers is an environment where communication does not entail intimate contact but the cold comfort of machine connections.

But machines are never simple, and Eliot's poem attests to that. The machine-driven world ("Trams and dusty trees. / Highbury bore me" [*CPP* 46]) may be disenchanted and hollow. Deserted by the nymphs of a long-gone era, the Thames "sweats oil and tar," and the people on its banks live in exile from meaning and transcendence. ("In Margate Sands. / I can connect / Nothing with nothing" [*CPP* 46]). And yet this disenchanted modernity is also a stage for the return of the dead. Madame Sosostris, "famous clairvoyante," summons them "with a wicked pack of cards" in an early part of the poem, and the dead respond in mass. The crowd that flows over London Bridge is a crowd of ghosts: "I had not thought death had undone so many."

At any turn one may run into one of the departed: "Stetson! / You who were with me in the ships at Mylae!" Michael Levenson points out that this eerie atmosphere contributes to making the poem into "a chamber of horrors—a gothic extravaganza" indebted at times to the atmosphere of Edgar Allan Poe's tales.[15] Following Eliot's own suggestions, critics have explained the poem's insistence on the return of the dead by reference to the fertility rites and myths analyzed in James G. Frazer's *Golden Bough* and in Jesse Weston's *From Ritual to Romance.* Without rejecting such explanations *tout court,* it is worth pointing out that there are also more immediate (if more complicit and definitely less Eliotic) sources for the ghostly: the voice media themselves and, notably, the gramophone.

The earliest uses of the gramophone were linked to preserving traces of the absent. Thomas Edison, who gave the phonograph, the immediate predecessor of the gramophone, its definite shape in 1878, building upon the work of earlier French pioneers such as Scott de Martinville and Charles Cros, conceived it at first as a means to record and repeat telephone conversations.[16] The invention emerged from a double absence—of the speakers who send their spectral voices through a cable, and of the original exchange itself. The Bell laboratories in Washington, D.C., restyled Edison's mechanism into a dictaphone, which would relay a disembodied voice and therefore bear witness to further absences. Edison suggested other uses for voice-recording technologies, among them, the production of "tone pictures" of a person's entire life, personal mementos condensing in a few minutes a sound panorama spanning from baby prattle to *the last words* of the dying member of the family."[17] (James Joyce may have been thinking of this when he had Leopold Bloom fantasize, in the tedium of a burial, about phonographically equipped tombs and families gathered around the voices of the dead: "Besides, how could you remember everybody? Eyes, walk, voice. Well, the voice, yes: gramophone. Have a gramophone in every grave or keep it in the house. After dinner on a Sunday. Put on poor old greatgrandfather. Kraahraak! Hellohellohello amawfullyglad kraark awfullygladaseeyouagain hellohello amwawf krpthsth"[18]).

With this technology, Madame Sosostris's conjuring could have been done by simply picking up the telephone (to have a ghost immediately inquire "Number, please?"), turning on the radio, or cranking up the gramophone. These media repopulate the world with "spirits"—from the Latin *spiritus,* breath—or, what is the same, with voices. Not in vain, the term "medium"—its most recent meaning, according to *Webster's,* was "a channel or system of communication, information, or entertainment"—had long been in use to designate an intermediary with "the beyond." For early users, there was something magical about the new media. Listening to the voices coming out of the telephone, the gramophone, or the radio felt at first like a séance of sorts, and naturally, those who trafficked in spirits took notice.[19] A Reverend Horatio N. Powers, from Piermont, New York, wrote a "Phonograph Salutation" in 1877 in which the gadget describes itself and extols its virtues and capabilities. Not the least of these is, "'I am a resurrection, men may hear / the quick and dead converse, as I reply.'"[20] Not for nothing was Edison widely known as "the wizard of Menlo Park." He was occasionally portrayed in the popular press in Merlin-like garb; and like Houdini, another contemporary sensation, he did not seem bound by the laws of nature. Even his collaborators agreed that something of the supernatural clung to the man and his milieu. Francis Jehl, one of Edison's assistants, recalled that the inventor's laboratory "'lighted up with a bewitching glimmer—like an alchemist's den.'"[21] In his biography of Edison, Neil Baldwin reports that Edison flirted with theosophy and spiritualism, owned many volumes of such lore, and openly admired Mme. Blavatsky. Blavatsky, in turn, was fascinated with the phonograph. She visited the inventor in his den, made him an honorary member of the Theosophical Society, and gave him a signed copy of her hulking bestseller, *Isis Unveiled* (1877). In the book she tries to bridge the gap between spiritualism and science—between the darkened parlors of the society's headquarters and Menlo Park—by claiming that magic simply derives from an intimate knowledge of magnetism and electricity.[22] In view of these connections, it is perhaps not surprising that the gramophonic *Waste Land* took the form of an extended séance. The return of the dead may be attributed to the poem's mythic substratum but also to the nebulous embodiments and the equivocal forms of absence-presence allowed by modern media.[23]

In addition to being ghostly, language, cut loose from bodies and their intentions and channeled through the media, appeared as an autonomous force, an energy without beginning, end, or direction. Radios, telephones, and gramophones multiplied exponentially the number of utterances floating through the air, contributing to the increased momentum of contemporary life. Their endless murmur was the sonic background of the second industrial revolution. One could try to shut off this murmur, or else tune in and ride the (Herzian) waves. Most modernist writers and thinkers did the latter. What such diverse figures as Sigmund Freud, F. T. Marinetti, Tristan

Tzara, Marcel Proust, Gertrude Stein, Ernest Hemingway, André Breton, James Joyce, John Dos Passos, and Marcel Duchamp, to name a few, endlessly recorded in their writing is precisely language unbound—nonsense, wordplay, unconscious rhymes and rhythms, strings of association, snatches of conversation caught on the run, glossolalia. Rather than create, they took dictation, their ears wide open to the world's unsuppressible cacophony.[24]

By doing this they fashioned themselves after recording-receiving devices—radios and telephones picking up the signal, and phonographs alternately recording and playing messages back. As a student at Radcliffe, Gertrude Stein took part in psychophysical experiments in automatic reading and writing conducted under Hugo Muensterberg's guidance. There is a direct line connecting the nonsense, randomly generated language used in these experiments and the cadenced audacities of *Tender Buttons* or *The Making of Americans*. Ernest Hemingway's style of "hard objectivity" was also labeled a "camera eye" style. Joyce's *Ulysses* and, especially, *Finnegans Wake* are radiophonic "tone poems" (McLuhan's term) that transcribe the densely layered speech of the world and its multiplicity of accents, dialects, languages, and memories. For Jacques Derrida, they are manic telephone exchanges hooked up to a soundbank ("a multiplicity of voices and answering machines") holding no less than "the entire archive of Western culture."[25] And here's how D. H. Lawrence described Dos Passos's *Manhattan Transfer:* "If you set a blank record revolving to receive all the sounds, and a film-camera going to photograph all the motions of a scattered group of individuals, at the points where they meet and touch in New York, you would more or less get Mr. Dos Passos's method."[26]

That Eliot was familiar with such methods of direct transposition is attested to by his first famous poem, "The Love Song of J. Alfred Prufrock": "It is impossible to say just what I mean! / But as if a magic lantern threw the nerves in patterns on a screen" (*CPP* 6). The transcription of neural engrams would be the straightforward, unequivocal manner of portraying subjectivity. Failing that, one may make do with the approximate notations poetry provides. These claim to be nearly verbatim transcriptions of the verbal stream that flows through consciousness.

The Waste Land, which grew from the themes and techniques of "The Love Song," can also be seen as one such attempt to record the drift of a speaker's mind. Its parallel with the earlier poem made the American poet Conrad Aiken wonder, "Isn't it that Mr. Eliot, finding it 'impossible to say exactly what he means,'—to recapitulate, to enumerate all the events and discoveries and memories that make up a consciousness—has emulated the 'magic lantern' that 'throws the nerves in patterns on a screen'?" (*CH* 160). The poem, he concluded, portrays a consciousness emptying itself; the only underlying unity for its jumbled contents is "the dim unity of the personality," which turns out to be no unity at all. The other source of unity, uncredited by Aiken, is the medium: the recording technology that traces the kaleidoscopic play of thought. In line with Aiken's comments, Elinor Wylie wrote: "Nothing could be more personal and direct than [Eliot's] method of presenting his weariness and despair by means of a stream of memories and images the like of which . . . runs through the brain of any educated and imaginative man whose thoughts are sharpened by suffering" (*CH* 155). And Harriet Monroe, updating the reference to the magic lantern, described *The Waste Land* as a moving picture of the mental processes of the poem's speaking persona: "While stating nothing, it [the poem] suggests everything that is in his [the speaker's] rapidly moving mind, in a series of shifting scenes which fade in and out of each other like the cinema" (*CH* 169). Edmund Wilson, Louis Untermeyer, and Helen McAffe explicitly posited that the flow of the unconscious was the raw material of Eliot's writing (*CH* 144, 153, 183).

All of these views gesture, more or less advertently, to the structure of the psychoanalytic session and to the media analogies that allowed Freud to conceptualize it. A "consciousness" compulsively empties itself, while another records it all to play it back in writing. Freud spoke of his gramophonic memory, which allowed him to store his patients' testimonies and to play them back for the record at the end of each day.[27] He further compared psychoanalytic communication to a telephone conversation where what was heard is not the speech of two individuals—doctor and patient—but an anonymous discourse: in Jacques Lacan's notation, the discourse of the Other, sending and receiving its own messages through them. In clinical psychology, machines sometimes worked as more than mere analogies; photographs and recordings were often used for diagnostic purposes—for differentiating, in the latter case, "the sob of hysteria from the sigh of melancholia."[28] In the recording one might spot the truth; sound could be better assessed when detached from the distracting mannerisms of the person.[29] In the poem, however, unlike in analysis, the writer is at once patient and analyst: speaker, listener, and recording device. Modernist literature coincided with psychoanalysis in its exploratory thrust and its interest in mental mechanisms. Psychoanalysis is a product of the machine age and of the modern media, which are, in a way, its unconscious—as Kittler put it, "the unconscious of the unconscious."[30] Just like the stylus of the phonograph or the radio receiver, the analyst is characterized by her or his nondiscriminatory receptivity; we have just seen that writers emulate this quality in the contemporary discourse network. In literature, however, there is no diagnosis. It further departs from (or contests) psychoanalysis by operating outside normativity and treatment. It may be relevant to recall that *The Waste Land* was indeed the product of "strained nerves" (in Edmund Wilson's phrase [*CH* 144]) and psychotherapy; it was composed during a particularly trying period of Eliot's life, when he was undergoing psychological treatment and a rest cure to overcome a nervous breakdown.[31]

Besides transcribing brain engrams and mental movements, *The Waste Land* is intent on recording sound as well. Take the following lines:

> HURRY UP PLEASE ITS TIME
> Well, that Sunday Albert was home, they had a hot gammon,
> And they asked me in to dinner, to get the beauty of it hot—
> HURRY UP PLEASE ITS TIME
> HURRY UP PLEASE ITS TIME
> Goonight Bill. Goonight Lou. Goonight May. Goonight.
> Ta ta. Goonight. Goonight.
> Good night, ladies, good night, sweet ladies, good night,
>   good night. (*CPP* 42)

Poetic discourse competes here with Edison's waxed cylinders and Emil Berliner's blank records. It seems to aspire to total inclusiveness; it automatically picks up the main conversation in the foreground and the calls in the background. It does not purge colloquialisms or correct mistakes and is therefore full of what Tim Armstrong calls "waste matter"—not only litter and detritus, but also verbal and sonic waste, even against Eliot's best intentions and Pound's severe editorship.[32] Pound admonished Eliot that some passages, particularly the women's speeches in "A Game of Chess," were too "photographic," too indiscriminate in their registration of quotidian utterance; but, it seems, Eliot could not bring himself to excise some of these verbal snapshots. Together with verbal waste, "alien" sounds and voices leak in and, as with a shift of the dial or a change of record, the "goonight" of the speakers shades off into Ophelia's poignant goodbye. The present quickly melts into the past; colloquial discourse transmutes into literature; and Lil blends in with Shakespeare's hapless character.

Such abrupt transitions are common in the poem. They are the feature that most disoriented early reviewers, and, consequently, much has been written about their meaning and motivation. What interests me here, however, is not what they mean (enough has been said about that) but the technological substratum that makes them possible. We have already pointed out how the voice media fragment the organic wholeness of oral and written communication. We may add that these media, particularly the gramophone, worked as data banks. They were information-storage devices—mechanical memories detached from self and psychology. They made all the speech and music of the world instantly retrievable. The gramophone made possible the existence of sound and music archives, like the *Musée glossophonographique,* created in 1900 by the Anthropology Society of Paris, or the phonographic collection of the Vienna Academy of Science, founded the same year.[33] Such aural memory banks were, in turn, the basis for the sound collages that would later be broadcast on the radio.

In the late 1920s, following up on the success of his film *Berlin, Simphonie der Großstadt,* the experimental German director Walter Ruttmann created several sound montages. He recorded them on the magnetic sound band of an unexposed film strip using the recently developed Tri-Ergon process, one of the most sophisticated at the time. The resulting pieces were *Wochenende,* a sound picture of leisure activities, and *Tönende Welle,* a simulation of radio zapping. Simultaneously, the Soviet avant-garde filmmaker Dziga Vertov was experimenting with similar ideas for his "Radio-Pravda" montages. These were the radio equivalents of his "Kino-Pravda" film newsreels: sounds and voices spliced together to depict, or comment on, contemporary events.

It is not difficult to see a kinship between these experiments and *The Waste Land.* Eliot's poem zaps through a sort of prerecorded literary archive that seems to be kept on the air at different frequencies.[34] As it runs through the length of the spectrum, the dial picks up some voices and frequencies while it skips others; the resulting collage is transcribed onto the page. It is small wonder that the messages transcribed are fragmentary. Mechanized communication does not respect the organic boundaries of grammar and sense. One may tune in and out in midsentence; the connection may be interrupted by leakage, power failure, or sudden malfunctioning. Or one may simply remove the record, turn the dial, or hang up the telephone whether the message has been completed or not.

> London Bridge is falling down, falling down, falling down
> *Poi s'ascose nel foco che gli affina*

Quando fiam uti chelidon—O swallow swallow
Le Prince d'Aquitaine à la tour abolie
These fragments I have shored against my ruins
Why then Ile fit you. Hieronymo's mad againe.
Datta. Dayadhvam. Damyata.
　　　Shantih shantih shantih. (*CPP* 50)

The poet himself is the tuning dial here, or else a disc jockey that delights in creating such mosaics of sound and language. The idea appears elsewhere in Eliot's work. In his famous essay "Tradition and the Individual Talent," written three years before *The Waste Land*, he repeatedly characterizes the mature poet as an impersonal "medium" for the storage and transmission of information: "The mind of the mature poet differs from that of the immature poet not precisely in any valuation of 'personality,' not by being necessarily more interesting or having 'more to say,' but rather by being *a more finely perfected medium* in which special, or very varied, feelings are at liberty to enter into new combinations."[35] He continues, "The poet's mind is in fact a receptacle for seizing and storing up numberless feelings, phrases, images, which remain there until all the particles which can unite to form a new compound are present together." This kind of writing is no longer based on *inventio* (imagination) or the rephrasing of experience. In the discourse network of 1900, writing means something akin to receiving, channeling, or playing back existing files. It is fashioned after the automatic receptivity of the electronic media; at its origin one finds the babble (the Babel) of machines, not the intimate pouring of the soul—that "infinitely gentle, infinitely suffering thing" (*CCP* 13). This was clearly perceived by Eliot's reviewers, who often criticized his writing for its excessive bookishness and apparent lack of "lived experience." Clive Bell's words are symptomatic in this respect: "He cannot write in the great manner out of the heart of his subject: birdlike he must pile up wisps and straws of recollection round the tenuous twig of a central idea. And for these wisps and straws he must go generally to books" (*CH* 188). What Bell and others fail to point out, however, is that the book is no longer the ultimate receptacle of discourse; wisps and straws of language and refracted experience also circulate through a variety of technological devices. The modern poet, whom Pound defined as "antenna of the race," is one of these.

Together with the voices of tradition, automatic receivers pick up noise as well: the communication channels often hiss with static, the sound may be garbled, and the gramophone needle may skip. This random, nonsignifying noise is faithfully transcribed. Noise travels through modernist literature as it does through the media. In part, the solipsism of the moderns may be attributed to the presence in their writing of obstreperous matter that does not yield meaning. The abrupt, seemingly haphazard transitions of *The Waste Land* are a way to encode the noise in the circuits, as are the occasional forms of glossolalia that punctuate the text:

> The barges wash
> Drifting logs
> Down Greenwich reach
> Past the Isle of Dogs
> > Weialala leia
> > Wallala leialala
>
> And further,
> > la la
> To Carthage then I came
> > Burning burning burning burning
> O Lord thou pluckest me out
> O Lord thou pluckest
> burning. (*CPP* 45)

More examples are available throughout Eliot's oeuvre: the epigraph of "Burbank with a Baedeker: Bleistein with a Cigar," which starts "Tra-la-la-la-la-la-laire" and continues, rather more ponderously, "nil nisi divinum stabile est" (*CPP* 23); the verses, "J'erre toujours de-ci de-lá / a divers coups de tra la la," in the frisky self-portrait "Mélange adultère de tout" (*CPP* 29); or the closing of "Fragment of an Agon," the second finished segment of *Sweeney Agonistes,* which ends by disintegrating into pure sound:

> Hoo ha ha
> Hoo ha ha
> Hoo
> Hoo
> KNOCK KNOCK KNOCK
> KNOCK KNOCK KNOCK
> KNOCK
> KNOCK
> KNOCK. (*CPP* 85)

At moments like these, literary discourse incorporates noise and momentarily sidesteps reason and understanding. It becomes a matter of pure externality, not a pathway to interiority, meaning, or a postulated "spirit." The media, in a way, displace all these and bring on the nonsignifying pleasures of pure sound—the grain of the voice, the whirrs, clicks, and grinds that always accompany communication relayed through circuits. At times, these "accidents" of signification took precedence over the message itself. This was happening widely in early twentieth-century music. In the 1910s, the futurist Luigi Russolo called for an "art of noise" that would integrate backfiring engines, ringing phones, clanging bells, slamming doors, and random footsteps. Some of his contemporaries quickly rose to the call. Edgar Varèse, a Frenchman transplanted to the United States, included sirens, cracking whips, and typewriters in his *Amérique* and later inserted blocks of noise, recorded on magnetic tape, in *Deserts* and synthesized electronic sound in *Ecuatorial* (he used Leon Theremin's early synthesizer, which he later replaced with an Ondes Martenot). George Antheil, an American transplanted to Paris and the composer of such scores as *The Airplane Sonata, Ballet Mécanique,* and *Transatlantic,* used propellers, doorbells, and elevators together with passages from well-known popular songs. In literature—although this is clearly no longer "literature" in any traditional sense—the dadaists in exile Hugo Ball, Richard Hülsenbeck, and Emil Janko "invented" (or transposed), in one of their evenings at the Cabaret Voltaire, the sound poem—a composition in several voices where all manner of inarticulate sounds alternated with crisply enunciated, perfectly meaningless syllables. Four decades earlier and in a more sedate mood, Edison, whose hearing, like Eliot's father's, was severely impaired, received his inspiration for the phonograph's recording device by feeling the vibrations of a telephone receiver on his fingertips. Touch and noise, traditionally on the outside of meaning, are now its harbingers. Woven with them, meaning itself becomes an intermittence. Discourse is at once message and massage—content *and* tactile stimulus that seems to skip sense and logic and caresses the ear and the skin.

It might be objected that the noise signals in *The Waste Land* are unduly amplified in this essay, that the poem's randomness *does* mean, and that even the least articulate, glossolalic moments respond to plan. However, the connections between fragments are so recondite and the meanings so far-fetched that, as *The Waste Land* first broke into print, it seemed to hover between attitudinizing and illegibility. Until the first efforts at explanation, led by Eliot's footnotes, the poem was consumed in the dark, noise and all. But the notes throw scarce light on the text and do little to filter out meaninglessness. Eliot himself dismissed them as "a monument of bogus scholarship"; they have primarily aesthetic rather than explanatory value. They prolong and amplify the moods and atmospheres of the poem by piling on further allusions and images and by suggesting further poetic and narrative departures. Where Eliot was aesthetic, others have tried to be didactic, yet after decades of hermeneutic exertions, scholarly glosses on sources and structure still fall short of explaining the work's fascination. This stems to great extent from its most tactile qualities—not from its message but from its massage. Edmund Wilson pointed out that Eliot's ear for rhythm and spoken language kept him readable even at his most abstruse. And Eliot himself once proposed, "It is a test (a positive test, I do not assert that it is always valid negatively) that genuine poetry can communicate before it is understood."[36] *The Waste Land* does communicate through its explosive (and, at times, still opaque) imagery, its energy, its moody atmospheres, and its dense allusiveness. While amenable to reasoned explanation, these qualities retain a power to move and suggest that short-circuits detached understanding; they promote the kind of total involvement typical of other forms of abstraction (Eliot was often called a cubist) and of the complex, multilayered textures of popular culture.[37]

Ragging, Jazzing, Sampling

The kinship between *The Waste Land* and popular culture was duly noticed by Eliot's contemporaries but later disappeared from discussion as the more respectable elements of the work claimed center stage.[38] At the time the poem was published, however, there was no doubt of its debt to the popular. We have already seen that for Harriet Monroe, the poem's transitions resembled cinematic fades (*CH* 169). Louis Untermeyer ruefully pointed out "the jumble of narratives, nursery-rhymes, criticism, jazz-rhythms, 'Dictionary of Favourite Phrases' and a few lyrical moments," and further, "the mingling of willful obscurity and weak vaudeville" (*CH* 152). This eclectic mix seemingly reproduced the varied strains of sound served up by blaring radios and gramophones. Rather than order or reduce such chaos—"an artist is, by the very nature of creation, pledged to give form to formlessness" (*CH* 152)—the poem writes it down. The result? A "documentary," or a direct transcription of the confusion of a media-ridden world. And even a critic as inimical to the popular as Lionel Trilling couldn't help but notice the poem's pop orientation: "[A]nyone who has heard a record of Mr. Eliot reading *The Waste Land* will be struck by how much that poem is publicly intended, . . . by how much the full dialect rendition of the cockney passages suggests that it was even shaped for the music hall, by how explicit the poet's use of his voice makes the music we are so likely to think of as internal and secretive."[39]

Trilling refers here to a series of recordings made in 1947. They present us with a curious loop: *The Waste Land,* once structured by gramophony, was later disseminated by it. (To be exact, rather than of the gramophone, we should speak here of one of its later mutations: magnetic tape, a spinoff of war-inspired communications engineering that made this particular late-1940s recording possible.) This is gramophony squared—Eliot doing "Eliot" in different voices. It was in a way a gesture of abdication: to be heard in the age of the media, poetry must be electrically amplified. Is this why Eliot's voice sounds so mechanical? He grinds out the lines with certain deliberateness, as if trying to stay in beat with an internal metronome.[40] His flat delivery may be, in this case, a way of mechanizing himself to confirm the machine origins of modern poetry. At the same time, there is something liturgical about his insistently regular cadence, perhaps inspired by a nostalgic attempt, so central in his late work, to endow his poetry with the binding power of collective ritual and imagery. But attempting this through a recording is already admitting defeat, acknowledging, in fact, an estranged audience, a fractured polity no longer reachable by the protocols of traditional religion. Like poetry, to get a hearing in the media era, religion has to become televangelism and showbiz, and this awareness may contribute further to the nostalgia audible between the lines.

From a different perspective, reading always stirred Eliot's subtle histrionic talents, and the recording is witness to that. As he dramatizes different dialects, languages, and intonations, he lends his own voice to the disintegration of poetic diction we have already glossed at some length. This is particularly perceptible in his rendering of the women's speeches in "A Game of Chess," the most theatrical of the poem's sections. His alternation between Lil's friends' chat, in a fairly credible cockney, and the background voices in the pub is especially memorable. Changes in volume and pitch evoke spatial distances; Lil's friends sound close and intimate, as if huddling around the microphone, while the bartender seems to bellow his calls from the back of a crowded room. In part the histrionism in these fragments stems from Eliot's self-conscious reproduction of "alien" words, "phonographed" by him and captioned as his but exceeding the limits of his discourse. But even when he is not in character and simply recites, in what is a sort of zero-degree voice in the recording, he still seems to be playing back accents and rhythms not quite his own. Not entirely British but no longer American, Eliot's is an obviously learned accent whose unnaturalness leads us back into the technological continuum and into electrical-aural loops. As contemporary DJs do with a mixture of analogical and digital means, Eliot's voice sampled the tones and rhythms of the metropolis, of traditional poetic diction, and of the (cultural, social) establishment, to play them back . . . with a difference. Now we call this sampling, and it is done with programmable machines; at the time when *The Waste Land* was written, such a defamiliarizing makeover of existing sounds often took the form of ragtime or jazz. This is the popular beat Trilling detected in Eliot's rather ponderous drone. The frequently invoked kinship between the poem and these forms of popular music was clinched by the dependence of both on the new communications media.

According to an anonymous reviewer (J.M.), *The Waste Land* was "the agonized outcry of a sensitive romanticist drowning in a sea of jazz" (*CH* 170). "Drowning" gives the phrase an ambiguous turn; it makes "the sea of jazz" antagonistic to the lyric but also underscores—or does it mourn?—the extent to which the poem is steeped in jazz culture. A few years earlier, after the publication of *Ara Vos Prec* (1920), Clive Bell had pronounced Eliot an eminent "product of the Jazz movement": his "agonizing labors seem to have been eased somewhat by the comfortable ministrations of a black and grinning muse," he wrote, seemingly unable to withhold the facile racial slur. The poet, he continued, "plays the devil with the instrument of Shakespeare and Milton"; his language is "of an exquisite purity as far as material goes, but twisted and ragged out of easy recognition."[41] More authoritative than Bell, the African American writer and jazz musician Ralph Ellison confirmed *The Waste Land*'s musical provenance: "Somehow, its rhythms were often closer to those of jazz than were those of the Negro poets, and even though I could not understand then, its range of allusion was as mixed and varied as that of Louis Armstrong."[42] (Armstrong, incidentally, started his recording career in the early 1920s, months before *The Waste Land* saw the light, when he was still based in Chicago's South Side.)

Twisting and ragging were what jazz was about. Its fractured melodies, audacious harmonies, and complex, driving rhythm twisted classical musical languages out of shape. "Ragging" meant modifying a melody to bring it closer to ragtime, an early jazz form. "Ragtime" was a heavily syncopated form of popular music whose roots were mainly in the African American tradition. Originally cultivated by black entertainers such as the pianist Scott Joplin (his bestselling "Maple Leaf Rag" dates from 1899), it was later adopted and further popularized by composers such as Irving Berlin, whose "Alexander's Ragtime Band" (1911) relaunched the turn-of-the-century ragtime rage. ("That Shakespearian Rag," written by Gene Buck, Herman Ruby, and David Stamper in 1912, cited in "A Game of Chess," was one of the spinoffs of this rage.)[43] "Ragging" a tune meant bringing it in line with the black musical idiom; it was an exercise in parody, defamiliarization, and racial masquerade dear to audiences in the 1910s and 1920s. Performer-composers such as Paul Whiteman and George Gershwin specialized in "ragging" or jazzing up classics and standards to wide acclaim. Clive Bell implicitly aligns Eliot's mischievous revamping of tradition with the work of these popular musicians (Ellison's invocation of Armstrong is more flattering, though).

Although jazz (like its predecessor, ragtime) was primarily a live musical form, its boom coincided with that of the gramophone and relied on it for its diffusion and full impact. Jazzing and ragging, like all parody, depend for their full effect on knowledge of the original being transformed. They presupposed a stock of musical references shared by the listener and performer, just like Eliot's poem presupposes the accessibility of the literary archive played back as a mélange of broken sound bites. In addition, jazz's strategies of defamiliarization and parody were favored by the distance that recordings created between the music itself, performers, and audiences. As music streams from metal tubes, horns, and pulsating membranes, it loses its aura—its uniqueness and unrepeatability—and loosens its ties to the personality, the genius, the body, and the nerves of the performer or composer.[44] It becomes more controllable by the listener than live music could ever be. Moreover, canned music is forced to commingle, indeed to compete, with the din of street life—"the sound of horns and motors." The performance is no longer bracketed off from daily routine; it may now happen any time, as when the typist in *The Waste Land* freshens up after "stooping to folly." Once all types of music are intimately woven with the ordinary, they appear ripe for parody and appropriation.

Like music, literature in the electronic age is subjected to a similar fall into the ordinary. And not only because literary mimesis has been making the quotidian its main focus of interest at least since romanticism. Literature loses some of its sacredness and solemnity when writing notes down the automatic speech of the world and thus imitates electronic receivers and transmitters. According to McLuhan, the electronic media have a leveling effect.[45] Once the channels are open, they carry any and all sounds, those of time-tested tradition as well as—mixed in with—the most ephemeral and mundane. A reporter present at the first demonstrations of Edison's phonograph at the offices of *Scientific American* put it as follows: "'With charming impartiality it [the phonograph] will express itself in the divine strains of a lyric goddess, or use the startling vernacular of a street Arab.'"[46] The gramophone's nondiscriminating ear explodes the queen's English and places it in open competition with all other dialects and inflections, and with sheer noise.[47] Hence in *The Waste Land* gramophonics blows up stylistic uniformity and, with it, extant cultural hierarchies. That's why Shakespeare and pub talk share the same frequencies, or why the Upanishads, Pope, and Dante blend in with jazz rhythms or the drone of city crowds, or why Ophelia and Lil, the cockney working-class woman, touch hands.

As do Eliot and the typist. She is, after all, the poem's originator: the one who gives Eliot his gramophone—electronic memory, language transmitter, verse generator—and his desire. She is the ultimate stand-in for authorship in the machine age—the medium who takes dictation; the conduit of voices, discourses, and noises that travel through her like through information channels; the one in whom language is detached from "the spirit" and its acrobatics and entangled in technological networks.[48] One could say that in his attempt to modernize the idiom of modern poetry, Eliot grafted onto an old medium the "minor," marginal vernaculars of modernity: the language of women, of machines, of popular culture—the language of those with no proper language. But as we will see, there were other peripheral collectives without a proper language whose sounds and images, also relayed through a variety of media, entered modernism's wave band.

5

Joseph Cornell and the Secret Life of Things

Cornell's Things

While Vachel Lindsay tried to regulate, by means of his film hieroglyphics, the proliferating disorder of the world of things, Joseph Cornell inhabited this disorder. He made strangely evocative assemblages of found objects and images that he frequently gleaned from second-hand bookstores and junk shops. Using ready-made objects as the basis of his work was a logical choice for Cornell, an untrained amateur with no artistic education or skills who was barely adequate at sketching or painting. Since "creating" was not an option for this retiring fabric salesman from Flushing, Queens, he could always manipulate the cultural archive by combining its fragments. The resulting oeuvre stands as a provocative meditation on the life of the object in modernity.

And yet, despite the prominence of objects in his work, the literature on

Cornell has been strangely evasive about them. This is not to say that critics have not studied his use of found materials, or that they have failed to comment on the specific things that go into his assemblages (many of which are titled *Object*). But the extensive commentary on the artist has consistently missed the thingness of Cornell's things: the fact that his work is a vivid demonstration of the vexing complexity of modern objects and that it constantly revolves around their inscrutability. Cornell's work gives things their due as things; it allows us to glimpse the life of material as well as the fact that a considerable part of this life is nocturnal and secretive and will not yield to enquiry. Oblivious of this—and following clues provided by Cornell himself—critics tend instead to humanize his objects by aligning them with artistic tradition, by reading them as autobiographical testimonies, or by interpreting them symbolically.

In terms of art history, surrealism has been invoked as the most immediate forerunner of Cornell's art. To this movement one can trace his use of found objects, his enigmatic iconography, and his fascination with the artifacts of popular culture. His connection with the movement was reinforced by his professional and personal trajectory: his work was first exhibited at the Julien Levy Gallery in New York City in 1932, and Levy, who was responsible for introducing the movement into the American art market, became Cornell's first dealer. The artist was a friend of Parker Tyler and Charles Henri Ford, two homegrown surrealists like himself, and a contributor to *View*, the journal they edited in the 1940s. He became acquainted with many of the European surrealists during their New York exile in World War II and remained interested in their work until the end of his life.

At the same time, surrealism does not completely account for Cornell's aesthetics. The art historian Dawn Ades has pointed out important differences between the American and his French counterparts—among them, Cornell's professed distaste for shocking subject matter and overt sexual reference—and has read him as a late descendant of nineteenth-century transcendentalism. Along similar lines, Dore Ashton claims that more than as a surrealist, Cornell must be seen as a late romantic and a symbolist, given his propensity to reverie and nostalgia and his conception of the material world as a vehicle for the ideal. Carter Ratcliff includes him in the picturesque tradition. And Deborah Solomon shows that, despite his aura of isolation and eccentricity, Cornell was a sensitive respondent to contemporary artistic currents whose style subtly incorporated features of 1940s magical realism, or neoromanticism, and 1950s abstract expressionism.[1] In addition, his use of popular iconography made him a forerunner of the 1960s pop artists and underground filmmakers.

These artistic references, however, do not fully explain Cornell's many idiosyncrasies, and scholars have turned to his life in search of further clues. Linda Roscoe Hartigan, Deborah Solomon, Mary Ann Caws, Diane Waldman, and Jodi Hauptman have related Cornell's imagery to the early loss of his father, his conflicted relationships with his mother and handicapped brother, and his erotic fixation with young women, ballet dancers, and movie stars.[2] Waldman, for example, reads the original box *Soap Bubble Set,* which later became the source of a whole series, as a staging of Cornell's family drama and early childhood memories: "The pipe is associated with memories of downtown Manhattan and old houses near the water; the egg is a symbol of life; the glass represents the cradle of life; the four cylinders are his family; and the doll head stands for Cornell himself. The moon, placed above the clay pipe, is both soap bubble and world."[3] Such self-assured interpretation rests on the widely spread assumption that Cornell's art is a heavily coded personal record. The notion has its origin in his abundant diaries and notes, where he often describes his work as an attempt to fix his circumstances and states of mind and therefore to counter the evanescence of experience. Besides a personal profile, Cornell's artifacts also sketch out elusive conceptual systems and historical connections. Sandra Leonard Starr has interpreted his assemblages—especially his ballet-inspired boxes—as religious reflections inspired by Christian Science, which he practiced throughout his life. And Hauptman has shown that the pieces that involve film actresses are informed by a sophisticated understanding of the history of the cinema and the psychosexual dynamics of spectatorship.[4]

Valuable as these interpretations are toward explaining a body of work that is as meticulously crafted as it is mystifyingly opaque, they consistently bypass that on the other side of art, the personal and the symbolic, Cornell merely gives us things—bits of obtrusively unreadable matter in odd combination. His constructions infuse quotidian things with cultural density and human circumstance and therefore lift them from their immediate materiality; yet at the same time, they simultaneously reassert them as matter—blunt remains that symbol and sense can never exhaust.

In this respect, Cornell's work is an example of a modernist attitude toward material culture that has only recently begun to be excavated. Douglas Mao describes it, in relation to such authors as Virginia Woolf, Wyndham Lewis, Ezra Pound, and Wallace Stevens, as a particular attention to objects, seen not as commodities or symbols—as props in a theater for the staging of the human—but as forms of radical alterity in the midst of the quotidian: "as not-self, as not-subject, as most help-less and will-less of entities, but also as a fragment of Being, as solidity, as otherness in its most resilient opacity." Mao sees the modernist concern with the opaque "otherness" of things as, at bottom, a concern with irreducible singularity, an ecological rapport with material not subordinated to consciousness but adjacent to it.[5] Parallel to Mao, Bill Brown attempts to trace in several examples of modernist and premodernist literature what he describes as "a life of things irreducible to the history of human subjects."[6] What he calls the "thing" is the object before subjective appropriation and before it becomes subordinated to perceptual routine and use and integrated into a history not its own. "Following things," a conceptual wager he glosses as "methodological fetishism," would entail looking at reality not from the centered perspective of the subject but from the far more acentric standpoint of material. And although Brown does not draw this conclusion, methodological fetishism may require that we balance the notion that humans call the world into being with the far less familiar one that the human—and its priced accoutrements of sense, culture, and selfhood—may be a way of responding to the constant solicitation of the world of things.

This may sound familiar to readers of Cornell's papers, the mostly private notes through which the artist endlessly responded to the world's solicitations, and where he painstakingly recorded ephemera, moods, the resonances aroused by an object or an anonymous face, a landscape, or an encounter. In these notes his writing moves in a wildly associative matter, as the simplest occurrences often bring to his mind other similar moments as well as literary and artistic allusions. On one occasion, the picture on the side of a delivery truck, a brightly painted still life of meat and fish, seen while riding his bicycle on a summer morning, brings to his mind the seventeenth-century Dutch still lives, Jan van Eyck's *Ghent Altarpiece* and Alan-Fournier's novel of childhood *Le Grand Meaulnes* (first published in France in 1913 and translated into English as *The Wanderer*). These associations heighten the symbolic potential of the original catalyst—the painted truck—and would seem to surpass its thingness. But in Cornell, matter is never entirely volatilized. Years after the original sighting, he glimpses the truck again, this time not in an idyllic setting but in the bleak parking lot of a shopping mall. He notices that, closely inspected, the design that had once inspired rapture barely covers the black lettering of a former picture (a "less picturesque version of a trade-mark") and finds it "as shabby and uninspired as the afternoon"—a piece of unassimilated material that will not lend itself to transcendence. This is not an isolated instance. Cornell's notebooks abound in comparable moments where things are at once richly symbolic and completely inscrutable; where symbolic flight is haunted by the return of matter to its place, and therefore by a sense of deflation that results in the inability to make anything out of certain deeply affecting fragments and events. As he once wrote, "'Miracles of life and beauty cannot be explained.'"[7] One could in fact conjecture that inscrutable materiality is not only what returns but also the starting point in Cornell's meditations and in his art. The endless symbolic resonances and flights of association in which he indulges are attempts to bind the primary alterity of the material world.

Since they provide a record of his creative process and often describe ideas that would later inform a piece, Cornell's notes have been attractive to scholars intent on deciphering the meaning of his work. But meaning is not the only thing these notes deliver; rather, meaning is a passing shadow in a frenzy of connections that Cornell himself is unable to control. He often complains that he needs more stringent discipline to keep the overflowing at bay. Rather than sense, Cornell's notes pursue "'the overcrowding of incident and experience ever opening paths leading ever farther afield . . . the ceaseless flow and interlacing of original experience.'"[8] Even his writing style, with its idiosyncratic punctuation and its omission of personal pronouns, seems designed to convey the automatism of things irrespective of his controlling consciousness. Mary Ann Caws has suggested that Cornell sets experience at a distance so that his reflections seem to come "from some outside source, to happen impersonally." Like in Eliot or even in Dos Passos, in Cornell we have again the artist as recorder, only here what is taken down is how the raw materials of experience connect through the artist, who acts as a registering surface. As things recall other things and any item is potentially connected to a myriad others through elliptical webs of association, the notes (more atomized and thinglike for being written on napkins, paper bags, old envelopes, or any available surface at hand) end up revolving upon the ultimate inapprehensibility of the material world in modernity, when the accumulation of things, and their ability to resonate against each other, completely overcomes the subject's ability to set them in order. The same could be said of Cornell's artworks. As arrangements of objects held together by barely articulated connections, they inhabit material without reducing its alterity or repressing its unconscious automatism. ("Who knows what these objects will say to each other?" he once wondered.) In this way of inhabiting modern matter, he was following, often despite himself, suggestions already developed in surrealism, the main forerunner of his take on things.

The Secret Objects of Surrealism

It seems that the example of French surrealism enabled Cornell to become an artist, and that the main catalyst in this transformation was the surrealists' manipulation of found images and objects.[9] Cornell's first known works were collages of nineteenth-century copper plates and steel engravings after the style of Max Ernst's collage novels *La femme 100 tetes* (1929) and *Reve d'un petite fille qui voulut entrer au carmel* (1930). They were immediately succeeded by pill boxes, glass bells, and shadow boxes, doubly suggestive of the surrealists' fascination with the outmoded and of Victorian domestic art. These artifacts, at once innocent and perverse, naive and sophisticated, would be hard to read without the antecedent of the French avant-garde. Yet the exact circumstances of Cornell's encounter with European surrealism are uncertain. His first work was produced in 1931, around the time when French surrealism premiered in the United States in a large-scale show ("The New Super-Realism"), which opened at the Wadsworth Athenaeum in Hartford, Connecticut, and then traveled to the Julien Levy Gallery in midtown Manhattan. But it is not clear that these events were the artist's first exposure to the movement. It is entirely probable that, as a Francophile and an avid reader, Cornell may have come across some of the surrealist reviews at the galleries he frequented or at the Gotham Bookstore, an important outlet for experimental literature at the time. Whatever the particulars of this enabling first encounter, to understand Cornell's engagement with objects demands a detour through surrealism.

Besides the year of surrealism's American debut and of Cornell's earliest work, 1931 was also the year of the official birth of the surrealist object.[10] This took place in the December issue of *Le Surréalisme au service de la révolution*. It featured Salvador Dalí's article on "the symbolically functioning object," which contained detailed descriptions and photographic reproductions of *objet-poems* by André Breton, Joan Miró, Gala Eluard, Valentine Hugo, Alberto Giacometti, and by Dalí himself.[11] (His was titled "Scatological Object Intended to Function Symbolically" and combined a glass of milk, a woman's shoe, a lump of sugar, a mechanism to lower the lump of sugar into the milk, and a plastic turd.) This may have been the occasion to give official sanction to the surrealist object, but the fact of the matter is that object play had accompanied surrealism from its inception. It had actually been inherited from dadaism, surrealism's immediate predecessor. The dada objects had been conceived (in Walter Benjamin's words) "as instruments of ballistics." Composed out of rubbish, newsprint cutouts, and similar degraded or perishable materials, they intended to deflate artistry, interiority, and personal vision and to explode the "aura"—that is, the exclusiveness and uniqueness— of the art work. The surrealists were not as interested in objects' percussive potential as in what they called their "lyrical" value: their capacity to derail automatized perception and to trigger unpredictable trains of association. In this capacity of objects they discovered a material unconscious of daily life. They thus extended the usual conception of the unconscious, a mental register initially anchored in individual subjectivity, to the world of objects and demonstrated that, despite its homogeneous, standardized facade, the material life of modernity was a porous terrain pitted with enigmas, pregnant with repressed histories, and driven by its own forms of automatism independent of consciousness and intention. As Benjamin put it, "The father of Surrealism was Dada; its mother was an arcade." Both parents traded in objects—some were intended for anarchic debunking; others were leftovers of a recent past still pregnant with obscurely intuited energies.[12]

Despite its importance, the role of the object-based unconscious in surrealism has been generally minimized. The surrealists themselves, and most historians and critics of the movement, have tended to emphasize the subjective dimension of notions like unconsciousness, automatism, surreality, and the image and to slight their application to the knowledge of the "objective" world.[13] In doing so, they have blunted the epistemological dimension of surrealism. They relocate its practice within the familiar realm of expressive, subject-centered aesthetics, and they confine the movement's revolutionary potential to an individualized, interiorized form of subversion difficult to articulate with collective social practice. By contrast, object-centered surrealism is anti-aesthetic and anti-expressive. Rather than create, it recontextualizes and (therefore) reinterprets the given, and because of this, it is best understood, following James Clifford's proposal, as a combination of ethnography and cultural critique whose purpose is the reinvention of the quotidian.[14]

The notion that there is a material unconscious parallel to the subjective unconscious was initially developed by the French critic Laurent Jenny.[15] Jenny associates the subjective unconscious with Breton and the early stages of the movement and the objective unconscious with Dalí's paranoid-critical method, developed largely in the early 1930s. He shows that the political tenor of the 1930s, when the movement sought to respond to charges of isolationism and disengagement, determined a shift from subjective, expressive theory to an objective "interpretive intervention" in the world. While I generally agree with this view, I think that Jenny turns into succession what is in fact simultaneity. From the start, surrealist discourse is traversed by the hesitation about where to locate automatism—in the subject, the object, or both—and the feasibility of an objective automatism is present in the earliest polemics of the movement. In his first manifesto, Breton defined surrealism as "psychic automatism in its pure state." Automatism designated "certain forms of previously neglected associations" produced "in the absence of any control exercised by reason." These associations were celebrated for their potential to "derange the senses," "bewilder sensation," and "reveal the marvelous in everyday life," and they were the main sources of "convulsive beauty," the ultimate goal of the movement.[16] Although Breton didn't put it so starkly, one can easily glean from his foundational manifesto two main modalities of automatism: subjective and objective. The former stemmed from the free-associative thinking unhinged within the individual consciousness. Its main (and often banal) application was *écriture automatique*—writing carried out with total spontaneity, often in a trancelike state, without filtering or censoring any connections that might come into the writer's mind. Object automatism was not so much produced as "perceived" in the disconcerting, incongruous resonances arising from single or haphazardly juxtaposed items: "[T]hings extravagant . . . the modern mannequin, or any other symbol capable of affecting the human sensibility for a period of time."[17]

The distinction between internal and external automatism is difficult to maintain largely because the surrealists were notoriously undecided as to where to locate surrealist affect. Receptivity to automatism often depended on the subject's *disponibilité*, a state of passive openness that was often sought in hypnotic states, in the identification with the hysteric, who acts out the symptom moved by elusive, uncontrollable forces, or, in Dalí's case, in paranoia. But it is undeniable that certain settings, objects, and events had the power to conjure the surreal and, so long as this power was acknowledged by the group and by subsequent critics of the movement, it cannot be regarded as the product of a solely private perception. The question remains: What makes certain objects laden with surrealist potential? Is it particular material properties in things, or a special mood of responsiveness on the part of the beholder? On the answer will depend to what extent we may consider surrealism a solipsistic, ultimately ineffectual style of rebellion or a blueprint for the subversion of the quotidian.

The most convincing attempts to answer this have come from Hal Foster and Joanna Malt, both of whom vindicate the political nature of the movement by demonstrating how private surrealist illuminations can become a critical way of inhabiting the everyday. For Foster, the surrealist object is a form of the Freudian uncanny—the return of psychic contents that were once familiar but have long been repressed. What returns in the object are precapitalist forms of sociality buried by capitalist rationality and, at a more personal level, a traumatic experience that he reads in subjective terms in the work of André Breton, Giorgio De Chirico, Alberto Giacometti, and Max Ernst as the threat of castration. The object arouses the memory of powerlessness and physical mutilation but also allows the subject to gain some distance from it and to work through this traumatic kernel by means of a fantasy. This is why objects combine anxiety and fascination; why, even though they evoke danger, they are also obsessively revisited.[18] Malt suggests that the surrealist object might be best understood in terms of fetishism, a term that collates social and psychic contents. It designates the workings of the commodity in the capitalist marketplace and factors bodily reality into the surrealists' confrontation with the material world.[19] For both critics, what defines the surrealist object is a particular style of symbolization that brings together the personal and collective past, the social and the psychic, and that would allow the individual subversions of a subjective surrealism to reverberate into the social. While I find these readings cogent and persuasive, there is another way to look at the surrealist object. Rather than a readable sign, as Malt and Foster propose, the surrealist object often resists symbolization altogether; it is a grimace of material reality that defies attempts to make it yield sense. In this respect, it is always already social and communal, the raw material of the public sphere at its most literal: the spaces, commodities, and practices that regiment public life, not as messages to be decoded but as obdurate lumps of matter we brush against in our daily doings.

Object automatism filled the pages of the surrealist periodicals and publications. It was explored, above all, by means of found objects: mysterious tools and implements, orthopedic and prosthetic devices, advertisement posters, ethnographic exhibits, and even quotidian debris, usually photographed against neutral backgrounds. Brassaï's photographic series, *"sculptures involuntaires,"* published in *Minotaure,* are representative. They are snapshots of torn tram tickets, bread crumbs, cigarette butts, and melting pieces of soap accidentally eroded by use into textures and shapes that evoke the human genitals, plant tissue, and art nouveau designs.[20] At times these objects were combined into assemblages that Breton labeled "object-poems" or "surrealist objects"—the direct antecedents of Cornell's boxes. Other times they were shown in isolation. The surrealist objects sought to re-create the surprise and unpredictability of the haphazard encounter by hiding obvious connections between their parts and by letting chance play a central role in their composition. They frequently transmitted the impression of randomness. Think, for example, of Hans Bellmer's dolls, whose limbs are carefully arranged to suggest accidental fractures; or of Cornell's *Taglioni's Jewell Casket,* where some of the glass cubes appear to have been dropped in haste, as if their examination had been suddenly interrupted.

The discovery and description of "automatic" objects was at times the main structuring principle in surrealist aesthetics. Breton's novel *Nadja,* for example, revolves around a found personality, the eponymous protagonist. It devotes long sections to the fantastic, often disturbing intimations accruing on advertising billboards ("the luminous Mazda sign on the boulevards"), shop signs, facades, film serials, "*bad*" plays, and "old-fashioned, broken, useless, incomprehensible, even perverse" objects accidentally encountered in flea markets. Among these last are a bronze cast of a glove; a white, shellacked cylindrical device (possibly a statistical representation); or "a brand new copy of Rimbaud's *Oeuvres Completes* lost in a tiny, wretched bin of rags, yellowed nineteenth-century photographs, worthless books, and iron spoons."[21] Objects also play an important part in Breton's later *L'Amour fou,* where the author returns to the flea market, this time in the company of the sculptor Alberto Giacometti, to find a wooden spoon resembling a slipper and an enigmatic iron mask that spurs Giacometti to finish his piece "The Invisible Object." Louis Aragon's *Paris Peasant* re-created the "underwater world" of the Passage de l'Opéra, a derelict arcade slated for demolition that housed public baths, a cheap hotel used for erotic rendezvous, some unfashionable cafés (like the Certá, where the surrealists held their meetings), a bookstore, a hair salon, a tobacco store, a theater, and number of other nondescript establishments. In this "dimly lit zone of human activity," objects and sights appear "to swing open . . . the gateway of mystery" and plunge the observer into "flights of dizzy speculation" and vertigo. Doors seem to hide truculent love affairs; heads of hair "pulse with hysteria"; a tailor's shop evokes the notorious serial murderer Landrú ("[T]hat sensitive experimenter . . . must have bought his clothes here, trying on his suits in the middle of luggage displayed like so many mysterious symbols of his destiny").[22]

Salvador Dalí was perhaps the most exhaustive explorer of the automatism of objects in a series of essays from the late 1920s and early 1930s. For him, surrealism was inseparable from object manipulation. It was born when the two-dimensional materials glued to the cubist *papier collés* swelled up into three-dimensional objects and eventually freed themselves from the flat canvas to start their "prenatal life out of it"—that is, their surrealist life. He periodized the history of the movement, taking as his basis the evolution of the surrealist object: from "external" and anthropomorphic, existing independently of the subject, to a second phase of "edible" objects, to a final stage characterized by objects purged of all symbolism or narrative, reduced to their "real," "material" presence and tactile qualities.[23] In his many essays, his critical gaze ranges widely across the material archive—from the latest fashions to outmoded styles; from kitsch pictures to classic examples of high art; from the iconography of mental pathology to homely quotidian castoffs (zits, nail clippings)—in search of convulsive objects. For Dalí, as for the other surrealists, their main characteristic is their resistance to interpretation—the convulsive is the unreadable.

Take, for example, the reports on Parisian life written in the late 1920s for a Barcelona newspaper, *La Publicitat*. In them Dalí completely forgoes the documentary or the picturesque and painstakingly describes instead the incongruous choreography of hands, glasses, bills, and assorted litter on the tables of the outdoor cafés; the number of (Adolphe) "Menjou moustaches" sighted in the crowd; and the transit of shoes, pushcarts, bags, pets, strollers, vehicles, and windswept trash seen at ground level on a busy intersection. He thus transforms ordinary city views into phantasmagorias of decontextualized objects floating in space, seemingly endowed with a life of their own, reminiscent of the artwork of the nineteenth-century cartoonist J. J. Grandville, a surrealist favorite. But while Grandville was allegorical, Dalí is purposefully opaque. His floating objects and body parts are (to quote his own words) "lyrical, irrational, and acute" affirmations of a materiality irreducible to meaning.

Another example of the convulsive-unreadable is his essay "Non-Euclidian Psychology of a Photograph," a commentary of a found (family?) snapshot of two women and a man at a storefront. The man stands between the women in a shady recess of the facade; only his face is visible and floats spectrally in a dark void. What draws Dalí's attention, however, is not the incongruity between the dowdy ladies and their ghostly male escort, or the improbable manner in which one of the ladies, who is probably standing on a step, seems to levitate a full foot above the pavement, but the disturbing presence of an unaccountable "*bare*" (his emphasis) spool of thread hardly visible in the gutter on the left foreground. This is "a crazy thing": "Delirious, flagrant, and incomprehensible," it poses a "universal problem for human intelligence" and shows the limitations of Kant's rationalistic epistemology, which Dalí fluently maligns.

> But neglible and feeble though it may be [the spool] no longer accepts the antipersonal and anti-anthropomorphic immobility of the metaphysical absolute; it is there, and of such insignificance as the ones whose solicitations we, surrealists, have, first and foremost, learned to listen to, solicitations revealed to us by dreams as characterizing our age, our life, with the utmost violence. These are precisely the threadless spools, these deplorably insignificant objects, that at this moment make us, the Surrealists, waste the most and best of our time, and the most and best of our space, because our works and our houses constitute a material and tangible proof of the pervasive cluttering of such objects and of the increasing number of strident solicitations they exert upon us, because, from their unnoticed state, they loudly trumpet their obvious physical reality. Psychology is nothing other than human behavior vis-à-vis this physics.[24]

A year later, Breton published "The Crisis of the Object," which rephrases many of Dalí's ideas. He explicitly links the exploration of objects to non-Euclidian geometry and to the role of undecidability in contemporary science. The new nonlinear geometry that hypothesized the existence of hidden dimensions and ambiguous spaces, and Heisenberg's principle of indeterminacy, seemed to legitimize the surrealists' fascination with illegible recesses in the quotidian: "Just as modern physics is increasingly based on non-Euclidean systems, so the creation of 'surrealist objects' derives from the necessity to establish, in Paul Eluard's masterful phrase, a genuine 'physics of poetry.'"[25]

By subjecting material life to a stop-motion view, the surrealists discovered a "non-Euclidean" everyday punctuated with opacities and blind spots that routine perception filters out. These blank spots solicit and obstruct the interpretive gaze. As Breton puts it in *Nadja,* they are "like doors left ajar"; they "present all the appearances of a signal, without being able to say precisely which signal, and of what."[26] What the surrealists extricate from them is not complete irrationality and unintelligibility but a regulated lack of meaning, a studied intertwining of the irrational with the recognizable and trivial. They see the irrational, enigmatic, and opaque as an undertow on familiar reality. Rather than confine these qualities to the otherworldly realm of the fantastic and paranormal, they regard them as a pervasive pulse in the real. Their point is not to separate the surreal from the real but to provide continued evidence of their vexing imbrication. As Breton explains in the first manifesto: "What is admirable about the fantastic is that there is no longer anything fantastic: there is only the real."[27]

And if there is only the real, then everything exists on the same plane, and external objects replicate mental processes so that the subject receives from them (from the Other) its own message backward.[28] The object world might be where the subjective and the objective coincide, where external reality becomes "humanized," a cipher for the inner mind, and the material unconscious is folded into a personalized, private unconscious. It might be that level, forecast by Breton in one of his most idealistic moments, where surreality becomes reality, polarities collapse, and opposites meet.[29] But such meetings never really take place. Plagued by opacities and enigmas, the "objective" is actually a realm of dislocation and missed encounters. The spaces, images, textures, and commodities that magnetized the surrealists are best read as instances of what Jacques Lacan called "the Thing"—what, in the real, "suffers" from the signifier. The Thing is what remains from the work of symbolization; or, differently put, what the agency of the signifier—the elemental symbolic unit—casts off as waste matter that does not contribute to meaning but still adheres to it, since all meaning is, after all, borne on matter. The "excremental" object was, for Dalí, central to the third and last phase of surrealism, and this phase came after a second one that revolved around "edible" objects. This succession may best be read as a dialectical relation, however. The edible object is the one the subject seeks to incorporate by ingestion, and ingesting, as Joanna Malt has pointed out, "is a means of imposing the individual's subjectivity on the recalcitrant thing"—in short, a metaphor for symbolization.[30] But, as Dalí is fond of remarking, incorporation (symbolic or not) generates waste, which becomes the privileged category in another stage of surrealism—the excreted object, by-product of two highly coded processes: eating and signification.[31] The excreted object belongs to the register of the Lacanian real: the impossible, what does not exist (in the symbolic) but only insists outside its grid in the form of irreducible excess, enjoyment astir between the lines or caught obliquely in the field of vision, like the spool in the corner of the picture or the enigmatic details that fill Cornell's boxes.

The appositeness of Lacan's terminology is not accidental since, to a great extent, his concept of the real formalizes surrealist ideas on the automatism of objects. Lacan's affinities with surrealism are well known.[32] His early research on paranoia found its most appreciative audience among the surrealists. The poet René Crevel, a member of Breton's group who had been unhappily in analysis for several years and was fond of taking jabs at the psychiatric establishment, praised Lacan's thesis, published in 1932, as a groundbreaking work and a true example of materialist psychiatry. Lacan was a long-standing friend of Georges Bataille's, an occasional participant in the meetings and activities of his group, and a regular at the events of the Collège de Sociologie, founded by Bataille, Michel Leiris, and Roger Caillois.[33] He published two essays in the surrealist review *Minotaure:* one, excerpted from his doctoral thesis, discussed the relationship between paranoia and aesthetics and was printed back to back with Dalí's famous exposition of the *méthode paranoïaque-critique;* the other dealt with the paranoiac component of the notorious murder perpetrated by the Papin sisters, two domestic servants who savagely killed their employers in Le Mans.[34] Lacan's doctoral thesis influenced Dalí, and Dalí's ideas had a lasting, if unacknowledged, afterlife in Lacan. Many of the concerns, examples, and even the concrete images that crop up in his seminars of the 1950s and 1960s can be traced back to Dalí's essays in *Minotaure.* In one example, the anamorphic skull in the foreground of Hans Holbein's "The Ambassadors," used to illustrate the notion of the *tache* in *Le Séminaire, Livre XI: Les Quatre concepts fondamentaux de la psychanalyse,* had been used by Dalí to illustrate his essay "Apparitions Aérodynamiques des 'Etre-Objets,'" which moves with slippery (Lacanian) (il)logic from the pleasure of popping blackheads to the contemplation of salivating, soft machines, to edible art—all examples of blots (*taches*) in the texture of reality.[35] And the very concept of the "real," as applied by Dalí to the objects of the excremental phase of surrealism, anticipates Lacan's subsequent use of the term.

As the mention of Lacan suggests, there is much more at stake here than traditionally conceived aesthetics. The exploration of object automatism involved the surrealists in interdisciplinary projects where "art" merged with science. Evidence of this is the lineage of surrealist ethnographers, including Marcel Griaule, Michel Leiris, Wolfgang Paalen, Jean Rouch, and even

Chris Marker, who mined non-Western art and culture as sources of alternative representational systems and cognitive styles. A further example is the peculiar perception of natural science that underlies surrealist play.

Science was the first vocation of many surrealists. Breton and Aragon studied medicine and met at the hospital of Val-de-Grace, a nerve clinic that specialized in treating shell-shocked soldiers, in 1917. One of these soldiers, the manic Jacques Vachè, who ended up committing suicide at the end of the war, was one of the formative influences on Breton. Breton's surrealism can be read as a formation of mourning, an attempt to come to terms with the loss of his friend by internalizing his *dèlire* in his own writing. Breton and Aragon instigated the homage to the discovery of hysteria published in an early issue of *La Révolution surréaliste,* and Aragon compared his attentive study of the life of the Passage de l'Opéra to the observation, through the microscope, of "magnificent bacterial dramas."[36] Other members of Breton's group were similarly invested in scientific discourse. Luis Buñuel had studied biology at the University of Madrid and was an expert entomologist. He and Dalí were fascinated with insects and natural processes such as death and decomposition. Accordingly, their first film, *Un Chien Andalou,* features rotting carcasses and crawling ants, and their second, *L'Age d'Or,* opens like a nature documentary. For his part, Max Ernst titled his *frottage* series, produced automatically by rubbing charcoals and crayons on paper placed on a variety of surfaces, *Histoire naturelle.* Like Cornell, Ernst was an avid bird-watcher and frequently included birds and birdlike creatures in his work. More marginal to the group, the French filmmaker Jean Painléve made peculiar nature documentaries infused with a taste for the grotesque, and Roger Caillois produced provocative readings of the death drive manifest in natural phenomena and animal behavior. In alliance with surrealism, natural science and ethnography purveyed counterdiscourses to the superficial deification of rationalism and total intelligibility characteristic of bourgeois technocratic society. They provided ample evidence of an unruly object realm that obeyed its own independent momentum, where meaning was often blocked off and held in abeyance.[37]

Yet as Cornell's work exemplifies, more than nature or anthropology, the main source of object automatism in the early phases of surrealism was popular culture. It has often been noted that the convulsive potential of the popular lay in its content, in the way it debunked all standards of propriety by purveying unbridled expressions of violence, eroticism, and fantasy. Some examples are the deranged plays performed at the Théâtre Moderne; in the

Passage de l'Opéra, described by Aragon and Breton; the truculent tabloid headlines, advertisements, and comic strips collaged by Julian Levy for the first surrealist show in New York; or the cartoons of George Herriman (the creator of *Krazy Kat*), Rube Goldberg, and Walt Disney. (Sketches by Goldberg and Disney were included in the 1936 Museum of Modern Art show, "Fantastic Art, Dada, Surrealism," curated by Alfred H. Barr.)[38] Popular film melodramas provided examples of mad passion, and the silent physical comedies of Mack Sennett, Buster Keaton, and Charles Chaplin wallowed in gleeful disruption of all established orders. But it has seldom been noted that there is *another* important reason for the surrealists' interest in popular culture: it was an important purveyor of object automatism.[39]

Advertisements, pulp literature, comic strips, pornography, tabloids, and films multiplied the tactile solicitations of the object horizon. At the same time, they underlined its radically estranged nature, its surplus of materiality that exceeded function and use and that media representations, with their lushness of detail, hyperbolic emotionalism, and enlarged scale, showcased to advantage. This was especially true of the films that entranced the surrealists: preclassical film, silent serials, westerns, adventure films, and comedies. Lacking complex plots, psychological depth, or intellectual ambition, these films highlighted the intricacy of the object horizon. For Aragon, these "dear old American adventure films . . . speak of daily life and manage to raise to a dramatic level a banknote on which our attention is riveted, a table with a revolver on it, a bottle that on occasion becomes a weapon, a handkerchief that reveals a crime, a typewriter that's the horizon of a desk, the terrible unreeling ticker tape with its magic ciphers that enrich or ruin bankers. . . . [O]n the screen, objects that were a few moments ago sticks of furniture or books of cloakroom tickets are transformed to the point where they take on menacing or enigmatic meanings."[40]

This perception was promoted by the new visual technologies that made mass culture possible: film and photography. This is why, as Aragon proposed in *Paris Peasant,* surrealism is "[t]he entrance to the realm of the instantaneous, the world of snapshot."[41] Likewise, for Breton, automatic writing provided "a photograph of thought." Writing for the third issue of *La Révolution surréaliste,* Pierre Naville, soon to defect to the orthodox Marxism of the Clarté group, listed the main sources of surrealist imagery: kiosks (a metonymy for the popular press?), automobiles, the cinema, and photographs. Rosalynd Krauss has explained the surrealists' fixation with photography in terms of "a rhyme between psychic automatism as a process of automatic recording and the automatism associated with the camera." The two reveal what she takes to be the key to surrealist convulsive beauty: reality as representation—as "the constant, uninterrupted production of signs"—inhabited by an internal spacing that prevents it from coinciding with itself and subjects it to the sequentiality of the signifier. Yet what photography reveals to the surrealists, what explains their fascination with the medium, is precisely those obtrusive aspects of reality—those automatisms—that will not submit to the defiles of the signifier and escape textualization and sense.[42]

Photography reveals the underlying strangeness of the object world by isolating things within a frame, and film produces an image of the world as inventory by means of editing. It yields a disjointed composite whose parts do not add up to a whole. The surrealist protocols of isolating particulars (as *objets trouvés*) and inventorying them in assemblages, art shows, and publications replicated the processes of photography and film. Framing and montage were at the root of surrealism's enumerative aesthetic. Montage was the source of the surrealist image and of convulsive beauty, whose famous example is "the fortuitous encounter of an umbrella and a sewing machine on an operating table." (Doesn't the sewing machine, which figures in one of Cornell's earliest collages, foreshadow the editing table?) Even in establishing a genealogy for their work, the surrealists practiced montage, as they disrupted chronological sequence and cultural hierarchies and grouped together wildly disparate figures—Hieronymus Bosch, E. T. A. Hoffmann, Edgar Allan Poe, Charles Baudelaire, Arthur Rimbaud, George Méliès, Emile Cohl, and Buster Keaton, to name a few—on the basis of their affinity to their aesthetic. Film is a surrealist medium as much as surrealism is a cinematographic aesthetic. Paraphrasing Friedrich Kittler, we could say that the image media are the unconscious of the surrealist exploration of the unconscious. By extension, they are the unconscious, the unspoken enabling agency, of Cornell's own work.

Photographer

While Cornell never learned to use a camera (the photographic reproductions included in his work were made to order, and his films were shot by his assistants), his confrontation with the object world was completely mediated by the photochemical media. Photography, for example, is directly referenced in his pervasive use of Photostat reproductions and in the pieces inspired in the daguerreotype—the portraits of Greta Garbo as Anna Karenina, whom she played on the screen, are case in point. In addition, the

Cornell scholar Jodi Hauptman has demonstrated that a concern with film was at the heart of a large number of his boxes, collages, and albums. This is most evident in the constructions dealing explicitly with film topics—his numerous homages to Hollywood actresses—and in the extensive album "The Crystal Cage," which re-creates a number of protocinematic technologies popular in the nineteenth century.[43] But even when visual technologies are not an explicit concern, Hauptman suggests, the gridlike placement of images in his assemblages evokes the seriality of Etienne Jules Marey's or Eadweard Muybridge's chronophotography or the frames in a strip of celluloid. Think of the "shots" of Lauren Bacall in the boxes that bear her name, or of the "decoupage" of the Medici boys in the *Medici Slot Machine* and *Pinturicchio Variant* series. Photographic framing and cinematographic editing are the basic methods of composition in Cornell's boxes.

Like photographs, Cornell's boxes capture objects and images within a frame, interrupting their daily transit, and like films, they regroup these objects into new assemblages. In the process their meanings mutate. For example, Bacall's face acquires different connotations by being included in a "penny arcade" portrait. Penny arcades were the first settings for the kinetoscopes. These coin-operated cabinets with a peeping hole patented by Thomas Edison were the earliest form of film exhibition in the United States. Placing the Hollywood star in the context of a penny arcade links her at once with the archaic and the illicit (since in the early 1940s, when the box was made, this form of film spectatorship only survived in erotic peep shows).[44] Further shifts in signification emerge from the "montage" of the actress's face with views of Manhattan skyscrapers and with the metal ball resting in the bottom of the box. Is this a penny arcade or a pinball machine? And if it is a bit of both, what is the meaning of their conflation?

In this construction, like in all of Cornell's works, the clash of individual components generates meanings that exceed their original ones. The procedure evokes Eisensteinian montage, but the results do not, since no straightforward content emerges from these collisions. The active viewing Cornell's works encourage is not geared toward revolutionary enlightenment but toward semiotic drift. Like other characteristically modern frames—show windows and display cases in department stores—they stimulate reverie and open up spaces of mystification. At the same time, and this is perhaps their most photographic quality, they capture incongruous details that generate indeterminacy and limit their readability.

In this respect, Cornell's work reflects his habitual way of looking at

Joseph Cornell, *Medici Slot Machine*, 1942.
Private Collection. © VEGAP, Madrid, 2004.

things, which he painstakingly recorded in his notes and journals. These show that his vision was completely modeled after image-recording technologies; it combined, cyborg-style, the human and machine-like. His seeing, for one, is often framed by windows, doors, and mirrors, or relayed by reflecting surfaces. He is not so much a man with a movie camera, which he never learned to use, but a man *as* a movie camera. As is the case with camera-mediated vision, Cornell's seeing is never neutral; it is always slightly distorting and transforming, and at times it becomes downright hallucinatory. In an interview published in *Art News* in December 1957, Cornell mentioned two events that changed his life. The first took place during a visit to a pet shop in Maspeth, Long Island: "'I heard a voice and I saw a light.'" The second overcame him at work. Looking out the window of his office at Traphagan Textiles, on Broadway and Fifty-Second Street, he saw the nineteenth-century dancer Fanny Cerrito dressed as a guard closing the windows of the Manhattan Warehouse, the building across the street.[45]

Can such visions be innocent of artistic and literary antecedents? In an essay on paranoia and creativity published in the first issue of *Minotaure,* Jacques Lacan argues that hallucination is never an entirely private affair but always draws on sensitive historical material. The psychotic is, at bottom, an eccentric cultural historian at work in reshaping the social imaginary. Was this the case here? Cornell's vision combines a romantic ballerina with Hedy Lamarr, who dressed as a guard in King Vidor's film, *Comrade X* (1938), one of her earliest vehicles. He brings together a nineteenth- and a twentieth-century star, the ballet and the cinema, and the spaces of art and commerce. Notice as well the carefully arranged topography: the double framings and telescoped windows. Throughout art history windows have thematized vision itself, and in symbolist and post-symbolist art, a spectrum that includes surrealism, they became emblems of subjectivism, solipsism, and separation—structures that, in Rosalynd Krauss's words, "freeze and lock the self into the space of its own reduplicated being." A man cut in two by a window seen during a hypnagogic reverie provided Breton with an entry into automatic thought processes. But, as should be clear by now, for the surrealists windows do not always look into the subject; they look out on collective phantasmagoria as well. In Max Ernst's collage novels, the monstrous (the symptom) springs into the well-padded Victorian interiors from windows, doorframes, paintings, and mirrors. In *Paris Peasant,* Aragon narrates that late one evening, before his astonished eyes, the canes in a shop window in the Passage de l'Opéra softened into seaweed consistency and swayed gently in the sea-green light of the arcade; a small-sized siren swam among them. Is this a merely private vision? The arcades were for Walter Benjamin "dream houses of the collective." They had "no outside—like the dream."[46]

Most of the time, however, Cornell's vision purveyed less hallucinatory spectacles—not of dead ballerinas but of live young women and men glimpsed during his frequent strolls through the city and always perceived through assorted framings. A diary entry from December 2, 1955, for example, recalls:

> cappuccino coffee (Grand and Mott?) shot of workman in mirror & pendulum clock strong in thought to start day . . . Young teenager in mirror framed by doily of glass shelf and mother ordering turkey sandwich—the magic of the camera eye (seeing with)—week ago watching on Grand Street—overemotionalism that comes with thawing out sometimes like this—certain "music"—later appreciation of faces in poorly lit subway stations, especially like an old one at 14th IRT—("now you(ll) see the guy with the violin again") chubby boy with glasses his sister asking directions, a little tableau that would have been magical on film—a kind of *"purgatorio"* climate of light for a series especially of fragile or interesting faces—an idea worth following up (Spanish girl).
>
> love of humanity—no matter how much might be taken on film this urge might not be satisfying—there is always the thing that the camera cannot catch.

Notice the peculiar staccato pace and the dashes, filmlike cuts that strive to register swarming associations. He once described this form of writing as "newsreel style" in a letter to the poet Marianne Moore.[47]

In this passage, the "magic of the camera eye (seeing with)" yields an oneiric view. Its unreal quality stems partly from the allusions Cornell piles on. The kids in a dark subway station evoke Dante's "Purgatory," or a tableau, reminiscent of early photography and film and of Victorian parlor games. The dreaminess of the scene is accentuated by the scrupulously recorded details that Cornell's (camera-like) eye refuses to filter out. Notice, for example, that the workman is uncannily duplicated in a mirror *and* a pendulum clock and that the chubby boy glimpsed in the subway wears glasses. Is this a sign of vulnerability, of disoriented vision, connected with the fact that his sister is asking for directions? Or is it simply a throwaway, accidental detail? Is this semiotic dross that crowds Cornell's description the background "music" that he hears through these scenes? Are these simply odd details that ruffle the surface of the picture, or are they essential to its meaning? And if they are essential, what is their meaning? More than his diaries, his collages and constructions abound in such incongruous oddities. What is, for example, the exact meaning of the compass at the bottom of the Medici slot machine? Of the branches that cover Bebé Marie? Of the images, often drawn from classical paintings (by Vermeer, by Parmigianino) or from sky charts, that fade out into the white walls of the hotel boxes? Why am I calling this withdrawal of meaning photographic?

The "truthfulness" of the photographic image is revealed most clearly by the contingent details that the camera, in its automatism, catches in flight and fixes within the frame. These details are at once real and touched with a degree of impenetrability; they belie the presumed transparency of the medium and its association with straightforward realism, and perhaps because of this, they have attracted the attention of a number of critics influenced by surrealism, such as Siegfried Kracauer, Parker Tyler, and Roland Barthes. In his writings of the 1940s, for example, Tyler underlined the weight of off-center details in the cinematic image and the extent to which they undercut the unified, realistic effect of the picture—"the movie city entertains a strange mathematics: the whole is equal to less than the sum of its parts."[48] His formulation had been anticipated by Kracauer, for whom the photograph, with its unconscious accumulation of unassimilated particulars, "dissolves into the sum of its details, like a corpse." The obtrusive elements on its surface make up a disintegrated unity. Because of this, photography and film are the emblematic media of modernity—a "fallen" time when experience is devoid of immanent sense.[49] And in *Camera Lucida,* Barthes names the obtrusive particular the *punctum.*[50] The punctum is a random element that "rises from the scene, shoots out from it like an arrow, and pierces me," provoking "a wound, a prick, a mark made by a pointed instrument" (26). It can only be encircled yet hardly explained or named. It plunges photographs into "the vast disorder of objects" (6) and forces the observer "to confront the wakening of intractable reality" (119).

The unnamable detail is a central ingredient in Cornell's boxes and films. The components of his boxes are fastidiously chosen and combined to evoke *and* withhold meaning, to suggest an unconscious that, refusing to be named, silently signals its presence. Analogously, his films hint at but do not deliver sense. *Rose Hobart,* his earliest and most widely seen film, is a recut version of George Melford's jungle picture, *East of Borneo,* that reduces the original from feature length to nineteen minutes. Cornell's version eliminates everything that contributes to narrative articulation and retains transitional, disconnected moments that evoke affect but not meaning or plot. Most of them showcase the actress Rose Hobart's haunting, vulnerable screen presence. She is usually fearful and tense, frowning, warily stepping around a luxurious palace, pulling a gun from the bottom of a dresser and hiding it in her purse, anxiously staring offscreen, or in earnest exchange with interlocutors we rarely see, since the matching shots are usually edited out.

Most of Cornell's other films are similarly fragmentary. His children's party reels—a trilogy comprising *Cotillion, The Children's Party,* and *The Midnight Party*—juxtapose footage from Hollywood films, acrobatic and vaudeville acts, and nature documentaries. The mixture suggests nocturnal, furtive, and at times frenzied rituals, especially the energetic scenes that show children dressed and made up as adults in what looks like a speakeasy. *Bookstalls* cross-cuts between a boy perusing through books at a stand in the street and the images these call up in his imagination; but with their changing geography and fragmented quality, these do not make up a coherent fantasy. Other titles, like *A Legend for Fountains,* made with Rudy Burkhardt, and the more abstract *Wonder Ring* (or *Gnirrednow*), a collaboration with Stan Brakhage, are equally invested on suggestive but largely opaque details.

Taken together, these films make up a catalog of cinematic puncta. They result from a characteristically modernist form of film spectatorship that disregards narrative wholes and focuses instead on the peripheral elements that accompany (and occasionally derail) the unfolding of the story. These bypaths and throwaway details tend to be the privileged objects of cultism and cinephilia.[51] They are a sort of optical unconscious of narrative film—involuntary moments that temporarily open up, within the linear flow of the story, a shadow realm, alternate paths of (non)sense and affect.

Collector and Historian

Cornell's boxes and films are opaque "snapshots," but they are also inventories of the material world and peculiar historical projects that conflate past and present, high and low culture, and intangible memory and solid objecthood, while they revolve around the intractable materiality of things.

A number of critics have pointed out that collecting is a central trope in Cornell's aesthetics. Each of his works was a curatorial project involving exhaustive research and gathering of images, objects, and quotations connected, often in a subterranean manner, to the box's subject matter.[52] Like museum exhibits, his boxes are carefully encased and often contain shelves, partitions, and slots for organizing their contents. Some of them were titled *Museum,* the collection's superlative format; others only evoked it in their formal arrangement. *L'Egypte de Mlle: Cléo de Mèrode* or *Pharmacy,* to name only two, are coffers with slots for closed, labeled glass jars purporting to contain in their reduced space an entire geography, a pharmacopoeia. But despite his use of the rhetoric of the collection and the museum, Cornell is far from a conventional collector, a fact that earlier analyses do not sufficiently take into account.

Collectors assemble traces of the material world and enlist vision to produce order. In a way, their goal is to correct the work of photography: to appropriate the frame as a site of containment while filtering out the contingency that inevitably taints the snapshot. For Jean Baudrillard, the collector substitutes a "formal" interest in order and seriality for a "real" interest in the objects as they exist in the world, but not out of empty formalism. The collection distils relations not immediately apparent in the world; it seeks to clarify the world by producing a simulacrum and therefore bears a metaphorical relationship to it. As Susan Stewart reminds us, the original model of the collection is Noah's ark, and its most spectacular modern incarnation is the museum, which strives to produce systematic knowledge through closure and exhaustiveness: "Like Noah's ark, those great civic collections, the library and the museum, seek to represent experience within a mode of control and confinement. One cannot know everything about the world but at least one can approach closed knowledge through the collection."[53]

Cornell's collections do not clarify the world of objects or reduce it to an intelligible system. The jars in *Museum, L'Egypte,* or *Pharmacy* contain, among other things, clock parts, glitter, sequins, nails, cuts of fabric, thread, colored sand, glass beads, dried herbs and flowers, stamps and cutouts of period postcards, and "mouse material" (dust balls). This capricious assortment is far from orderly or exhaustive. As collections, Cornell's boxes do not produce substantive knowledge, but their labels, orderliness, and seriality recall its "atmosphere" and topography. They turn knowledge into a style of presentation. They submit matter to a mode of classification that is completely inexhaustible (more elements could have been added) and mysterious (because of the arcane quality of containers and arrangements). Rather than delineate order, they succumb to the world's inherent disorder, to the fact that matter escapes all attempts to reduce it to system.

As is usually the case, Cornell's collecting was oriented to the past, perhaps because outmoded things, with their dated design and forgotten func-

Joseph Cornell, *Museum*, ca. 1944–48.
The Menil Collection, Houston. Bequest of
Jermayne MacAgy. © VEGAP, Madrid, 2004.

tionality, appear more immediately material than the self-evidently transparent objects of the present. The objects of his devotion belonged primarily to the nineteenth century—more specifically, to the romantic period and the 1890s. Like the French surrealists, he was receptive to the artifacts of the immediate past: Victorian velvet and rich fabrics, crowded interiors, early cinema, panoramas and dioramas, art nouveau, old postcards.[54] But unlike the surrealists, his antiquarian interests extended as well to the culture of the 1830s: the romantic opera and ballet; the music of Schumann, von Weber, and Jacques Offenbach; the Paris of the first arcades and the boulevards. He often manipulated and reinterpreted contemporary objects and images to relocate them within these eras, as if this were necessary to catalyze his desire and his creativity. He deliberately aged his boxes, by leaving them outdoors for days or cracking the paint, to give them an antique appear-

JOSEPH CORNELL AND THE SECRET LIFE OF THINGS

ance, and he subjected the likenesses of devoted film stars to a similar aging process. He repeatedly portrayed Greta Garbo in nineteenth-century apparel—as an aristocrat, in the role of Anna Karenina, and as an androgynous dandy in the destroyed *Crystal Mask*. In "Enchanted Wanderer," an homage to Hedy Lamarr, Cornell collaged the actress's face to a Renaissance painting (Giorgione's *Portrait of a Young Man*), and in the accompanying essay, he celebrated the actress's ability "to remind one again of the profound and suggestive power of the silent film to evoke an ideal world of beauty."[55] And, as we have seen, *Penny Arcade Portrait of Lauren Bacall* took the star out of contemporary Hollywood and repositioned her within a form of film viewing popular in the early 1900s. The same can be said of his film *Rose Hobart*, which turned a contemporary sound picture, *East of Borneo*, into a silent by eliminating the soundtrack, adding mood music (from Nestor Amaral's album *Holiday in Brazil*), and projecting it through a blue glass that recalled the tinting used in night scenes in silent film. In addition, Cornell's editing highlighted broad gestures and emphatic reactions, effectively turning Hobart's performance into the sort of pantomime typical of silent cinema. Cornell's fascination with the turn of the century is evident not only in the objects he made but also in those he collected. The largest part of his vast film collection belonged to the years between 1900 and 1923, but nickelodeon-era films were always his favorite, and among them, those by George Méliès and Emile Cohl—two surrealist cults.[56]

Critics have too often explained Cornell's antiquarian attachments in merely biographical terms as nostalgia, thus overlooking the fact that his fixation with the past is directly connected to his fascination with the opacity of material. Cornell's interest in the turn of the century, for example, certainly reveals a biographical investment in the historical period around his childhood—he was born in 1903—but also evokes a more general devotion to childhood as a time of fresh perception and untrammeled receptivity. As Walter Benjamin was fond of pointing out, childhood vision has not yet been reduced by purposive rationality and it is therefore more alert to the enigmatic quality of objects and to the webs of association in which they exist. It multiplies and transforms the object world instead of freezing it into routine: "'[The child's drawers] must become arsenal and zoo; crime museum and crypt. To "tidy up" would be to demolish an edifice full of prickly chestnuts that are spiky clubs, tin foil that is hoarded silver, bricks that are coffins, cacti that are totem poles, and copper pennies that are shields.'"[57] To see as a child is to see as a surrealist, fully attentive to the complexity of matter. This may be one reason for Cornell's intense fascination with children, who populate his notes and diaries, his boxes (think of the Medici boys and Bacall's girl pictures), his albums (*The Crystal Cage* revolves around a small girl, "Berenice"), his collages (to young actresses such as Deanna Durbin or Margaret O'Brien), and films (*Cotillion, Aviary, A Legend for Fountains, The Children's Party, Centuries of June,* and *Bookstalls*).

Childhood vision ties in with the vision of the new electronic media, still in their infancy at the beginning of the twentieth century. Hence to see like a child is, in a way, to see with the untutored eye of the new visual technologies at the time. Cornell's, and the surrealists', early years were a period when the emergent mass media had not yet erased residual forms of entertainment, and technologically mediated images and sounds still existed side by side and often in the same setting with traditional live acts such as the circus, fairground attractions, amusement-park rides, and magic shows. The new media had not yet streamlined their grammar and style. Preclassical cinema was characterized by what Tom Gunning calls an "aesthetics of astonishment" and "distraction," or what Noel Burch calls "a profuse simultaneity of signifiers." The flow of the image had not been subjected yet to strict narrative regulation or to the streamlining of the continuity style and was therefore full of obtrusive detail and tangential appeal. Rather than cut a clean path through the world of matter to follow a story, early cinema seemed entangled in the world's density, constantly sidetracked into the exploration of its strangeness and unpredictability.[58]

Cornell's fixation with the romantic period is another facet of his exploration of things. As Walter Benjamin sought to elucidate in his unfinished *Arcades Project,* this period was the prehistory of contemporary modernity. It was the time of the earliest institutions of consumer culture, such as the arcades, and of a media revolution brought about by new printing techniques (the cylinder press, the chromolithograph) and by the popularization of photography. Taken together, these developments multiplied the availability of images and commodities and thus gave material life an unprecedented complexity. At the same time, romanticism was the era of the consolidation of (Peter Bürger's term) "the institution of art"[59] as a realm separate from daily life, opposed to commercial culture (but supported by its own commodity logic), and reinforced by new institutions such as criticism, museums, salons, galleries, and academies. These often prompted a heightened awareness of things through their idealization of the work of art or of the archeological remain.

Cornell's main interest in this period attaches to the female stars of the romantic ballet: Fanny Cerrito, Maria Taglioni, Carlota Grisi, Fanny Elssler, Cléo de Mèrode, and Emma Livry. As a cultural phenomenon, their star status was symptomatic, on the one hand, of the bourgeois cult of individuality and skill, as opposed to inherited privilege, and, on the other hand, of the simultaneous, intertwined emergence of autonomous art and commodified culture. Romantic ballerinas were examples of art as autonomous practice, since the ballet, with its extreme stylization of costume, gesture, and decor, presents a fantasy realm isolated from daily praxis. At the same time, these stage idols were early pop-culture icons. Their acts were widely reviewed by the press; their likenesses circulated in postcards, daguerreotypes, and posters; their tours were eagerly followed; and their arrival in a city frequently prompted demonstrations of fan enthusiasm. Partly as an effect of their media presence, they became international cult figures, as the legend in Cornell's box *Taglioni's Jewell Casket* attests. In addition, the romantic ballerinas were early examples of the total commodification of the personality that stars embody. Not only their performances but their clothing and personal objects were invested with value for (and by) their fans, who often preserved them in glass-covered boxes and curio cabinets. In this respect, dancers were no different from other nineteenth-century divas also celebrated by Cornell, such as the singers Maria Malibran, Jenny Lind, and Giulia Grisi, all of whom were (in Benjamin's terms) "Ur-Formen" of a nascent, image-based, media-fueled celebrity culture that reached hyperbolic development in Hollywood stardom.[60] This may be the reason why Cornell occasionally brought nineteenth- and twentieth-century divas into dialogue. We have seen that his vision of Cerrito clothed the ballerina in the garb worn by Hedy Lamarr in one of her films. His show Romantic Museum, held at the Hugo Gallery in New York in December 1946, combined albums dedicated to Malibran, Cerrito, and Guidicia Pasta with boxes and collages devoted to Garbo, Bacall, and Jennifer Jones. They were all eminent examples of stardom, a particularly modern form of public presence that, in Cornell's view, stretched from the romantic ballet to contemporary Hollywood.

The juxtaposition of romantic ballerinas and contemporary movie stars suggests that Cornell's interest in the former cannot be explained by appealing solely to disembodiment and spirituality. For Sandra Leonard Starr, in one of the best works on the artist, the ballet represented for Cornell a spiritualization of the body akin to that proposed by Christian Science, and its stylization and narratives of impossible love naturally attracted Cornell, who was never comfortable with sexuality. However, idealization is only one moment in a dialectic that also includes its opposite: the reversion of the dancers' art, and of its symbolic, cultural, and historical connotations, to blunt materiality.[61] The nineteenth-century star cults can be seen as textbook illustrations of the workings of commodity fetishism, as in these cults—and in fandom, generally—relations between people (a performer and her adoring admirers) take the form of relations between things (presided by star memorabilia). In addition, they are examples of another kind of fetishism that Theodor Adorno conceptualized in relation to music and deplored as "regressive." In music, fetishistic listening was manifest by a series of displacements: from the appreciation of total structure to the superficial enjoyment of melodic lines, from the consumption of works as wholes to their sampling in fragments, and from actual musicianship to the celebration of the interpreter's, or composer's, personality or accoutrements. Extending Adorno's ideas to dance, one could conjecture that a mode of fetishistic spectatorship would consist in displacing attention from the ballerinas' art to their images or to those objects that had come in contact with them.

This type of displacement, whereby material comes to replace the ethereal quality of the dance, structures Cornell's reception of the ballet. During the 1940s and 1950s, through his friendship with Charles Henri Ford and Pavel Tchelitchew, who frequently designed sets for the New York City Ballet, Cornell became acquainted with some of the most prominent dancers of the time. Cornell saw Allegra Kent, Tamara Toumanova, and Tillie Losch, as reincarnations of the ballerinas of the previous century. His passion for their work was not limited to their stage acts but extended to their physical presence, the talismans that accompanied them in their dressing rooms, and their costumes. Tokens from their costumes found their way into the series of boxes *Homage to the Romantic Ballet*. The box subtitled *Swan Lake for Tamara Toumanova*, for example, includes white feathers from one of the dancer's costumes, while *Homage to the Romantic Ballet (Dream Fragments)* and *Homage to the Romantic Ballet (Little Mysteries)* gather cloth, glass jewels, slipper lace, and a hairpin. (*Dream Fragments* specifies with Cornell's characteristic preciosity that these keepsakes are "[g]old rain shed from garments of the dark fairy Tamara Toumanova in the Nutcracker Suite.") In the case of dancers from the past, the fetishistic fixation with objects may be read as a form of cultural preservation, since, in the absence of film or photographic records, a scattering of mementoes was all that remained of their performances. This is the concept behind the small box dedicated to "the Sylphide

Lucille Grahn," which offers a poignant metaphor for the fleetingness of the dancer's art and, by contrast, the relative durability of her traces. On the inside of the detachable lid there is a steel engraving of the star costumed for the stage with a flower diadem in her hair and gauze butterfly wings on her back, while at the bottom of the box lies what remains of this full, graceful presence after the passing of time: a pair of clunky wooden wings, a piece of tulle, a sprinkling of glass beads, and a few dried petals. The dancer's elusive artistry thus precipitates in an obtuse accretion of traces, the only remnants of her passage through the world.

These homages re-create cultural history in the private format of the souvenir.[62] They eschew monumental history and its narrative molds, instead transforming historical time into personal arrangements by taking hold of the debris of material culture—a broken toy, an anonymous card, a piece of fabric, a sequin. The ballet boxes implicitly show that these negligible objects and textures can be the support of unofficial histories, fueled by individual desire, that personalize collective time. But Cornell shows that also the reverse is true: even the most personal desires and fantasies are inevitably historical, mediated by collective iconography and impersonal commodities, clothed in perishable styles emanating from particular moments and locations. The world of things is revealed as a transitional territory, a passageway between the personal and the historical, psychology and cultural politics, Freudian and Marxian fetishism.

Cornell's fascination with the nineteenth century contains an implicit rejection of the material culture of his time. His beginnings as an artist coincide with the vogue of art deco and streamlined styles in the United States. Cultivated by such designers as Walter Dorwin Teague, Russell Wright, Norman Bel Geddes, and Gilbert Rohde, these styles revolutionized object culture; they introduced into mass-manufactured everyday utensils, clothing, and furnishings the machine-inspired designs that had been largely restricted to experimental coteries. The machine aesthetic became official culture as it was monumentalized in the World's Fair's "Century of Progress," celebrated in Chicago in 1934, and "World of Tomorrow," held five years later in Flushing, a short distance from Cornell's home. Its most durable and visible artifacts were such emblematic New York skyscrapers as the Chrysler Building (designed by William van Allen), the Empire State Building (the work of a team led by William Lamb), the Daily News Building, and Rockefeller Center (both by Raymond Hood), to name a few. All of these went up as Cornell was breaking into the art world. Industrially inspired styles were

Joseph Cornell, *Homage to the Romantic Ballet* (for the Sylphide, Lucille Grahn), 1945. The Menil Collection, Houston. Bequest of Jermayne MacAgy. © VEGAP, Madrid, 2004.

based on rationalization and simplicity. They stripped buildings and objects of unnecessary ornament and highlighted their underlying structure. In this way, modernist design contested the torpid clutter of nineteenth-century ornamentalism, an aesthetic that, according to one of its main detractors, the Austrian architect Adolf Loos, led to degeneration and crime and was symptomatic of cultural underdevelopment and femininity. The modernist revolution in design—called by some historians a "great masculine renunciation"—made objects lighter and more readable, but at the same time, it deprived them of their enigmatic aura and dense affect.[63]

Like the French surrealists, Cornell responded to the art-deco revolution by maintaining his commitment to the denser ("feminine") materiality of nineteenth-century object culture, with its ornamental vocation and its stylistic excess. His love for the soft textures and evanescence of the ballet is a clear example of this. And so are his constructions. They are frequently lined with rich velvets and antique wallpaper, show a distinct fascination with layering and depth, and place objects in multiple enclosures, rendering them at times distant and inaccessible. They strongly resemble the glass bells and curiosity cabinets once common in Victorian parlors. Their indebtedness to the design of an earlier time is most evident in their main trope: the glass-fronted box. This is a form of encasing that, in Walter Benjamin's eyes, was the central motif in nineteenth-century design: "[The nineteenth century] conceived residence as the receptacle for the person, and it encased him, with all his appurtenances, so deeply in the dwelling's interior that one might be reminded of the inside of a compass case, where the instrument with all its accessories lies embedded in deep, usually violet folds of velvet. It is scarcely possible nowadays to think of all the things for which the nineteenth century invented etuis: pocket watches, slippers, egg cups, thermometers, playing cards. What didn't it provide with jackets, carpets, wrappers! The twentieth century, with its porosity and transparency, has nullified dwelling in the old sense."[64] Dwelling "in the old sense" is what Cornell's boxes try to recover: the seclusion of the nineteenth-century bourgeois interior. With their profusion of drapery, padding, plush, and cushioning, they were conceived as refuges from public life, illusory last shelters of individuality in a world increasingly driven by the impersonal forces of industrial production. And yet, with their anarchic accumulation, they were allegories of the industrial modernity they were supposed to keep out. These indoor landscapes, with their multiple textures, surfaces, fabrics, folds, and tactile appeals, are the ultimate referent of Cornell's boxes.

In them, modernity appears, once more, as an automatic multiplication of objects, an uncontrollable warp of meaningless matter.

From Cornell to Subcultures: "What Form Do You Suppose a Life Would Take . . . ?"

What, in the end, is the political importance of traversing Cornell (and surrealism) through the paths of senselessness uncovered in the object world by visual technologies, the touch of the collector, and the gaze of the fan? What to make of this trail of unreadable traces and opaque signs? And what is the critical value of Cornell's obsession with the dated refuse of mass culture and the stories buried in it?

Highlighting the nonsignifying in daily objects is a way of wrenching them out of the narratives that govern custom and use and steer our traffic through the world. It is a form of ideological critique that elides the social totality and subjectivity—usual entry points into the political—to recode the molecular aspects of the quotidian, where ideology does its work most unconsciously and persistently. This form of critique does not take place at the ideal level of argumentation and concept but at the more material one of tactile manipulation and use. It is a form of (un)knowing where intellectual understanding is at times displaced, at times supplemented, by corporeal stimulation and affect. For Benjamin, only a type of knowledge that digs into the corporeal and is produced and received in distraction, bypassing traditional artistic means and media, can have any effect. Its main tools are the new media, with their power to reorganize the sensorial-perceptual apparatus and the material substratum of everyday life. "Only when in technology body and image so interpenetrate that all revolutionary tension becomes bodily collective innervation, and all the bodily innervations of the collective become revolutionary discharge, has reality transcended itself to the extent demanded by the 'Communist Manifesto.' For the moment, only the Surrealists have understood its present commands."[65] Understanding the commands, of course, is not the same as making them work. The surrealist revolution melted into air when, after a number of disastrous clashes with organized politics in the early 1930s, the movement fizzled out into individual celebrity trips, vapid séances, and arcane mythography. But the movement's tactile reactivation of the object and its emphasis on opaque affect have driven dissident formations ever since.

"What form do you suppose a life would take that was determined at a decisive moment precisely by the street song last on everyone's lips?" mused

Benjamin in his extraordinary assessment of surrealism. Surrealism itself is the reply to this question. With its "radical ideal of freedom," it is indeed the form such a "life" would take: one based on previous decades' fashions, old movies, formerly trendy haircuts and fabrics, pulp novels—in short, the castoffs of popular culture. No one before the surrealists had realized that these discards, these forms of "destitution," could be transformed into "revolutionary nihilism."[66] They could be the raw materials for a life that took seriously the utopian desires dormant in mass culture, desires that become most perceptible when the affect initially attaching to them wanes; desires whose utopian charge is often inversely proportional to their communicability. ("Nightmare alley of lower Broadway," Cornell wrote in one of his enigmatic notes, "the re-creative force of the dream images and illuminated detail seems very important albeit very difficult to do much about in terms of communication.")[67] Cornell, like the surrealists, brought "the immense forces of 'atmosphere' concealed in these things to the point of explosion" but failed to make them go off. What went wrong?

Benjamin again: "The trick by which this world of *things* is mastered—it is more proper to speak of a trick than of a method—consists in the substitution of a political for a historical view of the past."[68] That the surrealists failed to substitute action for contemplative nostalgia and introspection was as much their failure as it was the product of their historical situation. At a time when politics was class-defined party politics, their tactile interventions in the world of things could easily sound ineffectual and evasive. But from our present perspective, when party politics suffer an unprecedented crisis of legitimacy and new social movements have demonstrated the political import of such "personal" domains as bodily pleasures and commodity consumption, surrealism can be reread as what it always was—a subversion of the quotidian carried out at its most material level: the image, the randomly encountered object, the touch of a fabric, the cut of a dress, "the street song last on everyone's lips."

These forms of object-centered subversion have kept returning with the force of the repressed. They drove situationism in the 1950s and 1960s; an important segment of the underground cinema in the 1960s; the punk revolt of the late 1970s and early 1980s; the image manipulation of Barbara Kruger, Cindy Sherman, and Richard Prince in the 1980s; and the objects and photographs of Jimmie Durham and Gabriel Orozco in more recent years. And it still drives retro and trash cults everywhere. The otaku-like absorption of the cultist (increasingly a zine editor and reader and/or Web surfer) who builds up encyclopedic expertise on a number of private obsessions and assembles sample and after sample of despised genres and texts in pursuit of their intense yet often ineffable affect is prefigured in surrealism as well as in Cornell's work. And so are recent forms of dance music—house, electronic, hip-hop—based not on melodies and global structures but on the assemblage of break beats, tonal effects, scratches, and rhythms, aural leftovers recycled for their atmospheric effect and tactility.

While these artists and practices have not brought about the complete overturn "demanded by the 'Communist Manifesto,'" it would be myopic to claim that they have had no effect. Perhaps the historical mission Benjamin envisioned for surrealism, a total revolution entailing a conceptual and sensorial overhaul of the collective ushering into a nonalienated polity, is no longer possible (if it ever was). What is possible, what may be in fact indispensable, is to continue to practice those "commands" that Cornell, and the surrealists, knew so well, if not to bring about a total revolution then at least to articulate a plurality of "soft subversions"—to enlarge the possibilities for freedom, improvisation, and surprise in our inevitable, inexhaustible everyday.

The Murmur
of Otherness

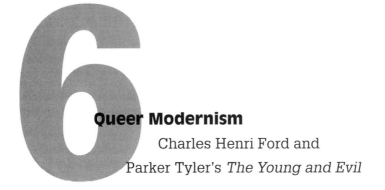

6

Queer Modernism

Charles Henri Ford and
Parker Tyler's *The Young and Evil*

For most of the authors studied so far, the noise of the quotidian was located in matter—objects, images, city spaces, sound, and technological automatism. This chapter and the two that follow explore another source of noise that is fleetingly registered but ultimately suppressed by *Manhatta,* Dos Passos's *USA* trilogy, and Lindsay's film criticism: the murmur that emanates from the peripheral subjects of modernity and from their manner of dwelling in material culture. They are the queers, ethnic subjects, folk communities, and inner-city dwellers in Charles Henri Ford and Parker Tyler's novel *The Young and Evil* (1933), in Zora Neale Hurston's ethnographic study of Haitian peasants, *Tell My Horse* (1938), in James Agee's report of southern tenant farmers, *Let Us Now Praise Famous Men* (1942), in the surrealist magazine *View,* and in Helen Levitt's photographs and her film *In the Street,* made in collaboration with Agee and Janice Loeb. Ford and Tyler's *The Young and*

Evil is the earliest of these texts. Set in New York's bohemia, it explores the manner in which queer identities and sexualities allow for a distinctive habitation of the languages, spaces, and images of modernity and modernism.

The Young and Evil was Ford and Tyler's first extended literary effort. At the time of the writing, Ford was known mostly as the editor of the short-lived *Blues* (a "Magazine of New Rhythms"), and Tyler as a poet and reviewer. They came together through *Blues*, which Ford launched in 1929 from Columbus, in his native Mississippi, after quitting high school to devote his life entirely to literature. *Blues* may have benefited from the recent demise of *The Dial*, the *Little Review*, and *transition*, the three most significant outlets for Anglo-American avant-garde writing in the 1920s. The gap they left may have been the reason why Ford, with no editorial experience and virtually no contacts in the art world, managed to secure contributions from established authors who had been featured prominently in these periodicals, including Ezra Pound, Gertrude Stein, H.D., Alfred Kreymborg, Eugene Jolas (the founder and editor of *transition*), Kay Boyle, Laura Riding, and William Carlos Williams. In addition, he recruited a number of promising beginners like Kenneth Rexroth, Paul Bowles, James T. Farrell, Erskine Caldwell, William Faulkner (the review folded before his short stories appeared), and Parker Tyler himself. Williams felt inspired enough by the new publication to write an endorsement declaring it the inheritor of earlier modernist audacities and encouraging it to stay firm in its revolt against prevailing "stupidity" and "regimentation."[1] And Gertrude Stein would later recall fondly that "of all the magazines which . . . have died to make verse free the youngest and freshest was the Blues."[2] Tyler's verse appeared in the first issue of the journal. He soon became the associate editor and New York correspondent. He and Ford would remain long-term friends and collaborators.

The Young and Evil is a fictional account of their adventures during Ford's first visit to New York early in 1930. It was written in 1931 and printed in 1933. Its open gayness and fairly explicit sexual episodes forced Ford and Tyler to look for a publisher outside the United States, since the 1927 raids on the Broadway plays *The Captive* by Edouard Bournet and *Sex* by Mae West, closed down for dealing openly with lesbianism and homosexuality, were still recent memories. The novel was eventually published in Paris by Obelisk Press, a small outfit run by the British émigré Jack Kahane and largely devoted to work in English that was either too commercially risky or too controversial to appear in Britain or the United States. The help of Ford's friends, Gertrude Stein and Djuna Barnes, may have been instrumental in securing a publishing contract. *The Young and Evil* is well within the purview of Obelisk, which specialized in works concerned with the sexual urban underworld.[3] In addition to some nondescript smut, it issued such polemical titles as Lawrence Durrell's *The Black Book,* Frank Harris's *My Lives and Loves,* Henry Miller's *Tropic of Cancer,* Radclyffe Hall's *The Well of Loneliness,* and Anaïs Nin's *Winter of Artifice,* the last book to appear from the press. This list suggests a close connection between aesthetic and sexual dissidence and further evokes the intellectual lineage of Ford and Tyler's novel. A mixture of experimental narrative and camp, *The Young and Evil* gestures to the transatlantic modernist idiom of Joyce, Stein, and Eliot and to the street languages and signifying strategies of a sector of the New York queer subculture at the time. In this respect it is a work of high modernism and a subcultural text, part experimental and part popular. And this boundary condition should prompt us to delineate the interface between modernism and the forms of popular textuality arising from queer subcultural practice.

This will be my approach to the cultural and gender politics of a work that remains relatively unexplored and, until recently, only sketchily discussed. Dickran Tashjian, who traces in some detail Ford's and Tyler's careers in his comprehensive study of American surrealism, does not mention *The Young and Evil.* The literary historian Roger Austen situates the work within the early 1930s vogue for commercial novels dealing with homosexual issues.[4] Catrina Neiman and George Chauncey pay Ford and Tyler's book passing attention in their discussions of the pre–World War II American avant-garde and urban gay male culture, respectively. The only substantial treatments to date are by Steven Watson and Joseph Boone. Watson's wonderfully informative introduction to the 1988 edition frames the genesis and publication history of *The Young and Evil* within the modernist and subcultural formations of its time and within its authors' careers. Joseph Boone groups Ford and Tyler's work with a number of noncanonical modernist narratives, such as Bruce Nugent's short story "Smoke, Lilies, and Jade," Djuna Barnes's *Nightwood,* and Blair Niles's *Strange Brother.* He cleverly relates their noninstitutionalized, "deviating and deviant" modernism to the queer urban sites of Harlem, the Left Bank, and Greenwich Village. Seeking to ground modernist writing in the strategies of everyday practice, Boone links the modes of occupation and use of these urban spaces to a peculiar textuality, "a deliberately perverse textual circuitry within whose spaces something akin to queer desire is produced and circulated."[5] These were spaces where normality was suspended, where alliances between social, racial, and sexual others created something akin to what we would call a queer polity based on a common fringe identity. In this respect, *The Young and Evil* offers "a phenomenology of queerness" that differentiates sexual outsiders from the norm and links them to other disenfranchised, marginal collectivities, thus enabling "a communal affiliation that cuts across and unites multiple categories of oppression" (Boone 254, 264).

Boone's interpretation folds into the novel a queer politics that belongs to our present, not to the text's fictional landscape or to the cultural formation from which it arose. As he acknowledges, this "ferment of queer attitudes and behaviors" ultimately foundered due to the lack of a concerted sexual politics beyond the individualized styles of subversion enabled by hedonism ("a politics of pleasure") or an aestheticized modernism ("the politics of art"). This lack is ultimately the reason why, rather than nodes of alliance and contact, the narrative offers scenarios of individual, communal, and aesthetic fragmentation. And it is precisely in the insistence on dissolution and undoing, and not in any form of coalition of marginals, that the particular queerness *and* (coextensive with it) political radicalism of *The Young and Evil* reside. Emblematic of this negative moment in the text's articulation of queerness are the vexing, unstable relations between modernist textuality and popular practice, between experimentalism and street culture. We could say that these instabilities characterize a queer modernism.[6]

Queer Modernism

Is there such a thing as queer modernism? A passing glance at the cultural archive discovers many instances of the confluence of queerness and modernism during the high decades of the movement. The setting of modernism on both sides of the ocean was bohemia, one of whose most scandalous characteristics was the flouting of Victorian gender and sexual conventions. Among the political radicals, nonconformists, and rebellious artists that inhabited this milieu, sexual outsiders could live their sexuality with relatively little fear of censure or attack. As the historians Shari Benstock, Steven Watson, George Chauncey, and Karla Jay, among others, have richly documented, many of the most prominent promoters of the new currents in art and literature were lesbians and gay men. On the Parisian Left Bank, for example, Gertrude Stein, Romaine Brooks, Djuna Barnes, Natalie Barney, Janet Flanner, Sylvia Beach, Renée Vivian, and Colette lived openly as lesbians; their writings, reviews, social activities, and publishing ventures advanced the cause of modernism.[7]

Some of their male counterparts also deserve mention. One of them was the publisher Robert McAlmon, the director of Contact Editions and a closeted bisexual who made a marriage of convenience with the rich British heiress Bryher (Winifred Ellerman). Like Sylvia Beach of Shakespeare and Company, he was instrumental in publishing some of the least conventional work of his generation.[8] Bryher, an open lesbian herself, would later divorce McAlmon and become H.D.'s lifelong companion. Living between London and Switzerland, she used her money and connections to publicize experimental art and literature. She also underwrote the activities of the experimental film collective Pool, which published the film magazine *Close-Up*. The journal's editor, who also directed Pool's film productions (*Borderline* is the best known of them), was Kenneth Macpherson. He was Bryher's nominal husband, and he had affairs with men and women. Another American editor in Paris was Monroe Wheeler, who would become director of publications at New York's Museum of Modern Art. Together with Barbara Harrison he launched Harrison of Paris in the early 1930s, a small press specializing in lavishly manufactured and illustrated limited editions. Wheeler was the novelist Glenway Westcott's partner at the time. They would soon meet the photographer George Platt-Lynes, with whom they lived in a three-way relationship for over a decade.

Many similar examples crop up in New York modernism. One of its main cultural activists was the socialite Mabel Dodge Luhan. In the early 1910s, she ran a successful salon at her Fifth Avenue apartment where political radicals of different persuasions, anarchists, feminists, free-lovers, and modern artists gathered to debate the issues of the day.[9] The main force behind these gatherings and the social magnet for many who attended was Carl Van Vechten, a gay man best known at the time as the music critic for the *New York Times*. He was also a noted participant in the salon of the Stettheimer sisters and in the activities of the Arensbergs' circle—both of which were hospitable to the French dadaists Marcel Duchamp and Francis Picabia during their stay in New York in the mid-1910s. Van Vechten's connections stretched across the Atlantic: he was a friend of Gertrude Stein and was instrumental in bringing her work before a broad readership in the United States. During the 1920s, he also attained celebrity as a bestselling novelist and was in addition a lively supporter of Harlem modernism.[10]

The painters Charles Demuth and Marsden Hartley, members of Alfred Stieglitz's circle, and the poet Hart Crane were also queer.[11] Crane was tormented about it and referred to his gayness cryptically in his published writing (not so in his private letters), but Hartley and Demuth were relatively open. The femme Margaret Anderson and the butch jane heap, editors of the *Little Review,* lived in a fairly public union during the high years of their magazine, when they published crucial texts by Ezra Pound and William Carlos Williams and they serialized James Joyce's *Ulysses* (they were eventually prosecuted for *Ulysses*'s alleged obscenity). Other members of the modernist New York circles were Djuna Barnes and Edna St. Vincent Millay. Before moving to Paris, Barnes was making a successful career as a journalist and writing short stories and one-act plays on the side. Millay was beginning to attain cult status as a little-magazine poet. Both were in lesbian relationships during these years.[12] And uptown, many of the artists and writers associated with the Harlem Renaissance were gay, among them Alain Locke, a philosophy professor at Howard University and the editor of the epochal volume *The New Negro;* the poet Countee Cullen; the novelist Wallace Thurman; and Bruce Nugent, whose intensely homoerotic "Smoke, Lilies, and Jade" provided a moment of scandal in the movement. The Jamaican-born Claude McKay, known for his collection of poems *Harlem Shadows* and for his bestselling novel *Home to Harlem,* was probably bisexual, and this may also have been the case with Langston Hughes.[13]

Given this roster, it may not be surprising that queerness and modern art became associated. The writer and critic Malcolm Cowley recalls in his memoir of the 1920s, *Exile's Return,* how *Broom,* the dada magazine he co-edited with Matthew Josephson and Harold Loeb, used to receive effusive letters from gay admirers of Oscar Wilde. This planted in him the fear that "a general offensive was about to be made against modern art, an offensive based on the theory that all modern writers, painters, and musicians were homosexual."[14] Cowley was quick to refute the connection, expressing his homophobic disdain for the Wilde school and his hate of "pansypoetical" literature. In a similar vein, the painter Thomas Hart Benton sought to ridicule what he called "the intellectual ballyhoo" of Greenwich Village in his 1932 murals for the Whitney Museum by depicting it as a frivolous gay fad devoid of artistic substance. The depiction of African Americans in this mural was also offensive and was the subject of protest by many of his students at the Art Students' League and by fellow artists like Stuart Davis.[15]

But this association between queer and modernist milieus was not merely drawn by outsiders to what the contemporary press knowingly called "the lavender world." The historian George Chauncey reports that, at about the time that Cowley was receiving unsettling mail by Wilde devotees, Eve

Kotchever, the Polish-born owner of a lesbian bar in Greenwich Village, who also called herself Eve Addams (or Adams), published under pseudonym a collection of stories called *Lesbian Love*. Popularly known as "the queen of the third sex," Addams and her successful club were eventually targeted by local authorities. In 1926 the club was raided, she was tried for writing obscene stories, convicted, and eventually deported. A few years later, a Village troupe put on a play based on her stories, titled *Modernity,* at the Play Mart, a basement theater on Christopher Street. Its successful run was cut short due to rumors of an imminent police raid.[16] The title might have been intended to divert the attention of morality watch groups and law enforcement, but it may also have been a wink to the initiated, as it insists on the connection between the queer and the modern. The scope of the term "modernity" points beyond modern art to an entire cultural and social logic that apparently was seen as fairly congenial to queer identities. Parker Tyler confirmed this as he reminisced in the 1970s about his and Ford's literary beginnings in the late 1920s: "'We were both dreadfully impressed with modern poetry, and we were trying to create our own brand of it. What we didn't realize too consciously was that we [young men leading openly queer lives] *were* modern poetry.'"[17] In the 1940s, Ford and Tyler may again have been playing with the ambiguity of the modern when they displayed Arthur Rimbaud's motto, "One must be absolutely modern," on the masthead of their camp, surrealist, glamorous magazine *View.*

If all these artists and writers are exponents of a queer modernism, what is common to them all? For scholars such as Eve Kosofsky Sedgwick, Joseph Boone, Colleen Lamos, Jonathan Weinberg, and Eric Haralson, it is the way in which their art and writing have been decisively shaped by contemporary forms of social and sexual insubordination.[18] These were not simply colorful extracurricular pursuits for the moderns; peripheral sexualities were social laboratories that produced concepts of identity and strategies of representation and encoding that became an integral part of modernist textuality. Moreover, as Sedgwick has generatively shown, queer sexualities pervaded, in unpredictable capillarity, a number of ideologies adjacent to aesthetic production. One of these is the ideology that postulates a sharp divide between high and low culture.

A recurring yet understudied trait in queer modernism is its receptiveness toward "low culture," manifest in the frequent attempt to fuse experimental modernism with popular energies. It is significant that the title of Charles Henri Ford's journal was *Blues,* a folk form whose first spurt of mass popularity in the early 1920s was largely due to the availability of gramophones and vinyl records. With this title, Ford claimed for the avant-garde poetry he published the same expressive force he must have relished in blues music. And "blues" also evokes the erotic writing and iconography of the clandestine pornography market (some reviewers picked up on this). Charles Demuth's work shows a similar tropism toward the popular. He affectionately portrayed homosexual scenes in beaches, baths, bars, and cruising spots, using his flowing line and slightly washed-off colors. One of his watercolors, *Cabaret with Carl Van Vechten,* shows a couple of men dancing animatedly among several heterosexual couples. The tall blonde in the foreground with his face turned toward the dancers is presumably Van Vechten. His inclusion in such a popular milieu may gesture toward the writer's fascination with popular music, manifest in his advocacy of jazz and ragtime. Van Vechten's music criticism for *The Seven Arts* attests to this. One of his pieces for this journal extolled the audacity and inventiveness of the musical programs accompanying film screenings in the recently popular movie palaces; the other defended the artistry and complexity of ragtime against the opinions of K. Hiram Motherwell, who had published an appreciative but patronizing analysis of this musical form in an early issue of the journal. Van Vechten's interest in popular forms is also perceptible in the successful novels he published in the 1920s, such as *Peter Whiffle* and *The Tattooed Countess.* His straightforward technique and realistic style, which often veer toward camp, implicitly reject the flights of experimentation practiced by other writers whom he admired and advocated, such as Stein and Joyce. His literary aesthetics and his fascination with black popular culture were shared as well by the British camp novelist Ronald Firbank, another contemporary queer cult.

The younger Paul Cadmus followed in Demuth's footsteps by portraying intensely homoerotic scenes in locker rooms, dance and banquet halls, and in the streets. Especially notorious is his *Sailor Trilogy,* which depicts sailors on shore leave cavorting with floosies or being propositioned by men. Cadmus was a friend of the photographer George Platt-Lynes, who was equally devoted to the high-art iconography of the ballet and classical mythology and to his own peculiar brand of aestheticized soft porn. The nudes he produced in this vein record a string of lovers, pickups, friends, and assistants, and remain one of the most provocative and exquisite bodies of homoerotic imagery from the pre-Stonewall years.[19]

Queer Harlemites frequently drew on popular molds such as blues, jazz, and oral storytelling traditions, and they praised the vitality of night clubs and cabarets—locations where the stringencies of a racist, heterosexist society were momentarily loosened. Editors and cultural sponsors would equally divide their attention between high and low culture. Monroe Wheeler and Babara Harrison's press issued classics such as Shakespeare's *Venus and Adonis* or a collection of Aesop's fables alongside popular works. One of their first editions was a selection of Bret Harte's eminently popular western short stories, which had given rise to "countless cowboys of Greek profiles, maidenly sturdy heroines, and poetical platitudinous films" but were only available in poorly edited volumes.[20] And Lincoln Kirstein, an American critic, editor, and cultural promoter, appeared equally fascinated with the ballet and with movie glamor. He was responsible for bringing George Ballanchine to New York and creating the American Ballet; he was also secretary and trustee of the Museum of Modern Art's Film Library, whose holdings contained avant-garde films and commercial titles of artistic merit. During his Harvard years in the late 1920s, Kirstein edited the little magazine *Hound and Horn*, which published modernist poetry as well as a series of appreciative essays on movie stars such as James Cagney, Greta Garbo, and Marlene Dietrich.

This fascination with popular modes and media was also common among queer modernists in other latitudes. We may remember in passing Jean Cocteau's work as a scriptwriter and director of experimental and popular films; the affinity, noted by Gregory Woods, between Marcel Proust's *A la Recherche du temps perdu* and gossip; or, in an earlier, more generative example, we may recall Oscar Wilde's practice of encrypting sexual rebellion in mundane forms like aphorisms, poses, styles of dressing, and lighthearted comedy.[21] Against the background of these examples, and many more are possible, the hybrid aesthetics of Ford and Tyler's novel appear not only as one more exponent of queer modernism; they actually belong in a relatively neglected strain where the articulation, more or less overt, of queer desires and subjectivities appears refracted through the attempt to fuse experimentalism and the popular, the spaces of the studio and art gallery and the irrepressible life of the streets, cruising grounds, and night clubs.

An image that encapsulates many of the issues raised so far is Charles Demuth's illustration for Robert McAlmon's story "Distinguished Air." It shows a group of people contemplating a sculpture reminiscent of Constantin Brancusi's outrageously phallic *Princess X*. A queer couple seen from behind—one man has flung his arm over the other man's shoulder—appears engrossed in the art work. To their left, visible in profile, stands a "hetero-

Charles Demuth, *Distinguished Air,* 1930.
Watercolor, 14 x 12 in. Collection of the
Whitney Museum of American Art.
Purchased with funds from the friends
of the Whitney Museum and
Charles Simon.

sexual" couple: a middle-aged man, exuding respectability, gazes intently at the crotch of one of the queers—incidentally, a sailor—while his female companion has her eyes fixed on a forlorn woman in slight dishabille who stands directly opposite her and seems to be returning her gaze.[22] The illustration draws attention to the uncertainty of appearances: is this gentleman "really heterosexual," whatever that might mean? What about his companion and the lonely woman? Do they always eye other men and women so openly? The picture turns an exhibition space into a queer site where desire transgresses the sanctions that link gender identity to a range of object choices and sexual behaviors. In addition, it cuts across a number of divides: public and private; generational difference; social class, since the sailor and the lonely bystander, coded as working-class through their appearance, are objects of desire of a number of middle-class characters; and cultural hierarchies, since what is represented is as much a street scene as a contemplative immersion in art. Further, the illustration insightfully comments on the textual character of queerness. It detaches desire from interiority and personal essence and projects it across a variety of external bodily presences and material supports. Does the sexual longing of the "hetero" man and woman stem, as René Girard might have it, from the contagious sight of someone else's desire? Does the desire of the two younger men arouse that of the other couple? Or is it the presiding phallus, with its inviting tumescence, that sets the libidinal currents adrift within the frame? In either case, one could invoke Judith Butler's popular thesis that imitation lies at the root of gender insubordination. And what is being imitated, the source of all the performative trouble and the equivocal comedy of gender/errors staged in this drawing, might be a high-art modernist object (the Brancusi-like creation), which is also a stylized rendering of corporeality, a "low" street sight (a queer couple in tender embrace), or a combination of both. It is crucial to my argument that these questions can only be posed and not answered. The wit of the scene partly stems from its indecisiveness; its figures remain frozen in an unfinished transaction, in a "not yet" that to our backward glance is always "already." More answerable questions remain to be addressed: What is the reason for this insistent engagement of a queer modernism with street life and the forms of popular culture enmeshed in it? What is the queer specificity of this way of crossing cultural, social, and spatial borderlines?

The popular has served queer experimental artists to signal their difference from an "orthodox" modernism that often upheld social and sexual conservatism. This is the kind of modernism most frequently associated with figures such as T. S. Eliot or Ezra Pound, but its sexual ideology cuts across political persuasions. It was shared, as we have seen, by a right-wing nationalist such as Hart Benton and a Popular Front leftist such as Malcolm Cowley. Even the French surrealists, who were politically and aesthetically radical, were notoriously misogynist and homophobic. In a ridiculous tirade in the March 1928 *Révolution surréaliste,* André Breton accused homosexuals of "confronting human tolerance with a mental and moral deficiency which turns itself into a system to paralyze every enterprise I respect," and he singled out Jean Cocteau and Max Jacob as targets of his scorn.[23]

These reactions show that despite modernism's critical rapport with the norm and the relative ease with which sexual outlaws played important roles in modernist culture, they often had to do so with a discretion that our confessional way of inhabiting queerness would call closeted. Sedgwick has pointed out that the importance of being discreet when it came to homoerotic matters resulted in modernism's overinvestment in self-reflexiveness and structure at the expense of content. It prompted, in other words, modernism's characteristic "antifigurality," "iconophobia," and abstraction. Thematically, this may also have allowed specifically queer modalities of alienation, desire, and self-knowledge—from *The Picture of Dorian Gray* to *Tonio Kröger* and from Henry James to Hart Crane—to be recoded as universal paradigms of the human condition. The aesthetics of modernism thus "substantively void[ed] . . . elements of a specifically and historically male homosexual rhetoric." This did not completely erase the queer features in modernist strategies; on the contrary, they remained "structuring fossil-marks," perpetuating sub rosa "the specificity of a desire that [modernism] exists to deny."[24] The queer subject is thus everywhere (which may explain the phobic disavowals just cited) and nowhere in modernism: it is the ultimately generalizable human exemplar but (consequently) hardly ever just a gay man or a lesbian concretely grounded in specific subcultural practice. If modernism provided an outlet for queer expression, it did so in a way that was intermittent and conditioned. Modernism was, in sum, as much a liberation as a closet.[25]

Against abstraction and antifigurality, the concreteness of popular modes allowed many artists to represent unorthodox desires openly. One of the characteristics of popular aesthetics, evident in commercial cinema, lifestyle magazines, competition sports, or dance culture, is its emphasis on the body, on its sensuous image and its pleasures. By immersing themselves in the aesthetics of the popular, queer authors and artists could embody modernism and attach bodily correlatives to urgent queer desires. There is considerable distance, for example, between the precisionist paintings of Charles De-muth, which depict depopulated buildings and urban landscapes in a stark geometrical style and saturated colors, and his more popular-oriented queer scenes, centered on human figures and their interactions. A similar difference may be observed between Platt-Lynes's modernist work, the photographs commissioned by the New York City Ballet and *Vogue* or intended for pub-lic exhibition, and those taken after hours in the privacy of his bedroom or his studio. The public pictures favor abstraction and evasion, particularly when their subject is the male body. Genitals are coyly shaded or covered by draped fabric, and queer rapport is obliquely rendered. However, his private portraits, especially his late ones, are far more concrete: homosexual contact is often explicit, genitals in full view, and the models often look straight into the camera, as if expressing their availability to the observer. Glenway Westcott's novels of the 1920s and early 1930s are good examples of mod-ernist indirectness; by contrast, his journals are written in a straightforward, journalistic style and contain numerous accounts of nights on the town, sexual encounters, gossip, and descriptions of lovers and friends (including a lengthy report on the shape, color, and texture of George Platt-Lynes's penis).[26] This split also structures *The Young and Evil:* while the modernist passages are nebulous and indirect, the streetwise sections brazenly express queer deportment.

But in the case of queer modernism, a popular idiom is not synonymous with popularity. In the early decades of the twentieth century, queerness forced a chiasmus that pushed the popular-styled work of these artists un-derground and their modernist work above ground. Hence their most pub-licized and institutionalized work is their modernist work, whose relative difficulty and abstraction made its circulation safe under cover of "art." And at the same time, the texts most indebted to popular aesthetics and poten-tially most consumable (Platt-Lynes's private portraits, Westcott's diaries, Demuth's gay drawings and watercolors, and, to an extent, Ford and Tyler's novel) were the most subversive and, as a result, seldom circulated. They were subject to self-censorship and institutional supression, and at times they only became available after the death of their authors. What made them unsuitable for the public eye was precisely their emphasis on (popular-in-debted) queer corporeality and the suggestions of the muscle gym, the cruisy comfort station, and the bath house that clung to these bedroom-eyed im-ages. It is ironic that these artists were secretly producing and suppressing their most "popular" and most radical work while thinkers and critics such as Max Horkheimer, Theodor Adorno, Clement Greenberg, and Dwight Macdonald were denouncing popular culture for its accommodating character and its collusion with the status quo.

Queer moderns met their like in popular culture. From the standpoint of modernist orthodoxy, there is something illicit and slightly shameful about indulging in popular pleasure, just as there may be about contemplating queer desires. For the queer artist disaffected with heteronormative orthodox modernism, mass culture opened up a line of escape through a range of class and ethnic identifications. As Richard Hoggart and Stuart Hall have pointed out, there is a strong class subtext in the devaluation of popular culture as the culture of the uneducated masses. Clement Greenberg regarded "kitsch" the preference of the newly literate and newly urbanized working- and lower middle-class crowds—those with some money and leisure but without enough instruction to enjoy the legitimate arts. And in Weimar Germany, Siegfried Kracauer considered factory workers, "little shop girls" (*kleine Ladenmädchen*), and low-standing clerical workers (*Angestellten*) to be the primary addressees of the entertainment industry.

If the devaluation of the popular has strong class connotations, its queer modernist revaluation may be driven by sexual desire. In the blanket logic of Greenberg's argument, kitsch is the culture of the sailor in Demuth's "Distinguished Air"; of the sailors and toughs in Platt-Lynes's photographs and Cadmus's paintings; of the hustlers and petty criminals in Cocteau's *Le Libvre blanche* and in Jean Genet's fiction; and of the workers, boxers, and con men that populate *The Young and Evil*. It is conceivable that desire for working-class men might eventually slide into a degree of identification with their tastes and an appreciative initiation into their cultural practice.

Class "otherness" is connected to further embodiments of alterity. The fascination with rough trade among modernists may be read as an appropriation of "exotic" bodies and locations as stages for sexual liberation. It has an uncomfortable colonizing edge connected with the imbalance in power and privilege between slummers and demimondaines, but it also signals a protest against the constrictive regulation of desire in bourgeois culture. As a number of historians, such as Michel Foucault, Anthony E. Rotundo, and Jonathan Ned Katz, have pointed out, the bourgeoisie's claims to social hegemony from the first third of the nineteenth century onwards were often propped upon a claim to superior morality, and this was made to rest on the exercise of exclusive, reproductive heterosexuality and on the demonization of queer entanglements. Michael Trask has recently shown that early twentieth-century social scientists attributed what they saw as the unsettling mobility and disengagement of "social others" to a range of perverse desires, including, but not limited to, sexual desires. Trask demonstrates that modernist literature frequently explores the connection between social and sexual fluidity. In this light, what may be at stake in the fixation with lower-class men and with ethnic others is nostalgia for a different social arrangement of the libido, for a system where the fixity of the homo-/heterosexual divide, and the stigmatization of all homosexuality, might give way to structures looser than those found in bourgeois society.[27] That this idealization of otherness may be more or less misguided or problematic does not invalidate the kernel of critical negation it contains.

The Most Beautiful Thing in Pants

At this point, it may begin to make sense that *The Young and Evil* mixed the popular gay idiom of camp and modernism, that it provided a fascinated record of parties, clubs, speakeasies, and street talk together with attempts to dig, through tortuous interior monologues, into what Virginia Woolf called "the dark places of psychology"—the purlieu of the modern novel. The mixture makes sense because Ford and Tyler were not exactly orthodox modernists—or orthodox anything, for that matter.

When *Blues* was still in the works, Katherine Tankersly Young, the magazine's first New York correspondent, described the prospective contributor Parker Tyler to her good friend Charles Henri Ford as "the most beautiful thing I ever saw in pants." With his long hair and mascara, his public persona was what the gay typology of the time called a "fairy." Ford's style seems to have been a bit more restrained, but apparently not restrained enough. From the beginning, *Blues* was as subject to literary attack as to gay-baiting. Dickran Tashjian reports that an unfriendly critic described it as "'the big blue blasphemous baby of Charles Henri Ford,'" and upon publication in the magazine, Gertrude Stein was called "'a literary jelly-bean of a she-man with a feminine name.'" Without missing a beat, the publishers incorporated the innuendo into their marketing strategies and began to advertise the review as a "bi-sexual bi-monthly."[28]

Ford and Tyler never escaped these suggestions; their gayness became a well-known part of their public personas. It placed them on the margins of the avant-garde, which is to say, on the margin of the margin, and often made them the target of trivializing comments and homophobic jabs. John Houseman, the experimental stage director (later to become an important

Hollywood producer) who collaborated with Orson Welles in the Federal Theater and "The Mercury Theater of the Air," narrates in his autobiography how Welles refused to allow Ford and Ford's lover (the painter Pavel Tchelitchew) to attend a dress rehearsal of *Doctor Faustus*. He simply would not come on stage with them sitting in the orchestra. As Houseman escorted them apologetically to the door, he could hear "Orson's voice from behind the curtain howling triumphantly of Russian pederasts and international whores."[29] Despite his adherence to surrealism, Ford always kept his distance from André Breton due largely to the latter's homophobia. After meeting the surrealist pope for the first time in Paris, Ford wrote Tyler that Breton "'is revolted by obvious Lesbians as well as "fairies" like we used to be. . . . Which does not obviate his looking like a woman in the first place without wearing his hair long in the 2nd.'" And he went on to point out Breton's resemblance to Oscar Wilde.[30] In many ways, Ford and Tyler's position within the American avant-garde was similar to that of Jean Cocteau (one of Breton's favorite peeves) among the French intelligentsia: grudgingly accepted but at the same time snubbed, trivialized, and belittled. (In the case of Cocteau, this snubbing came not only from heterosexual writers like Breton but also from André Gide, who could hardly countenance Cocteau's theatricality and his dabbling in commercial culture.) Ford and Tyler also shared Cocteau's propagandizing flair and versatility; they were editors as well as writers and worked in different media and formats, from literature, to film and photography, to the organization of glamorous "events" like balls, concerts, and multimedia performances.[31] And like the Frenchman, they often detached themselves from "serious" modernism and gave their work a popular turn.

Ford and Tyler's marginality within official modernism does not seem to have been particularly traumatic; it was often a subject for jokes. A picture of Ford taken in Paris by Henri Cartier-Bresson the year *The Young and Evil* was published, for example, might be interpreted as a joke: He is buttoning up as he leaves a *pissoir*, looking aloof and insouciant. Right behind him, a gigantic tongue on an advertising poster stretches urgently as if reaching for his crotch. And as Ford reported from Paris on the foundation of the International Federation of Revolutionary Artists, one of whose leaders was Breton, he stressed to Tyler that the federation's French acronym was "FIARI, not fairy," teasingly forestalling the possibility of a slippage from an orthodox (modernist-identified) political identity to a marginal (street-bred) one.[32] Such posing and joking suggest that being on the periphery of the modern seems to have given Ford and Tyler a critical distance from modernism's purported seriousness, its aesthetics, and its gender politics. In *The Young and Evil,* this distance took the form of a constant wavering between modernism and camp, the street vernacular of the queer outlaw, without fully embracing either. Outsiders to mainstream culture, Ford and Tyler were marginal as well to the queer and modernist milieus. Their novel at once chronicles and tries to come to terms with this homelessness, with their nearly impossible position in the culture.

The Art of Falling Apart

The Young and Evil is a *roman à clef* about the life of a group of devoted bohemians who fall in and out of love with each other, write, attend parties and drag balls, cruise in search of casual sex, and have occasional run-ins with street toughs and policemen. The plot centers on the triangle formed by Julian, Karel, and Louis. Aspiring writers, Julian and Karel are thinly fictionalized portraits of Ford and Tyler themselves. Early in the narrative, Julian, who has been living in the South, sails into New York from New Orleans, and Karel, with whom he has been corresponding for years, is expecting him on the pier. Karel is extremely flamboyant, as Tyler was in his twenties, while the younger Julian, just like Ford, is somewhat more subdued—except when he dolls up for a party or an outing. Their friendship, based on their shared literary ambitions, is temporarily clouded over by their common fascination with Louis, a petty grifter with intellectual interests and an abusive temperament who becomes Karel's lover for a time. In fact, one of the main plot lines concerns the estrangement of the two friends as Louis becomes part of their lives and their regained intimacy when Karel's relationship with him breaks up in the last third of the book.

The writing has a fragmentary texture due to the episodic storyline, the numerous elisions, and the constant oscillation between modernist experimentalism and camp. Each of these styles has specific functions and cultural politics. Camp is a language of communal identification, usually practiced in public spaces, whereas experimental modernism is associated with private spaces, introspection, and the portrayal of individual interiority. Camp allows for the expression of queer desire, while modernism is most often used in the expression of memory and dreamlike states. These two styles stand for the main modes of transgression that Jonathan Dollimore discerns in modern and postmodern queer literary and critical discourses. Dollimore calls them "the transgressive aesthetic" and "the revolt of authenticity," and for him they are most clearly embodied in the work of Oscar Wilde and André Gide, respectively.[33]

Both styles are juxtaposed from the beginning. As Julian and Karel meet on the docks, the narrative's campy observations on Karel's attire and looks are combined with elusive, lyrical passages of difficult exegesis. Immediately following a description of Karel's belabored eyebrows and make-up, for example, Julian enthuses: "You are the Karel who wrote me letters on nice long rotten sheets of paper Julian said. You made words on it that meant o sweet tight boy being in New Orleans *they* are the first madness of the age besides that which exists between an arctic bird's tongue and its beak."[34] And without pause, he adds, "Order some gin." Karel, unswerveable, intends to stay on track: "Shall I read you a poem" (16). Such shifts in tone make the gap between the two styles the central textual feature of the novel; at the same time, the gap between these two modes of writing evokes the impossibility of wholeness and the fractal nature of queer (ultimately of all) identity. Rifts and fissures are not only *how* the text means but also *what* it means. Its final message is of terminal fragmentation, not only of the narrative but of the couples, communities, and subjects that populate it.

Camp is a means to theatricalize gay identity, and this is most evident in connection with Karel's looks. "His eyebrows though Julian thought might cause an Italian laborer to turn completely around" (15–16), and they often do, and "his eyelashes were long enough now to catch in the boughs (should he go for a walk in Washington Square)" (56), at the time a popular pick-up spot. Karel's clothes (a hat "with an upward sweep on the left side" and a coat "that seemed to fit him desperately" [14]), his abundant hair, and his plucked eyebrows single him out as a fairy, the most visible gay type at the time. This identity overwrites biological masculinity with an artificial, contrived femininity often inspired by the iconography of mass culture. "Karel never did badly by his own face . . . Of course his eyebrows often looked the same as the week before. They could be pencilled into almost any expression: Clara Bow, Joan Crawford, Norma Shearer, etc. He thought he would choose something obvious for tonight. Purity" (56). Here synthetic corporeality displaces interiority, the special province of the high modernist writer, as "purity," an inner trait, boils down to a way of applying eye shadow. The identities that the fairy incorporates are mere surface effects that can be put on and taken off more or less at will. They are eminently cosmetic not only because they come out of Karel's "box of beauty" but because they are written on the skin. This writing—this peculiar way of "*being* modern poetry"—is at once a supplement and a debunking of biological gender, and in addition, it counters traditional models of bourgeois subjectivity. Against the idea that pose, gesture, and style express an interior quality, Karel glibly evokes the contrary possibility: that external particulars and contingent signifiers of identity articulate an inner subjectivity, which turns out to be the insubstantial projection of an external mask.[35]

As a theatrical mode, camp takes space; it is staged in public, at parties and cruising areas. It is performed, for example, through the gestures and inflections of Frederick, a friend of Karel and Julian's, as he cruises with them on Broadway ("Dont camp like that . . . or I'll leave," complains an unusually coy Karel [179]). In contexts like this, it functions as a code of queer self-presentation and identification in the mixed public spaces of the city.[36] As a form of speech, camp is most fully anthologized in the long chapter set at a drag ball in Harlem and titled "I Don't Want to Be a Doll." Julian and Frederick attend the party "made up within an inch of their lives." There, they meet some acquaintances, circulate, and enjoy the general revelry. As George Chauncey has shown in *Gay New York,* drags such as the one fictionalized here were important spaces for queer sociability. They reached their maximum splendor in the late 1920s and early 1930s. Although they were monitored by city police, who tended to clamp down on what they considered "indecent" behavior, they provided occasions where gender and sexual indeterminacy were given free rein. Gender inversion was the main trope at the balls. The central event was the "parade of the fairies" and the costume contest, with cash prizes awarded to the most imaginative outfits. Queens and fairies could indulge their feminine personas without fear of arrest or aggression, and some even attained short-lived fame, as the press frequently reported the brilliance of the balls and the sartorial feats of the winners.

Although these were largely visual affairs, *The Young and Evil* re-creates the ball as an aural space. Another example of modernist phonography, most of the chapter consists in a sound assemblage of snatches of conversation revolving largely around sexual gossip. The verse-like lines skillfully capture the arch humor and snappy rhythm of bitchy repartee, and constant line enjambment speeds up the pace of the text and communicates the kaleidoscopic shifts between overlapping conversations caught on the run:

> that the first thing I knew she was groping me like
> mad thinks she has the only bedroom back at the
> ball does he rent his brains my

dear just dirt you
silly! loose as a cut
jockstrap
still dead as far as my mouth
goes a
big chisler while he was here feature it
adores me to stick it in his and flew into a temper last night when
    after the regular party my poor thing wouldn't get a hard
    on enough to go in and STAY in but I promised to do my
    husbandly duty next. (161–62)

In addition to dishing out sexual gossip, as in this excerpt, the text frequently repeats common street witticisms or invents new ones: "I'd rather be Spanish than mannish"; "says he wears a flower in his buttonhole because it simply Wont stay in his hair!"; "she looks like death's daughter brought in backwards" (158).[37]

Rather than celebrate this verbal inventiveness and the intense affect of the scene, Julian, the implicit narrator, distances himself from it all. As he surveys the ball upon arrival, he ponders: "They all ought to be in a scrap-book. Would blood, paste and print make them stick together?" (155). "They" designates a collective he does not feel part of, and the mention of the scrapbook provides a metanarrative comment and a judgement. As a judgement, it is somewhat derogatory and insinuates that the heterogeneity of the crowd is somehow to be regretted. The gathering lacks unity beyond that provided by a shared desire for other men's bodies, but apparently this is no unity at all. The aspiration to wholeness alludes to an important modernist project: the establishment of wholes out of the fragments of experience. This may be what Karel means when, in a letter to Julian obliquely explaining his reasons for staying away from him and from the downtown scene, he writes: "O it isn't a world for scissors, for mallets; but for needle, thread and for paste" (85)—that is, for connection and togetherness, and art will supposedly provide the glue.

In Julian's eyes, the camp scene at the ball lacks the depth and authenticity that only self-conscious art might provide. One of the "found lines" reads, "sex is a false landscape only art giving it full colors," an idea later rephrased by Julian as he leaves the dance. On the way home he wonders whether he is "a doll" or a poet—whether he lives for his immediate pleasure and his good looks or for his art. "I have the will to doll which is a special way of willing to live my poetry may merely be a way of dolling up and then it may be the beginning of ego I think I would be nothing without my poetry unless a DOLL" (170). Dolling may be a way to live, or to live one's poetry, to bring it to bear on daily practice and the staging of one's identity. At the same time, poetry may be merely a pose, a way of "dolling up." But in any case, only the strenuous cultivation of this craft provides subjective depth, solidity, and awareness ("the beginning of ego"). If this is so, the surface subversions of camp ought to be subordinated to the commitment to art. The ephemerality, superficiality, and communal dimension of the former must be combined with the permanence, introspective depth, and individuality of the latter. *The Young and Evil* repeats a frequent motif in early twentieth-century gay literature: making camp, in Jonathan Dollimore's words, into "the quintessential expression of an alienated, superficial inauthenticity."[38] By maintaining the opposition between camp and art, the book further endorses the Arnoldian notion of culture as the realm of order and authenticity and further underpins the classic oppositions between high and low, the serious and the popular, high culture and subculture.

It is symptomatic of the novel's conceptual fluidity, however, that "art" does not quite live up to its promise. In fact, the more poetic—which is to say, the more self-consciously modernist—the writing, the more it reverts to the same scrapbook quality that Julian repudiates in "I Don't Want to Be a Doll." If the fragmentary style of the camp dialogues signifies a sort of interpersonal gap, the monologues that try to retrieve some form of personal authenticity end up connoting an intrapersonal gap, the lack of fit of the subject with itself. The most characteristic segments in this respect are the passages that close chapters 2, 3, and 6. If camp occupies space (streets, parks, ballrooms), these introspective passages condense and break up the temporal sequence. The first two are hypnagogic scenes. As Karel (in chapter 2) and Julian (in chapter 3) fall asleep, distant childhood memories merge with recent events. After the bustle of the day, each retreats into his consciousness and his past, and the movement of their thoughts is conveyed by a poetic prose that combines Stein's and Joyce's rhythmic play with an accumulation of loosely strung images that reads like surrealist automatic writing. These monologues are fragmentary and proceed in a seemingly arbitrary manner. Karel's monologue concerns memories of early friendships ("Before flowers or anything" [21]) and of a birthday: "fifty-one guests and the doll I got I got I got. I tear grass from the roots on my fifth birthday lawn and they imitate me and the other children and I am glad" (22). He recalls some of his favorite childhood toys, among them his doll, and abruptly juxtaposed with this memory, a move to a different city: "I think there must be a place called Philadelphia because I am going there. There. School" (23). School brings up memories of teachers dissolving lumps of sugar in tea, bitter cold winters, and snow fights with other children, and then, sickness and being forced to stay indoors during recess. The dark school corridors seem alive with breasts "offering but withholding stars planets alps one likes to climb or go through a valley skiing" (24). The passage closes with an Arthurian fantasy of "Guinevere or Elaine" hanging from a window, her heart fluttering with excitement. "There are many noises in the air not of birds no of nothing but Lancelot" (24). Fragments like this lift the characters from external circumstance and from the flow of the action into a realm of subjective "authenticity." Yet in the end, they also promote isolation and solipsism, since desire, memory, and fantasy remain enclosed within subjective boundaries, enmeshed in the subject's private images, and ineffectual in an impervious outside world. Rather than provide the "thread and paste" that Karel demanded in his letter, these artful passages depict the rift between individuals and their milieus, as well as the fractures within particular individuals, whose thoughts never add up to a whole.

Such monologues occasionally echo the florid eroticism of the ball and underline the disruptive workings of desire. The drunken hallucination that closes chapter 6, for example, revolves around Julian's longing for men, "the strange as it may seem pull toward the goodlooking ones": "*o murderpiss beautiful boys grow out of dung.* And wear padded shoulders. They push flesh into eternity and sidestep automobiles. I bemoan them most under sheets at night when their eyes rimmed with masculinity see nothing and their lymph-lips are smothered by the irondomed sky. Poor things, their genitals only peaceful when without visiting cards . . . I have often imagined the curve of them next to me in bed colored like coffee or like cream" (74–75). The objects of Julian's desire are vividly imagined but mostly unattainable, not only because they are dream images but because of the elusive manner in which they cross the homo-/heterosexual divide, which in the world of the novel, as in its historical context, appears much less definite than it would later become in the post-Stonewall, gay-liberation years.[39] Julian's fantasy flows across this divide, as it shifts from its homoerotic objects to the image of a beautiful woman: "There were violent shadows around her eyes and the nipples of her breasts were not large. . . . No hair anywhere except the long hair from her head" (77). As she walks by the sea, a sailor enters the scene; they have an elliptically described sexual encounter, and afterwards, he appears completely inapprehensible either to Julian or the girl: "They were warm to each other, he was pure. She was beautiful, it was sad to see the sailor-boy have to piss afterward and walk away" (77). The release of fluids highlights the bodily substratum and undercuts the sentimentality of the sequence. It further exposes the limitations of art—this is, after all, another lyrical monologue—to create workable wholes and to infuse depth and continuity into the self. Instead, it confirms the unmanageable instability of identity and desire. In *The Young and Evil,* streetwise camp and experimental writing do not supplement each other. "Art" does not make up for the lack of being a "doll." Art and dolling end up confirming each other's presumed deficiencies; in combination, they outline textual spaces of dissolution, where one can connect "nothing with nothing," no one with no one.

This lack of connection pervades the narrative. It is already insinuated in the extremely disjointed dialogues between Julian and Karel in the early chapters. The following lines come up shortly after the protagonists meet for the first time, as Karel stares at the new arrival with wonder:

> Tell me how southerners look now. Until I saw you I thought they were extinct.
> Not at all but the sky is different down there. In summer they peel something from it in huge slabs and nail it on you and call it the heat. I floundered in the sleek mirrors.
> Would it have been too much to have stolen a rose? Karel said.
> I only walked through the maples and plucked one green leaf.
> And in winter?
> On my left I'd see frozen birds, frozen last night too, on my right the shadows of smoke on the sides of buildings. (18)

The jumpy quality of this exchange may be attributed to the nervousness of a first encounter, complicated by the fact that, shortly after Julian and Karel meet, they jump into bed for an unsatisfactory tryst. But their choppy conversations might also signify their inability to come together due to the vagaries of desire. Karel and Julian understand that they are fit for each other in many ways but cannot jump-start their relationship. Neither is the other's type; the rougher, aggressive Louis is, and this forces them to choose between the sexless companionship they would enjoy with each other and the satisfaction of a sexual fantasy that Louis provides. "[Julian] had never known physical and mental love towards a single person. It had always been completely one or the other. With Karel it was the other. With Louis it was neither" (72). But the narrative suggests otherwise. Julian tries to seduce Louis after a party, while Karel, who has passed out drunk, lies next to them in bed. The main link between Karel and Louis seems to be sex. Their relationship is far from harmonious, with Louis constantly mocking, abusing, and stealing from Karel. In the last scene of the book, Louis strips Karel of his suit (to be pawned for some badly needed cash) and bites him in the neck, closing the relationship, and the novel, with a cruel vampiric gesture.

Similar mismatches recur throughout. After Karel, fearful of Julian's competition, moves uptown with Louis, Julian has several adventures, none of them satisfying. In one of the most erotic and best-paced, he cruises a young Italian worker—"the kind who makes homosexuality worthwhile" (141)—at a restaurant. Julian follows him down Fourteenth Street ("which only the good escape" [137]) and on to Union Square, where he continues his pursuit from a cab. He lures him into the car and ends up taking him home. Once there they cannot consummate because suddenly Julian's place is absurdly full of guests, and they can have no intimacy. The Italian eventually leaves after arranging to meet in the future, but they never do. Among the cast of secondary characters, there is Theodosia, a mutual friend of Julian and Karel's, who loves Julian. They are quite intimate and enjoy some intensely physical moments, but he cannot have an exclusive relationship with her. After sharing Julian's apartment for a while, she moves out. At one point, she hires the unpleasant Gabriel, Louis's friend and sidekick, to type her manuscripts and likes to watch him at work in her apartment through a door left ajar. One day Gabriel shows up drunk and decides to make love to her. As they writhe in hot embrace, Gabriel throws up on Theodosia. This degrading moment, where filth and despair are the outcome of desire, is one of the most emblematic in the book.

Lack of fulfillment is constantly accompanied by an unpleasant, violent underside at work in all desires and relationships. This is the aspect of the novel least attuned to the affirmative stances of contemporary gay art and politics, often geared to the production of positive images. "There is sex, a third flower whose shadow, too, is death" (207) is the melodramatic ending of the penultimate chapter, as Julian and Karel discover that Louis and Gabriel have hired a burglar to rob their apartment. At the drag ball, the crowd is fairly predatory, and the choral camp passage includes numerous intimations of violence and ends in what might be read as a note of abuse: "turn over kid I want to use you" (165). Through Julian's words, the narrative provides a sketchy explanation for this floating aggressiveness: "[H]omosexuality is just a habit to which I'm somehow bound which is little more than a habit in that it's not love or romance but a dim hard fetich [*sic*] I worship in my waking dreams it's more a symbol of power than a symbol of pleasure not a symbol inducing pleasure but exemplifying it not a specific symbol" (170).

The phallus, this "dim hard fetich," is the central element in this gridlocked view of (queer) desire. In terms that coincide with the familiar psychoanalytic formulation, the point in a relationship seems to be either to *have* it or to *be* it, options that always prove self-defeating for at least one of the parties involved. A symbol of power, not only of pleasure, the phallus is an emblem of domination. In the novel, being the phallus means being dominant, like Louis; possessing it means being subject to its power, as is the case with Karel, who "has" Louis and is subjugated by him. This problematic reading of homosexuality is offered, at different times in the narrative, as the reason why Karel and Julian can't desire each other and why they constantly gravitate toward rough trade.

Desire is also enmeshed in a visual economy that entails a fragmenting assault on the object of the look. Street cruising, a favorite practice among the book's characters, is a sexualized version of the voyeurism of that emblematic modern figure, the *flaneur*. It is about drifting through the city in search of inspiring, if fleeting, views, a practice characterized by detachment and vulnerable proximity—by a certain distance from the crowd and a simultaneous availability to the advances of others. In the same fashion, the *flaneur* posited himself above the mass but was simultaneously open to the stimuli it generated. Cruising, like the floating gaze of the dandified urban drifter, reaches fulfillment in intense, epiphanic moments when one recognizes one's kind, flashes a proposal, and registers a reply. The structure of these moments is eminently photographic. (The young Italian Julian picks up in Union Square is described as "a photograph" advancing toward him [139].) We could also describe it in cinematographic terms: the cruise starts with mobile establishing shots, then moves in for tighter frames, culminating in a close-up: "Have a place to go?" The work of the desiring gaze produces fragments out of the perceptual continuum of experience, and this is, to an extent, a mutilation, fetishistic cut-and-paste work. In Charles Baudelaire's influential description, the *flaneur*'s way of seeking artistic stimulus in the crowd is compared to fencing: a series of tactical moves of attack and defense. This has a correlate in the novel when Julian, Karel, and Frederick wander through a cruisy part of Broadway and their inquisitive stares fragment passersby into fetishized body parts: "A torso passed with a head";

"There are such things as eyes Karel thought such things as are not eyes as words as even arms"; "Broadway is a big long place like a hall . . . with new bodies and old doors that are not important but the bodies are and the clothes. And the faces" (179–80).

Parker Tyler's later film writings describe the desiring gaze as an aggressive intrusion. In his first film book, *The Hollywood Hallucination* (1944), he underlines the fragmentary quality of the film image and its tendency to disintegrate into a motley array of affects due to its composite character and multiple authorship. "Many a shot is a kind of three-ring circus, a contest for attention between the make-up man, the dialogue writer, and the star's personality." Another factor contributing to its disintegration is the work of desire: the spectator's fetishistic fixation on specific visual motifs, including parts of the actors' bodies. This fetishism, Tyler dramatically proclaims, "is capable of dismantling the human organism and separating one part from another as in a debacle."[40] Under the look of desire, the body of the film and the body of the lover dissolve into a collection of unbound objects.

Such puzzling insistence on the potential for violence and disintegration in queer desire should not necessarily be taken as the novel's homophobic last word. The text might simply be telling us that this is the bottom line in all sexuality. The family romance and the ideology of romantic love do much to gloss over this (perhaps unpleasant) truth, but such alibis are not so readily available to queers, for whom it may be clearer that coming together and falling apart are twin, often simultaneous moments in the embattled dialectics of sexuality. This idea reverses the closeting move that generalizes (and therefore erases) queerness; instead, it queers the generality. Ford and Tyler's work resonates with Leo Bersani's idea that queer sexuality uncovers the potential for dissolution and (self-)abolition latent in all sexuality, and this is ultimately the reason why queerness is so forcibly repressed. And more recently, through readings of André Gide, Marcel Proust, and Jean Genet, Bersani illustrates the antisocial potential of queerness, a potential that enables the articulation of a society of outlaws and radical others outside the recuperative normativity of the state machine.[41]

In *The Young and Evil*, only the negative, dissolving potential is present: the art of coming apart, not the capacity for social reconstruction. To an extent, this is a recurring motif in queer representation in early twentieth-century American culture. Glenway Westcott's novels and Tyler's and Ford's poetry insist on loneliness and disunion. Platt-Lynes's photographs frequently stage a complex circuit of gazes that fail to reciprocate each other or converge and clusters of bodies that touch in ways that seem forced and awkward. While not overly queer in subject matter, the 1930s and 1940s paintings by George Tooker and Jared French often represent groups where physical proximity conveys vast emotional distance, and Paul Cadmus's sailor paintings depict an overabundant, slightly disturbing fleshiness. Some of Cadmus's work, like "Floosies and Sailors," contains a subtle memento mori: next to the face of a cherubic sailor laid out in alcoholic slumber, a torn piece of paper announces the casualty count in a fascist bombing. Even the books issued by Monroe Wheeler and Barbara Harrison through Harrison of Paris showed a penchant for love stories full of obsessive, tragic relationships where sexual desire brings about violence and destruction. In *The Young and Evil*, this is thematized in a string of impossible relationships and encoded into the book's hybrid, self-split discourse, which pulls simultaneously toward seemingly opposite ends of the cultural spectrum that at times flow into each other but whose coming together, to paraphrase Theodor Adorno on the division between mass and high art, does not add up to a whole, to an integrated culture where things are in place.

In the last instance, the insistence on dissolution may be attributed to the lack of a collective consciousness that could turn queerness into a political gamble—a lack that Joseph Boone has rightly pointed out. In Ford and Tyler's novel, queer desire lacks a communal dimension, and without the political leverage this provides, cruising, desiring, having sex, fantasizing, and camping out cannot be sublated into an articulation of community or of an alternative polity. Instead, they may easily slide into the sadomasochistic dependencies endemic to everyday relationships. (This is not to say that politics would shelter anyone from that, but it might conjure a constructive moment from the emotional tangle.) When a community emerges, as in the camp balls, the bars, or the cruising areas, it is one *manqué*; its consciousness must come from aesthetics, which, in the logic of the novel, means modernist aesthetics. Yet an individualizing, hermetic modernism could not promote collective awareness, while a political aesthetic might, at least provisionally. Still, the novel cannot be faulted for its inability to posit a political front, since a politics of sexual dissidence, as we understand it today, was not such an available option in the early 1930s, a time when class, rather than bodily marks of identity, structured official political discourse and when an aestheticist bohemia, not community activism, subsumed social and cultural difference. Still, the missing element helps us see with greater clarity what is actually there and to discern the limits of the book's own discourse.

By 1933, when *The Young and Evil* came out and the Great Depression was hitting bottom, politics was certainly in the air. The novel reflects this through a number of topical allusions. One of them is a symposium, of the kind that punctuated the decade, on "political liberty and the artist." Karel is one of the featured speakers. In his talk, he rejects conventional politics because it only aims at the "removal of economic difficulties" and tends to erase individuality through its collectivist rhetoric. His main concern is "the conceptual realization of [people's] spiritual welfare" (120). In this, he maintains, only art can help, practiced by completely autonomous individuals only committed to aesthetics. In a way, the rejection of a political dimension for art, the defense of complete artistic freedom, and the assertion of individuality were familiar arguments for modernism and against the doctrinaire excesses of the socially engaged art of the time and the regressive rhetoric of the Popular Front. But as Karel argues his point, he performs a sort of disappearing act, since the high modernism he embraces can not suitably represent him. "Our adorable Kareletta," says Frederick fondly and admiringly as Karel, about to start his speech, asks for the lights to be lowered because they are shining into his eyes. This camp endearment uncovers the gap between Karel, the queer artist, and the straight scene in which he is now attempting to maneuver. Frederick's words remind us that it is in the popular discourse of camp, a third way between politically inflected social realism and solipsistic high modernism, where Karel, and those like him, most often found a voice.

Gone and Back

Karel's disappearing act seems to have been repeated by the work as a whole. This hybrid novel was too queer and experimental to be popular and too pop, too full of reference to street culture and quotidian messiness, to fit the hegemonic conception of the avant-garde as art "whose subject matter was art itself," in Clement Greenberg's famous formulation.[42] As a result, it has remained for decades a seldom visited ruin. Ford and Tyler never tried to repeat their experiment. In their later careers they withdrew into an elusive modernism that sublimated queer reference and cultivated difficulty and abstraction, whether in their poetry, in Tyler's essays and film criticism, or in their joint venture of the 1940s, *View* magazine. *The Young and Evil* failed to work out a viable queer aesthetic but gestured at possibilities that would be retried in the future, more concretely, in the 1950s experimental films of Gregory Markopoulos, Willard Maas, and Curtis Harrington and in the

1960s queer underground, represented by the filmmakers Kenneth Anger, Jack Smith, and Andy Warhol and by the writers and performers of the Theater of the Ridiculous. This "aesthetic"—"cultural practice" might be a better term—has subsequently endured in fiction by Dennis Cooper; contemporary film and video, from Rainer Werner Fassbinder to Bruce LaBruce; and photography, from Robert Mapplethorpe to Del LaGrace Volcano. The early twentieth-century antecedents of this tradition were consigned for years to the junk heap of history by a narrow way of theorizing and historicizing modernism. However, from the present standpoint, in which experimental art appears permeated with popular and subcultural reference, we may more easily track the meandering existence of this subterranean trend. This is what I have attempted in this chapter: to sketch out an archeology for the contemporary mixings of high and low art and for the queer matrix of postmodern textuality. The task seems all the more important because this provocatively unorthodox body of work still has much to say to our queer life today.

7

Walking with Zombies
Haitian Folklore and
Modernist Ethnography in
Zora Neale Hurston's *Tell My Horse*

Folk Culture and Hybridity

Zora Neale Hurston's contemporary fame rests largely on her novels and short stories, but in her lifetime she divided her energies between fiction writing and ethnographic research. She was trained as an ethnographer by Franz Boas and Ruth Benedict, her professors at Barnard College and foundational figures in modern anthropology. Boas in particular opened extremely important lines of inquiry in the field that point toward Hurston's later work. Starting in the 1890s, he questioned the evolutionism dominant at the end of the nineteenth century, which ranked cultures according to their presumed degree of "development," always defined in Eurocentric terms, and stressed instead the simultaneous coexistence of different evolutionary stages in any given culture. In his classic *The Mind of Primitive*

Man (1916), for example, he qualified the distinction between "primitive" and "civilized" communities and demonstrated that both share many mental and behavioral traits. He also attacked the tendency to see culture as a direct emanation of race. In numerous addresses, articles, and especially in a lengthy study requested by the U.S. Immigration Commission (also known as the Dillingham Commission), *Changes in Bodily Forms of Descendants of Immigrants* (1912), he stressed the plasticity of what were still being regarded as unchangeable "racial" traits and showed that mentality, culture, and even bodily configuration are highly dependent on context. Boas's object in this report was to undercut contemporary nativist arguments that the influx of Eastern and Southern European immigrants into the United States posed the threat of racial and cultural degradation. But his ideas had wider application. They tailgated with the attempts of contemporary black thinkers such as W. E. B. DuBois and Alain Locke to defend the intrinsic worthiness of African American culture and to study it not as an offshoot of an ahistorical "race spirit" but, in more materialistic terms, as the result of specific historical and social circumstances.[1]

Naturally, Boas's ideas attracted the attention of black intellectuals. In 1905 DuBois invited Boas to participate in one of the "Atlanta studies"—the yearly conference on different aspects of African American culture he organized at Atlanta University—and to give the commencement address at this institution. In his lecture, Boas recalled at length the history of ancient Africa and the technological sophistication of its past civilizations. Years later, and also at DuBois's initiative, Boas was present at the first gathering of the National Association for the Advancement of Colored People and afterward collaborated with its periodical, *The Crisis*. His ideas also left a deep imprint in Alain Locke's *Race Contacts and Interracial Relations* (1916) and, through Locke, in a younger generation of writers and thinkers.[2] Boas strenuously promoted the study of African American culture on his own turf. Probably inspired by DuBois's efforts, he lobbied in 1906 for the creation of an African Institute. Its objective, as he described it to Booker T. Washington, was to sponsor "scientific work on the Negro race." By divulging black achievement, the institute intended to deflate racism, increase racial pride, and further cultural development among the peoples of the black diaspora. The institute never materialized, but Boas found other ways of advancing the study of black culture. He served in the Executive Council of the Association for the Study of Negro Life and History, founded by the historian Carter G. Woodson, and sat on the editorial board of the organization's journal. And as a cofounder and officer of the American Folklore Society, established in 1888, he regarded one of the primary interests of the society and its organ, the *Journal of American Folklore,* to be the compilation and study of African American folklore, which ideally should make up about a fourth of the periodical's contents. Until then, the collection of southern black folklore had been too often in the hands of untrained amateurs whose treatment of the material was often tinged by racism and condescension. The *Journal* lived up to Boas's intentions; in 1925 Alain Locke listed more than fifty citations from this source in the bibliography he appended to *The New Negro.*[3]

Other members of Boas's school, such as Ruth Benedict, Otto Klineberg, and Miles Herskovits, often addressed racial issues in their work. Herskovits in particular studied black American culture, diasporic cultures, and African art and was, in addition, the author of the well-reputed *Life in a Haitian Valley* (1937), which Hurston would later mention in her own book on Haiti and to which her work on Caribbean folklore was often compared. Like Boas and Klineberg, Herskovits was an occasional contributor to *Opportunity.* Race was not only an academic interest for these intellectuals; it was a category that helped them conceptualize their position in society. Boas was a German Jew who moved to the United States in 1886 to escape the anti-Semitism rampant in German academic life, and many of his students belonged to ethnic, cultural, or sexual minorities and therefore had a tangential relation to the cultural norm.

These precedents gave academic legitimacy to Hurston's study of African American folklore. From the beginning of her studies, Boas encouraged her to study black folklore in the rural South, especially in her native Florida. The material she collected there in the late 1920s and early 1930s became the basis of her celebrated *Mules and Men* (1935) and wove its way into her fiction and drama. Two years after the publication of *Mules and Men,* she received a Guggenheim Fellowship to research Obeah religion in Jamaica and Haiti (Herskovits was one of her recommenders). During her stay there through 1937 and 1938, she toyed with the idea, later abandoned, of completing a Ph.D. in anthropology at Columbia University under Boas's direction.[4]

In her two roles as ethnographer and creative writer, Hurston exemplified the notion, put forward by Houston Baker Jr., that the specific modernism of the Harlem Renaissance, within which Hurston is usually framed, was not only aesthetic but discursive at large. The goal of the (loose) Harlem movement was not only the expansion of black literary and artistic tradition but also the "broadening and enlargement of the field of traditional Afro-American discursive possibilities."[5] This was the purpose of Alain Locke's collection *The New Negro* (1925), which reputedly launched the Harlem movement. The volume combined art (by Aaron Douglas and Weinold Reiss), pictures of African masks, creative writing (by Countee Cullen, Langston Hughes, Claude McKay, Jean Toomer, Eric Walrond, and Zora Neale Hurston, among others), and pieces on sociology, history, journalism, cultural criticism, and folklore. The overall goal was the promotion of black cultural nationalism on the basis of a common inheritance. As Locke put it in his preface, "[I]mmediate hope rests on the revaluation . . . of the Negro in terms of his artistic endowments and cultural contributions, past and prospective." Perhaps inspired by DuBois's analysis of spirituals in *The Souls of Black Folk,* the visibility of the Jubilee Singers, and the success of James Weldon Johnson's poetic homage, *God's Trombones,* he singled out "folk art, music especially," as the realm where African Americans had already made "substantial contributions." A shared folklore might bring together audiences and artists. At a time when cultural production and consumption were frequently atomized into a profusion of "classes, cliques, and coteries," this cohesive heritage could grant black creations "almost the conditions of classical art."[6] The reassessment of folk materials was then a means to clear the path for a modern(ist) black culture whose existence was, to an extent, dependent on giving folklore its due and on mining it as a source of expressive possibilities.[7] Hence we must consider the folklorist Arthur Huff Fauset's contribution to *The New Negro,* "American Negro Folk Literature," together with the abundant graphic evocations of the African past sprinkled throughout the book, of a piece with the examples of literary modernism that made up most of the volume.[8]

The twin orientation toward the folk past and toward modernity are closely linked in the work of 1920s Harlem writers, who updated and modernized the tradition by assimilating the African American vernacular—think, for example, of Langston Hughes's use of blues measures and rhythms in *The Weary Blues* (1926) or of Jean Toomer's evocations of black southern lifestyles in *Cane* (1923). A similar fusion of old and new also characterized contemporary black music and performance arts. In their northern urban mutations, jazz, blues, and the black musical theater recast a number of rural traditions in modern formats and media. In the new city settings, rural styles acquired more complex structures and arrangements and were disseminated through phonographs, electrically amplified instruments, and radios and integrated into the commercial theatrical circuits. But under the new sophistications one could still spot the essential folk idiom—what Locke called "a fresh distinctive note that the majority of [the artists] admit as the instinctive gift of the folk spirit."[9]

Most of Hurston's ethnographic writings appeared in the 1930s, when the reclaiming of the vernacular received additional impulse from the New Deal government, particularly from the Work Projects Administration (WPA), a state agency that sponsored, among many other cultural activities, the research and compilation of American popular art and folklore. Hurston was the head of the Florida unit of the Federal Writers' Project (FWP; a sub-unit of the WPA) and carried out part of her studies under its auspices. She was involved in collecting and editing material for a work tentatively titled "The Florida Negro," which she never completed. According to Hurston's biographer, Robert Hemenway, this volume would have contained many stories and songs gathered by Hurston and a number of important slave narratives collected by the Florida FWP staff. It was part of a national project, coordinated from Washington, D.C., by the writer Sterling Brown, to research and document the history and the contemporary state of black culture. Its main achievement was the impressive *The Negro in Virginia,* after which the Florida book was to be modeled. Hurston's position as a sponsored writer and researcher was by no means unique; a number of contemporary African American writers, including Richard Wright, Arna Bontemps, Margaret Walker, Frank Yerby, and Ralph Ellison, were also on the WPA payroll in various federal projects. The choreographer and folklorist Katharine Dunham's early ethnomusicology studies were also funded by this agency.

The critic and historian Hazel V. Carby has described this widespread concern with traditional lore as "the Harlem Renaissance's interest in establishing a folk heritage as the source of, and inspiration for, authentic African-American art forms."[10] Whether or not authenticity is essential to the folk interests of black modernists, it is clear that they were engaged in an urgent struggle over the relevance of traditional African American culture at a time when this was being transplanted into unfamiliar urban milieus and altered by commercialization, electronic transmission, and by its unprecedented visibility. Carby characterizes Hurston's interest in black folklore as nostalgic, an attempt "to preserve the concept of Negroness, to negotiate and rewrite its cultural meanings, and, finally, to reclaim an aesthetically purified version of blackness" (79). Hurston presumably located this version in the South of her childhood, to which she repeatedly returned to film and record vanishing ways of life. Hence her anthropological work (like all anthropology) can be seen as a particularly modern undertaking. It sought to preserve traditional communal ties and practices before they died out under the pressure of industrialized modernity and to salvage from among those forms on the brink of extinction whatever might be of use for forging new social bonds and enriching the present.

It is less clear that a purified version of blackness was the goal of Hurston's folklore studies or that any kind of "purity" could be derived from (black) folk culture. In addition to Carby, Hurston has often been regarded as a folk "purist" by critics who have picked up on her occasional defenses of "authenticity." She was indeed fond of contrasting the "genuine Negro" music and singing she heard from amateur singers in logging camps or rural churches to the more polished Broadway or glee-club renditions, and she often enthused about using this material as the basis of a "*real* Negro theater."[11] But at the same time, Hurston repeatedly emphasized the hybrid character of black popular expression, which was distinguished in part by its ability to rework and make its own a great variety of styles, characters, icons, and fashions. Everything was grist to its mill, even "the Sheik haircut made famous by Rudolph Valentino" (838). This was not to deny its creativity and originality—after all, originality, as Hurston put it, "is the modification of ideas. The most ardent admirer of the great Shakespeare cannot claim first source even for him. It is his treatment of the borrowed material" (838). From this perspective, she continues, "The Negro is a very original being. While he lives and moves in the midst of a white civilization, everything that he touches is re-interpreted for his own use. . . . Nothing is too old or too new, domestic or foreign, high or low for use" (838). Rather than in pure essences, black folklore trades in subtle forms of intertextuality and collage, a quality that makes it both premodern and fully modern(ist), at once more and less than the basis for a "pure" identity.

This was not only Hurston's view, and it was not only applicable to African American folklore. Around the time when Hurston was doing field work in Florida in the late 1920s, the Chicago anthropologist Robert Redfield published *Tepoztlan*. In this ethnographic study of rural Mexico, Redfield noted the presence of a number of phonographs in the remote village that gives the book its title; their sound competed with and ended up influencing, but not erasing, the local musical languages. Back in the industrialized world, the new sound media did not eliminate folk culture either but actually helped to preserve and spread it. The cultural historian Lizabeth Cohen has pointed out that folk-music recordings helped immigrants in

Chicago preserve a sense of community and strengthen their ethnic alliances in new settings by making available the sounds of home away from home. Record players were often at the center of social gatherings, and rather than stifle popular expression, they often prompted listeners to keep the beat, dance, and sing, at times comparing alternative versions of the same song or musical piece. It is not surprising that cities like Chicago and Los Angeles, where many African Americans flocked during the Great Migration, ended up becoming two of the main centers of the "race record" industry during the 1930s and that, during the same decade, New York rose as an important production and distribution center for folk music.[12]

It is hard to imagine an aesthetically purified version of blackness—or of any other ethnic or cultural identity—when its basis, folk culture, turns out to be an unstable process of cut and mix; when it is in constant dialogue with other forms; and when it depends on industrial technology for its dissemination and preservation. Could Hurston have afforded to be a folk purist? In her research trips she combed southern Florida in her second-hand Chevrolet, "Sassy Susie," wielding cameras and recording devices, using, as she put it, the "spy-glass" of anthropology and its auxiliary technologies to capture, caption, and get to know what, in a way, she had always already known but, as she puts it in *Mules and Men,* "couldn't see for wearing it" (9). This dependence on technology to limn out identity will be familiar to readers of her fiction. Janie Woods, the protagonist of *Their Eyes Were Watching God,* becomes aware of her color by seeing herself in a photograph with a group of white children. The black girl she does not recognize in the center of the picture turns out to be herself. Ascertaining identities, whether individual or collective, in modernity inevitably involves a technological supplement. As a result, identity can hardly be "essential"; it is relational, mediated by machines, and differentially articulated. And the folk culture on which collective identity rests is perforce hybrid and unstable. In the terms Hurston used to describe herself in the essay "How It Feels to Be Colored Me," it is "a brown bag of miscellany," "a jumble of things" (829).

In any case, folk culture was a central concern in Hurston's early books. Most representative among them are the folk collection *Mules and Men* (1935) and the now-classic novel, *Their Eyes Were Watching God* (1937). The former is nostalgic, the second dialectic. The former seeks to preserve the voice of the community. To do so, "Zora," the narrator and protagonist, returns to southern Florida, the landscape of her childhood, where she visits small towns, saw mills, turpentine camps, and juke joints. In the last part of the book, she travels to New Orleans to be initiated in hoodoo and magic. The book narrates the process of collecting and displays the material she digs up—a rich compilation of stories, songs, games, jokes, recipes, home remedies, and conjuring practices. *Their Eyes Were Watching God* features a confrontation and eventual reconciliation between an individual, Janie, and her small-town milieu. Reconciliation comes about largely through the oral narration of the protagonist's life. Raised by her grandmother and married off, when still an adolescent, to a much older farmer, Janie has to forfeit her romantic idea of love to the realities of a marriage of convenience that, predictably, does not make her happy. After years of misery, she leaves her first husband for Jody Starks, a charming wanderer on his way to the recently incorporated all-black community of Eatonville. Businesslike and charismatic, Starks organizes the town, makes provisions for street lighting, opens a store, runs the post office, and is soon elected major. The relationship between him and Janie grows increasingly tense, as an aging, jealous Jody keeps Janie tied to the store and the home while she chafes under constraint. Eventually Jody dies, and shortly afterwards Janie meets the love of her life: a younger man, Tea Cake, with whom she discovers equality (roughly), companionship, and romance. When she leaves the town to live with him in nearby Jacksonville, she earns the animosity of the community. In the end, her happiness is short-lived; Tea Cake dies after being bitten by a dog with rabies during a flood in the everglades, and Janie returns to Eatonville to a sullen welcome. By the close of the narrative, when Janie completes the account of her experiences to her friend Phoeby, the only town-dweller who comes out to greet her, Phoeby decides to accept and forgive her, even if this means defying the rest of the community: "'Lawd! Ah done growed ten feet higher from jus' listenin' tuh you, Janie. . . . Nobody better not criticize yuh in mah hearin.'"[13] Oral communication, in the form of Janie's personal testimony, works as an integrating agent, harmonizing the "modern" imperative for independence and self-fulfillment—present in Janie's unconventional relationship with Tea Cake—and communal cohesion. In closing, the moral Janie offers of her own story is not of rupture; in her defense of the right of the individual to go down the least-traveled path, there is also a gesture of reconciliation: "'Now Pheoby, don't feel too mean wid the rest of 'em 'cause dey's parched up from not knowin' things. . . . Yo' papa and yo' mama and nobody else can't tell yuh and show yuh. Two things everybody's got tuh do fuh theyselves. They got tuh go tuh God, and they got tuh find out about livin' fuh theyselves.'"[14]

These books were only two of the many projects undertaken by Hurston in the 1930s that focused on the representation of popular heritage. She wrote several scholarly pieces on black folk expressiveness, including her famous essay, "Characteristics of Negro Expression," published in Nancy Cunard's anthology *Negro* (1934), and a long essay on hoodoo for the *Journal of American Folklore*. She co-authored, with Langston Hughes, the play *Mule Bone,* and worked on three musicals, all with rural topics and settings. She wrote dialogue for the revue *Fast and Furious,* with music by J. Rosamond Johnson and Porter Grainer, and featuring the black vaudevillians Jackie Mabley and Tim Moore. She also contributed lyrics and dialogue for *Jungle Scandals,* a show with music by Grainer that never opened. And she wrote *The Great Day.* Its loose story line, which depicts a day in the life of a railroad camp, serves as a frame for songs, tales, and dialogues that dramatize some of the material later published in *Mules and Men.* Alain Locke wrote the program notes praising the authenticity of the material. Yet despite the contemporary vogue of the black musical, the troupe had to be disbanded after only a few performances, as no producer would pick up the show. In addition, Hurston set up a number of gospel concerts, assisted Alan Lomax with folk recordings for the Music Division of the Library of Congress, helped Orson Welles and John Houseman organize the Federal Theater Project Harlem unit and wrote a play for them, and during 1936 and 1937, she lived in Jamaica and Haiti studying Caribbean society and folklore, which later became the subjects of a new book.[15]

This book was *Tell My Horse,* and it remains vastly underrated and misunderstood. Contemporary reviews were often positive; they praised its entertaining character and Hurston's perceptiveness and gift for storytelling. While questioning at times her conclusions, Harold Courlander, writing for the *Saturday Review of Literature,* pronounced the book "exceedingly good folklore." For the influential scholar C. G. Woodson, it was amusing and of scholarly value. And Carl Carmer, of the *New York Herald Tribune,* declared it "the best that I know in the field of contemporary folklore" and proposed that Hurston should be put to work immediately on other corners of the Caribbean.[16] *Tell My Horse* has fared otherwise with recent scholars. Robert Hemenway calls it her poorest work and points out its embarrassing nationalism and conservatism.[17] In his review, Courlander had also noted that Hurston's view of the United States' occupation of Haiti was too benign and apparently written in oblivion of the widespread denunciation, by black intellectuals, of American interventionism on the island. It certainly differed from James Weldon Johnson's exposés for *The Nation,* in which he revealed rampant abuse and the collusion of the occupation forces and the corrupt local elite. More recent researchers, such as Hazel V. Carby, Karen Jacobs, and Lynda Hill, allude to *Tell My Horse* in passing when discussing Hurston's more standard folklore work, but an in-depth assessment is still not available.[18] The closest one comes to this is in essays by Wendy Dutton and Gwendolyn Mikell. Mikell shows that Hurston's Haiti book was informed—as was most of her ethnography—by feminist concerns. Gender relations, rather than racial or cross-cultural relations, were the primary focus of Hurston's research. She demonstrated that voodoo replicates the patriarchal bias of Caribbean society but also offers women a number of empowering female figures—such as the goddess Erzulie—and some protagonism in the rituals.[19] While I agree with Mikell's views, the focus on gender is not the only distinctive contribution of *Tell My Horse,* and it is certainly not the reason for its marginalization, especially since gender studies and feminism have played a decisive role in the recovery of Hurston's work in recent decades. Wendy Dutton reveals the centrality of voodoo in Hurston's oeuvre, from her early scholarly articles, to *Mules and Men,* to her autobiography, *Dust Tracks on a Road,* to the column ("Hoodoo and Black Magic") that she wrote for the *Fort Pierce Chronicle* at the end of her life. She offers a thoughtful and sympathetic account of Hurston's interest in the subject, yet her characterization of *Tell My Horse* is largely negative, dominated by a sense of failure and incompleteness. Instead of "the definitive book on voodoo" projected in her Guggenheim grant application, Dutton writes, Hurston delivered a work that is "confusing," "murky," that "fails as serious anthropology," and "does not fly as fiction either." Dubious as to how to present her material and caught between the scorn of her intellectual peers and the hostility of the underground world of voodoo, Hurston's "confusion" mars her writing. At the same time, Dutton acknowledges that Hurston's approach "need not be seen as flawed, but as unprecedented, innovative, and ahead of its time," but she does not specify why.[20]

There are important reasons for such misunderstanding and neglect. *Tell My Horse* is a puzzling, uncomfortable work. It was hastily planned and written and has a rough finish and a ragged feel to it. Formally, its mixture of written and photographic reportage is reminiscent of other 1930s documentary books, such as *You Have Seen Their Faces,* by Erskine Caldwell and Margaret Bourke-White, *Let Us Now Praise Famous Men,* by James Agee and Walker Evans, and *Twelve Million Black Voices,* by Richard Wright and Edwin

Rosskam. All of them depicted rural poverty during the Depression. Like these, *Tell My Horse* deals with an impoverished rural society (that of Haitian peasants), but Hurston's writing is more whimsical than that of other documentarists, and it abounds in personal impressions and humor. *Tell My Horse* shifts from travelogue and political commentary in the first part, devoted to Jamaica and Haiti, to Haitian folklore and religion in the second. It contains some fairly unaccountable moments: Hurston's encounter with a zombie; her reports on the atrocities of Haitian secret societies; and her initiation into voodoo, which continues her apprenticeship at the end of *Mules and Men*. Yet the main puzzle posed by *Tell My Horse,* and the reasons for its remaining largely unclaimed by contemporary cultural criticism, are its vexing conceptualization of the folk community and its modernist ethnography. While in earlier works (like *Mules and Men* and *Their Eyes Were Watching God*) the folk community is more or less embattled yet readily found and representable, in *Tell My Horse* it edges toward the unrepresentable, becoming a site of loss and dissolution that defies conventional mimetic modes.

Writing Haiti

Hurston's move from black America, the main subject of her previous work, to the Caribbean landscapes of *Tell My Horse* signals a transnational, globalizing view of the black community consonant with the pan-African awareness of Locke's *The New Negro* and of Cunard's *Negro.* In a gesture toward what Paul Gilroy calls "the black Atlantic," *The New Negro* included an essay by Willie A. Domingo ("Gift of the Black Tropics") about the West Indian community in Harlem. Cunard's *Negro* was even more cosmopolitan. In addition to the United States and Africa, it covered extensively black culture in Latin America (Brazil and Uruguay) and the entire Caribbean, and its collaborators were drawn from Europe (especially France, where Cunard was living at the time), Africa, and the Americas.

Like Locke's and Cunard's compilations, *Tell My Horse* contains an implicit homage to the historical significance of Haiti as the first black state in the Northern Hemisphere and the setting of the earliest anticolonial black rebellion. This important historical antecedent was also chronicled in the 1930s by the Trinidad intellectual C. L. R. James, who was living at the time in New York. His landmark study *The Black Jacobins* appeared the same year as *Tell My Horse,* and his play *Touissant L'Overture,* about the leader of the revolt that freed Haiti from French rule, was produced a few years later in London with Paul Robeson in the lead. The African American artist Jacob

Lawrence was at work in the 1930s on a sequence of historical paintings also on Touissant, and a number of novels and plays, such as Arna Bontemps's *Drums at Dusk,* Guy Endore's *Babouk,* Langston Hughes's *Emperor of Haiti,* and Orson Welles's *Voodoo Macbeth,* for the Federal Theater, all dealt with Haiti's war for independence.

Hurston's interest in the area may have been further motivated by the influential West Indian presence in Harlem—more than 20 percent of the population, according to some accounts—and current Caribbean anticolonialist militancy.[21] According to Willie A. Domingo, West Indians in Harlem tended to be educated, entrepreneurial, and militant defenders of their rights. Accustomed to slightly more egalitarian societies, they bridled under the racism they encountered in the United States.[22] This is borne out by the political activism of Harlem-based West Indians such as Marcus Garvey, the founder of the short-lived United Negro Improvement Association, and Cyril Briggs, a Left radical, the editor of *The Crusader,* and founder of the African Blood Brotherhood, intended as the black arm of the international proletariat revolution.[23] Traces of West Indian militancy are also visible in literature. In the Jamaican Claude McKay's *Home to Harlem,* the most articulate and politically committed character is Ray, a Haitian immigrant who works as a Pullman porter; his sense of responsibility and his social concerns contrast with the freewheeling, apolitical attitude of the roguish African American protagonist, Jake. Ray reappears in McKay's *Banjo: A Story without a Plot* as the intellectual leader of a transnational community of blacks stranded in Marseilles. Writing in the 1960s, C. L. R. James recalled the generative role of 1930s Caribbean activism to the anticolonialism movement at large: "Today the emancipation of Africa is one of the outstanding events of contemporary history. Between the wars, when this emancipation was being prepared, the unquestioned leaders of the movement in every public sphere, in Africa itself, in Europe and in the United States, were not Africans but West Indians." He goes on to mention George Padmore's African Bureau; Andrew Cipriani's antiracist reform government in Trinidad and his Caribbean Labour Congress; and, on the cultural front, the publication of Aimé Césaire's *Cahier du retour au pays natal* (1939), where the poet coined the influential term *négritude.*[24]

But in addition to all these factors, Hurston's interest in the Caribbean was primarily spurred by her folklore research. In her autobiography, *Dust Tracks on a Road,* she states that her encounter with Bahamian immigrant workers in southern Florida made her aware of the many cultural features shared by black communities in the United States and the Caribbean, and this awareness prompted her first research journeys abroad (700). In "Characteristics of Negro Expression," she repeatedly acknowledges the African origins of possession in African-derived forms of spirituality (851). In *Their Eyes Were Watching God,* Janie and Tea Cake listen with fascination to the drumming of Bahamian harvesters "on the muck," with whom they quickly become friends (294). And in the fragments for the work in progress "The Florida Negro," Hurston elaborates on the influence of Cuban and Bahamian music and folklore on the black communities of western Florida (889–90).

Despite the contemporary emancipationist ferment, however, the Caribbean Hurston describes in *Tell My Horse* is far from heroic. She evokes its rebellious past in her visit to the maroon communities in the mountains of Jamaica. The present, however, is dominated by corruption and strife. In the chapters on Jamaica, Hurston focuses mostly on gender conflict and social inequality; in the early chapters on Haiti (a section called "Politics and Personalities of Haiti"), conflict is social, political, and ethnic—between mulattos and blacks, the north and the south, the capital and the country, the middle and upper-middle classes and the peasants, and the governing elites and the masses of the governed. These accounts convey an impression of keen dissension, of interests and factions that fail to coalesce into a harmonious social project.

An account of such a conflict-ridden society seemed to require a fluid chronology and a wide repertoire of mimetic modes. Accordingly, the text intertwines history and contemporary commentary; it intersperses narratives of the Haitian past with passages on current conditions. In both one finds a mixture of fact, legend, and rumor. Emblematic in this connection are the chapters "Rebirth of a Nation" (360–67) and "The Black Joan of Arc" (331–38). They deal with the rise and fall of two political regimes: that of General Simon after 1908, allegedly upheld by the witchcraft of his daughter, the magic powers of his goat, Simalo, and the connivance of the landowning class, and the later regime of General Jean Vilbrun Guillaume Sam, doomed by mountain prophets and ended by a bloody popular rebellion that culminated in 1911 in military occupation by the U.S. army (337).

Such a mixture of narrative perspectives and mimetic modes resembles the "magic realism" cultivated by Latin American writers in the second half of the twentieth century. Hurston's Haiti can be seen as an early example of what the Cuban writer Alejo Carpentier would famously call *lo real maravilloso.* Carpentier, like Hurston, was interested in ethnography and folklore;

he conceived this term in the late 1940s during his stay in Haiti, where he had been destined as a member of the Cuban diplomatic delegation, and he defined it in the preface to *El Reino de este mundo* (1949), a historical novel on the Haitian Revolution that allegedly inaugurated Latin American magic realism. (Some later representatives of this current are Gabriel García Márquez, Miguel Angel Asturias, Juan Rulfo, Carlos Fuentes, and Jorge Luis Borges.) For Carpentier, *lo real maravilloso* is the literary style best suited to the American social and cultural experience, whose baroque complexity and excess demand a combination of the factual with the mythic and the fantastic.[25] From a more materialist perspective, Fredric Jameson has described magic realism as a mode of representation grounded in the embattled history of Latin America and the Caribbean. It is constitutively dependent on the existence of "structural disjunction," and in the American context, the main form of disjunction is the coexistence of precapitalist and "nascent capitalist" systems of production, a coexistence that brings about a constant clash among the diverse conceptions of society, labor, time, and history attached to each of these systems. Moreover, as the postcolonial critic Kurkum Sangari has shown, disjunction based on modes of production is further complicated by ethnic diversity, a mosaic of local and migrant cultures spread across the continent that contribute diverse "historical sedimentations." Hence the heterogeneity of Latin American societies results as well "from the physical coexistence over time of different ethnic groups (Native-American-Indian, Arab, African, Indochinese, Asian, Spanish), each laden with its respective cultural freight of myth, oral narrative, magic, superstition, Roman Catholicism, Cartesian education, and Western rationalism. Simultaneity is the restless product of a long history of miscegenation, assimilation and syncretization *as well as* of conflict, contradiction, and cultural violence." The resulting cultural space is composite and multilayered; it constitutes a sort of postmodernity before the postmodern that, as cultural critics such as Néstor García-Canclini and Celeste Olalquiaga point out, throws into crisis Eurocentric history and its periodization and chronology.[26] Hurston's account reflects this heterogeneity. Rather than try to produce order, a hierarchy of truth between the different discourses and perspectives, *Tell My Horse* situates them all on the same level of credibility, thus flattening them out and relativizing their claims. Mixed with myth, legend, and rumor, historical study and anthropological commentary remain open questions rather than purveyors of answers. The ironic relativism of Hurston's approach is emphasized by the Creole expression placed at the end of most Haiti chapters, "Ah Bo Bo!"—a phrase at once dismissive and jocular, a playful squiggle that casts a shadow of doubt and mockery over the sections it closes.

Yet not all is conflict in Hurston's account. Haitian folklore and religion often seem to counter the factionalism that characterizes history and public life. In particular, voodoo (the cult of the *loa,* or native deities) occasionally acts as powerful social cement: "As someone in America said of whiskey, voodoo has more enemies in public and more friends in private than anything else in Haiti. None of the sons of voodoo who sit in high places have yet had the courage to defend it publicly, though they know quite well and acknowledge privately that voodoo is a harmless pagan cult that sacrifices domestic animals at its worst" (358). Commonality is the dominant note in chapters describing the *loa* gods and the rituals attached to them. In highly regimented services, peasants, members of the local bourgeoisie, and city arrivals come together under the direction of the *houngan,* or voodoo priest, to chant, dance, and invoke the deities. In such moments, the cult acts as a great leveler of class and color differences. Even when difference does not disappear entirely, the cult creates a space for fairly indiscriminate social communion. Hence in the ceremonies of the *tete l'eau,* designed to honor the gods that inhabit the heads of streams and in those consecrated to the goddess Erzulie, upper-class Haitians often throw lavish banquets in honor of the *loas* to which all devotees, rich and poor, are welcome (500–502). And in the yearly pilgrimage to the hallowed *Saut d'eau,* Haitians from all social extractions, naked except for pieces of white cloth wrapped around their waists and heads, mingle in the ascent to the top of the waterfall (503–8). Here the universal near-nudity of the pilgrims is a sign of purity and respect for the local gods, but it also has the effect of dissolving the most visible marks of social status.

But if voodoo cults have an integrating character, they also register the divisiveness of Hatian society. This is particularly manifest in the existence of zombies, in the workings of possession (the *parlay cheval ou,* or "tell my horse"), and in the secret societies, all of which exemplify the anticommunitarian workings of the cult. As tradition has it, zombies, or living dead, are recently dead bodies recalled from the tomb through a series of spells to be used as slaves. They are often exploited as beasts of burden or sent out on evil errands by their masters. They are created as acts of revenge against the deceased or their families, or as part of a pact with the evil gods contracted through priests who may grant supplicants particularly ambitious wishes in exchange for control over the bodies of their defunct relatives. The existence of zombies introduces into society an element of terror and mistrust: "[T]he fear of this thing and all that it means seeps over the country like a ground current of cold air. This fear is real and deep. . . . Sit in the market place and pass a day with the market women and notice how often some vendeuse cries out that a Zombie with its invisible hand has filched her money, or her goods. Or the accusation is made that a Zombie has been set upon her or some one of her family to work a piece of evil. Big Zombies who come in the night to do malice are talked about" (456). In such an anxious climate, those suspected of retrieving dead bodies are often threatened with mob violence, and families organize all-night watches by the tombs of the departed to thwart the work of the zombie-callers (or *bocors*).

The *parley cheval ou* also instills communal division. The term refers to the central moment in voodoo rituals, when a devotee is "mounted" (or possessed) by the *loa* and, turned into a mouthpiece of the divinity, "does and says many things that he or she would never have uttered un-ridden" (495). The mischievous god Guedé, for example, dictates "the most caustic and belittling statements concerning some pompous person who is present. A prominent official is made ridiculous before a crowd of peasants" (495). This evidences the critical potential of the rituals, which allow ordinary folk to air their discontent under cover of divine possession. Because of this, Hurston sees voodoo celebrations as examples of cunning and creativity under pressure. Yet she is also aware that they operate at times as forms of social control, as possession may turn into a means of repressing unorthodox behavior: "A woman known to be a lesbian was mounted one afternoon. The spirit announced through her mouth 'Tell my horse I have told this woman to stop making love to women. It is a vile thing and I object to it. . . .' The woman pranced and galloped like a horse to a great mango tree, climbed it far up among the top limbs and dived off and broke her neck" (497). It is worth noting, however, that voodoo deities are not always so ready to punish sexual transgression. The Haiti scholar Karen McCarthy Brown has pointed out that nowadays the female *loa* Erzulie Freida is often assumed to have an unconventional sexuality that includes occasional lesbian affairs; hence the life her devotees attribute to her is capable of accommodating the widening range of behaviors present in Haitian communities.[27] But even when the *loa* do not induce discord or repression, the act of invocation is always risky. It may attract the wrong divinities, the Petro gods, prone to evil and not always easily controllable by the *houngan*. On one occasion, Hurston witnessed a man possessed by one of the evil spirits. His face grotesquely distorted, he smashed objects and pushed against other celebrants. As this happened, the *hounfort,* a space of commonality and healing, threatened to become a death space dominated by a presence of "unspeakable evil"—"the fear was so humid you could smell it and feel it in your tongue" (411–12).

The secret societies do not partake of the anti-authoritarian bent of *loa* possession, but they, too, function as systems of surveillance. They are devoted to destructive deities that often demand human sacrifices and the consumption of the victim's flesh. These sects practice extortion and blackmail and enforce a rule of silence that makes them comparable to American gangsters or the Ku Klux Klan (483). Their disintegrating effect on the social fabric is similar to that brought about by the zombies. Hurston's attempts to study their activities repeatedly bump against a wall of silence and evasiveness. Eventually, she is warned by an informant against asking too much and trusting casual acquaintances: "Furthermore, it was not possible for me to know whom to trust without advice. All was not gold that glittered. There were different kinds of priests. Some of them worked with two hands. . . . I must make no contacts nor must I go anywhere to stay unless I let my friends advise me" (479–80). She may have disregarded this advice or taken a wrong turn in her inquiries. In June 1937, while deep into her research, she experienced a "violent gastric disturbance" and saw in it the hand of a secret society or of a *bocor* made uncomfortable by her curiosity. "'It seems that some of my destinations and some of my accessions have been whispered into ears that heard,'" she wrote to a friend.[28] She broke off her voodoo studies, spent months recovering and ordering her material, and eventually abandoned the island with the intention of wrapping up her writing in the United States.

The Martinican theorist of colonialism Frantz Fanon has explained zombies, leopard-men, ecstatic dance, and possession—one might add to the list the secret leagues described by Hurston—as part of the "magical superstructure that permeates native societies" and fulfills "certain well-defined functions in the dynamism of the libido."[29] Characteristic of the prepolitical consciousness of colonial societies, these ideological forms help sublimate or vent the frustration of the colonized. They integrate the native peoples in a history and a mythological universe distinctly their own, in traditions not controlled by the colonizer. Moreover, the stark horrors embodied by monsters and sects dwarf those represented by the settlers. The dominant culture (that of the invader or the powerful elite) is thus minimized; but this symbolic victory also saps the strength to resist it. "We," writes Fanon, mockingly impersonating the native, "no longer need to fight against them [the colonizers] since what counts is the frightening enemy created by myths. . . . Believe me, the zombies are more powerful than the settlers; and in consequence, the problem is no longer that of keeping oneself right with the colonial world and its barbed-wire entanglements, but of considering three times before urinating, spitting, or going out into the night" (56).

Following Fanon's clues, one could make a case for other interpretations of these phenomena. Most zombies reported by Hurston were "set to toiling ceaselessly in the banana fields," where they worked "ferociously and tirelessly without consciousness of [their] environment and conditions and without memory of [their] former state" (457, 459). In addition, they remained dumb unless fed salt. Silenced and exploited, they can be seen as the ghostly counterparts of the colonial subjects, extreme embodiments of their alienated citizenship. At the same time, zombies incarnate a form of popular, albeit ultimately complicit, resistance. The system of belief spun around them replicates, within native society, the division between exploiters and exploited that characterizes colonial or, as is the case with Haiti, neocolonial nations. Only this time, those subjugated in the larger picture can occasionally play at being subjugators by enslaving zombies at their will. A similar function could be attributed to the secret societies, analogs of the repressive forces (secret police, spies, and undercover agents) frequently responsible for clamping the (neo)colonial system in place. Their rule of terror is transferred from alien "others" (the colonizers, the local elites) to native "same" (the folks down under); thus the former are symbolically annihilated and displaced, and the latter deviously empowered. As Fanon pointed out, however, such empowerment is purchased at the cost of communal cohesion and solidarity. Only the project of decolonization, impelled by widespread political awareness, can bridge the rifts introduced in the colonized society by magic superstructures and mobilize their libidinal power for the common good (57, 59).

Fanon's ideas help to locate one of the most disturbing aspects of Hurston's account: the stark portrayal of the decomposition and fractiousness of a deprived neocolonial society at the mercy of imperialist powers and of its own internal divisions. In the words of one of Hurston's informants: "Our history has been unfortunate. First we were brought here to Haiti and enslaved. We suffered great cruelties under the French and even when they had been driven out, they left here certain traits of government that have been unfortunate for us. Thus having a nation continually disturbed by revolution and other features not helpful to advancement we have not been able to develop economically and culturally. These things being true, we have not been able to control certain bad elements" (482–83). This statement reveals that, as *Tell My Horse* demonstrates at every turn, the real tragedy of colonialism is that violence does not flow exclusively from the invader to the invaded; it tends to ricochet unpredictably and exponentially within the ranks of the subjugated, to the extent that, after a certain point, they become the custodians of their own dispossession and end up doing the job of the colonial police.

The confrontations so prominently pictured with regard to Haiti are not entirely new in Hurston's folk communities. In *Mules and Men* and, more often, in *Their Eyes Were Watching God,* the social unit is occasionally disturbed by tension and violence. In *Mules and Men,* the threat of violence rises most often because of jealousy and competition between women, competition for a male and, figuratively, for the control of enunciation and meaning—for the right to "signify" against a rival. But in these early works, commonality is restored by popular practice—by the recurring storytelling, playing-the-dozens, dancing, singing, joking, and feasting that mark moments of forgiveness and integration. At the end of *Mules and Men,* hoodoo also acts as a communal restorative, a means to regulate social life, apportion justice, and mend relationships. It restores the bonds of female solidarity largely thanks to the work of priestesses who help other women regain their status and dignity or take revenge on injurious lovers. Around the codes of "conjure," the community may heal; it may cease being prey, in Houston A. Baker Jr.'s words, "to random violence and disorderly rivalry."[30] Yet despite its salutary potential, conjure is still an aggressive, volatile practice that can kill and maim and "turn the trick back on the one who set it." This violent underside of conjure, which in *Mules and Men* is kept at bay, tends to dominate Hurston's description of Haitian cults. As a form of popular practice, it does not offer an "aesthetically purified version" of the local culture or the national character but an embattled combination of healing and death, at once cohesive and dissolving, integrating and disintegrating, and, overall, more destructive than constructive.

Modernist Ethnography—or Voodoo?

Perhaps because of its divisive, disintegrating potential, voodoo presents a problem of visibility and definition and generates a discourse rich in negatives. In *Mules and Men,* the narrator, "Zora," states that "nobody knows how [hoodoo] started. . . . Nobody knows for sure how many thousands in America are warmed by the fire of hoodoo." (176). The cult itself can be so intricate that "[n]obody can say where it begins and ends" (177). In *Tell My Horse* we are told that the *loa* are usually represented by images of Catholic saints, but "even the most illiterate peasant" knows that this is only an approximation, yet more faithful depictions are not proffered (377). The gods are too many and too varied to be fully known: "*No one* knows the name of every *loa* because every major section of Haiti has its own local variation" (377). They are associated through complex family trees that the popular imagination keeps in flux by inventing further relations of kinship among the members of the pantheon—relations that change from place to place. And the *loa* are prone to become linked to figures in other religious systems (especially to Catholic saints), to historical figures, and to particularly distinguished late *houngans* and *mambos,* so that each Haitian deity can be seen as a node in a proliferating network of associations. The difficulties of representation inherent in such plurality are compounded by the obstacles that priests and devotees place in the path of the researcher. Hurston's questions about Erzulie, for example, are only partly answered—"Nobody in Haiti told me who she was but told me what she was like and what she did" (383)—and the same happens when she tries to pry into the existence of secret societies, only this time, she is physically injured. As an object of research, voodoo presents considerable resistance; the paths to knowledge are circuitous, and proximity to the core of the cult brings about the threat of annihilation. The dangers of nearness are prefigured in *Mules and Men,* where, after several months of coexistence with her "informants," "Zora" comes close to being knifed by Lucy, a jealous local, in a barroom brawl. Such scenarios of danger thematize the impossibility of fully knowing one's object of inquiry, an impossibility that always haunts the ethnographic—or any epistemological—adventure.

As a result of these difficulties, what Hurston offers in *Tell My Horse* is perforce a partial version of voodoo: "This work does not pretend to give a full account of either voodoo or voodoo gods. It would require several volumes to attempt to cover completely the gods and Voodoo practices of one vicinity alone. Voodoo in Haiti has gathered about itself more detail of gods and rites than the Catholic church has in Rome" (397). Perhaps because it is aware of its incompleteness, the book moves in fits and starts; it oscillates from lavish profusion of detail to exasperatingly elliptical passages. Events are distanced from their explanation, or they are never explained at all—

like the Jean Valou, a dance that is mentioned and photographed but never glossed. "[T]he subject of poisons or poisonings [is] . . . too important to omit altogether," but rather than an interpretation of the phenomenon we are rushed through a number of poisoning methods that ends with the assurance that the topic has "an infinite sinister future" (518).

All this adds up to a hesitant, fragmentary—or modernist—way of writing about culture. Hurston's text sharply differs from the classical anthropological writing of her time in form and method. After hesitant beginnings, cultural anthropology was solidifying, in the late 1920s and early 1930s, into a legitimate academic discipline. Its central genre was the ethnography, whose goal was to provide as complete a picture as possible of the community under observation. Typically, the ethnographer selected an event, practice, or institution that brought into play a large number of cultural or semiotic codes and thus served as a point of entry into the study of an entire society. Margaret Mead saw the parent-child relationship as one such point of entry into the peculiarities of the Samoan social system; Bronislaw Malinowski regarded the regulation of sexual relations as the most resonant social arrangement among South Pacific peoples; Claude Levi-Strauss conferred particular importance to the kinship system; and Clifford Geertz studied the Balinese through the staging rituals and social relations established around cockfights.[31] The idea underlying this inevitable selectivity is that cultures are organic webs of meaning and action, so that any one point in the net naturally connects with all others. In James Clifford's words: "In the predominantly synecdochic-rhetorical stance of the new ethnography, parts were assumed to be microcosms or analogies for wholes."[32] For Hurston, however, voodoo, the central motif in her study of Haiti, does not allow the same sort of approach. It hardly constitutes an apprehensible entity, and it does not contain a picture of the totality *en abyme*. Around the cult of the *loa*, Haitian culture does not unfold as a structured whole but reveals its rifts and cracks as it comes apart at the seams.

At this point, we can perhaps begin to understand the peculiar brand of ethnography at work in *Tell My Horse*. Foregoing wholeness, closure, and transparency, Hurston's account embraces isolated intensities and highlights their opaqueness and irreducibility; it does not provide interpretation, the traditional ethnographic pursuit, but something else that, following the anthropologist Michael Taussig, we could call mimesis. Rather than explain what it all means, Hurston seems more intent on conveying how it feels. That may be the point of the detailed and, for the most part, surprisingly uncritical descriptions that fill her book: to transmit, for example, the excruciatingly formulaic nature of voodoo rituals, the rapture of the dance, the chilling deliberation of murder societies and poison makers, the gaps and hesitations in the research, the devastation and vacantness of the female zombie she meets and photographs in a hospital yard in broad daylight, and the shock she experiences as the body of a dead *houngan* suddenly sits up and opens its eyes. Writing about his own work, Taussig has explained this descriptive mode as the attempt to preserve the "graphicness," the particular feel, density, and texture, of the culture under study. The point, he claims, is "to penetrate the veil while retaining its hallucinatory quality," a task that begins at the uncertain border where holistic explanation founders and unruly details obtrude.[33]

For Hurston, this ethnographic mode did not start with *Tell My Horse,* although it may have climaxed there. It was already present in the early essays and in *Mules and Men,* all characterized by her reliance on narrative and anecdote over analysis and her occasional short-circuiting of interpretation. Her descriptions of hoodoo rites in *Mules and Men,* for example, are punctuated with deadpan descriptions of ghosts (they "feel hot and smell faintish" [213]) and with recommendations about how to handle them: "speak gently to them," and do not answer when they call (214). At a particularly grim ceremony intended to give her the power of invisibility she experiences unexpected hallucinations and "unearthly terrors," and in the end she knowingly professes ignorance: "Maybe I went off in a trance. Great beast-like creatures thundered up to the circle from all sides. Indescribable noises, sights, feelings. Death was at hand! . . . Many times I have thought and felt, but I always have to say the same thing. I don't know. I don't know" (208). Critics such as Dutton and Mikell read this rejection of standard anthropological protocol as a gender-coded resistance to the patriarchal authority of "papa Boas" and an attempt to carve a distinctive niche for women's perspectives in a field that was largely male-dominated. This attitude can be spotted as well in the work of Elsie Clews Parson, Margaret Mead, Ruth Benedict, and Gladys Reichard. Like Hurston, they were all Boas's disciples, students at Barnard and Columbia who dabbled in literature, straying from "straight" science into poetry and fiction. However, their ethnographic work has more in common with Boas's or Herskovits's than with Hurston's "mimetic" approach.

Hurston's fascination with the opaque, irreducible quality of cultural practice is close to a contemporary form of cultural anthropology that the anthropologists George Marcus and Michael Fisher label "modernist."[34]

This mode of cultural description contests the "realistic" conventions of classical ethnography, which assumed cultures to be fully intelligible totalities, and assumes instead that much of what matters in culture is fragmentary, incoherent, and ultimately undecidable, and the ethnographic account must accommodate this fact. Hurston's text foreshadows this methodological stance.[35] Following Ross Posnick's suggestions, one might attribute her openness to the open-ended and inconclusive to the influence of William James's pragmatism and Wilhelm Dilthey's historicism, two contemporary intellectual currents that met in Boas and in black intellectuals like DuBois and Locke.[36] Pragmatism and historicism defended the primacy of concrete experience over abstract ideas and the need for philosophy and cultural analysis to address particulars in context, rather than to try to establish universal standards of rationality and truth. In Boas, this led to a vexed relationship with systems of classification and universalizing explanations. He focused on the exception, the singular instance: "[T]he object of our study is the individual, not abstractions from the individual under observation." Historicism and pragmatism allow for the notion that "life" (as Dilthey puts it) is not fully rational—a suggestion that rhymes with Hurston's obsessive return to magic and religious phenomena.

Within its own historical moment, *Tell My Horse* is closely related to a rogue tradition of cultural critique that James Clifford calls "surrealist ethnography."[37] According to him, a peculiar kind of "negative ethnography" is at play in surrealist juxtapositions, collages, games, and "irrational analyses of objects." The point of these practices was not to clarify but to defamiliarize reality, to question received usages, and to point out the arbitrariness and contingency of all cultural forms, starting with those most seemingly natural: our own. In the late 1920s and early 1930s, this debunking impulse spilled into the nascent field of cultural anthropology through figures like Michel Leiris, Marcel Griaule, and Georges Bataille, who were active in the two camps. When applied to the analysis of "cultural otherness," as in Bataille's essays or in Michel Leiris's groundbreaking *L'Afrique fantôme* (1934), surrealism as a mode of cultural research yielded texts that avoided "the portrayal of cultures as organic wholes" and emphasized the strangeness and disorientation produced by what is alien.[38] Rather than the reduction of incongruities, these texts sought their proliferation. In them, anthropology is being born not as a discipline but as an *indiscipline,* a study in interrupted meanings, unsolved enigmas, social disintegration, and fear.

But is this surrealism or voodoo? There seems to be a deep structural affinity between Hurston's method and object, between her way of doing anthropology and the cult she researched. Something like this was suggested fifteen years later by the filmmaker and choreographer Maya Deren, who became interested in voodoo in the late 1940s and early 1950s and authored the volume *Divine Horsemen: The Living Gods of Haiti* (1953).[39] Just like Hurston, many of whose photographs illustrate *Tell My Horse,* Deren assembled a painstaking visual record of the voodoo rituals, posthumously assembled into a film by her husband, the musician Teiji Ito, and she was also initiated into the cult. The narrative of her initiation and her first-person descriptions of possession, much more restrained than Hurston's and coyly confined to the endnotes, accompany her ethnographic analysis. At the beginning of her book, Deren self-consciously justifies her incursion into the field despite her lack of academic credentials. As an artist, she felt well equipped to study a religion that was, above all, sensuous and was based on tactile qualities like rhythm, the direct experience of the *loa,* and the frenzy of the dance, rather than on cold dogma.

Recent anthropologists have confirmed Hurston's and Deren's perceptions. In an important study, *Mama Lola: A Vodou Priestess in Brooklyn,* Karen McCarthy Brown similarly underlines the concreteness of voodoo. It is less an abstract body of doctrine than a cast of humanized forces (the divinities), a practice of invocation and trance, and a therapeutic space for reflection and healing. The priests and priestesses Brown interviewed avoided engaging in formal discussions of their practice. They tended to answer by means of stories, anecdotes, and examples whose meaning is not always univocal. As a result, and perhaps due to a sort of epistemological contagion, Brown's book (much like Deren's and Hurston's) relies on storytelling, autobiography, and fiction as much as on traditional forms of interpretation. The work of the anthropologist comes close to that of the *houngans* or of the *loa* who speak through them. As Brown tells it, when called upon for help or consultation, the gods seldom give direct advice; they speak in "lean, enigmatic ways," in open-ended messages that must be completed by the addressee. "Through possession-performance, the spirits explore all the potentialities, constructive and destructive, in a given life situation. In this way they provide the images that allow [the believer] to reflect on problems and to make her own choices about the most appropriate and effective ways of dealing with them" (112). Images without comment, lean messages, unexplained anecdotes: again, more than ethnography, this seems a description of surrealist montage—or is it voodoo?

It is also an apt description of the work of photography: the automatic registration of the disorder of the world, the collection of particulars that do not always yield univocal sense—that often yield no sense at all. Is it a coincidence that *Tell My Horse* is abundantly illustrated with photographs, many taken by Hurston herself, rather than with drawings, as was the case with *Mules and Men?* Hurston's work has much less in common with the "orthodox" work of contemporary professional anthropologists than with an experimental text such as the film *Haiti,* also made in 1938 by Rudy Burkhardt, a Swiss-born filmmaker then residing in New York City who would later make a number of stylized city films. As an assistant to Joseph Cornell in the 1940s—they worked together on the films *Aviary, Legend for Fountains,* and *What Mozart Saw on Mulberry Street*—Burkhardt had some ties with New York surrealism. *Haiti* is a lyrical travelogue. Rather than a well-rounded view of its subject, the film purveys small, seemingly insignificant details: people on their way to the market, a group talking in the shadow of a tree, the bustle of the streets in Port-au-Prince, whitewashed facades, a cornice, a street sign. The soundtrack, featuring Erik Satie's famous *Gymnopédies,* gives the images a slightly oneiric quality. Two energetic dance scenes with diegetic drum music, possibly part of a voodoo ceremony, momentarily immerse the viewer in documentary immediacy, but the return to Satie's sound afterward restores the dreamy perspective sustained through most of the film. The point is not to "explain" Haiti but to re-create its fragments and convey the exhilarating strangeness of a foreign land. At the same time, the soundtrack and editing, containing mismatches and abrupt transitions, foreground the film's textuality—the fact that it is a constructed artifact—and therefore foreswear any claims to transparency and objectivity.

And we should not forget Hurston's own films, such as the ones she made during 1928 and 1929 around Eatonville. In their extant form, they appear as a number of unedited scenes portraying children at play, a christening in the river, a crowd milling around during a baseball game, even some Méliès-like trick shots. One scene is devoted to Kossula, "last of the Tikkoi slaves in America," on whom Hurston wrote an article for *Journal of Negro History.* (She mentions him again in *Tell My Horse* [514] and devotes several pages to him in *Dust Tracks on a Road* [707–11]). The white-haired gentleman steps out of his house, greets courteously, chops some wood, sits down, and smiles patiently at the camera. The most elaborate footage re-creates a porch scene, perhaps predictably, given the importance of this domestic setting in Hurston's fiction. It opens with long shots of a clapboard house seen through the foliage and then cuts to closer shots of two young women sitting on a swing and talking. These are spliced with takes of the floorboards, abandoned tools, a bucket, a pump, a close-up of feet next to a dog's paws.[40] With their intense re-creation of detail and their refusal to gloss, these film fragments embody Hurston's ethnographic method. In them, like in much of her writing, observation results in an open-ended visual text that captures the rich textures and imagistic quality of everyday life.

But we seem to have strayed far afield from the purportedly integrated communities of *Mules and Men* to the unreconciled ones in *Tell My Horse;* from Harlem to Parisian modernism; from black cultural nationalism to surrealist countercultural agitation. Have we really strayed that far? Recall that Hurston's early essays on black folklore appeared in Cunard's *Negro* anthology, a work that the historian Jane Marcus has placed at the crossroads of modernism and anthropology, and which contained a contribution by the surrealist poet René Crevel and a collective text by André Breton's group.[41] Indeed, the parallels between Hurston and the surrealists are considerable. Possession, one of Hurston's pet obsessions, also fascinated Leiris and Bataille and, in a way, was also explored by the members of the Breton group in séances, hypnoses, and *écriture automatique.* Mother Catherine, the cult leader Hurston describes in a section of "Characteristics of Negro Expression," is the Florida equivalent of the shamanic figures that recur in Leiris's African memoirs. She lives in a compound worthy of *facteur* Cheval, the protosurrealist figure revered by Breton's coterie: a mail carrier who assembled over the years a fantastic structure made up of randomly encountered odds and ends, which stood for them as the apotheosis of the *objet trouvé.* And Huston's fascination with (human) sacrifice and murder (as practiced by the Haitian secret societies, for example) also resonates with Bataille's interest in ritualized violence. But perhaps the most important parallel lies in their common conception of the everyday as an uncertain terrain pitted with enigmas and inconsistencies that may be registered but cannot be easily explained. (And, cautiously bracketed, here is a coincidence worthy of Salvador Dalí's paranoid-critical method: as Cunard was putting together the *Negro* anthology, between 1931 and 1933, she moved the Hours Press from a farmhouse in Réanville, on the outskirts of Paris, to a small shop at 15 Rue Guénégaud, just around the corner from the Gallerie Surrealiste on Rue Jacques Callot.[42]) Granted, the anthology is a motley affair, and copresence in a publication does not imply ideological concurrence. Still, the juxtaposition of Hurston's essays with surrealist work gestures toward the peculiar ethnographic mode of *Tell My Horse* and demands a series of remappings that I'd like to sketch out in conclusion.

In light of the preceding analysis, we should probably revise the received truth about Hurston: that she traded in authenticity and nostalgia; that she was bent on distilling an "essence of blackness"; and that her work showcases the restorative effect of the popular. Alongside these impulses, one can uncover the pull of a second set of ideas in her writing: her questioning of authenticity and "purity"; her relish in collage-like cultural activity; and her ambivalence about the popular, which she saw as an integrating and disintegrating practice. Ultimately, Hurston's folk communities are not seamless, unproblematic, and organic but plural, conflict-ridden, and unstable. From this perspective, the polemic that erupted between Hurston and Richard Wright after the publication of *Their Eyes Were Watching God* might be, on certain points, moot. Wright certainly exaggerated the extent to which Hurston simply reproduced minstrel stereotypes in her fiction; under a festive exterior, Huston's communities and characters have a tragic, fatalistic dimension that is more commonly associated with Wright's fiction. At the same time, showing that all communities are streaked with difference, Hurston refused to abide by the racial divisions that, in her view, like in that of other contemporaries like Locke, DuBois, and Toomer, drastically simplified the inexaustible complexity of African American life. In a well-known passage from *Dust Tracks on a Road,* she writes: "If you have received no clear cut impression of what the Negro in America is like, then you are in the same place with me. There is no *The Negro* here. Our lives are so diversified, internal attitudes so varied, appearances and capabilities so different, that there is no possible classification so catholic that it will cover us all" (733). For Ross Posnick, such a statement signals that, beginning with *Dust Tracks on a Road,* Hurston chose to short-circuit "the destructive dymanic of identity/difference that undergirds Jim Crow" and to inhabit "the unclassified residuum."[43] But the desire to be outside classification is a constant in Hurston's work; it becomes more noticeable in her later writing, in *Tell My Horse* and *Dust Tracks,* but it is already present in the early essay "How it Feels to Be Colored Me" (1928) and recurs in *Mules and Men.*

Contradictory and conflict-ridden, at times willfully "unauthentic" and syncretic, folk cultures in Hurston's writings are not necessarily the opposite of, or correctives for, modernity but operate in constant dialogue with it. As can be seen in her essays for Cunard's *Negro,* for example, Hurston stresses the easy passage between the folk and the modern, to the extent that the folk appears like untutored modernism and modernism incorporates the mimetic forms of peripheral traditions—folk culture being one of them. The hieroglyphic quality of the modern everyday that Vachel Lindsay attributed to the profusion of mass-mediated images Hurston discovered in black folk expression, where everything is "illustrated" and kinetic. The free circulation of the hieroglyphic makes it exceedingly difficult—not to say useless—to determine the exact borderline between folklore and modernity and suggests continuity between the two.

Hurston's combination of modernism and ethnography is part of a transatlantic, interdisciplinary dialogue about the peripheral cultures of modernity that ought to make us expand the usual frames of reference used to discuss her work. The French surrealists were important participants in this exchange; still others were surrealist-indebted Caribbean writers like Alejo Carpentier and Miguel Angel Asturias; the black Martinican Aimé Césaire; and the West Indian critic-historian C. L. R. James, to name a few. In Mexico, the modernist exploration of the peripheries was developed by the great painters of the 1930s, a roster that includes Miguel Covarrubias, who illustrated *Mules and Men,* wrote ethnographies, and researched popular art. In the United States, this exploration was furthered by 1940s journals like *View, Tiger's Eye, VVV,* and *Dyn* (which was published in Mexico but was well known in New York circles); by the mythopoetic painters of the war and postwar years (Adolph Gottlieb, Mark Rothko, or Jackson Pollock); by the novelist and documentarist James Agee (who still has to be reread as a surrealist ethnographer); by the African American dancer-ethnographer Katrina Dunham; and by the filmmaker-anthropologist-cultural theorist Maya Deren.

The interface of ethnography and modernism in these examples forces us to expand the usual scope of modernism, which, as James Clifford, George Marcus, Jane Marcus, and others have suggested, should perhaps be seen not only as an aesthetic but also as an epistemological mode characterized by multiperspectivism, relativism, fragmentation, and formal self-consciousness. For Hurston, and for many critics after her, modernist epistemology provided mobile, nuanced positions of enunciation from which to describe cultures in a nonreductive, nonessentialist fashion. Because of this, it may help us to interrupt certain forms of cultural globalization in the present. It may prompt us to question the tendency to promote universal cross-cultural translatability. This project is often justified, by thinkers such as Jürgen Habermas and Richard Rorty, by the need to establish a common ground for communication and understanding across difference, but it also ends up dissolving local peculiarities, integrating them into the larger metanarratives of modernity, not on their own terms but as one more choice in a sort of multicultural supermarket. We need, today more than ever, to rethink the imperialistic gesture of imagining others as ourselves—even as fully available to our inspection—and here is where Hurston may be a great help: with her awareness of an inassimilable element in culture, a sublime object that resists translation and epistemic closure, she still has much to teach us about perceiving difference without trying to reduce it to sameness.

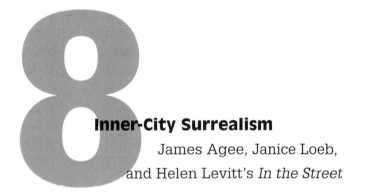

Inner-City Surrealism

James Agee, Janice Loeb, and Helen Levitt's *In the Street*

In the Street

Like Hurston's book on Haiti, the experimental film *In the Street* can be described as a modernist ethnography that, while seeking to document the real, overshoots its mark and ends up delivering the surreal.[1] Ostensibly a film about life in the streets of a poor neighborhood, it portrays an everyday dotted with opacity and ghostliness. It was a collaboration among the writer James Agee, the photographer Helen Levitt, and the painter Janice Loeb. Agee is usually credited for the scenario and Loeb and Levitt for most of the shooting; Loeb financed the production, and Levitt edited the film and was responsible for its visual style, which has numerous continuities with her photographs. It was shot in East Harlem and on New York's Lower East Side during 1945 and 1946 using hidden cameras and a right-angle view-finder, a device that allowed for unobtrusive filming and that had been used by Paul Strand for his pictures of street characters published in *Camera Work* in 1917 and, after him, by two of Levitt's main influences, Ben Shahn and Walker Evans. Levitt produced a preliminary version of the film in 1947, with the title *I Hate 104th Street* (the message of the chalk-scrawled graffito in the opening shot, later removed), and reedited it into its present form in 1952. At that time, a piano soundtrack composed by Arthur Kleiner, who played the accompaniment at silent film screenings at the Museum of Modern Art (MoMA), was added to the final cut. By this time, the filmmakers were relatively well known in New York intellectual circles. Agee, the oldest and most established of the three, had been on the payroll of Henry Luce's *Fortune* magazine for several years but was mostly known for the documentary book *Let Us Now Praise Famous Men* (1941), with photographs by Walker Evans, and for his film reviews for *Time* and *The Nation*. Levitt had shown her photographs at MoMA and enjoyed considerable esteem, and Loeb was a painter who often freelanced as a researcher for MoMA publications.[2]

The film opens with a statement of its main conceit: "The streets of the poor quarters of great cities are, above all, a theater and a battleground. There, unaware and unnoticed, every human being is a poet, a masker, a warrior, and a dancer, and in his innocent artistry he projects, against the turmoil of the street, an image of human existence." The images that follow illustrate this characterization of the street as stage and battlefield and record the spontaneous role-playing and inadvertent theatricals of daily life. In the course of the film, theatricality modulates into warfare as the antics of a group of children gradually turn into a humorous street fight.

The film weaves together a number of motifs that recur in no particular order or pattern. As Jan-Christopher Horak has pointed out, most of its images could function as stills, "with little syntactic connection to each other," and *In the Street* could be seen as a cinematic transposition of Levitt's photographs.[3] At the same time, there are few completely disconnected images or loose ends. Like a musical composition, the film has a structure of theme and variation. Almost every shot can be related to others that play a formal or thematic variation on it. The film opens with a boy on a bicycle threading his way around traffic, moving left to right. The next shot shows a baby in a stroller (another child on wheels); this time the vehicle is motionless, but passersby move in the same direction as the boy in the previous shot. And later on, there is a take of a car with a child riding on the rear bumper and moving in the same direction as the boy on the bike. The links between these shots are graphic and thematic. Other times, a thematic connection

In the Street. Production still.
Courtesy of Cecile Starr.

predominates. There are, for example, numerous shots of couples: children, teenagers, young adults, and adults. They play, flirt, or merely stand next to each other, glumly leaning against doorways and stoop railings. One of these couples, a man and a woman in their twenties, stroke each other in a way that recalls an early shot of two cats engaged in mutual licking. Three shots show as many different dressed-up women seemingly on the way to a date. One, a lithe black woman, appears easy-going and self-possessed as she strolls around trading banter with a neighbor who remains offscreen; the other two appear a little more stiff in their finery. The last one to appear is thick-set and overdressed in a thick fur collar on what seems like a warm, sunny day; she shifts uneasily inside her clothes, itchy and tight, fidgets with her gloves, then turns away and deftly picks her teeth, spontaneity eventually gaining the upper hand. These interrelated shots are never spliced together to form compact thematic blocks but are scattered throughout the film.

The main protagonists of the film are children, Levitt's dominant photographic interest at the time. They are seen mostly at play by an open hydrant, flitting about in Halloween masks and costumes, and engaged in a street

INNER-CITY SURREALISM

fight. The fight is the only narrative episode in the film, and the only one that evokes a relatively coherent chronology and spatiality. But even this episode is crosscut with unrelated shots and disseminated throughout the film. The children are first shown in a demolition site filling up stockings with what looks like chalk. Shortly afterward, they start hitting each other with this improvised weaponry, and the fight spreads quickly across the street. The scenes of the fight are intensely kinetic, with the camera giddily following the children's fluid movements. They are also somewhat oneiric due to the eerie clouds of white dust punctuating the blows and the incongruous juxtaposition of the dismal environment and the children's creativity and playfulness. Such effects are reminiscent of the famous dormitory pillow fight in Jean Vigo's *Zéro de conduit* (1932), another dreamlike sequence in which the feathers of a torn pillow fill the air like snowflakes while the children continue their scuffle. (Levitt saw this film in the late 1930s at a screening organized by the Film and Photo League and counted it among her favorites, and Agee reviewed it for *The Nation* in 1947.[4]) Like *Zéro, In the Street* contrasts the intoxicating energy of the children to the stiffness of dull, disapproving adults: an ill-humored woman chases some kids away from her stoop; a surly middle-aged man is seen scorning a group of boys; and, during the fight sequence, there are some cutaway shots of frowning onlookers. Yet unlike Vigo, who unambiguously celebrates the children's ability to disrupt the oppressive adult order, Agee, Loeb, and Levitt attach to their play some destructive overtones.

Due to its matter-of-fact recording of actuality, *In the Street* has often been described as a documentary. Siegfried Kracauer regarded it as an example of "imaginative" documentary, which he contrasts with the coolly factual *Housing Problems* (1935), a British film by Anthony Elton and Edgar Anstey advocating slum clearance and housing reform.[5] The underground filmmaker and critic Jonas Mekas considered Agee and Levitt's film the starting point for a realistic trend culminating in the 1960s cinema verité of the Maysles brothers, Don Pennebaker, and Ricky Leacock.[6] And Ken Kelman, a critic close to Mekas, regarded it as "the quintessential documentary" whose open-endedness makes it "literally credible and utterly immediate."[7] But *In the Street* is clearly more than straight reportage. In the only thorough assessment of Helen Levitt's filmmaking to date, Horak discusses *In the Street* as an avant-garde work that fuses Levitt's interests in children at play with a taste for the carnivalesque, yet he does not say much about what kind of avant-garde the film might be aligned with, nor about the scope of this label in the film's cultural context.[8] More specific in this respect, Manny Farber suggests its links with surrealism, and Sandra S. Phillips and Maria Hambourg document some of Levitt's connections with this form of cultural practice.[9] *In the Street* does have surrealist and documentary traits. Its surrealism is the result of taking documentary factualism at its word; or, differently put, it is the result of exploring popular practice (children at play) and everyday life (ordinary street interaction and city spaces) by means of an automatic recording device that does not discriminate between sense and nonsense, information and noise. Like most texts studied in this book, *In the Street* shows that automatic registration yields an undecidable real and that popular practice, even seemingly innocuous children's games, contains undertones of disintegration and fear.

The film also brings together a number of strands in American modernism already discussed in previous chapters: the fascination with urban spaces and street life, the use of ready-made materials ("found" people and scenes), an ethnographic interest in the quotidian, and a surrealist eye for discovering unsettling undertows in its midst. At the same time, the film summarizes many modernist attitudes toward mass culture. Like *Manhatta,* it is a throwback to the actualities of the nickelodeon era and confirms the avant-garde's indebtedness to early cinema. Like Charles Henri Ford and Parker Tyler, who chronicled the queer life of Greenwich Village in the early 1930s, Loeb, Levitt, and Agee are fascinated with the vitality of marginal urban groups—blacks, Hispanics, immigrants, the poor, and children—and like Hurston, they do not romanticize their spontaneous culture. In addition to looking back to earlier modernism, *In the Street* anticipates a number of attitudes toward the popular and the everyday arising after the late 1950s in Beat literature and visual culture, in pop and junk art, installations and assemblages, happenings and performance, and in the underground cinema. In this respect, it is a liminal work that stands between two phases of modernism (or, in a different terminology, between a receding modernism and an emerging postmodernism) and their different ways of conceptualizing vernacular culture and portraying everyday life.

Graffiti: "Button to Secret Passage"

In the Street appears at first sight to be a belated example of 1930s documentary expression. This was one of the dominant aesthetics of the decade, an aesthetic that, as William Stott has shown in his classic study, influenced movies, high and low literature, journalism in all media (including radio), painting, sociology, and even dance. For Stott, the vogue of documentaries reflected "the consummate need of the thirties' imagination . . . to get the texture of reality."[10] This meant recording the actual, postulating the continuity between aesthetics and public life, and mobilizing an analytical, exploratory dimension through art. The main motivation for this impulse was the pressure of the Depression. The crisis compelled artists to explore contemporary living conditions with the idea that if society were better known, its problems might be more easily solved.

Responsive to this cultural climate, Agee and Levitt embraced documentary expression early on in their careers. While they remained mostly independent from New Deal state agencies and Left political parties, the main promoters of documentary work in the decade, their sympathies were closer to Left radicalism than to government-sponsored reform. They refused to instrumentalize their work by aligning it with any particular ideology but still took for granted a certain degree of social responsibility on the part of the cultural producer. This attitude prompted them to avoid solipsistic aestheticism and to give testimony of inequality and conflict in their work. Hence, for all the disavowals invoked by critics of Levitt's work, who insist—as if it weren't a political claim—that her work be read on "merely" aesthetic terms, her pictures have obvious social resonances: they catch fleeting moments of grace under the pressure of poverty, against the background of derelict tenements, trashed sidewalks, and industrial landscapes.[11] In her choice of topics she is quite close to the committed photographers of the New York Film and Photo League, such as Arthur Leipzig, Aaron Siskind, and Ben Shahn, whose city scenes showed the lives of the most disenfranchised. She was actually associated with the league from the mid-1930s on. She attended league-sponsored screenings of foreign films, used the league's darkroom, and became friends with some league members, such as Willard Van Dyke, Sidney Meyers (also known as Robert Stebbins, a film reviewer for *New Theater*), Ben Marrow, and Leo Hurwitz. But she never became a member herself and remained detached from organized politics.[12]

Agee's trajectory reflects a similar tendency toward qualified engagement. He progressively turned from the lyrical poetry of his Harvard years (inspired by Hart Crane, T. S. Eliot, and the Elizabethans) to documentary prose in *Let Us Now Praise Famous Men*—an unclassifiable report on the lives of southern tenant farmers that he started in 1936 but did not publish until five years later. But he took pains to stay unaligned and to keep his engagement a philosophical attitude rather than a concrete political choice. Thus the book's epigraphs are the closing sentence from Marx and Engels's *Communist Manifesto* ("Workers of the world unite . . .") and some verses from *King Lear*. Still in the preface, the roster of "Persons and Places" includes, under the heading "unpaid agitators," William Blake, Céline, Jesus Christ, Ring Lardner, Sigmund Freud, and the blues musician Lonnie Johnson, none of them conventional revolutionaries by contemporary standards.[13] And in case there was any doubt about his independent stance, toward the end of the volume Agee includes his response to one of the questionnaires that the *Partisan Review* frequently circulated to poll intellectuals on culture and politics. Rather than answer, Agee largely questioned the questions and excoriated the "self assumed 'vanguard'" journal for being "as bad, or irrelevant to good work, as *The New Masses* or *The Saturday Review* or Clifton Fadiman or most of the parlor talkers or the publishers," effectively dismissing in one sentence the entire political spectrum from radical to moderately liberal and remaining proudly isolated, a critical voice on the outside (*LUS* 352). (Agee's replies were not published but were kindly returned to him by his friend Dwight Macdonald, one of the *Partisan* editors.)

In their choice of subject matter and in their perspective, Agee and Levitt were responsive to the tenor of contemporary American intellectual life but kept their distance from institutional allegiance. If the America that painters, photographers, filmmakers, commentators, reporters, and writers sought to document was populated by the unprivileged—in Stott's words, by "the worker, the poor, the jobless, the ethnic minorities, the farmer, the sharecropper, the Negro, the immigrant, the Indian, the oppressed, and the outlaw"[14] the protagonists of *In the Street,* who inhabit some of the poorest neighborhoods in New York City, are a likely addition to the list. Although the film was produced in the late 1940s and premiered in the early 1950s, its topic and feel of recorded actuality stem directly from the 1930s documentary tradition, but with a difference.

The film's ethnographic attention to popular culture—the children's games and ways of relating, their improvised Halloween masquerade, their playful fighting, their way of turning refuse into toys—also stems from 1930s documentary. An important part of documenting "the people" was in fact documenting their culture, an enterprise promoted from official quarters by New Deal agencies and governmental institutions. The Library of Congress, for example, under the direction of the writer Archibald MacLeish, one of Agee's senior colleagues at *Fortune,* created in the early 1930s a Recording Division devoted to accumulating a vast sound archive of popular music that was still being orally transmitted and, it was feared, might soon disappear under the onslaught of commercial culture. The folklorist Alan Lomax was its coordinator, main fieldworker, and ideologist. The Federal Writers Projects Guides series, which recorded the ethnic, social, and historical peculiarities of different regions across the country together with legends, traditions, and other oral lore, was equally concerned with the preservation of folk culture. Perhaps the most impressive accomplishment of the Work Projects Administration (WPA) in this field was the monumental Index of American Design. Coordinated by the cultural historian Constance Rourke, the author of *American Humor,* a pioneering study of popular literature, the index gathered over ten thousand paintings and illustrations of furniture, tools, clothes, household utensils, and architecture, among other crafts, which documented the variety of the popular decorative arts in America.

One witnesses in these developments the institutionalization of a shift from Culture to culture(s), from what in cultural studies has been called an Arnoldian, evaluative notion of culture ("the pursuit of perfection," "the best that has been thought and known") to an anthropological conception of culture as a whole way of life, a set of strategies for everyday practice and the articulation of its meanings (and opacities). This generalized shift and the heightened attention to the quotidian and to the folk culture it prompted were complexly overdetermined. They were not only the result of political strategy or cultural nationalism; another determining influence was what George W. Stocking Jr. calls the "ethnographic sensibility" of the 1920s and the contemporary consolidation of modern cultural anthropology.[15] Stocking points out that this sensibility was intimately tied to the rise of modernism, whose exploration of new modes of representation was frequently accompanied by the discovery of "primitive" and peripheral art. Among the protagonists of the first wave of modernism in the United States, the artists Marsden Hartley and Georgia O'Keeffe, for example, drew considerable inspiration from Native American design; the gallery owners Robert Coady, Alfred Stieglitz, and Marius de Zayas exhibited contemporary art together with oceanic and African sculptures and objects; and little magazines such as *The Soil* and *The Dial* customarily showcased new writing and painting along with ethnographic essays and exhibits. The interest in nonwestern art was, at bottom, motivated by the nostalgia for popular expressive forms integrated in the life of the collectivity—forms that could be upheld as alternatives to the isolationism and separateness of traditional high art in the West.

The search for alternatives to conventional art and the consequent fascination with non-Eurocentric otherness frequently contributed to an increased appreciation of the domestic vernaculars. The critic and novelist Waldo Frank was an exponent of this double interest during the 1910s and 1920s. A progressive cultural critic aligned with Van Wyck Brooks and Randolph Bourne, he wrote abundantly on what he called the "buried" cultures of North America, on Latin America, and Spain and was a sensitive observer of popular forms such as jazz. Other contemporaries driven by similar interests were William Carlos Williams, John Dos Passos, and Archibald MacLeish. And in the 1930s and early 1940s, as the *indigenista* Mexican muralists Diego Rivera and José Clemente Orozco worked and exerted a considerable influence in the United States, American artists, musicians, and ethnographers—Paul Strand, Zora Neale Hurston, Aaron Copland, Walker Evans, and Helen Levitt are some of them—traveled through South America and the Caribbean, often on Guggenheim Fellowships, documenting everyday life and studying popular practice. The experience of foreign travel and immersion may have prompted in many of them a desire to study the home site, paying renewed attention to neglected forms of domestic culture.

It is significant that before they produced their most personal, sophisticated art, Evans and Levitt, whose work was eminently concerned with the quotidian, immersed themselves in peripheral cultures. Evans traveled in the early 1930s to Tahiti and Cuba. Maria Hambourg and Sandra Phillips have suggested that his Cuban photographs of Havana street life, commissioned as a photo-essay to accompany Carleton Beals's political exposé of the tyrannical Machado regime, *The Crime of Cuba* (1933), opened Levitt's eyes to the aesthetic richness of unscripted city actualities. Levitt resided in Mexico City for a few months in the early 1940s and produced a record of its street life. Unlike Evans or Levitt, Agee did not spend much time outside the United States, yet he frequently masquerades in his writing as an ethnographer of the (un)familiar. He wrote an essay on Brooklyn, where he lived for long periods of his life, for a special issue of *Fortune* on New York City, and titled it "Southeast of the Island: Travel Notes."[16] In this way, he placed his extraordinary rendering of the quiet and slightly provincial ways of the borough under a heading redolent of faraway travel and exploration, and in addition, he appropriated the title of a short film Evans had made with footage taken during a stay in Tahiti (*Travel Notes*). In *Let Us Now Praise Famous Men*, he detected in the farmers' homemade clothes and utensils suggestions "of the orient or what is named the savage" (*LUS* 272), and elsewhere, he described

Levitt's photographs of children's games and street drawings as a "record of an ancient, primitive, transient, and immortal civilization."[17]

Against this ethnographic perspective, *In the Street* can be read as an instance of what Walter Benjamin calls "botanizing on the asphalt." The eminent pursuit of the nineteenth-century flaneur, it consisted in looking for exotic, unexpected moments in the inner city, or rather, in turning to the inner city the distancing gaze of the botanist or the anthropologist, intent on discerning the strange in the familiar and the familiar in the strange.[18] I use "strange" deliberately to designate a sort of excess present in *In the Street* but also in Agee's and Levitt's work at large. This is an excess they glimpsed in the popular scenes they wrote up and photographed, a quality that pulls their peculiar variants of ethnography and documentary not only toward the real but also toward the surreal.

For example, one of Levitt's earliest series, produced between the late 1930s and mid-1940s but not collected until several decades later, consists of pictures of chalk drawings and graffiti from the streets of East Harlem. She encountered these on her way to the public school where she taught art briefly in 1937 under a Federal Art Project initiative, and, captivated by their combination of naïve design and intense affect, she decided to study and photograph them. Levitt's interest in these forms of inscription was shared by other contemporary photographers like Arthur Leipzig, who also documented children's games and drawings for the Workers' Film and Photo League, and by Levitt's mentor Walker Evans, who projected, but never made, a similar series at the time. Her interest in graffiti also connects with Evans's fascination with vernacular design and found popular artifacts, a fascination to which she had been amply exposed, since by the time she started to photograph children's art she had already been working as Evans's assistant. She helped him prepare the prints for his 1938 MoMA show, "American Photographs," and for the companion book of the same title. Evans's book, like the show, was a testimonial to the involuntary artistry of found materials. The first two plates are homages to commercial photography: one of them shows the window of a photographer's storefront completely covered with penny portraits. Other plates reproduce posters and advertisements (of movies, minstrel shows, and merchandise), native architecture, store signs in a great variety of letterings, and interiors (a black barber shop, guest-house bedrooms, homeless shelters, and modest parlors). Similarly, his pictures for *Let Us Now Praise Famous Men* devote close attention to the farmers' material culture—their homes' interiors, heirlooms, object assortments used as decorations.[19] Evans's reproductions of these objects frequently emphasize texture and composition and avoid sentimentalism; they combine the formalism characteristic of his earliest work with the codes of ethnography or documentary. They stand as a point of reference for Levitt's own work, but others are important as well. The most important reference point is surrealism.

From its beginnings, surrealism championed marginal cultural expression, from the "primitive" art exhibited in the evocative Trocadero Museum, where the surrealists loved to lose themselves, to industrial objects (what Dalí called "the poetry of the useful-standardized"), to old-fashioned kitsch, to a vast array of "local aberrations" (Roger Cardinal's phrase) such as mediumistic expression and the art of children and the lunatic.[20] The two main retrospectives of surrealism held in New York in the 1930s—at the Julien Levy Gallery in 1932 and MoMA's "Fantastic Art, Dada, Surrealism" in 1936, for which Janice Loeb worked as a researcher—contained examples of unorthodox art. Neither show contained graffiti, but it seems that these inscriptions were of considerable interest to New York–based surrealists. In his autobiography, written in the mid-1970s, Levy bills himself as a pioneer in the study of graffiti and children's street art. He claims that in 1939, he and Matta Echaurren, a prominent painter in the New York surrealist group, roamed Greenwich Village, where they were living at the time, photographing and studying graffiti and later recognized in them one of Jean Dubuffet's main inspirations.[21] A picture of one of these drawings is reproduced in his memoirs. In addition, the photographer George Platt-Lynes, whose work was included in "Fantastic Art, Dada, Surrealism," was also interested in these anonymous inscriptions and had a wooden door in his studio where he encouraged visitors to write their own graffiti. Many of his private pictures of male models in the nude are taken against this defaced background, which suggests a public lavatory.[22]

Perhaps the best exponent of the surrealists' interest in graffiti is the article and the photographs that Brassaï published in the surrealist review *Minotaure* a few years before Levitt started photographing chalk messages and graffiti in East Harlem. His fascination was the result of a typically surrealist illumination triggered by the accidental discovery on the walls of a factory of a number of inscriptions and rough animal and human figures, among them a deeply scored heart with a date ("1928") scratched across. For him this modality of ephemeral "*art bâtard*" was deeply instinctive and obeyed a vital function like breathing or eating: it vented out the frenzy of unconscious desires. The same "anguish" and fear that guided the cave dwellers' hands in prehistoric times also drove the hands that marked the crumbling mortar of the factory walls. These coarse sketches overlaid a space governed by production and rationality with deeply rooted instinctual demands and were therefore a point of convergence of modernity and prehistory.[23] Levitt may have known this article, if not directly, perhaps thorough Loeb's research or through her friend Henri Cartier-Bresson, the French photographer who was affiliated with surrealism and became one of her formative influences. She met him in 1935 at Willard Van Dyke's studio during Cartier-Bresson's residency in New York, where he became involved with the Film and Photo League as a cinematographer and cameraman. He arrived in the United States after prolonged sojourns in Spain, Africa, and Mexico. Despite his association with the league and his obvious sympathies toward the underprivileged, his work could not simply be read as protest or social exposé. As was also the case with Levitt, even his most socially conscious images always have a strong undercurrent of oneiric lyricism.[24]

Brassaï's ideas could be used as an appropriate caption for Levitt's photographs. Rather than present the children's graffiti as detached ethnographic evidence, as is often the case in Arthur Leipzig's pictures, or in similar ones made by the filmmaker Maya Deren in the following decade, Levitt's snapshots tend to emphasize instead their instinctual force. While Leipzig, for example, showed the children at work drawing and lettering, Levitt preferred to show the finished product tightly framed and generally pulled out of context. In this fashion, they acquired a sense of urgency as they communicated inchoate but deeply felt longings and fears. Many of these chalk drawings show luminous, bucolic landscapes or smiling figures on board sailing ships; others depict figures kissing tightly or sexualized women, invariably smoking, with prominent bosoms; and others present violent scenes, gangster- and western-style shootouts presumably inspired by Hollywood films. As one of the photographed graffiti promises, they are a "button to [a] secret passage"—a passage to the children's unconscious.[25] These pictures became part of surrealist culture. The "secret passage" photograph, for example, was published in the first issue of *VVV*, the surrealist review edited by David Hare, André Breton, Max Ernst, and Marcel Duchamp, among others, during their New York exile in World War II. It accompanied an article by Roger Caillois on "the myth of secret treasures" in childhood. But more than with *VVV*, Levitt's and Agee's work and the film they made must be connected with the peculiar surrealism of *View*.[26]

"This Is All a Colon":

Agee was equally receptive to spontaneous, untutored cultural production, and, as is the case with Levitt, his perception of popular culture was influenced by the 1930s documentary-ethnographic vogue and by surrealism. Some of his journalism for *Fortune* dealt with cockfighting, the modern interior, "the American roadside," and holiday cruises (the last two were illustrated with photographs by Evans). In these articles Agee evidences an encyclopedic knowledge of the history, economics, and psychology of these popular formations, and perhaps because of this, he is never patronizing or dismissive. "The point that the satirist misses when he lampoons American folkways is that most folkways make sense," he warns in his essay on cockfighting. He also highlights the wanton unconventionality of popular practices. Roadside culture, for example, exists as the result of a manic desire for unimpeded movement that he regards as typically American and traces back to the 1920s, when motor vehicles became household possessions. And cockfighting owes its subterranean popularity, and above-ground notoriety, to the highly ritualized death trip it provides.[27] His application for a Guggenheim grant submitted in 1937 lists, among his plans for future work, the compilation and edition of a collection of found letters, another of found news items, newsreels (based, again, on existing material), a cabaret ("cheap drinks, hot jazz by record, and occasional performers"), collections and analyses of faces in news pictures ("the nearest word for such a study is anthropological"), a "true account of a jazz band" modeled after his "Alabama report," a collection entitled "City Streets. Hotel Rooms. Cities," and a history of the movies based on "exhaustive inventory." As is the case with Levitt's photographs of graffiti, Agee's interests coincide with the vogue of Americana promoted by the New Deal and the Popular Front, but they also sound close to a catalog of surrealist raves, particularly because of his intention to use found materials and his awareness of the unconventional, disorienting poetry embedded in them. Agee's fascination with found letters resonates, for example, with a wonderfully incongruous moment in Luis Buñuel and Salvador Dalí's *L'Age d'Or:* in the montage sequence of Rome streets that opens the second part of the film, there is a prolonged close-up of a handwritten missive taped on a storefront window detailing some obscure family business. And "City Streets. Hotel Rooms. Cities" reads as a compact summary of *Nadja, Paysan de Paris,* Joseph Cornell's art, or even of surrealism itself.[28]

In *Let Us Now Praise Famous Men,* Agee indulged at greater length in the surrealist charge of found popular materials. His record of the farmers' lifestyles contained extremely detailed descriptions of their houses, tools, clothes, and belongings. Like Evans did in his photographs, Agee delved into the way the farmers modified found objects—from clothes to store-bought ornaments to magazine illustrations—to suit their own purposes and to aestheticize their surroundings. These interventions expressed desires and fears, revealed an entire conception of the world, and bore testimony to the determination to survive and to wrench a measure of beauty from an inhospitable environment. In this respect, their objects, like their economics, leisure activities, style of relationships, and work, which Agee meticulously researched and detailed, might serve to typecast and "signify" them as a particular social group—cotton tenant farmers, a particularly disadvantaged sector of the rural proletariat.

The term for this kind of semiosis, which goes from the particular to the general and subsumes singular traces and scattered particulars under a label, is "naming." Naming consists in finding equivalents, or metaphorical substitutes, with the purpose of tabulating, classifying, and ordering reality. However, it has the unwanted effect of evacuating experience, since it postulates that meaning is always elsewhere: in abstractions, beyond the multitude of immediate particulars in which everything is given. "Naming" is precisely what conventional documentaries and ethnographies do: they sublate the material traces of reality into a label or a type. Agee resisted this kind of evacuation in his report and through the rest of his oeuvre. Instead of naming, of fixing the drift of the given into meaning, he pursued what the work of naming must cast aside: the irreducible singularities that jam the naming machinery and make (in this case) the farmers and their material culture not only an ethnographic "case" or an illustration of a sociological category but something unrepeatable and distinct. Addressing the farmers in his imagination, he wonders, "[E]ach of you is a creature which has never in all time existed before and which shall never in all time exist again and which is not quite like any other and which has the grand stature and natural warmth of every other and whose existence is all measured upon a still mad and incurable time; how am I to speak of you as 'tenant' 'farmers,' as 'representatives' of your 'class,' as social integers in a criminal economy, or as individuals, fathers, wives, sons, daughters, and as my friends and as I 'know' you?" (*LUS* 100). Similarly, in an extended section that attempts to describe George Gudger, one of the farmers Agee and Evans stayed with during their spell in Alabama, Agee is repeatedly confronted with the inability of abstractions—of language at large—to give an accurate account of the actual person in front of him: "George Gudger is a man, et cetera. But obviously, in the effort to tell of him (by example) as truthfully as I can I am limited. . . . I am confident of being able to get at a certain form of the truth about him, only if I am as faithful as possible to Gudger as I know him, to Gudger as, in his actual flesh and life . . . he is. But of course, this will only be a limited truth" (*LUS* 239). To tell "of him (by example) as truthfully as I can" is to dwell on the multiple singularities that accrue on him as an individual; to dissolve the person—or the thing, as the case may be—into an endless chain of circumstantial evidence: "A chain of truths did actually weave itself and run through: it is their texture that I want to represent, not betray, nor pretty up into art" (*LUS* 240).

Rather than the work of naming, Agee's writing pursued the work of the "colon"—after the comma, the most widely used punctuation mark in the text and the title of a central section devoted to metacommentary that attempts to explain why his project, "a book only by necessity," cannot come together as such. What I am calling "the work of the colon" is highly duplicitous. In the *Webster's* definition, the colon "directs attention to matter (list, explanation, or quotation) that follows." While it promises an endpoint of signification, the definitive statement that will rest the case, it often keeps the utterance adrift by excreting more explanatory material, making language double upon itself and turn into an endlessly self-generating mechanism. In a way, the colon proves, much like *Let Us Now Praise Famous Men* does, that naming is by definition incomplete and that observation never yields the comfort of orderly categories but, in Agee's words, "multitudes within each granular instant" (*LUS* 106). And much like the anatomical colon, it generates (linguistic) dirt, excreta, (semiotic) noise: mere matter indeed—asignifying, obtrusive, inert, so excessive that it must be flushed out of sight and made to disappear since its unwanted presence marks one of the limits of social life. But in Agee's report nothing is flushed; "waste" matter keeps piling up. The textures and the material density that envelop the farmers' existence keep goading Agee into overwhelmingly detailed digressions. Hence, on describing their homes, he reports at length on the grain of the wood in the walls, the scratches and erosions on the floorboards, the dust under the beds, the garbage shoved under the porch, the sweat stains and wrinkles in the clothing. This unmanageable proliferation, provoked by the fractal granulation of reality, is the result of taking literally the observational rhetoric of documentary and ethnography: "It is intended that this record and analysis be exhaustive, with no detail, however trivial it may seem, left untouched" (*LUS* xv). And later: "If I could do it I'd do no writing at all here. It would be photographs; the rest would be fragments of cloth, bits of cotton, lumps of earth, records of speech, pieces of wood and iron, phials of odor, plates of food and of excrement" (*LUS* 13). Because of statements like this, Miles Orvell has read the book as an exponent of "the modernist drive to produce [in William Carlos Williams's phrase] 'not realism but Reality itself.'"[29] But reality for Agee, as for most of the writers and artists I examine in this study, is not a solid foundation of fact but an inapprehensible horizon, the site of an always missed encounter. The closer one observes and listens, the more it all appears an unknowable accretion of mere substance. Early on in the book, Agee recommends that the reader listen to music ("Beethoven's Seventh Symphony or Schubert's C-Major Symphony") by turning up the volume as far as it will go and jamming the ear into the loudspeaker, until the recognizable consistency of the compositions disintegrates into vibration: "You won't hear it nicely. If it hurts, be glad of it" (*LUS* 15–16). The book itself ends up dissolving into noise; it closes with Evans and Agee intently listening to an undecipherable high-pitched animal sound in the night. It is precisely the attempt to capture the real in extreme close-up and with photographic precision that uncovers such instances of noise and entangles the report in the opaqueness of matter, in the haptical automatism of things. And it was one of the primary goals of surrealism to locate and amplify this irreducible quality of the material horizon. Hence, in the spirit of *Let Us Now Praise Famous Men*, I am further (unnecessarily?) complicating Agee by adding yet another label—another term after the colon—to his major work. There is no shortage of characterizations for it: for William Stott, it is an exponent of self-conscious documentary; for Miles Orvell and Peter Cosgrove, it is a modernist masterpiece; for Paula Rabinowitz, it is a postmodern text; for T. V. Reed, it is the predecessor of a "postmodern realism"; for Jean-Christopher Agnew, it is an antecedent of the contemporary crisis in anthropology; and for Michael Staub, it is a critique of 1930s ideals of objectivity.[30] To this list I would add that it is also a surrealist work along the lines of Breton's *Nadja* or Aragon's *Paris Peasant*.

How do Agee's colonic labors translate into the aesthetics of the film? If *In the Street* is deeply indebted to 1930s documentary expression, it is also quite different from it. Documentaries in the 1930s steered spectators to foreordained conclusions and messages.[31] While they used experimental devices like montage and collage and are best understood as a brand of political modernism, they were not conceived as open texts. The films of collectives like the Workers' Film and Photo League (*Bonus March, Scottsboro Demonstration*) and Frontier Films (*Heart of Spain, Return to Life*) presented unambiguously stated theses, partly through forceful visuals and partly through the use of self-assertive voice-over commentary. So important was the voiceover that for many contemporary critics, the spoken text and the visuals of such films as Pare Lorentz's popular documentary *The River* (1937)—in many ways a trendsetting film—were equally important and actually interchangeable.[32] By contrast, *In the Street* refuses to direct the viewers' attention. It forgoes the "voice of God" and gives spectators for all lead a rather poetic thesis at the outset and an atmospheric piano score in the soundtrack. Moreover, its editing patterns are fairly open and vague; they do not build up coherent space or time coordinates or univocal conceptual relations. Seen without context, the film tells little about its location and subjects, apart from the fact that they look poor and urban. It offers no information about the people portrayed or their reasons for being where they are. Such information was always clearly stated in 1930s documentary film and writing, whose main goal was to present common people's particulars. However, we are spared all such knowledge in *In the Street,* which presents without captioning and shows without telling.

Such elision has the effect of making characters and actions in the film at once near and distant: near because their presence is immediate and physical, unmediated through knowledge of their social and personal circumstances; and distant because, without such knowledge, they remain somewhat remote, obscurely perceived, as in a dream. Because of this double telescoping, characters are for the most part irreducible to anything but their screen presences, their physiques, and kinetics. The film thus eschews the stereotyping and sentimentalizing typical of much 1930s documentary work, where people are viewed in terms of wider social groups, as stand-ins for "the suffering proletariat," "the toiling farmer," or "the migrant field worker." As in Agee's written report, the text of *In the Street* refuses to gather a scattering of traces under a name, preferring instead to inhabit a dispersed plurality. This refusal to typecast promotes a certain thickening of the physicality and materiality of subjects and background. Unhinged from wider signifying frames, people and their milieus appear objectified, inert, a swelling of the real that is impervious to interpretation.

Inertness is especially visible in the vacant air of the film's adult subjects,

In the Street. Frame enlargement.
Courtesy of Anthology Film Archives.

emphasized by their seemingly meaningless (because decontextualized) gestures and in the dead time they inhabit. If the children are mostly seen at play, the adults are usually waiting: loitering, ambling, looking through windows, or sitting on stoops. Notice the transitional character of these locations: like colons, they separate and connect, promising finitude (a destination) but also postponement. Such a suspended state accentuates idiosyncrasies of body and behavior. While the film does show sympathy for those it portrays, it does not edit out the ugly or quirky in them. In fact, it seems to emphasize sagging bodies and coarse countenances in aging women and men. One can read under the film's sympathy, lyricism, and social awareness a muted fascination with the bizarre and the irreducibly odd in faces and gestures: a lame woman in a slightly pretentious broad-brimmed hat suddenly breaks into an unbalanced, precarious lope; a bulky old woman totters along on bowed legs, out with her dog for a walk; a much older woman, her face disfigured into bleary-eyed grotesque, stands before a gloomy facade. This perception extends to the streets themselves, where the children's creative play coexists with squalor and dereliction. Paradoxically, these are surpluses of actuality that make *In the Street* "too real," too unstable and uncertain in tone for the heavily typologized kind of reality conveyed by 1930s documentary conventions. Uncertainty, ambiguity, and a vaguely unnamable excess make the film a record of untutored popular expressiveness *and* a surrealist artifact, but according to Agee and to the native brand of surrealism espoused by the magazine *View,* these are one and the same thing.

Agee's Film Criticism, or the Real: A Pop (Anti-)Aesthetic

As Levitt's photographs implied and Agee's writing explicitly articulated, popular culture and surrealism frequently exceed conventional notions of reality and its representation. Or, differently put, the popular and the surreal contain an (anti-)aesthetic quality that Agee's film criticism frequently detected and intensified. What is this quality? Here are some hints.

In a review of Frank Capra's *Prelude to War,* the first installment of the Office of War Information series "Why We Fight," Agee praised the use of documentary footage taken by anonymous cameramen in the following terms: "There is an eye for the unprecedented powers which can reside in simple record photographs—the ferocious, inadvertent caricature, the moment when a street becomes tragic rather than a mere street, the intricate human and political evidence in unknown faces—which is here equaled only by the quiet dry-touched forcefulness with which such images are cut in" (*AF* 40). Watching *Screen Magazine,* a war documentary that included shots of daily life on a ship taken by the crew, he was drawn to "the frequent, intelligent use of an excellent device which ought to be recognized as basic to decent film grammar: the shot introduced and given its own pure power, for a few seconds—it ought often be minutes—without sound, music, explanation, or comment" (*AF* 79). The Hollywood production *The Seventh Cross* was "glossy lard" only cut by expert star performances and by a memorable frame: "[O]ne street shot of coarse legs in black cotton stockings, walking with casual peculiarity, has a suddenness, sadness, and individuality which should have taught those who made this film how to create and photograph a city" (*AF* 86). And on *A Tree Grows in Brooklyn,* he stated, "[M]y heart goes out to the people who reproduced the Brooklyn streets" (*AF* 142), but recommended further "submerging your actors in the real thing, full of its irreducible present tense and its unpredictable proliferations of energy and beauty" (*AF* 142)—the very qualities that *In the Street* sought to capture.

Judging from these quotations, what makes particular films, or moments in films, valuable to Agee is the extent to which they convey fragments of "unimagined existence" or of the "unimagined world." "Unimagined" here is analeptic and proleptic: it refers to the fact that they were not the result of purposeful design and that they cannot be anticipated or planned. They can only be recorded as found, in part because they outstrip the ability of existing symbolic systems to encode them. These cinematic moments, like the lives of the tenant farmers in *Let Us Now Praise Famous Men,* explode all attempts to "name" and typecast. What Agee celebrates in them is a realistic aesthetic of sorts, but one that differs sharply from traditional realism. If *Let Us Now Praise Famous Men* sought to formalize and clarify experience and to map in the process the social and historical forces underpinning it, the kind of realism that Agee promoted in his film criticism and that also characterizes Levitt's photographs and *In the Street* bears witness to everything unstable and inscrutable and implicitly exposes the inability of inherited representational codes to signify it. It shows that "reality" as such cannot be contained or explained; it signals obscurely, beckoning the interpreter but also blocking his or her gaze. That is why the only valid form of realism is murky, contradictory, incomplete, always only an approximation, and flawed (but here is precisely where it succeeds) by the inevitable failure to reduce the complexity of what is. (It is crucial not to remove the inexplicable, Agee admonished in his glowing review of *The Story of G.I. Joe* [*AF* 172]).

According to Agee, this kind of realism can only be found in the margins of cultural expression, high and low. Sanctioned mainstream culture does not challenge existing ideological and representational repertoires but tends to ratify them. Widespread circulation and acceptance of cultural artifacts, whatever their provenance, always entails the flattening of affect and the erasure of the most dangerous, antisocial implications. In this way, high culture may be turned into a parlor game and a source of merchandising ideas: "[P]eople hear Beethoven in concert halls, or over a bridge game, or to relax; Cézannes are hung on walls, reproduced in natural wood frames; van Gogh is the man who cut off his ear and whose yellows became recently popular in window decorations . . . Kafka is a fad; Blake is in the Modern Library; Freud is a Modern Library Giant" (*LUS* 14). This kind of dilution was the plight of Hollywood as well. As the movies tried to gain cultural legitimacy and to appeal to all social classes, everything risky, extreme, or unpredictable about them was eradicated. And as he detailed in his article "Pseudo Folk," written for the *Partisan Review* in 1944, the same had happened to jazz and folk music. Their commercial versions only supplied impoverished, if technically proficient, work: "the evocation, the third-remove sensuous hint, the exquisite sub-detail, the romantic actor's catch-in-the throat, the dying fall which the worst of such writers emphasize with dotdotdot" (*AF* 406).

Close to their sources on the social and geographical margins, high and popular art were still forceful, driven by an uncompromising sense of the complexity of emotion and experience and capable, as Agee puts it, of "embodiment and statement." Hence the "pure" jazz idiom could still be heard "in the back country South and on the best records by Mitchell's Christian Singers . . . in street bands and dives, now and then, and now and then for a moment on the 'race records' of little known and unknown musicians" (*AF* 405). This purity was absent from the work of established figures like Louis Armstrong, Duke Ellington, or Cab Calloway, even though it was still there in their first recordings and performances, before they became bestselling acts. On film, there are the liminal moments quoted earlier, scenes in which a few feet of stock footage, a face, a gesture, or a line of dialogue evoke depth and complexity and stand out from the general banality. Like the felicitous, intensely ambiguous scenes captured in *In the Street,* these moments are "found" rather than planned. They are less the good work of a director or a crew than the compound product of chance, an unprejudiced openness to the real, and the recording apparatus that preserves them. Like "most good photographs," Agee observed, they are "battles between the artist and luck, and the happiest victories for the artist are draws."[33] The fact that Agee conceives these moments as disconnected intensities that can hardly be sustained over an entire work also explains his affinities with Levitt, a "mini-cam" snapshot photographer, and the loose construction and deliberately minor format of *In the Street.* Larger formats betraying intellectual ambition are more easily appropriated—as art, for example—and at the same time, they hinder the quick notation from actuality that Agee and Levitt made the benchmark of their aesthetics. (Aesthetics, yes, but "above all else . . . do not think of it as Art" [*LUS* 15].) Besides, the fragments where reality appears in all its "cruel radiance" had to remain deliberately unhinged—remember those celebrated shots without "sound, music, explanation, or comment"—since clear-cut syntactic connection curtails their evocativeness and manipulates their inherent affect. That is why the film is so fragmentary. It almost feels like a collection of finds culled from a cinephile's memory bank, made up of moments that slip through the cracks, since commercial film—like commercial culture at large—tends to repress them in favor of artificial sets, conventional storytelling, and polished performance. One has to wait patiently for these instances of revelation.

Now Panic: View Magazine

Revelation of what? In part, of the inexhaustibility of experience, of the fact that "the unimagined world is itself an artist"—that is, a discourse generator—and "constantly brings to the surface its own signals and mysteries."[34] Only the signals are themselves mysterious, and their opacity is tinged with fear. Hence the moments where the world reveals itself obscurely to the eye hint at unplumbed depths of terror in quotidian objects and spaces. And, once more, it is the privilege of the camera to capture this quiet obduracy of the real. According to Agee, Alfred Hitchcock's *Spellbound,* for example, contains a haunting point-of-view shot: "In one crisis of mental dereliction, in which the camera flicks its eye forlornly around a bathroom, you get a little of the unlimited, cryptic terror which can reside in mere objects" (*AF* 104). In *Forty-Eight Hours,* a war film made in England by Alberto Cavalcanti, "As the audience watches from a hill, with the eyes at once of a helpless outsider, a masked invader, and a still innocent defender, a mere crossroads imparts qualities of pity and terror which, to be sure, it always has, but which seldom shows us except under titled circumstances" (*AF* 104). And Jean Renoir's *The Southerner,* about a Texan cotton farmer, contains an extraordinary re-creation of a small-town main street. "I have seldom, in a movie, seen the corner of a brick building look at once so lonely and so highly charged with sadness and fear" (*AF* 166).

For Agee, Levitt's pictures often convey a similar affect. He expatiates on this in an essay he wrote in 1946, near the end of the filming of *In the Street,* that was intended as an introduction to a compilation of Levitt's photographs of children. (The book, *A Way of Seeing,* was not published until 1966 and has been reedited several times since.) These photographs are a perfect counterpart to *In the Street,* since they re-create many of the same settings and motifs (children in Halloween costumes and at play; the contrast between the children's creativity and the adults' somber despair). In Agee's reading, Levitt's scenes communicate a strong undercurrent of dejection and fear. In one of them, for example, the spacing between two black children, one sitting on a doorstep, another standing on the edge of the sidewalk, arms crossed, slightly defiant, has "a quality of mystery—a strong undertone even, against the picture's brave and practical melancholy, of terror." In another, the conjunction of the "rifted asphalt," a burnt match, and a chalk drawing "testify to the silent cruelty of nature." Elsewhere, "a woman, crossing a street, can seem to beckon towards blind alleys of unthinkable sorrow and fright." These scenes generally exemplify that "there seems to be much about modern cities which of itself arouses in artists a sensitiveness, in particular, to the tensions and desolations of creatures in naked space."[35]

Such undertones of tension and desolation are present as well in the film. Over the funny sights and the children's good humor hovers a sense of threat as subtle as it is haunting. There is an early shot, one of the few that do not seem to connect with any other, where a man filmed from behind and slightly off frame stands at a street crossing wielding a bottle: is he drinking in peace, waving hello, or threatening someone? An old yenta interrupts her conversation and gestures admonitorily in the direction of the camera: has she discovered she is being filmed, or is she just asking a child to stop doing something? A young woman rests her hands on her beau's chest and smiles at him; as her face turns away from him, her expression changes into a mixture of deep worry and dread. These moments are passing disturbances on the surface of the film that make its tone uncertain and unsettling.

The children, the affective center of the film, are not exempt from this instability. Funny and playful as they are, they also appear aggressive and cruel. The fight with chalk-filled socks results from their overbrimming energy, but it is still a destructive burst, no matter how stylized. The tone of the fight shifts momentarily from the humorous to the tragic when a boy is hit in the eye and is shown lying on the ground, contracted with pain, and later crying, standing aside from the scuffle. The smooth transition from cooperative play to battle contradicts idealized views of childhood innocence and suggests as well that even among children—or especially among them?—a measure of violence always lurks under the surface, ready to pop up unannounced. Their Halloween costumes do not connote aggression, but they are still unsettling, partly because they introduce icons of death—memento mori such as skeletons and skulls—into their games. As many of the children seem Hispanic, this iconography may contain deliberate echoes of the Mexican Day of the Dead, a celebration that fascinated the surrealists and Sergei Eisenstein alike and that found its way into a famous sequence of Eisenstein's Mexican film. In any case, the death effigies and ghoulish masks make their games somewhat somber, akin to baroque allegories of human finitude. These masks also make the children somewhat opaque, and not only because their faces are covered; the masks suggest depths that adults are not used to seeing in children—like an easy rapport with death, whose iconography they wear as

In the Street. Production stills.
Courtesy of Cecile Starr.

naturally as they do their clothes. Because of this, the children infuse the urban landscape with a mixture of enchantment and fear. They also confirm an intermittent quality of the city in the film. While it is portrayed as a setting for neighborly interaction, it is also shadowy, quite close to the inner city as re-created at the time by film noir or by the surrealist magazine *View*. With *View*, Agee and Levitt also share their peculiar perception of popular expressiveness as a realm of creativity tinged with tragedy and death.

Published between 1940 and 1947, *View* was coedited by Charles Henri Ford and Parker Tyler. Both of them had been active in the literary scene since the late 1920s and had co-authored the novel *The Young and Evil* (1933), which combined experimental modernism with the camp idiom of gay street culture. Both editors claimed as *View*'s predecessors such surrealist periodicals as *Documents, Varieté, Verve, London Bulletin,* and especially the Parisian *Minotaure*, whose glossy format and luxurious advertisements it imitated. Since all of these journals disappeared with the onset of World War II, *View* presented itself as one of the last bastions of surrealism. It shared the stage of surrealist activity in New York with *VVV*, whose two only issues came out in 1944 and 1946. *VVV*, which imitated *View*'s name and design, was the European exiles' response to Ford and Tyler's publication. But despite initial rivalry, both journals ended up sharing contributors (Max Ernst, Eduard Roditi, Kurt Seligmann, Roger Caillois, and André Breton) and interests (mythology and magic, experimental writing, and nonwestern art and cultures). *View* was the more eclectic of the two, however, as it was more invested in untagged experimentation than in enforcing surrealist orthodoxy, as the Breton group was notorious for doing.[36]

View's disregard for any surrealist hard line can be seen in the way the journal romanced the world of high fashion only a few years after Dalí had been excommunicated from Breton's group ostensibly for doing exactly this. Cosmetics and fashion companies were *View*'s main sources of funding; their lavish full-page advertisements generated the revenue that kept the magazine afloat and gave it a peculiar combination of glamor, high living, and avant-gardism.[37] This combination was not entirely alien to the European avant-garde, since Man Ray had already worked as a photographer for Chanel and Helena Rubinstein in the 1930s, but it is particularly pronounced in the post-Depression United States. Its main causes were the expansion of the glossy magazine empire, led by Condé Nast publications, and the influence of these magazines' art directors. Many of them—Alexander Liberman at *Vogue* is perhaps the best-known example—had solid artistic credentials and sought the collaboration of some of the most advanced artists of the time, like George Platt-Lynes, Salvador Dalí, and Joseph Cornell. As a result, the borderline between experimentalism and commercial art became extremely thin in 1940s New York, as Dalí was designing shop windows for Saks Fifth Avenue, film sequences for Hollywood studios, and fabrics for Schiapparelli; Platt-Lynes and Man Ray were photographing Schiapparelli's and Adrian's gowns for *Vogue* and including some of these pictures in their art shows; Cornell designed fabrics at Traphagan Textiles, advertisements for *Vogue,* and collages for Hollywood studios; the former Film and Photo League radical Ben Shahn was becoming a major commercial illustrator (a young Andy Warhol faithfully imitated his style); and several designers launched couture and interior-decoration lines based on Mondrian's austere geometries or on Pollock's drips. In addition, the Museum of Modern Art periodically featured commercial design in shows like "Useful Objects under $5" (1938), "Color Prints under $10" (1939), and "Organic Design in Home Furnishings" (1940), set up in collaboration with department stores.[38]

Despite its ties to the high life, *View* was insistently devoted to "the death instincts," and for the journal's writers, illustrators, and editors, these cropped up with particular clarity in popular culture. Issues on vertigo, "Tropical Americana," "Americana Fantastica," and "The American Macabre," together with numerous articles on Hollywood films, amateur art, jazz, folk aesthetics, and even sports, characterized the popular as a realm of violence, grotesqueness, and despair. An exponent of these ideas is the special issue "Americana Fantastica." It opened with a short essay by Parker Tyler, who defined the fantastic as "the city of the irrational. The irrational plus architecture." Its sociological roots are "the imagination of the underprivileged aware of a fresh and overpowering strength. . . . The fantastic is the inalienable property of the untutored, the oppressed, the insane, the anarchic, and the amateur, at the moment when these feel the apocalyptic hug of contraries."[39] Among the examples of this aesthetic quoted by Tyler are the "the photographs of Harlem children by Helen Levitt," which he considered a conduit for unchronicled expressiveness rather than an authorial statement. The rest of the issue is taken up with somber bizarreries by a number of highly self-conscious professionals: found photographs and collages by George Platt-Lynes, a short story by Paul Bowles, and two albums (collections of texts, found illustrations, and collages) by Joseph Cornell: "The Glass Cage: Portrait of Berenice" and "Fantastic America, or the Land We Live In." The latter includes a picture by Helen Levitt, "Harlem Knight," which echoes some motifs from *In the Street*. It shows a masked boy drawing a toy sword in a derelict hallway, his demeanor at once wary and threatening.

Subsequent issues remained invested in "fantastic Americana" and published art by children—the "Children's Page" became a lasting feature—and amateurs. Some examples are the dense, minutely realistic drawings by Siegfried Reinhardt, a nineteen-year-old *"View* find" who was in the army; poems by Joe Massey, a convicted murderer serving time at the Ohio State Penitentiary; poems and short stories by Paul Childs, a porter and construction worker from Cleveland; a short story by Leo Poch, a miner from New Jersey, and another one by Joan Doleska, a housewife from Berwyn, Illinois, both gathered under the heading "Modern Folk"; and a number of anonymous, probably spurious pieces like "The Alienation of Language: Letters from a Corsican Boy to his English Sweetheart," in a passionate but slightly demented English. *View* also rescued past exponents of the popular-fantastic, such as the nineteenth-century American painter William Harnett or the "Comte de Permission," an illiterate sixteenth-century French shepherd-become-court-jester who dictated his prophecies and visions to the scribes of the court.[40]

Through all these examples of the untutored fantastic runs a streak of violence and morbidity. Massey's poems are intensely necrophiliac, and Poch's "The Watermelons" contains moments of unabashed sadism. But the apotheosis of the morbid is the special "Tropical Americana" issue guest-edited by Paul Bowles. His introduction, illustrated with a woodcut of a human sacrifice, states that tropical America "offers the tragic, ludicrous, violent, touching spectacle of a whole vast region still alive and kicking, as here it welcomes, there it resists the spread of so-called civilization." And because of this resistance, it is close to the spirit of the metropolitan avant-garde. The issue is largely a collection of found texts (their sources are scrupulously credited), pictures, and collages that frequently showcase the violence and grotesquerie that supposedly characterize everyday life in this vaguely defined region. A news story, for example, tells of a woman who, in an effort to get rid of her skin disease, had eaten a human heart every day for the last few years, while on the facing page, another chronicles the "horrendous crime" of Gabino Chan, who murdered his paralytic mother. An ethnographic text (avowedly from Bernard Flornoy's *Haut Amazone*) describes a gruesome head-shrinking ceremony in lush detail. And a report on the *chicleros* (rubber harvesters) expatiates on the sickly jungle environment where they are forced to live: "When one is in contact with this kind of nature, one feels the danger of physical degeneration and moral perversion." (A picture of a Cheiw chewing-gum packet, a side-product of the rubber industry, graces the bottom of the page.) The issue also includes a "scrapbook" with photographs and collages by Rudy Burkhardt, based on images taken during his stays in Haiti and Central America in the late 1930s.[41]

View's examples of the popular-fantastic seem intended to highlight a sinister underside of popular life and to contest the patriotic idealization of folk culture promoted in WPA projects like the Library of Congress's Recording Division, the Farm Security Administration photographs, or the guide series. As *View* presents it, the spontaneous art of amateurs warps the wrong way; instead of national essences and community spirit, it yields terror and death. In this respect, the journal resonates with Agee's *Let Us Now Praise Famous Men,* which frequently uncovers a "noir" streak in southern life. In his description of Bud Woods, one of the farmers with whom he became intimate during his stay in Alabama, Agee notes his "dimly criminal" face (*LUS* 89). When fantasizing about the dreams of Annie Mae, married to another farmer, George Gudger, Agee conjures up a nightmarish scene of domestic violence: "[S]he is dreaming now, with fear, of a shotgun: George has directed it upon her: and there is no trigger" (*LUS* 77). And all over the region, he finds "rare and inexpiable cities: New Orleans; Birmingham; whose facades stand naked in the metal light of their fear" (*LUS* 85). This tantalized stare at the frightening potential of folk culture, at what one might label a sort of "hick sublime," has a long history, and these texts make up merely one of its late moments. This history stretches back at least to the explosion of sensationalistic literature in the 1830s and 1840s; it is a salient ingredient in nineteenth-century frontier literature, from the almanacs and tall tales to classics by Mark Twain; and it still circulates nowadays under several guises, not the least popular of which is the contemporary horror film. Think, to name only a few, of *The Texas Chainsaw Massacre, Friday the Thirteenth, Kalifornia, The Blair Witch Project,* or *Wendigo,* where rural communities appear as theaters of horror.

As reported in *View,* inner-city life is similarly sinister. For example, Eduard Roditi's "California Chronicle" offers a demystifying view of a state run amok with vigilantism, virulent xenophobia, fanatic conservatism, and urban poverty: "In Los Angeles one faces the facts: the garish illusions and conflicting ideas which give our age its neurotic drive. . . . Los Angeles poverty is more sordid than the slumlife of any other city except Shanghai." And further, "The notion has got around, amongst vigilantes in Modesto,

Visalia, Salinas, Ukiah, and elsewhere, that all immigrants from the dust-bowl are undesirable aliens, that all aliens are homosexual, that all homosexuals are Jews, that all Jews are nazis, that all nazis are communists, and that all communists are dangerous drivers. So drive slowly if you come to California." Published in the same issue, Troy Garrison's "Plaza of the Psycophathic Angels" reinforces Roditi's dystopian perception of Los Angeles. His description of a park at the intersection of several old Los Angeles neighborhoods renders the glamor mecca as a capital of the grotesque. "The southward tides of traffic and pedestrians move past rotted ancient structures whose windows reflect no light, past what must be the oldest cafe (where an Arab serves fairly good Mexican food at very reasonable prices) and, some five or six blocks away, flow through the backwash of 'B-girl' cafes, burlesques, pawnshops, and human wreckage." Around the square, a number of demented soapbox preachers hold forth. And a similar sensibility informs "That Secret Look," by Brion Gysin, who would later become William Burroughs's cut-up collaborator, only this time the setting is a hallucinatory New York: "The streets below are like the stream of 'The Old Mill' or 'The Tunnel of Love' at Luna Park or Coney Island through whose fog of carbon monoxide you are swept clutching your neighbor, past bright tableaux; the desert island, the cemetery by moonlight, the axe murderer in the kitchen or famous scenes from fiction."[42]

These descriptions are examples of what, in the 1960s, the French situationists retrospectively labeled "psychogeography": an extremely subjective habitation of urban places that consists in traversing the city in search of spaces that trigger unfamiliar feelings and associations. Psychogeographical research saw the city as a spatialized unconscious, a vast *combinatoire* endlessly generating coincidences, surprising juxtapositions, and intimations of eroticism and death. The direct antecedent of situationist psychogeography was French surrealism. Works such as André Breton's *Nadja* and *L'amour fou,* or Louis Aragon's *Paysan de Paris,* show that the surrealists rejected official, monumental Paris and dwelled instead in a subterranean city composed of disorienting constructions and spaces, such as "the very handsome and very useless Porte Saint-Denis";[43] dated locations such as the Passage de l'Opera; macabre ones such as the slaughterhouses at La Villette; wildly heterogeneous settings like the flea markets or a shanty town called the Zone; or indefinite locations like *banlieue,* "the fringe," Aragon writes, "where, in our opinion, freedom and secrecy had the best chance of flourishing—that is to say, along the stretches of that great equivocal suburb that rings Paris, the setting for those supremely disconcerting scenes in French serial stories and films in which a special kind of drama takes shape."[44] The surrealists studied these locations with the hovering attention of the analyst, pursuing and amplifying details that intimated irrational, unaccustomed latencies. These pockets of the city were especially suggestive because they were difficult to read; they were incongruous composites of, for example, old and new, nature and technology, the trivial and the horrific, the familiar and the unknown. This indeterminacy often yielded an undertone of fear—a quality that Walter Benjamin caught perfectly when he wrote that the photographer Eugène Atget, who was not a surrealist but whose pictures were frequently featured in surrealist periodicals, photographed cityscapes as if they had been the scenes of a crime. Much like Atget, the surrealists read the city as if it were pregnant with either the memory or the premonition of tragedy; it was seen as a terrain that leaned toward some sort of undoing, the key to which was in the past (in the murder just committed) or in the future (the one about to happen).

A similarly defamiliarized perception of the city was present in 1940s film noir, a genre contemporary with *View* and, as James Naremore has brilliantly shown, intimately connected with surrealism.[45] John Huston's film *The Maltese Falcon* (1941), often taken as the "first" title of the genre, premiered shortly after *View,* and Parker Tyler published an essay on the film—"Every Man His Own Private Detective"—in an early issue.[46] Film noir unfolds in a deceptive space where everyday appearances hide an underworld of corruption and violence. The existence of this underside has a peculiarly enchanting effect. Through its influence, the modern city seems no longer a scenario of standardization and rationality; it becomes tinged with tragedy and heroism as the possible setting for an unnerving discovery, a decisive coup, or a murder. This noir sensibility was not exclusive to 1940s film. It also appears in contemporary pulp fiction (by Cornel Woolrich and Mickey Spillane) and "hard-boiled" photography (think of Weegee's famous book *Naked City*), and it certainly impregnates as well Levitt's images, Agee's ethnography, and, in a slightly more muted manner, *In the Street,* whose indeterminate tone hovers between the cuteness of the children and the doomed quality of the adults; between the exhilaration and the violence of the street games.

The noir and surreal qualities of *In the Street* are also heightened by the film's ambiguous treatment of class. *In the Street,* like *View,* revisits some of the motifs and protagonists of 1930s proletarian art without resorting to the abstractions ("the people," "the proletariat") that traditionally gave this social stratum a historical meaning. The creators of *In the Street* avoided such abstractions because they refused to simplify and typecast their "subjects" and preferred to let them exist independently of the partisan interests that drove much cultural production at that time. Yet in the context of the late 1940s and early 1950s, when the film was made and first shown, a working class without class politics was a symptom of the erosion and eventual disappearance of the Left under the compound pressures of the cold war and McCarthyism; and it was equally symptomatic of the avowed emergence of a "consensus" society where leftist categories were presumed obsolete. From this perspective, the individuals who people *In the Street* are a bit like zombies, occupying a realm between two lives: dead to the rhetoric of an earlier time but not yet born into a new one. They are a message whose meaning is at once forgotten *and* not yet cracked, and because of this, they are fairly illegible: empty ciphers easily filled by uncertainty and fear. This fear is the fear of ghosts—another name for the memory of trauma, for what is excluded from symbolic articulation and (therefore) returns in the real in hallucinatory form. I am not suggesting that the film is deranged (it is not), only that the gap that repression creates in the contemporary repertoire of socially expressive forms has a way of letting in the "unimagined existence" of real people in the form of an unreadable excess, a sublime insistence that distorts the surface of *In the Street* and obtrudes in the dejected countenances, the unfathomable gaping doors and shadowed windows, the playful yet threatening games of the children, in the closing shot of two spectral women encased in dark coats, heads veiled, toiling uphill toward an immense grey emptiness.

Aftermaths

In the Street outlines the scene of a historical eviction but also clears the ground into which most experimental art would subsequently move. Starting in the late 1950s, Beat literature, underground film, junk and assemblage art, happenings, and minimalist dance similarly embraced the landscapes and culture of the inner city. "The streets of the poor quarters of great cities" were the milieu of Jack Kerouac's and William Burroughs's fiction and of Allen Ginsberg's poetry. Their writing reported the unchronicled life of an unassimilated urban proletariat made up of hipsters, hobos, migrant workers, queers, petty criminals, and bohemians. A similar cast populated the contemporary underground cinema: Andy Warhol's Factory films, Kenneth Anger's *Scorpio Rising,* Ron Rice's *The Flower Thief,* and Jack Smith's *Flaming Creatures,* to name a few titles. Beat and underground "deviance"—to use the sociological parlance of the period—was more deliberate and theatrical than the otherness of the urban dwellers of *In the Street*. It did not arise from being stranded in the sidelines of history, orphaned by the rhetoric of the times, but from the active rejection of normality.

In a different manner, the unofficial city of *In the Street* reappeared in the work of a number of young artists living in Lower Manhattan in the late 1950s—artists like Jim Dine, Allan Kaprow, Red Grooms, and Claes Oldenburg. They built installations and environments out of materials scavenged in the streets and showed their work in alternative, nonprofit exhibition spaces, such as the basement of the Judson Church on Washington Square or Grooms's home-studio-exhibition space on Delancey Street. Simultaneously, a number of dance theorists and performers, such as Trisha Brown, Yvonne Rainer, and Merce Cunningham, started to reject the dramatic, introspective vocabulary of modernism and to incorporate everyday gestures and tasks (walking, running, sitting down, and getting up) into their choreographies. As they explored the untapped expressiveness of quotidian movement, they were following in the steps of the creators of *In the Street,* who had framed children's games and movements as spontaneous dance.

In what became a widely accepted interpretation, the artist Allan Kaprow saw this new avant-garde as the extension of the gestural idiom of abstract expressionism—more specifically, the idiom of Jackson Pollock, with its use of chance and randomness—into object manipulation in three-dimensional space.[47] At the same time, since the new art incorporated quotidian materials and objects and drew on vernacular expressiveness, its genealogy should also include 1930s documentarism and proletarian aesthetics, surrealism, Walker Evans's and Helen Levitt's photographs, and James Agee's exploration of the inexhaustibility of matter. The experimenters of the new generation shared with the makers of *In the Street* the conviction that uncharted recesses of the everyday were the last repositories of expressiveness and originality in the exhaustively administered, technocratic society of the cold-war era. And they also shared the submission to their materials. Found "objects" (in the broadest sense of the word as anything detachable, discrete, or portable) were the foundation of their aesthetics. In Kaprow's words: "Objects of every sort are materials for the new art: paint, chairs, food, electric and neon lights, smoke, water, old socks, a dog, movies," even "the vastness of Forty-Second Street" (25–26). Rather than create, this "new art" sought to capture and transpose pieces of the actual with a minimum of tampering, in the belief, shared equally by the two main ideologues of this avant-garde constellation,

Jack Kerouac and John Cage, that reality itself is, as Agee had already proposed, "its own artist," and one merely needs to stop and watch—or listen. Watching and listening, however, do not imply understanding or, even less, the ability to chart reality down to its ultimate details. Another important element that connects *In the Street* with Kaprow's generation, as well as with earlier forms of cultural production, from Lindsay to Hurston, is the attentiveness to an unconscious of the quotidian—an uncontrollable automatism that turns the everyday into a repository of vaguely intuited possibilities for discovery and transformation. As Kaprow puts it: "Not only will these bold creators show us, as if for the first time, the world we have always had about us, but ignored, but they will disclose entirely unheard of happenings and events, found in garbage cans, police files, hotel lobbies, seen in store windows and on the streets, and sensed in dreams and horrible accidents" (26).

Kaprow's words, written in 1958 and intended as a call for the art of the future, might also be read as a retrospective manifesto for the modernist formations that I have been tracing in these pages. As Kaprow draws attention to slightly defamiliarized, commonplace objects, his words recall Lindsay's and Cornell's awareness of the subterranean latencies of things. His appeal to "the vastness of Forty-Second Street" and to events glimpsed about the city resonates with *In the Street* and *Manhatta*. Dos Passos's *USA* offers stories that might have been dug up from police files (on labor agitators and vagrants) or from yesterday's newspapers (the source of most of his Newsreels). The fact that these materials seem to Kaprow pervaded with mystery is contiguous with the emphasis that early twentieth-century modernists placed on noise—the unreadable contingencies that punctuate the everyday. And finally, although Kaprow did not relate the neglected materiality he championed to nonaligned—we might call them "queer"—identities, the Beats and underground filmmakers did. In their work, material dereliction, the disused spaces of the inner city, and marginal identities came together in an antinormative front that replayed, in some ways, the queer modernism of Ford and Tyler's *The Young and Evil*. It is no coincidence that Ford and Tyler experienced a revival of sorts in the 1960s, Ford as an occasional filmmaker and general *animateur* in New York's underground circles, and Tyler as one of the most prominent film critics of the time.

These concerns do not only link early twentieth-century modernism with the 1960s neo-avant-gardes; they also flow into the present, when art still obsessively revolves around the "thingness" of things, city spaces, and (social, sexual) non-normativity with the intention of reshaping quotidian perceptions. The sculptures of Rachel Whiteread, who casts everyday objects such as chairs, sinks, bathtubs, and even entire houses in rubber and resin; the objects of Gabriel Orozco and Jimmie Durham, and, in my own country, of Txomín Badiola or Eulalia Valldosera, reexamine and defamiliarize common things in ways that evoke examples discussed earlier. The fascination with the street as a sign generator and purveyor of opaque occurrences recurs in Chantal Akerman's video installations and films. The conception of the street as a stage, central to Helen Levitt, is revisited by the many artists who set their actions and images in the midst of the urban flow, and by the subcultural formations—from break-dancers to graffiti artists to skateboarders—who reinvent the metropolitan environment just as Levitt's children did. Found personalities and radical lifestyles are the central subject of the photographers Nan Goldin, Del LaGrace Volcano, and Cathie Opie, just as they held the floor in Ford and Tyler's pioneer novel and in Hurston's book on Haiti. And noise of the kind I have been amplifying in these pages has become a newly valued material with the emergence of "sound art." It is the main ingredient in the oeuvre of Christian Marclay, a gallery artist; but it also thrives in popular music, as electronica and rap abundantly incorporate all sorts of aural detritus. In this manner, the early twentieth-century experiments of George Antheil, Luigi Russolo, and Edgar Varèse in music have gone pop and now shake the dance floors. In a wider sense, noise—as opaque residue impregnable to sense—is a much wider issue. It may be one of the defining characteristics of contemporary art, which embraces the unsignifying in a variety of ways: by emphasizing texture and matter over concept, by rejecting completion and absolute formalization, by showcasing partial perspectives, and by insistently representing otherness.

Common to all these recent artistic manifestations—and another thematic link between them and early modernism—is the concern with the everyday as a realm that is familiar yet ultimately unknown, pervaded by modalities of difference and transformative forces that we are still trying to plumb. The insistence on the everyday has the character of the unsolved—the symptom that keeps recurring until it is untied by interpretation. The everyday is, after all, a fraught terrain; it is where we make ourselves at home in the world, where the political becomes personal, ideologies are adapted to individual conditions, and where wide-ranging, global changes percolate into the here and now. It is, at the same time, an elusive horizon, always in motion, and therefore difficult to map—a constant source of disturbance and instability. As a realm of contingency and singularity in a maximally rationalized modernity, it is where systemic imperatives jam against the intricacy of lived experience. Despite (or because of?) these complexities, the quotidian has often been neglected by traditional politics—what some thinkers have called macropolitics, the politics of national interests and class destinies, of ascertainable historical actors and spectacular macro-events. But it has always figured prominently in art.

It seems that critics and historians have only recently begun to recover art as a set of instructions for exploring and reinventing the quotidian. The examples were ubiquitous in experimental art, but it has taken a long time to begin to decipher them. For years, scholars had (in Benjamin's terms) a historical rather than a political attitude toward modernism and the avant garde, reading them through the kinds of concepts routinely applied to traditional art, but attitudes have started to shift in recent decades. There are several reasons for this. Macropolitics has been undergoing an unprecedented crisis of legitimation since at least May 1968. Situated critiques like feminism, queer theory, and postcolonial and ethnic discourses have shown that culture is far from a universal standard of excellence untainted by political interest; it has often been an alibi for exclusion and inequality. In addition, the so-called new social movements that gained momentum since the 1960s have placed on the map issues like the environment, sexuality, gender and ethnic identities, the effect of the media, and the management of public space. They have brought minute and polemical attention to the micropolitical—the material, bodily, and spatial components of our lives—and have forced a reconsideration of "art" as an *art de faire:* a plurality of strategies for practicing and inhabiting the immediate.[48]

This conception of art—although this is no longer art in any conventional sense—has a long genealogy, and one of my purposes in writing this book has been to excavate some of its significant moments. Along the way, I have tried to recast somewhat the image of modernism and to connect recent forms of cultural practice with analogous ones in the early decades of the twentieth century. It seems important to me not to cut our present off from these modernist antecedents. From its beginnings, modernism tried to make good the promise of a better life contained in the objects, spaces, and images of modernity, in noise, and in the energies of unassimilated others. It contested regimentation and depletion and acted out the modes of difference intermittently enabled by the electronic media, by peripheral traditions, and by the contours of everyday life. Because of this, we can only forget it at our own risk; the forces it sought to counter have certainly not forgotten us.

INNER-CITY SURREALISM

Notes

Introduction

1. For an influential differentiation between modernism and postmodernism on the basis of their attitude to mass culture, see Andreas Huyssen, *After the Great Divide: Modernism, Mass Culture, Postmodernism* (Bloomington: Indiana University Press, 1986), vi–xii, 178–221.

2. The most rigorous attempt to differentiate between modernism and the avant-garde is Peter Bürger, *Theory of the Avant-Garde,* trans. Peter Shaw (Minneapolis: University of Minnesota Press, 1984). While there are important reasons to make this distinction, I have come to think that the overlaps between modernism and the avant-garde are more important than the differences. The attempt to dissolve the art institution and the desire to merge art and everyday life, which according to Bürger are the driving motivations of the historical avant-gardes, also crop up in modernism (Vachel Lindsay and Ezra Pound are two examples). And conversely, the institutional investment normally associated with modernism occasionally crops up in the avant-garde, which then resorts to a rhetoric of "art for art's sake" and aesthetic ineffability. Because of this, I have chosen to use "modernism" as an encompassing label that ranges from the radical, materialist avant-gardism of John Dos Passos and James Agee to the more institutional, idealist experimentalism of Lindsay and T. S. Eliot.

3. One of the most recent results of this rereading of modernism is the journal *Modernism/Modernity.* Some other important titles in "postmodern" modernist

studies include Marshall Berman, *All That Is Solid Melts into Air: The Experience of Modernity* (London: Verso, 1982); Warren Susman, *Culture as History: The Transformation of American Culture in the Twentieth Century* (New York: Pantheon, 1984); Shari Benstock, *Women of the Left Bank, Paris, 1900–1940* (Austin: University of Texas Press, 1986); Houston A. Baker Jr., *Modernism and the Harlem Renaissance* (Chicago: University of Chicago Press, 1987); Cary Nelson, *Repression and Recovery: Modern American Poetry and the Politics of Cultural Memory* (Madison: University of Wisconsin Press, 1989); Bonnie Kime Scott, ed., *The Gender of Modernism* (Bloomington: Indiana University Press, 1992); Walter Kalaidjian, *American Culture between the Wars* (New York: Columbia University Press, 1994); Ann Douglas, *Terrible Honesty: Mongrel Manhattan in the 1920s* (New York: Farrar, Straus and Giroux, 1995); Dickran Tashjian, *Skyscraper Primitives: Dada and the American Avant-Garde* (Middletown, Conn: Wesleyan University Press, 1975); Dickran Tashjian, *A Boatload of Madmen: A History of Surrealism in the United States, 1920–1950* (New York: Thames and Hudson, 1995); Cecelia Ticchi, *Shifting Gears: Technology, Literature, and Culture in Modernist America* (Chapel Hill: University of North Carolina Press, 1987); Peter Wollen, *Raiding the Icebox: Reflections on Twentieth-Century Culture* (Bloomington: Indiana University Press, 1993); Michael North, *The Dialect of Modernism: Race, Language, and Twentieth-Century Literature* (New York: Oxford University Press, 1994); Rita Felski, *The Gender of Modernity* (Cambridge, Mass.: Harvard University Press, 1995); Thomas Crow, *Modern Art in the Common Culture* (New Haven, Conn.: Yale University Press, 1996); Michael Denning, *The Cultural Front: The Laboring of American Culture in the Twentieth Century* (New York: Verso, 1997); Bill Brown, *The Material Unconscious: American Amusement, Stephen Crane, and the Economies of Play* (Chicago: University of Chicago Press, 1996); Bill Brown, *A Sense of Things: The Object Matter of American Literature* (Chicago: University of Chicago Press, 2003); Douglas Mao, *Solid Objects: Modernism and the Test of Production* (Princeton, N.J.: Princeton University Press, 1998); Tim Armstrong, *Modernism, Technology, and the Body* (Cambridge: Cambridge University Press, 1998); Wanda Corn, *Great American Thing: Modern Art and National Identity, 1915–1935* (Berkeley: University of California Press, 1999).

4. Wollen, *Raiding the Icebox,* 206–9.

5. See, for example, T. J. Clarke, *The Painter of Modern Life: Paris in the Art of Manet and His Followers* (Princeton, N.J.: Princeton University Press, 1984); David S. Reynolds, *Beneath the American Renaissance: The Subversive Imagination in the Age of Emerson and Melville* (Cambridge, Mass.: Harvard University Press, 1988). The crucial text on the proto-history of the modern is Walter Benjamin, *The Arcades Project,* trans. Howard Eiland and Kevin McLaughlin (Cambridge, Mass.: Harvard University Press, 1999).

6. T. J. Jackson-Lears, "From Salvation to Self-Realization: Advertising and the Therapeutic Roots of the Consumer Culture, 1880–1930," and Christopher

Wilson, "The Rhetoric of Consumption: Mass-Market Magazines and the Demise of the Gentle Reader," in *The Culture of Consumption,* ed. Richard Wrightman-Fox and T. J. Jackson-Lears (New York: Pantheon, 1983), 3–38, 40–64; Roland Gelatt, *The Fabulous Phonograph, 1877–1977: From Edison to Stereo* (New York: Macmillan, 1977); Claude Fischer, *America Calling: A Social History of the Telephone to 1940* (Berkeley: University of California Press, 1992); Charles Musser, *The Emergence of Cinema: The American Screen to 1907* (New York: Scribner, 1990); Richard Koszarski, *An Evening's Entertainment: The Age of the Silent Feature Picture* (New York: Scribner, 1990); Lary May, *Screening Out the Past: The Birth of Mass Culture and the Motion Picture Industry* (Chicago: University of Chicago Press, 1983).

7. Miriam Bratu Hansen, "The Mass Production of the Senses: Classical Cinema as Vernacular Modernism," in *Reinventing Film Studies,* ed. Linda Williams and Christine Gledhill (London: Arnold, 2000), 332–35.

8. For Coney Island as a form of modernism, see John Kasson, *Amusing the Millions: Coney Island at the Turn of the Century* (New York: Hill and Wang, 1978), 88–98; Brown, *Material Unconscious,* 239–43, 251–54; and Rem Koolhaas, *Delirious New York: A Retroactive Manifesto for Manhattan* (1978; reprint, New York: Monacelli Press, 1994), 29–79.

9. Michel de Certeau, *The Practice of Everyday Life,* trans. Steve Rendall (Berkeley: University of California Press, 1984).

10. George Simmel, "The Metropolis and Mental Life," in *On Individuality and Social Forms,* ed. and trans. Donald Levine (Chicago: University of Chicago Press, 1971), 409–24.

11. De Certeau, *Practice of Everyday Life,* 40–41.

12. North, *Dialect of Modernism,* 8–34; Gilles Deleuze and Félix Guattari, *Kafka: Toward a Minor Literature,* trans. Dana Polan (Minneapolis: University of Minnesota Press, 1986).

13. See, for example, Bill Brown, "The Secret Life of Things (Virginia Woolf and the Matter of Modernism)," *Modernism/Modernity* 6.2 (1999): 1–28; and Bill Brown, "Thing Theory," *Critical Inquiry* 28 (Autumn 2001): 1–16.

14. Walter Benjamin, "The Work of Art in the Age of Mechanical Reproduction," *Illuminations: Essays and Reflections,* trans. Harry Zohn (New York: Schocken, 1969), 245–37 (further references are given parenthetically in the text).

15. Walter Benjamin, "A Short History of Photography," in *One-Way Street and Other Writings,* trans. Edmund Jephcott and Kevin Shorter (London: New Left Books, 1979), 240–57.

16. See, for example, Roland Barthes, *Image-Music-Text,* ed. and trans. Stephen Heath (New York: Hill and Wang, 1978); Roland Barthes, *Camera Lucida,* trans. Richard Howard (New York: Hill and Wang, 1981); Roland Barthes, *The Rustle of Language,* trans. Richard Howard (New York: Hill and Wang, 1986);

Friederich Kittler, *Discourse Networks 1800/1900* (1985), trans. Michael Mettier with Chris Cullens (Stanford, Calif.: Stanford University Press, 1990); Friederich Kittler, *Gramophone, Film, Typewriter,* trans. Geoffrey Winthrop-Young and Michael Wutz (Stanford, Calif.: Stanford University Press, 1999); and Michael Taussig, *Mimesis and Alterity: A Particular History of the Senses* (New York: Routledge, 1993). Mary Ann Doane, *The Emergence of Cinematic Time: Modernity, Contingency, the Archive* (Cambridge, Mass.: Harvard University Press, 2002).

17. Deleuze and Guattari, *Kafka,* 6.

18. Bill Brown, *Sense of Things,* 12–13, 133–43, 171.

19. On the concept of the real, see Jacques Lacan, *The Four Fundamental Concepts of Psychoanalysis,* trans. Alan Sheridan (New York: Norton, 1978), esp. sections 4 ("On the Network of Signifiers") and 5 ("Tuché and Automaton"), 42–64. For the connection between the Lacanian real, noise, and the analogical media, see Kittler, *Discourse Networks 1800/1900,* 177–346; Friederich Kittler, "The World of the Symbolic—A World of the Machine," *Literature, Media, Information Systems: Essays* (Amsterdam: OPA, 1997), 130–47; Kittler, *Gramophone, Film, Typewriter,* 1–114. I am generally indebted to Kittler's work for many of the ideas that circulate through this book.

20. Kittler, *Discourse Networks 1800/1900,* 304.

21. Benjamin, *Arcades Project,* 456–57.

22. Hansen, "Mass Production of the Senses," 334.

23. Greil Marcus, *Dead Elvis: A Chronicle of a Cultural Obsession* (New York: Doubleday, 1991), 7–8, 122.

24. Benjamin, *Arcades Project,* 482

25. Taussig, *Mimesis and Alterity,* 44.

26. Michael Taussig, *Shamanism, Colonialism, and the Wild Man: A Study in Terror and Healing* (Chicago: University of Chicago Press, 1987), 10.

27. Theodor Adorno, *Negative Dialectics* (1973), trans. E. B. Ashton (New York: Continuum, 1983), 189, 191.

28. Walter Benjamin, "Surrealism: The Last Snapshot of the European Intelligentsia," in *One-Way Street and Other Writings,* trans. Edmund Jephcott and Kevin Shorter (London: New Left Books, 1979), 239.

Chapter 1: Reading Modernity

1. Vachel Lindsay to Arthur Davison Ficke, November 11, 1913, in *The Letters of Vachel Lindsay,* ed. Marc Chénetier (New York: B. Franklin, 1978), 81.

2. Stanley Kauffmann, Introduction to *The Art of the Moving Picture,* by Vachel Lindsay (New York: Liveright, 1970), ix–xix.

3. Vachel Lindsay, *The Progress and Poetry of the Movies,* ed. Myron Lounsbury (Lanham, Md.: Scarecrow Press, 1995) (herafter cited in the text as *P*). Lounsbury's editorial work is remarkable, and his lengthy introduction is indispensable to anyone interested in Lindsay's work.

4. Three excellent examples of cultural history that use Lindsay's idea of modernity as a "hieroglyphic civilization" are Warren Susman, *Culture as History: The Transformation of American Society in the Twentieth Century* (New York: Pantheon, 1989); Douglas Tallack, *Twentieth-Century America* (London: Longman, 1991); and Miles Orvell, *The Real Thing: Imitation and Authenticity in American Culture, 1880–1940* (Chapel Hill: University of North Carolina Press, 1989), 244. None discusses Lindsay at any length.

5. See Myron Lounsbury, *Origins of American Film Criticism, 1909–1939* (New York: Arno Press, 1973), 50–58, 67–77, and Glenn J. Wolfe, *Vachel Lindsay: The Poet as Film Theorist* (New York: Arno Press, 1973).

6. Laurence Goldstein, *American Poet at the Movies* (Ann Arbor: University of Michigan Press, 1994), 19–35.

7. Rachel O. Moore, *Savage Theory: Cinema as Modern Magic* (Durham, N.C.: Duke University Press, 2000).

8. Nick Browne, "Orientalism as an Ideological Form: American Film Theory in the Silent Period," *Wide Angle* 11 (October 1989): 23–31; Miriam Hansen, *Babel and Babylon: Spectatorship in American Silent Film* (Cambridge, Mass.: Harvard University Press, 1991), esp. 76–89, 188–98.

9. Hansen, *Babel and Babylon*, 78–94.

10. Vachel Lindsay, *The Art of the Moving Picture* (New York: Liveright, 1970), 45 (hereafter cited in the text as *A*).

11. Warren Susman, *Culture as History*, 116–17.

12. Tom Gunning, "The Cinema of Attractions: Early Film, Its Spectator, and the Avant-Garde," *Wide Angle* 8.3–4 (Fall 1986): 63–70.

13. Ernst Bloch, *Das Prinzip Hoffnung*, vol. 1 (Frankfurt: Suhrkamp Verlag, 1959), 471–73; Walter Benjamin, "The Work of Art in the Age of Mechanical Reproduction," in *Illuminations: Essays and Reflections*, trans. Harry Zohn (New York: Schocken, 1969), 217–51.

14. Peter Marzio, *The Democratic Art: Pictures for Nineteenth-Century America* (Boston: David R. Godine, 1979).

15. Christopher Wilson, "The Rhetoric of Consumption: Mass Market Magazines and the Demise of 'The Gentle Reader,' 1880–1920," in *The Culture of Consumption*, ed. Richard Wrightman-Fox and T. J. Jackson-Lears (New York: Pantheon, 1983), 40–64.

16. Robert Park, "The Natural History of the Newspaper," in *The City*, by Robert Park, Ernest W. Burgess, and Roderick D. McKenzie (Chicago: University of Chicago Press, 1925), 91, 96–98.

17. Wolfgang Schivelbusch, *The Railway Journey: Trains and Travel in the Nineteenth Century* (New York: Urizen Books, 1979), 180–88; Tom Gunning, "An Unseen Energy Swallows Space," in *Film before Griffith*, ed. John Fell (Berkeley: University of California Press, 1983), 355–66; Charles Musser, "The Travel Genre in 1903–1904: Moving towards Fictional Narrative," in *Early Cinema: Space,*

Frame, Narrative, ed. Thomas Elsaesser (London: British Film Institute, 1990), 49–62; Lynn Kirby, *Parallel Tracks: The Railway and Early Cinema* (Durham, N.C.: Duke University Press, 1997).

18. Raymond Fielding, "Hale's Tours: Ultra-Realism in the Pre-1910 Moving Picture," *Cinema Journal* 10.1 (Fall 1970): 34–47.

19. Paul Virilio, *Esthetique de la disparition* (Paris: Andre Balland, 1980), 77, 120; Paul Virilio, "Cinema Isn't I See, It's I Fly," in *War and Cinema,* trans. Patrick Camiller (London: Verso, 1989), 11–30.

20. On placelessness, or atopicality, see Avital Ronell, *Finitude's Score: Essays for the End of the Millenium* (Lincoln: University of Nebraska Press, 1994), 83–103, 219–35.

21. 1970s *Screen* theory, following Louis Althusser's influential, and partial, reading of Jacques Lacan, focused on how the classical cinema, through the interplay of the imaginary and symbolic registers, lured spectators into a (masculine-identified) position of centrality and power. Starting in the late 1980s, new readings of Lacan have inflected these views by highlighting the importance of the real as a manic core of enjoyment, a destabilizing, formless undergrowth that gives filmic pleasure a destructive edge. In fact, without this edge there would be no pleasure at all. See, for example, Slavoj Žižek, *Looking Awry: An Introduction to Jacques Lacan through Popular Culture* (Cambridge: Massachusetts Institute of Technology Press, 1991); Slavoj Žižek, *Enjoy Your Symptom: Jacques Lacan in Hollywood and Out* (New York: Routledge, 1992); and Slavoj Žižek, *The Plague of Fantasies* (London: Verso, 1997). From non-Lacanian perspectives, others have also departed from *Screen* by highlighting the masochistic components in spectatorship. See Gaylyn Studlar, *In the Realm of Pleasure: Dietrich, Sternberg, and the Masochistic Aesthetic* (Urbana: University of Illinois Press, 1988); Kaja Silverman, *Male Subjectivity at the Margins* (New York: Routledge, 1992); and Carol Clover, *Men, Women, and Chainsaws: Gender in the Modern Horror Film* (Princeton, N.J.: Princeton University Press, 1992).

22. Vachel Lindsay, "Rhymes to Be Traded for Bread," in *Adventures, Rhymes, and Designs,* ed. Robert F. Sayre (New York: Eakins Press, 1968), 231–46. See also Elizabeth Ruggles, *The West-Going Heart: A Life of Vachel Lindsay* (New York: Norton, 1959), 110–19, 129–33, 178–99.

23. As Lounsbury shows, Lindsay worked hard in the 1920s to shake his reputation as a "jazz poet" and a "jazz evangelist" (*P* 74–80). Yet he had been the artificer of this persona through his early advocacy of ragtime and the syncopated rhythm of his verse, which he stressed in his spirited recitals. But what in the 1910s had been a way to reject a corseted gentility had become in the 1920s an oppressive cultural dominant. Hence his frequent complaints in the introduction to the 1925 edition of his *Collected Poems* that his business was not jazz but hieroglyphics—not shallow entertainment but cultural exegesis.

24. Karl Marx, "The Fetishism of Commodities and the Secret Thereof," in

The Marx-Engels Reader, ed. Robert Tucker (New York: Norton, 1978), 319, 321–23.

25. Ibid., 320. Moore also brings up Marx's discussion of fetishism (and the example of the table) in relation to modern primitivism, rather than in relation to the disorder of modern materiality, as I do here. See Moore, *Savage Theory,* 57–58.

26. George Simmel, *The Philosophy of Money,* ed. David Frisby, trans. Tom Bottomore and David Frisby (New York: Routledge, 1990), 457.

27. Stuart Ewin and Elizabeth Ewin, *Channels of Desire: Mass Images and the Shaping of American Consciousness,* 2nd ed. (Minneapolis: University of Minnesota Press, 1992), 49.

28. Michael Taussig, *Mimesis and Alterity: A Particular History of the Senses* (New York: Routledge, 1993), 22–23; Jacques Lacan, *El Seminario de Jacques Lacan, Libro 7: La ética del psicoanálisis (1959–60),* trans. Diana S. Rabinovich (Buenos Aires: Paidós, 1992), 141.

29. Bill Brown, *A Sense of Things: The Object Matter of American Literature* (Chicago: University of Chicago Press, 2003), 34. See also Orvell's analysis of Victorian material culture in *Real Thing,* 40–72.

30. On Lindsay's connection to a number of early film theorists such as Béla Bálazs, Sergei Eisenstein, and Jean Epstein, who also reflected on the peculiar qualities of filmed objects, see Moore, *Savage Theory,* 62–72.

31. Passages like this relativize Walter Benjamin's assumption that the "auratic" disappears under mechanical reproduction (whether iconic, as in film and photography, or industrial, in the case of mass manufacturing). For some objections to Benjamin's thesis, see Jürgen Habermas, "Consciousness-Raising or Redemptive Criticism," *New German Critique* 17 (Spring 1979): 30–59.

32. For Freud's earliest theorization of the object, see "Three Essays on the Theory of Sexuality" (1905), in *The Standard Edition of the Complete Psychological Works of Sigmund Freud,* vol. 7, ed. and trans. James Stratchey (London: Hogarth, 1955), 123–243. It was later elaborated in "Instincts and their Vicissitudes" (1915), in *The Standard Edition of the Complete Psychological Works of Sigmund Freud,* vol. 14, ed. and trans. James Strachey (London: Hogarth, 1953), 117–40. See also Sigmund Freud, "Fetishism" (1927), in *Collected Papers,* vol. 5 (London: Hogarth, 1949), 198–204.

33. Quoted in David Curtis, *Experimental Film* (New York: Universe Books, 1971), 27.

34. Siegfried Kracauer, "Cult of Distraction: On Berlin's Picture Palaces," trans. Thomas Y. Levin, *New German Critique* 40 (December 1987): 94 (further references are given parenthetically in the text).

35. On Kracauer's 1940s film theory, see Miriam Hansen, "With Skin and Hair: Kracauer's Theory of Film, Marseille 1940," *Critical Inquiry* 19 (Spring 1993): 437–69.

36. The term "linearize" is Noel Burch's. See his "Primitivism and the Avant-Garde: A Dialectical Approach," in *Narrative, Apparatus, Ideology: A Film Theory Reader,* ed. Philip Rosen (New York: Columbia University Press, 1986), 483–506. See also Hansen, *Babel and Babylon,* 79–89; Kristin Thompson, "The Formulation of the Classical Style, 1909–1928," in David Bordwell, Janet Steiger, and K. Thompson, *The Classical Hollywood Cinema: Film Style and Mode of Production to 1960* (New York: Columbia University Press, 1985), 155–239. More recently, see Mary Ann Doane, *The Emergence of Cinematic Time: Modernity, Contingency, the Archive* (Cambridge, Mass.: Harvard University Press, 2002), 141–71; and Robert B. Ray, *The Avant-Garde Finds Andy Hardy* (Cambridge, Mass.: Harvard University Press, 1995), 28–30.

37. Nicolas Vardac mentions how a Boston theater advertised the 1924 version of *Ben-Hur* with a timetable specifying when particularly spectacular scenes were to take place. Nicolas Vardac, *Stage to Screen: Theatrical Method from Garrick to Griffith* (Cambridge, Mass.: Harvard University Press, 1949), 232.

38. Lindsay's use of the hieroglyphic connects with other conceptualizations of mass culture as "hieroglyphic writing." One of the most influential of these was by Theodor Adorno, who also identifies "hieroglyphs" with certain stability of meaning; but while Lindsay praises the univocal hieroglyph as an antidote to the disorder of the present, Adorno condemns it for freezing cognition, subjectivity, and sociality into reified forms. See Miriam Hansen, "Mass Culture as Hieroglyphic Writing: Adorno, Derrida, Kracauer," *New German Critique* 56 (1992): 43–73.

39. For an extended comment on the writerly aspects of hieroglyphics in relation to Freud's conception of mental representation, see Jacques Derrida, "Freud and the Scene of Writing," in *Writing and Difference,* trans. Alan Bass (Chicago: University of Chicago Press, 1978), 196–231. Miriam Hansen discusses this ambiguity of hieroglyphic writing in relation to D. W. Griffith's *Intolerance,* one of Lindsay's fetish texts, in *Babel and Babylon,* 188–98.

40. Hansen, *Babel and Babylon,* 194; see also 146–51.

41. See Marc Chénetier, "L'Obsession des signes: L'Esthetique de Vachel Lindsay (1879–1931), Prose, Poems et Dessins" (Ph.D. diss., Université de Paris, 1979); and Marc Chénetier, "Vachel Lindsay: Modernity and Modernism," in *American Poetry between Tradition and Modernism, 1865–1914,* ed. Roland Hagenbuchle (Regensburg, Germany: Pustet, 1984), 197–207. Some of Lindsay's favorite hieroglyphics include Abraham Lincoln, Lindsay's home town of Springfield, Illinois, the state of California, William Jennings Bryan, the actress Mae Marsh, the soul of the butterfly, the soul of the spider, and Johnny Appleseed. Their extremely personal quality connects Lindsay to another sublime eccentric, the New York–based filmmaker and performer Jack Smith, who constructed a peculiar image repertoire similar to Lindsay's. The coincidences between them deserve more room than I can give them here: they were both of rural origin but

loved urban culture, they idealized female stars, were fascinated with chintzy Hollywood Orientalia, developed peculiar stage personalities, and ended up succumbing to them.

42. Vachel Lindsay, *Complete Poems* (New York: Macmillan, 1925), 340 (hereafter cited in the text as *C*).

43. F. O. Matthiessen, *American Renaissance: Art and Expression in the Age of Emerson and Whitman* (1941; reprint, New York: Oxford University Press, 1968), viii.

44. On the modernist poetics of (re)assemblage, see Sanford Schwartz, *The Matrix of Modernism: Pound, Eliot, and Early Twentieth-Century Thought* (Princeton, N.J.: Princeton University Press, 1985).

45. R. A. Sanborn, "The Fight," *The Soil* (January 1917): 67–68; J. B., "To the Bronx Zoo," *The Soil* (January 1917): 73; Adam Hull-Shirk, "Prestidigitation," *The Soil* (January 1917): 86.

46. H.D., "The Borderline Pamphlet" (1930), in *The Gender of Modernism*, ed. Bonnie Kime Scott (Bloomington: Indiana University Press, 1992), 110–25 (see esp. 115–16); H.D., "Cinema and the Classics," *Close-Up* 1.1 (July 1927): 22–33; H.D., "Russian Films," *Close-Up* 3.3 (September 1928): 18–29. These are reprinted in *Cinema and Modernism: Close-Up, 1927–33*, ed. James Donald, Anne Friedberg, and Laura Marcus (Princeton, N.J.: Princeton University Press, 1998).

47. Charles Baudelaire, *Oeuvres completes* (Paris: Gallimard, Bibliothèque de la Pleiade, 1969), 296–97.

48. See Ben M. Hall, *The Best Remaining Seats: The Golden Age of the Movie Palace* (1966; reprint, New York: DaCapo, 1988); Robert W. Rydell, *All the World's a Fair: Visions of Empire at America's International Expositions, 1876–1915* (Chicago: University of Chicago Press, 1984); John Kasson, *Amusing the Millions: Coney Island at the Turn of the Century* (New York: Hill and Wang, 1978); and Lewis A. Erenberg, *Steppin' Out: New York Nightlife and the Transformation of American Culture, 1890–1930* (Chicago: University of Chicago Press, 1984). On Dreamland and Murray's Roman Gardens, see Rem Koolhaas, *Delirious New York: A Retrospective Manifesto for Manhattan* (1978; reprint, New York: Monacelli, 1994), 101–4.

49. Goldstein, *American Poet at the Movies*, 23–30.

50. Heinrich Heine's phrase is quoted by Freud in "Femininity" (1933), in *The Standard Edition of the Complete Psychological Works of Sigmund Freud*, vol. 22, ed. and trans. James Strachey (London: Hogarth Press, 1949), 112.

51. Hugo Muensterberg, *The Film: A Psychological Study* (1916; reprint, New York: Dover, 1970), esp. 73–81 (originally published as *The Photoplay: A Psychological Study*).

52. Ruggles, *West-Going Heart*, 90, 107–9, 122.

53. Vachel Lindsay, "Explanation of the Map of the Universe," in *Adventures, Rhymes, and Designs*, ed. Robert F. Sayre (New York: Eakins Press, 1968), 253.

54. On the connections between cinema, transit, and architecture, see Giuliana Bruno, *Streetwalking on a Ruined Map: The City Films of Elvira Notari* (Princeton, N.J.: Princeton University Press, 1993), 35–57.

55. Benjamin, "Work of Art in the Age of Mechanical Reproduction," 239–40.

56. Evidence of how thin Lindsay's dream of unity is and how much it rests on a repression of ethnic difference is provided by embarrassingly racist passages in his correspondence (*P* 419–21; Ruggles, *West-Going Heart*, 310–11). It must be borne in mind, however, that these statements were made late in Lindsay's life, at a time of considerable psychological distress, after he had been diagnosed with epilepsy and his mood was often extremely irascible and paranoid. Early in his youth, he had vehemently protested lynchings, and poems such as "The Congo" (*C* 178–84) and his "Booker Washington Trilogy" (*C* 161–74) show a heartfelt, if problematic, idealization of black culture.

57. Van Wyck Brooks, *America's Coming of Age* (1915), in *Three Essays on America* (New York: Dutton, 1934), esp. "Highbrow and Lowbrow," 5–24.

58. Editorial, *The Seven Arts* 1 (November 1916): 52–53; Peter Minuit, "291 Fifth Avenue," *The Seven Arts* 1 (November 1916): 61–65.

59. Randolph Bourne, "Trans-National America," in *Critics of Culture: Literature and Society in the Early Twentieth Century*, ed. Alan Trachtenberg (New York: John Holt, 1976), 145–61.

60. Robert Coady, "American Art, Part I," *The Soil* (December 1916): 3–4; Robert Coady, "American Art, Part II," *The Soil* (January 1917): 54–55.

61. Vachel Lindsay, "An Editorial to the Art Student Who Has Returned to the Village," in *Adventures, Rhymes, and Designs,* ed. Robert F. Sayre (New York: Eakins Press, 1968), 269.

62. Ruggles, *West-Going Heart,* 160–61.

63. Robert F. Sayre, Introduction to *Adventures, Rhymes, and Designs,* by Vachel Lindsay, ed. Robert F. Sayre (New York: Eakins Press, 1968), 10.

Chapter 2: Reading the Modern City

1. The first Whitman quotation comes from "A Broadway Pageant" (1860), the second is from "Mannahatta," in the section "From Noon to Starry Night," and the last is from "Crossing Brooklyn Ferry" (1856). These poems are the main sources for the film's intertitles. Walt Whitman, *Complete Poetry and Selected Prose by Walt Whitman,* ed. James E. Miller (Boston: Houghton Mifflin, 1959), 177, 330, 119.

2. For the production and exhibition history of *Manhatta,* see Jan-Christopher Horak, "Paul Strand and Charles Sheeler's *Manhatta*," in *Lovers of Cinema: The First American Film Avant-Garde, 1919–1945,* ed. Jan-Christopher Horak (Madison: University of Wisconsin Press, 1995), 267–86 (further references are given parenthetically in the text). See also an updated version of the same essay, Jan-Christopher Horak, "Paul Strand: Romantic Modernist," in *Making Images*

Move: Photographers and Avant-Garde Cinema (Washington, D.C.: Smithsonian Institution Press, 1997), 79–108; this version emphasizes Paul Strand's contribution to the film and studies his post-*Manhatta* film career.

3. Quoted in Horak, "Paul Strand and Charles Sheeler's *Manhatta*," 270–71.

4. On the New York art world around the time of the Armory Show, see Steven Watson, *Strange Bedfellows: The First American Avant-Garde* (New York: Abbeville, 1991). On the Stieglitz group, see Edward Abrahams, *The Lyrical Left: Randolph Bourne, Alfred Stieglitz, and the Origins of Cultural Radicalism in America* (Charlotesville: University Press of Virginia, 1986), which focuses on the early years; Celeste Connor, *Democratic Visions: Art and Theory in the Stieglitz Circle* (Berkeley: University of California Press, 1999), focuses on the group in the 1920s and 1930s. On Sheeler, I have found especially useful Karen Lucic, *Charles Sheeler and the Cult of the Machine* (Cambridge, Mass.: Harvard University Press, 1991); and Theodor E. Stebbins Jr. and Norman Keyes Jr., *Charles Sheeler: The Photographs* (Boston: Museum of Fine Arts, 1987). These can be supplemented by the more recent Theodor E. Stebbins, Gilles Mora, and Karen E. Haas, *The Photographs of Charles Sheeler: American Modernist* (Boston: Bullfinch, 2002). On Strand, I have used Margaret Sange, ed., *Paul Strand: Essays on His Life and Work* (New York: Aperture, 1990), esp. Naomi Rosenblum, "The Early Years" (27–46); Sarah Greenough, "An American Vision," in *Paul Strand: An American Vision* (Washington, D.C.: National Gallery of Art, 1990), 31–49; and Maria Morris Hambourg, *Paul Strand circa 1916* (New York: Metropolitan Museum of Art/N. H. Abrams, 1998).

5. The phrase comes from M. Christine Boyer, *Dreaming the Rational City: The Myth of American City Planning* (Cambridge: Massachusetts Institute of Technology Press, 1983), 59–82.

6. Walter Benjamin, "On Some Motifs in Baudelaire," in *Illuminations: Essays and Reflections,* trans. Harry Zohn (New York: Schocken, 1969), 174–76.

7. In his pioneering survey of American experimental film, Lewis Jacobs regards *Mannahatta* (one of the film's alternate titles) as the first significant title in this tradition and regards it a forerunner of the documentary school of the 1930s. Lewis Jacobs, "Experimental Cinema in America, 1921–1947," in *The Rise of the American Film, a Critical History* (New York: Columbia Teacher's College, 1974), 545. See also Dickran Tashjian, *Skyscraper Primitives: Dada and the American Avant-Garde* (Middletown, Conn.: Wesleyan University Press, 1975), 221–23; Lucic, *Charles Sheeler and the Cult of the Machine,* 47–54; Miles Orvell, *After the Machine: Visual Arts and the Erasure of Cultural Boundaries* (Jackson: University Press of Mississippi, 1995), 13–29; Connor, *Democratic Visions,* 147–48; Wanda Corn, *The Great American Thing: Modern Art and National Identity, 1915–1935* (Berkeley: University of California Press, 1999), 182–85; Scott Hammen, "Sheeler and Strand's *Manhatta:* A Neglected Masterpiece," *Afterimage* 6 (January 1979): 6–7; Horak, "Paul Strand and Charles Sheeler's *Manhatta.*"

8. On the idealization of nature in the Stieglitz group, see Connor, *Democratic Visions,* 107–40; on the group's romantic Americanism, see Corn, *Great American Thing,* 3–40.

9. On Coady and *The Soil,* see the personal reminiscences of Robert Alden Sanborn, "A Champion in the Wilderness," *Broom* 3.3 (October 1922): 174–79; and Gorham Munson, *The Awakening Twenties: A Memoir-History of a Literary Period* (Baton Rouge: Louisiana State University Press, 1995), 39–47. For critical studies, see Dickran Tashjian, *Skyscraper Primitives,* 71–74; Judith Zilc(zer, "Robert J. Coady: Forgotten Spokesman for Avant-Garde Culture in America," *American Art Review* 27 (November 1975): 77–90; and Judith Zilczer, "Robert J. Coady, Man of the Soil," in *New York Dada,* ed. Rudolf Kuenzli (New York: Willis, Locker, and Owen, 1986), 31–43.

10. Alfred Turner-Keller, "Mispronunciation," *The Soil* (January 1917): 80.

11. J.B., "The Woolworth Building," *The Soil* (January 1917): 61–62.

12. Miles Orvell, *The Real Thing: Imitation and Authenticity in American Culture, 1880–1940* (Chapel Hill: University of North Carolina Press, 1989), 141–56.

13. Paul Strand, "Photography," in Alfred Stieglitz, *Camera Work: The Complete Illustrations, 1903–1917* (Köln: Taschen, 1997), 780–81.

14. Tashjian, *Skyscraper Primitives,* 71–84; Zilczer, "Forgotten Spokesman," 88.

15. The most easily accessible sources on Cravan (born Fabian Avernarius Lloyd in 1887) in English are Francis Naumann, *New York Dada* (New York: H. N. Abrams, 1994), 162–67; and Carolyn Burke, *Becoming Modern: The Life of Mina Loy* (New York: Farrar, Straus and Giroux, 1999), but the most complete is Maria Lluisa Barrás, *Arthur Craván: Una biografía* (Barcelona: Quaderns Crema, 1993). See also Iñaki Lacuesta's speculative documentary film, *Cravan vs. Cravan* (Spain: Benecé Produccions, S.L., 2002). For a selection of Cravan's writings in English, see *Four Dada Suicides: Selected Texts of Arthur Cravan, Jacques Rigaut, Julian Torma, and Jacques Vaché,* ed. and intro. Roger Conover, Terry Hale, and Paul Lenti (London: Atlas Press, 1995).

16. R. J. Coady, "American Art, Part I," *The Soil* (December 1916): 3–4.

17. R. J. Coady, "American Art, Part II," *The Soil* (January 1917): 55.

18. F.M., "Dressmaking," *The Soil* (December 1916): 26.

19. R. A. Sanborn, "The Fight," *The Soil* (January 1917): 67; R. A. Sanborn, "Notes on the Fight," *The Soil* (January 1917): 68–70; and R. A. Sanborn, "Fight Nights," *The Soil* (March 1917): 116–18.

20. Georg Simmel, "The Metropolis and Mental Life," in *On Individuality and Social Forms,* ed. and trans. Donald Levine (Chicago: University of Chicago Press, 1971), 410.

21. Robert E. Park, "The City: Suggestions for the Investigation of Human Behavior in the Urban Environment," in Robert E. Park, Ernest W. Burgess, and Roderick D. McKenzie, *The City* (Chicago: University of Chicago Press, 1925), 23.

22. Louis Wirth, "Urbanism as a Way of Life," in *Louis Wirth on Cities and Social Life: Selected Papers,* ed. Albert J. Reiss (Chicago: University of Chicago Press), 71.

23. Anonymous, *The Soil* (March 1917): 124.

24. "The scent of this arm-pits aroma finer than prayer" is a line from "Song of Myself"; "This Compost" is a poem in "Autumn Rivulets." Whitman, *Complete Poetry and Selected Prose,* 42, 260–61.

25. On the relationship between Coady and Duchamp, see Corn, *Great American Thing,* 85–87.

26. Craig Adcock, "Marcel Duchamp's Approach to New York: 'Find an Inscription for the Woolworth Building as a Ready-Made,'" in *New York Dada,* ed. Rudolph Kuenzli (New York: Willis Locker and Owen, 1986), 52–65.

27. Tashjian, *Skyscraper Primitives,* 222.

28. Strand, "Photography," 781.

29. Robert J. Coady, "Censoring the Motion Picture," *The Soil* (December 1916): 38 (further references are given parenthetically in the text).

30. Robert Alden Sanborn, "Motion Picture Dynamics," *Broom* 5.2 (September 1923): 80 (further references are given parenthetically in the text).

31. On the aesthetic of the urban panoramas, see Tom Gunning, "An Unseen Energy Swallows Space," in *Film before Griffith,* ed. John Fell (Berkeley: University of California Press, 1983), 355–66; Tom Gunning, "The Cinema of Attractions," *Wide Angle* 8.3–4 (Fall 1986): 63–70; and Tom Gunning, "The Whole Town's Gawking: Early Cinema and the Visual Experience of Modernity," *Yale Journal of Criticism* 7.2 (1994): 189–201. See also Charles Musser, "The Travel Genre in 1903–1904: Moving towards Fictional Narrative," in *Early Cinema: Space, Frame, Narrative,* ed. Thomas Elsaesser (London: British Film Institute, 1990), 123–32; and Lynne Kirby, "The Urban Spectator and the Crowd in Early American Train Films," *Iris* 11 (Summer 1990): 49–62.

32. Gunning, "Unseen Energy Swallows Space," 362.

33. Corn, *Great American Thing,* 140–41.

34. Kenneth Macgowan, "Beyond the Screen," *The Seven Arts* (December 1916): 166 (further references are given parenthetically in the text).

35. Man Ray, "Cinemage," in *The Shadow and Its Shadow: Surrealist Writings on the Cinema,* ed. Paul Hammond (London: British Film Institute, 1979), 84–85.

36. Quoted in Horak, "Paul Strand and Charles Sheeler's *Manhatta*," 272. The film's abstraction and schematism were highlighted in a photomontage, "Manhattan—The Proud and Passionate City: Two American Artists Interpret the Spirit of New York Photographically in Terms of Line and Mass," *Vanity Fair* 18 (April 1922): 51.

37. Quoted in Hambourg, *Paul Strand circa 1916,* 37.

38. For the larger context of these photographs, see ibid., 31–37. For Greenough these shots only "superficially resemble" Lewis Hine's pictures of im-

migrants on Ellis Island and are closer in conception and style to Edgar Lee Masters's *Spoon River Anthology* (Greenough, "American Vision," 37). I am more convinced by Naomi Rosenblum's dating the influence of Masters to the early 1930s, the time of Strand's falling out with Stieglitz and of his incipient friendship with Harold Clurman and the Group Theater. Naomi Rosenblum, "The Early Years," in *Paul Strand: Essays on His Life and Work,* ed. Margaret Sange (New York: Aperture, 1990), 46. Peter Conn also emphasizes the Strand-Hine connection in the early pictures. See Peter Conn, *The Divided Mind: Ideology and Imagination in America, 1898–1917* (Cambridge: Cambridge University Press, 1983), 287–91.

39. Siegfried Kracauer, "The Mass Ornament" (1927), trans. Barbara Correll and Jack Zipes, *New German Critique* 5 (Winter 1975): 67–76 (further references are given parenthetically in the text).

40. Kracauer borrows this idea from Georg Lukacs, *History and Class Consciousness,* trans. Rodney Livingston (Cambridge: Massachusetts Institute of Technology Press, 1969), 101.

41. Horak, "Paul Strand and Charles Sheeler's *Manhatta,*" 279.

42. Frederick Lewis Allen, *Only Yesterday: An Informal History of the Twenties* (1931; reprint, New York: Harper and Row, 1959), 59–61.

43. Wilhelm Worringer, *Abstraction and Empathy* (1908), trans. Michael Bullock (New York: International Universities Press, 1953), 36.

44. Marshall Berman, *All That Is Solid Melts into Air: The Experience of Modernity* (London: Verso, 1982), 312–29.

45. Jane Jacobs, *The Death and Life of Great American Cities* (New York: Vintage, 1961), esp. 48–60.

46. Michel de Certeau, *The Practice of Everyday Life,* trans. Steve Randall (Berkeley: University of California Press, 1984), 91–99.

47. Gilles Deleuze and Felix Guattari, *One Thousand Plateaus,* trans. Brian Massumi (Minneapolis: University of Minnesota Press, 1987), 208–31, 474–500.

48. Roland Barthes, *The Pleasure of the Text,* trans. Richard Howard (New York: Farrar, Straus, and Giroux, 1975), 49.

Chapter 3: John Dos Passos's *USA*, the Popular Media, and Left Documentary Film in the 1930s

1. John Dos Passos, "Why Write for the Theater Anyway?" in *Three Plays: The Garbage Man, Airways, Inc., Fortune Heights* (New York: Harcourt Brace and Co, 1934), xix.

2. John Howard Lawson, Introduction to *Processional* (New York: T. Seltzer, 1925), v–vi.

3. John Dos Passos, "Did the New Playwrights Theater Fail?" in *John Dos Passos: The Major Non-Fiction Prose,* ed. Donald Pizer (Detroit: Wayne State University Press, 1988), 118–20.

4. Kenneth Macgowan, *Continental Stagecraft,* illus. R. E. Jones (New York: Harcourt, Brace and Co., 1922), 198–212 (on the Cirque Medrano).

5. Huntley Carter, *The New Theater and Cinema of Soviet Russia* (London: Chapman and Dodd, 1924); Huntley Carter, *The New Spirit in the Russian Theater, 1917–1928* (London: Brentano's Ltd., 1929).

6. *Little Review,* special issue on "The International Theater Exposition" 11.2 (Winter 1926). In a footnote under the table of contents, jane heap claims responsibility for the idea and acknowledges Tristan Tzara's help: "[H]e advised me to invite the cooperation of Friedrich Kiesler, director of the Theater Exposition of the city of Vienna, 1924, and famous theatre architect . . . in the organization of the project." She also acknowledged the help of the Theater Guild, Provincetown Playhouse, Greenwich Village Theater, and Neighborhood Playhouse. Friedrich Kiesler would later become a New York City resident, where he designed the Film Guild Theater, devoted to showing experimental productions and run by Symon Gould, in 1929, and Peggy Guggenheim's gallery "Art of This Century" in the early 1940s.

7. Dos Passos, "Why Write for the Theater Anyway?" xiv.

8. Miles Orvell, *The Real Thing: Authenticity and Imitation in American Culture, 1880–1940* (Chapel Hill: University of North Carolina Press, 1989), 268; Donald Pizer, *Dos Passos's* USA: *A Critical Study* (Charlottesville: University Press of Virginia, 1988), 58–70.

9. Compton Mackenzie, "Film or Book?" in *John Dos Passos: The Critical Heritage,* ed. Barry Maine (New York: Routledge, 1988), 109–10; Malcolm Cowley, "The End of a Trilogy," in *The Merrill Studies in* USA, ed. David S. Sanders (Columbus, Ohio: Charles Merrill, 1972), 4–7; Edmund Wilson, untitled review, in *John Dos Passos: The Critical Heritage,* ed. Barry Maine (New York: Routledge, 1988), 84–87; Mike Gold, "The Education of John Dos Passos," in *John Dos Passos: The Critical Heritage,* ed. Barry Maine (New York: Routledge, 1988), 115–17; Upton Sinclair, review of *The 42nd Parallel,* in *John Dos Passos: The Critical Heritage,* ed. Barry Maine (New York: Routledge, 1988), 87–90.

10. Gretchen Foster, "John Dos Passos's Use of Film Technique in *Manhattan Transfer* and *The 42nd Parallel,*" *Literature/Film Quarterly* 14.3 (1986): 186–94; David Seed, "Media and Newsreels in Dos Passos's *USA,*" *Journal of Narrative Technique* 14.3 (Fall 1984): 182–92.

11. John Trombold, "John Dos Passos's *USA:* Futurist Avant-Garde and Popular Culture" (Ph.D. diss., Columbia University, 1995); Townsend Ludington, *John Dos Passos: A Twentieth-Century Odyssey* (New York: Dutton, 1980); William Earl Dow, "John Dos Passos and the French Avant-Garde" (Ph.D. diss., University of Delaware, 1992).

12. Michael Spindler, "John Dos Passos and the Visual Arts," *Journal of American Studies* 15.3 (December 1981): 391–405.

13. The classic study of the documentary book is William Stott, *Documentary*

Expression and Thirties America (1973; reprint, Chicago: University of Chicago Press, 1986). More recently, see Paula Rabinowitz, *They Must Be Represented: The Politics of Documentary* (New York: Verso, 1994), which ranges across 1930s documentary, cinema verité, feminist documentary, and the videotape of Rodney King's beating.

14. Warren I. Susman, "The Culture of the Thirties," in *Culture as History: The Transformation of American Culture in the Twentieth Century* (New York: Pantheon, 1986), 160–61.

15. Among the recent reassessments of the culture and literature of the 1930s that build upon Susman's focus on contemporary media, I have found most useful Michael E. Straub, *Voices of Persuasion: Politics of Representation in 1930s America* (New York: Cambridge University Press, 1995); Laura Browder, *Rousing the Nation: Radical Culture in Depression America* (Ahmerst: University of Massachusetts Press, 1998); and William Solomon, *Literature, Amusement, and Technology in the Great Depression* (Cambridge: Cambridge University Press, 2002).

16. Pierre Macherey, *Toward a Theory of Literary Production,* trans. Geoffrey Wall (London: Routledge and Kegan Paul, 1978), 77 (further references are given parenthetically in the text).

17. Hans Robert Jauss, "Literary History as a Challenge to Literary Theory," *New Literary History* 2.1 (Autumn 1970): 11–14.

18. David Platt, "The New Cinema," *Experimental Cinema* 1.1 (February 1930): 1–2; Seymour Stern, "The Idea of Montage," *Experimental Cinema* 1.1 (February 1930): 12–15; Seymour Stern, "A Working Class Cinema for America?" *The Left* 1.1 (Spring 1931): 70–71. The epigraph from Lenin is quoted in Carter, *New Theater and Cinema of Soviet Russia*, 247. Joseph Freeman, "The Soviet Cinema," in *Voices from October,* by Joseph Freeman, Joshua Kunitz, and Louis Lozowick (New York: Vanguard Press, 1930), 217–64.

19. For surveys of the proletarian fiction of the time, not limited to Proletkult influence, see Barbara Foley, *Radical Representations: Politics and Form in U.S. Proletarian Fiction, 1929–1941* (Durham, N.C.: Duke University Press, 1993); and, focused on women's writing, see Paula Rabinowitz, *Labor and Desire: Women's Revolutionary Fiction in Depression America* (Chapel Hill: University of North Carolina Press, 1991).

20. Lewis Jacobs, "The New Cinema: A Preface to Film Form," *Experimental Cinema* 1.1 (February 1930): 13–14.

21. Kenneth Macpherson, "As Is," *Close-Up* 1.1 (July 1927): 5–15; H.D., "Russian Films," *Close-Up* 3.3 (September 1928): 38; Bryher, *Film Problems of Soviet Russia* (Territet, Switz.: Riant Chateau, 1929).

22. Harry Alan Potamkin, "Populism and Dialectics," *Experimental Cinema* 1.2 (June 1930): 16–17.

23. Bert Hogenkamp, "Workers' Films in Europe," *Jump-Cut* 19 (1978): 16–22.

24. John Dos Passos, "Wanted: An Ivy League for Liberals," *New Republic* 63 (August 13, 1930).

25. Russell Campbell, "Radical Cinema in the 1930s: The Film and Photo League," in *Jump-Cut: Hollywood, Politics, and Counter-Cinema,* ed. Peter Steven (New York: Praeger, 1985), 124.

26. Quoted in William Alexander, *Film on the Left: American Documentary Film in the 1930s* (Princeton, N.J.: Princeton University Press, 1981), 6, 5.

27. Leo Hurwitz, "One Man's Voyage: Ideas and Films in the 1930s," *Cinema Journal* 15.1 (Fall 1975). 9.

28. W. Needham, "The Future of American Cinema," *Close-Up* 2.6 (June 1928): 45.

29. Robert Elson, "De Rochemont's *March of Time,*" in *The Documentary Tradition,* ed. Lewis Jacobs (1971; reprint, New York: Norton, 1979), 107.

30. Meyer Levin, "The Candid Cameraman," *Esquire* 8.98 (September 1937): 125.

31. Brody and Potamkin quoted in Campbell, "Radical Cinema in the 1930s," 125.

32. Harry A. Potamkin, "A Movie Call to Action," in *The Compound Cinema,* ed. Lewis Jacobs (New York: Columbia Teacher's College, 1977), 585.

33. Campbell, "Radical Cinema in the 1930s," 126–27.

34. Dziga Vertov, "Kino-Eye," in *Kino-Eye: The Writings of Dziga Vertov,* trans. Kevin O'Brien, ed. Annette Michaelson (Berkeley: University of California Press, 1984), 62 (further references are given parenthetically in the text). Metaphors of narcosis and addiction as the effect of the bourgeois Hollywood cinema appear as well in the early 1930s writings of Lewis Jacobs, Mike Gold, and H. A. Potamkin. See Paul R. Gorman, *Left Intellectuals and Popular Culture in Twentieth-Century America* (Chapel Hill: University of North Carolina Press, 1996), 119–23.

35. Dziga Vertov, "On *The Eleventh Year,*" in *Kino-Eye: The Writings of Dziga Vertov,* ed. Annette Michaelson, trans. Kevin O'Brien (Berkeley: University of California Press, 1984), 87.

36. Quoted in Alexander, *Film on the Left,* 57.

37. Leo Hurwitz, "The Revolutionary Film—Next Step," in *The Documentary Tradition,* ed. Lewis Jacobs (1971; reprint, New York: Norton, 1979), 93. See also Alexander, *Film on the Left,* 56; and Leo Hurwitz and Ralph Steiner, "A New Approach to Filmmaking," *New Theater* (September 1935): 22–23.

38. Lewis Jacobs, "Experimental Cinema in America," in *The Rise of the American Film: A Critical History* (New York: Columbia Teacher's College, 1974), 558; Charles Wolfe, "Straight Shots and Crooked Plots: Social Documentary and Avant-Garde in the 1930s," in *Lovers of the Cinema,* ed. Jan-Christopher Horak (Madison: University of Wisconsin Press, 1995), 234–65.

39. The roster of Frontier Films' board of members and advisors is in Alex-

ander, *Film on the Left,* 146. On *Spain in Flames* and *The Spanish Earth,* see Tom Waugh, "Joris Ivens' *The Spanish Earth:* Committed Documentary and the Popular Front," in *Show Us Life: Toward a History and Aesthetic of the Committed Documentary,* ed. Thomas Waugh (Metuchen, N.J.: Scarecrow Press, 1984), 112–13. On Dos Passos's break with the official Left, see Daniel Aaron, *Writers on the Left* (1961; reprint, New York: Oxford University Press, 1977), 343–53; Linda Wagner, *John Dos Passos: The Artist as American* (Austin: University of Texas Press, 1979), 112–14; Ludington, *John Dos Passos,* 265–71.

40. Campbell, "Radical Cinema in the 1930s," 129–30.

41. Hurwitz, "Revolutionary Film—Next Step," 92.

42. John Dos Passos, *USA: The 42nd Parallel, 1919, The Big Money,* ed. Daniel Aaron and Townsend Ludington (New York: Library of America, 1996) (further references given parenthetically in the text).

43. Quoted in Pizer, *John Dos Passos's USA,* 80.

44. In what follows I am departing from William Solomon's interpretation. In an allegorical (in Paul de Man's sense) reading that primarily concerns itself with the work's signifying strategies, Solomon sees the "critical movement" of the trilogy as leading from the expressive aesthetic style of the Camera Eyes, "based on a faith in the phenomenality of the linguistic sign," to the dismemberment of language and undercutting of referentiality in the Newsreels, to the allegorical sublation of both these styles in the biographies and in the work's compositional strategy. Solomon, *Literature, Amusement, and Technology,* 214. Solomon transforms what I see as a simultaneity of mutually canceling moves into a hierarchy of discourses and into a dialectical transit from the Camera Eyes to the Newsreels and their decomposition of reference to their sublation in the biographies and the work's overall structure. His interpretation is compelling and well argued, yet it underplays the role of the narratives and Dos Passos's faith in the "speech of the people."

45. Staub, *Voices of Persuasion,* 28–32. Staub's comments refer to Dos Passos's use of a newsreel style in *Facing the Chair* (1927), his exposé of the Sacco and Vanzetti trials, but can be applied to *USA.* See also Solomon, *Literature, Amusement, and Technology,* 182–224, esp. 184 and 192.

46. Kazin, *On Native Grounds,* 355–56.

47. Orvell, *Real Thing,* 268; Cowley, "End of a Trilogy," 5.

48. Pizer, *John Dos Passos's USA,* 42–44.

49. The allusion here is to three prominent Boston citizens appointed by Governor Fuller of Massachusetts to reconsider the evidence against Sacco and Vanzetti: President Lowell of Harvard, President Stratton of MIT, and Judge Robert Grant. They validated the evidence and upheld the death sentence. See Frederick Lewis Allen, *Only Yesterday: An Informal History of the Twenties* (1931; reprint, New York: Harper and Row, 1959), 71.

50. Gorman, *Left Intellectuals and Popular Culture,* 124–26.

51. See Michael Goldstein, *The Political Stage: American Drama and Theater of the Great Depression* (New York: Oxford University Press, 1974), esp. 90–106.

52. William Barrett, "*I Am a Fugitive from the Chain Gang,*" *National Board of Review Magazine* 7.8 (November 1932): 8–9. Good overviews of Hollywood in the 1930s are Neil Roddick, *A New Deal in Entertainment: Hollywood in the 1930s* (London: British Film Institute, 1983); Andrew Bergman, *We're in the Money* (New York: Harper, 1972); and Saverio Giovacchini, *Hollywood Modernism: Film and Politics in the Age of the New Deal* (Philadelphia: Temple University Press, 2001).

53. Dugan and Stebbins quoted in Myron Lounsbury, *The Origins of American Film Criticism, 1909–1939* (New York: Arno Press, 1973), 453, 455.

54. Quoted in ibid., 434.

55. Dwight Macdonald, "Soviet Cinema, 1930–1940, a History," and "The Eisenstein Tragedy," in *Dwight Macdonald on Movies* (Englewood Cliffs, N.J.: Prentice Hall, 1969), 192–255.

56. Denning, *Cultural Front,* 163–99.

57. Foley, *Radical Representations,* 193–202 (other examples she examines are Mary Heaton Vorse's *Strike,* Albert Halper's *Union Square,* and Josephine Johnson's *Jordanstown*); Denning, *Cultural Front,* 197.

58. Quoted in Staub, *Voices of Persuasion,* 29.

59. Ludington, *John Dos Passos,* 217.

60. Kenneth Burke, "Revolutionary Symbolism in America," in *American Writers' Congress,* ed. Henry Hart (New York: International Publishers, 1935), 87–94.

Chapter 4: The Art of Noise

1. Vachel Lindsay, *The Progress and Poetry of the Movies,* ed. Myron Lounsbury (Lanham, Md.: Scarecrow Press, 1995), 182.

2. On the influence of sound technologies in experimental culture, see Allen S. Weiss, *Phantasmatic Radio* (Durham, N.C.: Duke University Press, 1995); Douglas Kahn and Gregory Whitehead, eds., *Wireless Imagination: Sound, Radio, and the Avant-Garde* (Cambridge: Massachusetts Institute of Technology Press, 1992); Douglas Kahn, *Noise, Water, Meat* (Cambridge: Massachusetts Institute of Technology Press, 1999); and Brian Reed, "Hart Crane's Victrola," *Modernism/Modernity* 7.1 (1999): 99–125.

3. Evan Eisenberg, *The Recording Angel: Explorations in Phonography* (New York: McGraw-Hill, 1986), 11–13; Jacques Attali, *Noise: Toward a Political Economy of Music,* trans. Brian Massumi (Minneapolis: University of Minnesota Press, 1985).

4. Béla Balázs, *Theory of the Film* (1952), trans. Edith Bone (New York: Arno, 1972), 65. Balázs's "microphysiognomy" was eminently visual; it would lead to minute knowledge of facial gesture and to receptivity toward the face of the

other (72–75). Balázs had similar hopes for sound on film: it should "reveal to us our acoustic environment . . . the speech of things and the intimate whisperings of nature" (197). For him, such revelations were always on the side of meaning.

5. Andy Warhol, "What is Pop Art?" interview by G. R. Swenson, *Artnews* 62 (1963): 24–60. Warhol's actual words are: "The reason I'm painting this way is because I want to be a machine. Whatever I do, and do machine-like, is because it is what I want to do."

6. John Crowe Ransom, "Waste Lands," in *T. S. Eliot: The Critical Heritage,* vol. 1, ed. Michael Grant (London: Routledge and Kegan Paul, 1982), 176 (subsequently cited parenthetically in the text as *CH*).

7. Friedrich A. Kittler, *Discourse Networks 1800/1900* (1985), trans. Michael Mettier with Chris Cullens (Stanford, Calif.: Stanford University Press, 1990), 369.

8. T. S. Eliot, *The Complete Poems and Plays, 1909–1950* (New York: Harcourt Brace Jovanovich, 1971), 44 (subsequently cited parenthetically in the text as *CPP*).

9. It seems to me that the reader is invited to cringe at the invitation ("in demotic *French*," no less!), whose placement reveals that, for Eliot, this kind of homoerotic possibility sounds the depths of contemporary decadence. For another example of Eliot's homophobic anxieties, see Peter Akroyd, *T. S. Eliot: A Life* (London: Hamish Hamilton, 1984), 243–44.

10. T. S. Eliot, "Eeldrop and Appleplex. II," *The Little Review* (September 1917): 16. Part 1 had appeared in the May 1917 issue.

11. T. S. Eliot, "Mary Lloyd," in *Selected Prose of T. S. Eliot,* ed. Frank Kermode (London: Faber, 1975), 174.

12. This inverts somewhat Marshall McLuhan's idea that the content of a new medium is always an older one: the content of radio is the written word; of cinema, the theater; of television, both the cinema and the radio, and so on. Marshall McLuhan, *Understanding Media: The Extensions of Man* (New York: Vintage, 1964).

13. Clement Greenberg, "Avant-Garde and Kitsch," in *Pollock and After,* ed. Francis Frascina (New York: Harper and Row, 1985), 23.

14. According to Dave Laing, this turned music from an audiovisual to an exclusively aural experience. Dave Laing, "A Voice without a Face: Popular Music and the Phonograph in the 1890s," *Popular Music* 10.1 (1991): 7–8.

15. Michael Levenson, *A Genealogy of Modernism: English Literary Doctrine, 1908–1922* (Cambridge: Cambridge University Press, 1984), 172. The debt to Poe is more obvious in earlier pieces such as "Sweeney Erect." Helen Sword has written insightfully on the importance of spirit possession to the poem's composition and how mediumship is postulated on sexual instability and transgression. Helen Sword, *Ghostwriting Modernism* (Ithaca, N.Y.: Cornell University Press, 2002), 93–102. For another insightful take on the ghostly in Eliot's (and Pound's) poetics, this time explained in relation to historicism, see James Lon-

genbach, *The Modernist Poetics of History* (Princeton, N.J.: Princeton University Press, 1987), 3–28.

16. Thomas A. Edison, "The Phonograph and Its Future," in *Democratic Vistas, 1860–1880,* ed. Alan Trachtenberg (New York: Brazillier, 1970), 234–35. See also McLuhan, *Understanding Media,* 241–48; and Roland Gelatt, *The Fabulous Phonograph 1877–1977: From Edison to Stereo* (New York: W. W. Norton, 1977).

17. Edison, "Phonograph and Its Future," 234.

18. James Joyce, *Ulysses,* ed. Hans Walter Gabler with Wolfhard Steppe and Claus Melchior (New York: Vintage, 1986), 93.

19. Friedrich Kittler, *Gramophone, Film, Typewriter,* trans. Geoffrey Winthrop-Young and Michael Wutz (Stanford, Calif.: Stanford University Press, 1999), 12. See also Avital Ronell, "The Walking Switchboard," in *Finitude's Score: Essays for the End of the Millenium* (Lincoln: University of Nebraska Press, 1994), 239–40; and Lisa Gitelman, *Scripts, Grooves, and Writing Machines* (Stanford, Calif.: Stanford University Press, 1999), 189–99.

20. Quoted in T. Lindsay Buick, *The Romance of the Telephone* (Wellington, N.Z.: N.p., 1927), 52.

21. Quoted in Neil Baldwin, *Edison: Inventing the Century* (New York: Hyperion, 1995), 89.

22. Ibid., 92–93.

23. Apparently Eliot was introduced to the tarot pack in 1920, and later that year he and his wife Vivienne attended several séances organized by Lady Rothermere, who would later fund *The Criterion.* By that time, the Eliots were reportedly avid, if solemn, dancers who were quite familiar with the hits of the day, blaring out of gramophones. Akroyd, *T. S. Eliot,* 113.

24. Kittler, *Discourse Networks,* 225. Duchamp's whimsical writings are collected in *Marchand du Sel: Écrits de Marcel Duchamp,* ed. Michel Sanouillet (Paris: Terrain Vague, 1958).

25. Jacques Derrida, "Ulysses Gramophone: Hear Say Yes in Joyce," in *Acts of Literature,* ed. Derek Attridge (New York: Routledge, 1992), 273, 275.

26. D. H. Lawrence, Review of *Manhattan Transfer,* in *Dos Passos: The Critical Heritage,* ed. Barry Maine (New York: Routledge, 1988), 75.

27. Sigmund Freud, "Recommendations for Physicians on the Psychoanalytic Method of Treatment," in *Therapy and Technique,* ed. Philip Rieff, trans. J. Bernays, James Strachey, and Joan Riviere (New York: Collier, 1963), 121–22; Kittler, *Gramophone, Film, Typewriter,* 87–94.

28. McLuhan, *Understanding Media,* 246.

29. On the use of recorded sound, film, and photography in psychiatric practice, see Kittler, *Gramophone, Film, Typewriter,* 85–95, 140–49; Felicia McCarren, "The 'Symptomatic Act' circa 1900: Hysteria, Hypnosis, Electricity, Dance," *Critical Inquiry* 21.4 (Summer 1995): 748–74; Sander L. Gilman, "The Image of the Hysteric," in Sander L. Gilman, Helen King, Ray Porter, George Rousseau,

and Elaine Showalter, *Hysteria beyond Freud* (Berkeley: University of California Press, 1993), 345–52.

30. Kittler, *Discourse Networks,* 285.

31. Lyndall Gordon, *Eliot's Early Years* (New York: Oxford University Press, 1977), 102–5; Akroyd, *T. S. Eliot,* 115–18.

32. Tim Armstrong, *Modernism, Technology, the Body* (Cambridge: Cambridge University Press, 1998), 68–74.

33. Stephen Kern, *The Culture of Time and Space, 1880–1918* (Cambridge, Mass.: Harvard University Press, 1983), 38.

34. Daniel Albright has applied this image to Ezra Pound's *Cantos.* See Daniel Albright, "Early Cantos, I-XLI," in *The Cambridge Companion to Ezra Pound,* ed. Ira B. Nadel (Cambridge: Cambridge University Press, 1999), 60–61.

35. T. S. Eliot, "Tradition and the Individual Talent," in *The Sacred Wood* (London: Faber and Faber, 1972), 53–54, 55.

36. T. S. Eliot, "Dante," in *Selected Essays* (New York: Harcourt Brace, 1950), 200.

37. For Charles Sanders, the poem "invites active collaboration and continuing performance. And if we perform it, the ritual will communicate feelings before we can understand or explicate the words." Charles Sanders, "*The Waste Land:* The Last Minstrel Show?" *Journal of Modern Literature* 8 (1980): 38.

38. In the last decade or so, the traces of the popular in Eliot's writing have been receiving considerable attention again. See, for example, Michael North, "Old Possum and Brer Rabbit: Pound and Eliot's Racial Masquerade," in *The Dialect of Modernism: Race, Language, and Twentieth-Century Literature* (New York: Oxford University Press, 1994), 77–99; Sanders, "*The Waste Land*"; David Chinitz, "T. S. Eliot and the Cultural Divide," *PMLA* 110.2 (March 1995): 236–47; Gregory S. Jay, "Postmodernism in *The Waste Land:* Women, Mass Culture, and Others," in *Rereading the New: A Backward Glance at Modernism,* ed. Kevin Dettmar (Ann Arbor: University of Michigan Press, 1992), 221–46; and Manju Jaidka, *T. S. Eliot's Use of Popular Sources* (Lewiston, N.Y.: Edwin Mellen Press, 1997). While greatly attentive to Eliot's popular textual sources, these works do not point out to what extent the popular (and modern) elements in his work take shape dialogically against the media and technological environment of the time—more specifically against phonography.

39. Lionel Trilling, "Kipling," in *The Liberal Imagination* (New York: Harcourt, Brace, Jovanovich, 1975), 117–18.

40. My thanks to Laurence Erussard for lending me a copy of the recordings and to A. Robert Lee for his comments on Eliot's accent and delivery. On Eliot's accent, see also Christopher Ricks, "An English Accent," in *T. S. Eliot and Prejudice* (Berkeley: University of California Press, 1988), 154–203; and Michael North, "The Dialect in/of Modernism: Pound and Eliot's Racial Masquerade," *American Literary History* 4.1 (1992): 71–72.

41. Clive Bell, "Plus de jazz," *New Republic* 28 (September 21, 1921): 94.

42. Ralph Ellison, "Hidden Name and Complex Fate," in *Shadow and Act,* (New York: Random House, 1964), 159–60.

43. For the text and music of the song, see *T. S. Eliot's* The Waste Land: *Authoritative Text, Contexts, Criticism,* ed. Michael North (New York: Norton, 2001), 51–54.

44. See, for example, Béla Bartók, "Automatic Music" (1937), in *Essays,* ed. Benjamin Suchoff (Lincoln: University of Nebraska Press, 1976).

45. McLuhan, *Understanding Media,* 247.

46. Quoted in Martin W. Laforse and James A. Drake, *Popular Culture and American Life* (Chicago: Nelson and Hall, 1981), 3.

47. Kittler, *Discourse Networks,* 233.

48. On typing, automatic writing, and authorship, see Gitelman, *Scripts, Grooves, and Language Machines,* 211.

Chapter 5: Joseph Cornell and the Secret Life of Things

1. Dawn Ades, "The Transcendental Surrealism of Joseph Cornell," in *Joseph Cornell,* ed. Kynaston McShine (New York: Museum of Modern Art, 1980), 15–39; Dore Ashton, *A Joseph Cornell Album* (New York: Viking, 1974); Carter Ratcliff, "Joseph Cornell: Mechanic of the Ineffable," in *Joseph Cornell,* ed. Kynaston McShine (New York: Museum of Modern Art, 1980), 42–56; Deborah Solomon, *Utopia Parkway: The Life and Work of Joseph Cornell* (New York: Farrar, Straus, Giroux, 1997), esp. 110–12, 184–86.

2. Lynda Roscoe Hartigan, "Joseph Cornell: A Biography," in *Joseph Cornell,* ed. Kynaston McShine (New York: Museum of Modern Art, 1980), 95–113; Mary Ann Caws, Introduction to *Joseph Cornell's Theater of the Mind: Selected Diaries, Letters, and Files,* ed. Mary Ann Caws (New York: Thames and Hudson, 1994), 9–52; Jodi Hauptman, *Joseph Cornell: Stargazing in the Cinema* (New Haven, Conn.: Yale University Press, 1999); Diane Waldman, *Joseph Cornell* (New York: Brazillier, 1977); Diane Waldman, *Joseph Cornell: Master of Dreams* (New York: H. N. Abrams, 2002).

3. Waldman, *Master of Dreams,* 25.

4. Sandra Leonard Starr, *Joseph Cornell and the Ballet* (New York: Castelli, Feigen, Corcoran, 1983); Hauptman, *Joseph Cornell,* 76–83, 103–13.

5. Douglas Mao, *Solid Objects: Modernism and the Test of Production* (Princeton, N.J.: Princeton University Press, 1998), 4, 7–8.

6. Bill Brown, "The Secret Life of Things (Virginia Woolf and the Matter of Modernism)," *Modernism/Modernity* 6.2 (April 1999): 1–28.

7. Quoted in Lindsay Blair, *Joseph Cornell's Vision of Spiritual Order* (London: Reaktion, 1998), 52.

8. Quoted in ibid., 41.

9. Solomon, *Utopia Parkway,* 57.

10. Ades, "Transcendental Surrealism of Joseph Cornell," 25.

11. Dalí catalogues surrealist objects as follows: "functioning symbolically," "transubstantiated," "to be thrown," "wrapped," "diurnal fantasies," "objects-machines," and "objects-moldings (hypnagogic origin)." "Objets surréalistes," *Le Surréalisme au service de la révolution* 3 (December 1931): 77–78. In the same issue Breton published "L'objet fantôme," a fragment later included in *Les Vases communicants*.

12. Walter Benjamin, *The Arcades Project*, trans. Howard Eiland and Kevin McLaughlin (Cambridge, Mass.: Harvard University Press, 1999), 82.

13. This is the case, for example, in Anna Balakian, *Surrealism: The Road to the Absolute* (New York: New York University Press, 1963); Maurice Nadeau, *History of Surrealism* (Cambridge, Mass.: Harvard University Press, 1969); Marcel Jean, ed., *The Autobiography of Surrealism* (New York: Viking, 1980). Hal Foster also notes that despite its anti-artistic practice and its materialist/ethnographic vocation, surrealism is often still "reduced to painting" and "folded into discussions of iconography and style." This tendency elides its critical charge as the "nodal point of three fundamental discourses of modernity: psychoanalysis, Marxism, and ethnology—all of which inform surrealism and it in turn develops them." Hal Foster, *Compulsive Beauty* (Cambridge: Massachusetts Institute of Technology Press, 1993), xiii.

14. James Clifford, "Ethnographic Surrealism," in *The Predicament of Culture: Twentieth-Century Ethnography, Literature, and Art* (Cambridge, Mass.: Harvard University Press, 1988), 117–51.

15. Laurent Jenny, "From Breton to Dalí: The Adventures of Automatism," *October* 51 (Winter 1989): 105–14.

16. André Breton, *Manifestoes of Surrealism*, trans. Richard Seaver and Helen Lane (Ann Arbor: University of Michigan Press, 1972), 258, 263, 275.

17. Ibid., 16.

18. Foster, *Compulsive Beauty*, 57–98.

19. Joanna Malt, *Obscure Objects of Desire: Surrealism, Fetishism, and Politics* (Oxford: Oxford University Press, 2004), 101–12.

20. Brassaï, "Sculptures Involuntaires," *Minotaure* 3–4 (1933): 68.

21. André Breton, *Nadja,* trans. Richard Howard (New York: Grove Press, 1960), 52, 129.

22. Louis Aragon, *Paris Peasant,* trans. Simon Watson Taylor (Boston: Exact Change, 1994), 17, 39, 40, 45.

23. The texts excerpted here are Salvador Dalí, "Cher Breton (Letter to André Breton)" (1933), "The Object as Revealed in Surrealist Experiment" (1932), and "Psychoatmospheric-Anamorphic Objects" (1934), in *The Collected Writings of Salvador Dalí,* ed. and trans. Haim Finklestein (Cambridge: Cambridge University Press, 1998), 249–53, 234–44, 244–48.

24. Salvador Dalí, "Non-Euclidian Psychology of a Photograph" (1935), in *The*

Collected Writings of Salvador Dalí, ed. and trans. Haim Finklestein (Cambridge: Cambridge University Press, 1998), 302–6.

25. André Breton, "The Crisis of the Object" (1936), in *Surrealism and Painting,* ed. and trans. Simon Watson Taylor (New York: Harper and Row, 1972).

26. Breton, *Nadja,* 19.

27. Breton, *Manifestoes of Surrealism,* 15.

28. See the forum "The Encounter," *Minotaure* 3–4 (1933). The introduction to this survey of surrealist attitudes toward chance states: "Le hasard c'est le rencontre d'une causalité externe et d'une finalité interne" (Chance is the encounter of an external causality with an internal determination). This formulation is repeated in André Breton, *Mad Love = L'amour fou,* trans. Mary Ann Caws (Lincoln: University of Nebraska Press, 1987), 21.

29. "Everything tends to make us believe that there exists a certain point of the mind at which life and death, the real and the imagined, past and future, the communicable and the incommunicable, high and low, cease to be perceived as contradictions." Breton, *Manifestoes of Surrealism,* 123.

30. Malt, *Obscure Objects of Desire,* 118.

31. For an insightful exploration of the role of the real in Dalí's autobiographical writings, see David Vilaseca, "In Dalí More Than Dalí: *Un diari, 1919–20* and the Real of Salvador Dalí's Autobiography," in *Hindsight and the Real: Subjectivity in Gay Hispanic Autobiography* (Bern: Peter Lang, 2003), esp. 66–69.

32. David Macey, *Lacan and his Contexts* (London: Verso, 1988).

33. Elizabeth Roudinescu, *Jacques Lacan,* trans. Barbara Brey (New York: Columbia University Press, 1997), 31–32, 135–36.

34. Jacques Lacan, "Le Problème du style et la conception psychiatrique des formes paranoïaques de l'expérience," *Minotaure* 1 (1933); Jacques Lacan, "Motifs du crime paranoïaque—Le Crime des soeurs Papin," *Minotaure* 3–4 (1933).

35. Salvador Dalí, "Apparitions Aérodynamiques des 'Etre-Objets,'" *Minotaure* 6 (1935): 33–34.

36. Aragon, *Paris Peasant,* 30.

37. In many respects, surrealist-object research has foreshadowed the ideas of a number of contemporary theorists of science. For Bruno Latour, for example, modernity made an arbitrary distinction between subjects and objects, when in reality the world is made up of interactive assemblages of (Michel Serres's terms) "quasi-subjects" and "quasi-objects." Bruno Latour, *We Have Never Been Modern,* trans. Catherine Porter (Cambridge, Mass: Harvard University Press, 1995), 10–11. For Haraway, social relationships include humans and nonhumans as "sociotechnically active partners." Donna Haraway, *Modest_Witness@Second_ Millennium. FemaleMan Meets OncoMouseTM. Feminism and Technoscience* (New York: Routledge, 1997), 8.

38. Alfred H. Barr, ed., *Fantastic Art, Dada, Surrealism* (1936; reprint, New York: Museum of Modern Art, 1968). Goldberg and Disney are included in the

catalog in the section, "Artists Independent of the Dada and Surrealist Movements" (205–24), and the filmography of "Fantastic or Surrealist Films" at the MoMA library at the end of the book lists Walt Disney's *The Skeleton Dance* (1929) next to titles by Buñuel and Dalí, Man Ray, Hans Richter, and Marcel Duchamp (262).

39. Paul Hammond's excellent introduction to the most recent edition of his anthology of surrealist film criticism acknowledges this fact. Paul Hammond, Introduction to *The Shadow and Its Shadow: Surrealist Writings on the Cinema,* ed. Paul Hammond (San Francisco: City Lights Books, 2000), 9–14.

40. Louis Aragon, "On Decor," in *The Shadow and Its Shadow: Surrealist Writings on the Cinema,* ed. Paul Hammond (San Francisco: City Lights Books, 2000), 51–52.

41. Aragon, *Paris Peasant,* 78.

42. Rosalynd Krauss, "The Photographic Condition of Surrealism," in *The Originality of the Avant-Garde and Other Modernist Myths* (Cambridge: Massachusetts Institute of Technology Press, 1986), 115.

43. Hauptman, *Joseph Cornell,* 176, 188.

44. Ibid., 57–83.

45. Quoted in Solomon, *Utopia Parkway,* 250.

46. Lacan, "Problème du style"; Krauss, *Originality of the Avant-Garde and Other Modernist Myths,* 16–17; Breton, *Manifestoes of Surrealism,* 21; Foster, *Compulsive Beauty,* 177; Aragon, *Paris Peasant,* 22; Benjamin, *Arcades Project,* 405–6.

47. Joseph Cornell, *Joseph Cornell's Theater of the Mind: Selected Diaries, Letters, and Files,* ed. Mary Ann Caws (New York: Thames and Hudson, 1994), 193 (the letter to Moore is quoted on p. 112).

48. Parker Tyler, *The Hollywood Hallucination* (1944; reprint, New York: Simon and Schuster, 1970), 15.

49. Siegfried Kracauer, "Photography," in *The Mass Ornament: Weimar Essays,* ed. and trans. Thomas Y. Levin (Cambridge, Mass.: Harvard University Press, 1995), 55, 62.

50. Roland Barthes, *Camara Lucida,* trans. Richard Howard (New York: Hill and Wang, 1981), 4 (subsequent references are given parenthetically in the text).

51. According to Umberto Eco, a film's cult status depends on the existence of numerous such byways and corners. See Umberto Eco, "*Casablanca*: Cult Movies and Intertextual Collage," *Substance* 14.2 (1985): 3–12. For other discussions of cultism, see Paul Willemen and Nöel King, "Through the Glass Darkly: Cinephilia Reconsidered," in Paul Willemen, *Looks and Frictions: Essays in Cultural Studies and Film Theory* (London: British Film Institute, 1994), 223–57; and Roger Cardinal, "Pausing over Peripheral Detail," *Framework* 30–31 (1986): 112–33.

52. The centrality of collecting to Cornell's working method was first mentioned by Thomas Lawson, "Silently, by Means of a Silent Light," *October* 15

(1980): "It was as a collector that Cornell first came to understand art, not as an art collector, but as a collector of . . . incomplete memories" (52). See also Hauptman, *Joseph Cornell*, 22.

53. Jean Baudrillard, *The System of Objects,* trans. James Benedict (New York: Verso, 1996); Susan Stewart, *On Longing: Narratives of the Miniature, the Gigantic, the Souvenir, the Collection* (Baltimore: Johns Hopkins University Press, 1984), 161.

54. Cornell must be aligned here with Breton, who, according to Benjamin, "was the first to perceive the revolutionary energies that appear in the 'outmoded,' in the first iron constructions, the first factory buildings, the earliest photos, the objects that have begun to be extinct, grand pianos, the dresses of five years go, fashionable restaurants when the vogue has begun to ebb from them." Walter Benjamin, "Surrealism: The Last Snapshot of the European Intelligentsia," in *One-Way Street and Other Writings,* trans. Edmund Jephcott and Kingsley Shorter (London: Verso, 1985), 229.

55. Joseph Cornell, "Enchanted Wanderer: Excerpt from a Journey Album for Hedy Lamarr," in *The Shadow and Its Shadow: Surrealist Writings on the Cinema,* ed. Paul Hammond (San Francisco: City Lights Books, 2000), 206–9.

56. Cornell's film exhibition practice was equally archaic. He ran several film screenings at Subjects of the Artist, an informal art workshop established by Robert Motherwell, Mark Rothko, David Hare, and William Baziotes that operated in 1949. According to Deborah Solomon, in these screenings, "Cornell's dream was to re-create the vanished world of the nickelodeon." Solomon, *Utopia Parkway,* 200–201.

57. Quoted in Susan Buck-Morss, *The Dialectics of Seeing: Walter Benjamin and the Arcades Project* (Cambridge: Massachusetts Institute of Technology Press, 1989), 263.

58. Tom Gunning, "The Cinema of Attractions," *Wide Angle* 8 (Fall 1986): 63–70; Tom Gunning, "An Aesthetic of Astonishment: Early Film and the (In)credulous Spectator," *Art&Text* 34 (Spring 1989): 31–45; Noel Burch, "How We Got into Pictures," *Afterimage* 8–9 (Spring 1989): 29.

59. Peter Bürger, *Theory of the Avant-Garde,* trans. Michael Shaw (Minneapolis: University of Minnesota Press, 1984).

60. On some examples of celebrity culture in the nineteenth-century United States, see David S. Reynolds, *Walt Whitman's America: A Cultural Biography* (New York: Knopf, 1995). Cornell's fascination with the stars of the romantic ballet was stimulated by the contemporary vogue of the ballet in New York City. Colonel de Basil's Ballets Russes de Montecarlo had been performing in the city since the early 1930s. The American Ballet, founded by Lincoln Kirstein and Edward M. M. Warburg in 1935, was an instant success and provided a forum for the influential work of George Balanchine, trained in Paris in Sergei Diaghilev's Russian Ballet. Nearly simultaneously, a number of scholars were recovering the

history of the romantic ballet. The periodical *Dance Index,* ancillary to the American Ballet and founded by Kirstein himself, started publication in 1942. It was edited by Kirstein and the writer Donald Windham, and Cornell was one of its steady collaborators. He designed numerous covers and dossiers and guest-edited special issues on Maria Taglioni (summer 1944), Hans Christian Andersen (September 1945), and "Clowns, Elephants, and Ballerinas" (June 1946). Another Kirstein project was the creation of a Dance Archive at the Museum of Modern Art, for which he sought the collaboration of Paul Magriel, who had studied with Michel Fokkine in Paris. According to Sandra Leonard Starr, the two works that revealed to Cornell the charms of the romantic ballet and evoked numerous connections between its New York present and its European past were Cyril W. Beaumont, *Complete Book of Ballets* (New York: Grosset and Dunlap, 1938), which has gone through many editions since, and Sacheverell Sitwell, *The Romantic Ballet in Lithographs of the Time* (London: Faber and Faber, 1938). See Starr, *Joseph Cornell and the Ballet,* 18–20.

61. For another materialist, and far more sexual, reading of Cornell's attitude toward women performers, see Michael Moon, "Oralia: Hunger, Sweets, and Women's Performances," in *A Small Boy and Others: Imitation and Initiation in American Culture from Henry James to Andy Warhol* (Durham, N.C.: Duke University Press, 1998), 132–54.

62. On the rhetoric of the souvenir, see Stewart, *On Longing,* 163–78.

63. On the new industrial design in the United States, see Richard G. Wilson, Diana H. Pilgrim, and Dickran Tashjian, *The Machine Age in America* (New York: Brooklyn Art Museum/Harry N. Abrams Inc., 1986); and Terry E. Smith, *Making the Modern: Industry, Art, and Design in America* (Chicago: University of Chicago Press, 1993). Adolf Loos, "Ornament and Crime," in *Ornament and Crime: Selected Essays* (Riverside, Calif.: Ariadne Press, 1998).

64. Benjamin, *Arcades Project,* 865. For another translation and an extensive analysis of this perception by Benjamin, see Buck-Morss, *Dialectics of Seeing,* 293–95.

65. Benjamin, "Surrealism," 239.

66. Ibid., 229.

67. Quoted in Blair, *Joseph Cornell's Vision of Spiritual Order,* 83.

68. Benjamin, "Surrealism," 230.

Chapter 6: Queer Modernism

1. William Carlos Williams, "For a New Magazine," *Blues* 1.1 (February–July 1929): 30–32.

2. Gertrude Stein, *The Autobiography of Alice B. Toklas* (1933; reprint, New York: Random House, 1961), 241. Stein continues: "Its editor Charles Henri Ford has come to Paris and he is young and fresh and also honest which also is a pleasure.

Gertrude Stein thinks that he and Robert Coates alone among the young men have an individual sense of words."

3. Hugh Ford, *Published in Paris: American and British Writers, Printers, and Publishers in Paris, 1920–1939* (New York: Macmillan, 1975), 345–89, esp. 357–59; Shari Benstock, *Women of the Left Bank: Paris, 1900–1940* (Austin: University of Texas Press, 1987), 429–30.

4. Some of these titles include Robert Scully, *A Scarlet Pansy* (New York: Royal, n.d.); Blair Niles, *Strange Brother* (New York: Horace Liveright, 1933); André Tellier, *Twilight Men* (New York: Greenberg, 1931); Richard Meeks, *Better Angel* (New York: Greenberg, 1933); Kennilworth Bruce, *Goldie* (New York: William Godwin, 1933); and Lew Lewenson, *Butterfly Man* (New York: Castle, 1934). These books escaped censorship probably because their treatment of homosexuality lacks the confrontational directness of *The Young and Evil*. See Roger Austen, *Playing the Game: The Homosexual Novel in America* (1977; reprint, New York: Garland, 1991), 59–60.

5. Joseph Boone, *Libidinal Currents: Sexuality and the Shaping of Modernism* (Chicago: University of Chicago Press, 1998), 205, 254, 211 (further references appear parenthetically in the text); Steven Watson, Introduction to Charles Henri Ford and Parker Tyler, *The Young and Evil* (London: GMP Publishers, 1989), n.p.

6. Dickran Tashjian, *A Boatload of Madmen: Surrealism and the American Avant-Garde, 1920–1950* (New York: Thames and Hudson, 1995), esp. 137–201; Austen, *Playing the Game*, 60–62; James Levin, *The Gay Novel: The Male Homosexual Image in America* (New York: Irvington, 1983), 30–32; Catrina Neiman, "*View* Magazine: A Transatlantic Pact," in View: *Parade of the Avant-Garde*, ed. Charles Henri Ford (New York: Thunder's Mouth Press, 1991), xi–xvi; George Chauncey, *Gay New York: Gender, Urban Culture, and the Making of the Gay Male World* (New York: HarperCollins, 1994), 168–69, 191n., 242–43.

7. Benstock, *Women of the Left Bank*; Steven Watson, *Strange Bedfellows: The First American Avant-Garde* (New York: Abbeville Press, 1991); Karla Jay, *The Amazon and the Page: Natalie Clifford Barney and Renée Vivien* (Bloomington: Indiana University Press, 1988).

8. Robert McAlmon compiled three of his short stories with a homosexual theme in *Distinguished Air* (Paris: Contact Editions, 1925). They attest at once to McAlmon's fascination with the queer scene and to his rabid homophobia. See Austen, *Playing the Game*, 42–46. They are now most easily available in Robert McAlmon, *Mrs. Knight and Others*, ed. S. N. Lorusso (Albuquerque: University of New Mexico Press, 1992).

9. Mabel Dodge Luhan, *Movers and Shakers* (1936; reprint, Albuquerque: University of New Mexico Press, 1985).

10. Bruce Kellner, *Carl Van Vechten and the Irreverent Decades* (Norman: University of Oklahoma Press, 1968); Watson, *Strange Bedfellows*, 134–38, 253–59.

11. On Demuth and Hartley, see Jonathan Weinberg, *Speaking for Vice: Homosexuality in the Art of Charles Demuth, Marsden Hartley, and the First American Avant-Garde* (New Haven, Conn.: Yale University Press, 1993).

12. Philip Herring, *Djuna: The Life and Work of Djuna Barnes* (New York: Viking, 1995), 106–7, 134–35; Lilian Faderman, *Odd Girls and Twilight Lovers: A History of Lesbian Life in Twentieth-Century America* (New York: Penguin, 1992), 85–87.

13. Eric Garber, "A Spectacle in Color: The Lesbian and Gay Subculture of Jazz Age Harlem," in *Hidden from History: Reclaiming the Gay and Lesbian Past,* ed. Martin Duberman, Martha Vicinus, and George Chauncey (New York: New American Library, 1989), 319–31; F. Amitai Avi-Ram, "The Unbearable Black Body: 'Conventional' Poetic Form in the Harlem Renaissance," *Genders* 7 (1990): 32–45; Alden Reimonenq, "Countee Cullen's Uranian 'Soul Windows,'" *Journal of Homosexuality* 26 (1993): 143–65; Henry Louis Gates Jr., "The Black Man's Burden," in *Fear of a Queer Planet: Queer Politics and Social Theory,* ed. Michael Warner (Minneapolis: University of Minnesota Press, 1993); Chauncey, *Gay New York*, 227–67.

14. Malcolm Cowley, *Exile's Return* (1936; reprint, Harmondsworth, Middlesex: Penguin, 1976), 62.

15. Peter Wollen, *Raiding the Icebox: Reflections on Twentieth-Century Culture* (Bloomington: Indiana University Press, 1992), 84; Erika Doss, *Benton, Pollock, and the Politics of Modernism* (Chicago: University of Chicago Press, 1991), 91–98.

16. Chauncey, *Gay New York*, 241.

17. Quoted in Watson, Introduction.

18. See Boone, *Libidinal Currents;* Weinberg, *Speaking for Vice;* Eve Kosofsky Sedgwick, *Epistemology of the Closet* (Berkeley: University of California Press, 1990); Collen Lamos, *Deviant Modernism: Sexual and Textual Errancy in T. S. Eliot, James Joyce, and Marcel Proust* (Cambridge: Cambridge University Press, 1998); and Eric Haralson, *Henry James and Queer Modernity* (Cambridge: Cambridge University Press, 2001). Extending one of Sedgwick's insights, Lamos shows that modernism was "shaped by the turmoil in male gender and sexual identity and by disputes over masculine authority" (9). Boone's wide-ranging study also covers texts affected by the turmoil over feminine gender and sexuality. Haralson extends queerness to the "internal heterogeneity" present in a number of facets of contemporary life, including sexuality.

19. As Platt-Lynes was progressively displaced as a fashion photographer in the postwar years by rising, younger photographers, and his commissions dwindled, he was forced to sell most of his private photographs. Many were bought by Alfred Kinsey, who was ostensibly interested in them as records of homosexual iconography and sexual practice. Some have been published in James Crump, *George Platt-Lynes: Photographs from the Kinsey Institute* (New York: Bullfinch

Press, 1993); and David Leddick, *Nude Men: Pioneers of the Male Nude, 1935–1955* (New York: Universe, 1997). The former is a surprisingly tame collection, more invested in showcasing aesthetic and formal values than in documenting an underground queer culture. Despite its title, Leddick's book is mostly a compilation of nudes by Platt-Lynes with some shots by the PAJAMA collective (Paul Cadmus, Jared French, and Margaret French) and by such photographers as Holland Day, Horst P. Horst, and Raymond Voinquel. Both volumes contain wonderfully informative essays by their editors. On the aesthetics of pre-Stonewall homoerotic photography, the indispensable reference is Tom Waugh, *Hard to Imagine: Gay Male Eroticism in Photography and Film from Their Beginnings to Stonewall* (New York: Columbia University Press, 1996), esp. chap. 2.

20. Anatole Pohorilenko, *When We Were Three: The Travel Albums of George Platt Lynes, Monroe Wheeler, and Glenway Westcott* (Santa Fe, N.M.: Arena Editions, 1998), 72.

21. Gregory Woods, "High Culture and High Camp: The Case of Marcel Proust," in *Camp Grounds: Style and Homosexuality,* ed. David Bergman (Amherst: University of Massachusetts Press, 1993), 125.

22. According to Barbara Haskell, Demuth took McAlmon's story as "a springboard for a totally personal creation," since the humor of the scene is completely alien to McAlmon's tortured version of the queer scene. Barbara Haskell, *Charles Demuth* (New York: Harry N. Abrams, 1988), 204. Haskell's volume contains reproductions of the paintings described here and of other works with queer subjects (see esp. plates 20–26 and 104–8). For a reading of "Distinguished Air" as a satire on the audiences of modern art, see Weinberg, *Speaking for Vice,* 195–200.

23. José Pierre, ed. *Investigating Sex: Surrealist Research, 1928–1932,* trans. Malcolm Imrie (London: Verso, 1992).

24. Sedgwick, *Epistemology of the Closet,* 163, 165. See also Lamos, *Deviant Modernism,* 225.

25. On the sublimation of queerness into supposedly universal paradigms of the human, see Jonathan Dollimore, *Sexual Dissidence: Augustine to Wilde, Freud to Foucault* (New York: Oxford University Press, 1991), 31; and Woods, "High Culture and High Camp."

26. Glenway Westcott, *Continual Lessons: The Journals of Glenway Westcott, 1937–1955,* ed. Robert Phelps with Jerry Rosco (New York: Farrar, Straus and Giroux, 1990) (the description of Platt-Lynes's penis is on 23–24).

27. See Michel Foucault, *The History of Sexuality,* vol. 1, trans. Robert Hurley (New York: Random House, 1978); Jonathan Ned Katz, *The Invention of Heterosexuality* (New York: Dutton, 1995); Anthony E. Rotundo, *American Manhood: Transformations in Masculinity from the Revolution to the Modern Era* (New York: Basic Books, 1993); and Michael Trask, *Cruising Modernism: Class and Sexuality in American Culture and Social Thought* (Ithaca, N.Y.: Cornell University Press, 2003).

28. Quoted in Tashjian, *Boatload of Madmen,* 138.

29. John Houseman, *Run-Through: A Memoir* (New York: Simon and Schuster, 1972), 239.

30. Quoted in Tashjian, *Boatload of Madmen,* 170–71. In the early 1970s, Ford told the *Gay Sunshine* interviewer Ira Cohen that the suicide of the surrealist poet René Crevel, the one gay member of the Breton group, in 1935 probably had to do with his inability to combine his homosexuality with his allegiance to surrealism and communism. A friend of Platt-Lynes, who made several portraits of him, Crevel had been Pavel Tchelitchew's partner before Ford. *The Gay Sunshine Interviews,* ed. Winston Leyland (San Francisco: Gay Sunshine Press, 1978), 35–65. John Bernard Myers, a *View* insider between 1944 and the demise of the journal in 1947, writes in his memoirs that Breton had "extremely rigorous sexual ideas, among them a strong anti-homosexual bias," and because of this he was suspicious of Charles Henri Ford and disapproved of Nicolas Calas's "continuing bachelorhood." John Bernard Myers, *Tracking the Marvelous* (New York: Random House, 1983), 35, 42.

31. Like Pavel Tchelitchew, Ford's partner and an assiduous illustrator for *View,* Cocteau made numerous designs for ballet productions. Cocteau's multimedia collaboration with Francois Poulenc in the cabaret *Le Boeuf sur le toit* is analyzed by Bernard Gendron, "Jamming at *Le Boeuf:* Jazz and the Paris Avant-Garde," in *Between Montmartre and the Mudd Club: Popular Music and the Avant-Garde* (Chicago: University of Chicago Press, 2002), 83–101. In a similar fashion, Ford and Tyler frequently organized lectures, concerts, and balls as part of their activities at *View.* They organized a costume ball with décor by Tchelitchew in Alice DeLamar's country estate in 1945 to celebrate the fifth anniversary of the publication. To advertise the "Existentialism" issue, *View* organized a lecture by Jean-Paul Sartre at Carnegie Hall. And they frequently organized fundraising jazz concerts organized by Barry Ulianov, the journal's jazz critic. Myers, *Tracking the Marvelous,* 29–30, 48–49, 60–67.

32. Ford's initial contacts with the French surrealists took place around the time when Breton, Leon Trotsky, and Diego Rivera issued their "Manifesto for an Independent Revolutionary Art," first published in English by *Partisan Review* in 1938. FIARI was the cultural organization that was to lobby for putting the ideas of the manifesto in practice; it meant to counter the influence of the Popular Front and of the Soviet Union's cultural policies. The American branch of FIARI was the short-lived, erratic League for Cultural Freedom and Socialism, headed by Dwight Macdonald, in which Tyler initially took part. The league never really got off the ground. Tashjian, *Boatload of Madmen,* 167–68; Christopher Lasch, "The Cultural Cold War: A Short History of the League for Cultural Freedom," in *Toward a New Past: Dissenting Essays in American History* (New York: Vintage, 1969), 322–60; Alan Wald, *The New York Intellectuals: The Rise and*

Decline of the Anti-Stalinist Left from the 1930s to the 1980s (Chapel Hill: University of North Carolina Press, 1987), 146, 199.

33. Dollimore, *Sexual Dissidence,* 39–73.

34. Charles Henri Ford and Parker Tyler, *The Young and Evil* (London: GMP Publishers, 1989), 16 (further references will be given parenthetically in the text).

35. On the pose and queer identity, see Moe Meyer, "Under the Sign of Wilde: An archaeology of posing," in *The Politics and Poetics of Camp,* ed. Moe Meyer (New York: Routledge, 1994), 75–109.

36. On camp as a communal language, see Chauncey, *Gay New York,* 280–99.

37. This last sentence was apparently Djuna Barnes's, according to Ford's unpublished autobiography, "I Will Be What I Am." Herring, *Djuna,* 180. "[L]oose as a cut jockstrap" was also Barnes's description of freewheeling Ford upon his arrival in Paris (ibid., 174).

38. Dollimore, *Sexual Dissidence,* 54.

39. On the mobility of desire and the open-ended character of sexual identification at the time, see Chauncey, *Gay New York,* 65–66, 96; Watson, Introduction; and Herring, *Djuna,* 106–7, 174–75.

40. Parker Tyler, *The Hollywood Hallucination* (1944; reprint, New York: Simon and Schuster, 1970), 63, 71.

41. Leo Bersani, "Is the Rectum a Grave?" in *AIDS: Cultural Analysis/Cultural Activism,* ed. Douglas Crimp (Cambridge: Massachusetts Institute of Technology Press, 1989), 197–222; Leo Bersani, "The Gay Outlaw," in *Homos* (Cambridge, Mass.: Harvard University Press, 1995), 113–81.

42. Clement Greenberg, "Avant-Garde and Kitsch," in *Pollock and After: The Critical Debate,* ed. Francis Frascina (New York: Harper and Row, 1985), 23.

Chapter 7: Walking with Zombies

1. Lee D. Baker, *From Savage to Negro: Anthropology and the Construction of Race* (Berkeley: University of California Press, 1988), 120–26. For a slightly more critical view of Boas, see Michael E. Staub, *Voices of Persuasion: Politics of Representation in 1930s America* (New York: Cambridge University Press, 1994), 82–85.

2. Ross Posnick, *Color and Culture: Black Writers and the Making of the Modern Intellectual* (Cambridge, Mass.: Harvard University Press, 1998), 208–10.

3. Baker, *From Savage to Negro,* 145–47.

4. The best sources on Hurston's life are Robert E. Hemenway, *Zora Neale Hurston: A Literary Biography* (Urbana: University of Illinois Press, 1977); and Valerie Boyd, *Wrapped in Rainbows: The Life of Zora Neale Hurston* (New York: Scribner's, 2003).

5. Houston Baker Jr., *Modernism and the Harlem Renaissance* (Chicago: University of Chicago Press, 1987), 73. On the Harlem Renaissance at large, the clas-

sic study is Nathan Huggins, *Harlem Renaissance* (New York: Oxford University Press, 1971). See also James de Jongh, *Vicious Modernism: Black Harlem and the Literary Imagination* (New York: Cambridge University Press, 1990); Steven Watson, *The Harlem Renaissance: Hub of African-American Culture* (New York: Pantheon, 1995); and Cheryl A. Wall, *Women of the Harlem Renaissance* (Bloomington: Indiana University Press, 1995). A good documentary collection is David Levering Lewis, ed., *The Portable Harlem Renaissance Reader* (New York: Viking, 1994). For an insider's account, see Langston Hughes, *The Big Sea* (1940; reprint, London: Pluto Press, 1986), 223–335.

6. Alain Locke, "The New Negro" and "The New Negro Speaks," in *The New Negro,* ed. Alain Locke (1925; reprint, New York: Atheneum, 1970), 15, 47.

7. For a thoughtful study on the role of folklore in African American modernism that avoids the pitfalls of vernacular criticism, with its tendency to romanticize and to postulate folk culture as an ahistorical bedrock of authenticity, see David Nicholls, *Conjuring the Folk: Forms of Modernity in African America* (Ann Arbor: University of Michigan Press, 2000).

8. Arthur Huff Fauset, "American Negro Folk Literature," in *The New Negro,* ed. Alain Locke (1925; reprint, New York: Atheneum, 1970), 238–44.

9. Locke, "The Negro Youth Speaks," in *The New Negro,* ed. Alain Locke (1925; reprint, New York: Atheneum, 1970), 51.

10. Hazel V. Carby, "The Politics of Fiction, Anthropology, and the Folk: Zora Neale Hurston," in *New Essays on* Their Eyes Were Watching God, ed. Michael Awkward (Cambridge: Cambridge University Press, 1990), 71–93 (further references are given parenthetically in the text).

11. For some of Hurston's defenses of "genuine Negro material," see *Dust Tracks on a Road* and "Characteristics of Negro Expression," both in *Folklore, Memoirs, and Other Writing,* ed. Cheryl A. Wall (New York: Library of America, 1995), 701–2, 869–74. All ethnographic writings by Hurston cited in this chapter, including *Tell My Horse,* are contained in this volume; further references are given parenthetically in the text. For critics who class Hurston as a purist, see, in addition to Carby, Jerrold Hirsch, "Modernity, Nostalgia, and Southern Folklore Studies: The Case of John Lomax," *Journal of American Folklore* 105 (Spring 1992): 183–207; and Shelley Eversley, "Racial Hieroglyphics: Zora Neale Hurston and the Rise of the New Negro," in *The Real Negro: The Question of Authenticity in Twentieth-Century African-American Literature* (London: Routledge, 2004), 21–39.

12. Lizabeth Cohen, "Encountering Mass Culture at the Grassroots: The Experience of Chicago Workers in the 1920s," *American Quarterly* 41.1 (March 1989): 6–33. On the "race music" market, see Ed Ward, Geoffrey Stokes, and Ken Tucker, *Rock of Ages: The Rolling Stone History of Rock and Roll* (Englewood Cliffs, N.J.: Rolling Stone Press/Prentice-Hall, 1986), 17–32. On folk music in 1930s New York, see Joe Klein, *Woodie Guthrie: A Life* (New York: Ballantine, 1980).

13. Hurston, *Their Eyes Were Watching God,* in *Novels and Stories,* ed. Cheryl A. Wall (New York: Library of America, 1995), 332.

14. Ibid.

15. For more information about these episodes, see Hemenway, *Zora Neale Hurston,* 178–83; Boyd, *Wrapped in Rainbows,* 260–97; and Hurston, *Dust Tracks on a Road,* 713–14, for her own accounts of the gospel concerts she produced in the decade. On Hurston's collaboration with the Negro Theater Project, John Houseman described her as "our most talented writer on the project" who "had come up with a Negro *Lysistrata* updated and located in a Florida fishing com munity. It scandalized Left and Right by its saltiness, which was considered injurious to the serious Negro image they both, in their different ways, desired to create. So I [as director of the project] had to give that one up." John Houseman, *Run-Through: A Memoir* (New York: Simon and Schuster, 1972), 205.

16. Harold Courlander, "Witchcraft in the Caribbean Island," *Saturday Review of Literature* 18 (October 15, 1938): 6; C. G. Woodson, untitled review, *Journal of Negro History* 24.1 (January 1939): 116–18; Carl Carmer, "Haiti and Jamaica," *New York Herald Books* (October 23, 1938): 2; all in *Critical Essays on Zora Neale Hurston,* ed. Gloria I. Cronin (New York: G. K. Hall and Co., 1998), 139–46.

17. Hemenway, *Zora Neale Hurston,* 248–49.

18. Carby, "Politics of Fiction, Anthropology, and the Folk," 87; Karen Jacobs, "From 'Spyglass' to 'Horizon': Tracking the Anthropological Gaze in Zora Neale Hurston," in *The Eye's Mind: Literary Modernism and Visual Culture* (Ithaca, N.Y.: Cornell University Press, 2001), 111–44; Lydia Marion Hill, *Social Rituals and the Verbal Art of Zora Neale Hurston* (Washington, D.C.: Howard University Press, 1996), 131–55.

19. Gwendolyn Mikell, "Feminism and Black Culture in the Ethnography of Zora Neale Hurston," in *African American Pioneers in Anthropology,* ed. Ira E. Harrison and Faye V. Harrison (Urbana: University of Illinois Press, 1999), 51–69.

20. Wendy Dutton, "The Problem of Invisibility: Voodoo and Zora Neale Hurston," *Frontiers* 13.2 (1992): 131–52 (quotes on pp. 133 and 136). A more positive but sketchy estimate is Ishmael Reed, Introduction to *Tell My Horse,* by Zora Neale Hurston (New York: Harper and Row, 1990), xi–xv.

21. Jervis Anderson, *This Was Harlem* (New York: Farrar, Straus and Giroux, 1981), 299–304.

22. Willie A. Domingo, "Gift of the Black Tropics," in *The New Negro,* ed. Alain Locke (1925; reprint, New York: Atheneum, 1970), 341–49.

23. Lawrence Levine, "Marcus Garvey and the Politics of Revitalization," in *The Unpredictable Past: Explorations in American Cultural History* (New York: Oxford University Press, 1993), 107–35; Michelle A. Stephens, "Black Transnationalism and the Politics of National Identity: West Indian Intellectuals in Harlem in the Age of War and Revolution," *American Quarterly* 50.3 (September 1998): 592–608.

24. C. L. R. James, "From Touissant L'Overture to Fidel Castro," in *The C. L. R. James Reader,* ed. Anna Grimshaw (Oxford: Blackwell, 1990), 296–314.

25. The piece where Carpentier defines magical realism, "De lo real americano," appeared in the first edition of the novel but was omitted from later editions. For an English translation, see Alejo Carpentier, "On the Magical Real in Latin America," in *Magical Realism: Theory, History, Community,* ed. Louis Parkinson Zamora and Wendy B. Faris (Durham, N.C.: Duke University Press, 1995).

26. Fredric Jameson, "On Magic Realism in Film," *Critical Inquiry* 12 (Winter 1986): 301–25; Kurkum Sangari, "The Politics of the Possible," *Cultural Critique* 7 (Fall 1987): 157–86; Néstor García-Canclini, *Culturas Híbridas: Estrategias para entrar y salir de la modernidad* (1990; reprint, Barcelona: Paidós, 2001); Celeste Olalquiaga, *Megalopolis* (Minneapolis: University of Minnesota Press, 1991).

27. Karen McCarthy Brown, *Mama Lola: A Vodou Priestess in Brooklyn* (Berkeley: University of California Press, 1990), 228–29 (further references will be given parenthetically in the text).

28. Quoted in Hemenway, *Zora Neale Hurston,* 247. See also Boyd, *Wrapped in Rainbows,* 298–99.

29. Frantz Fanon, *The Wretched of the Earth* (1961), trans. C. Farrington (New York: Grove Press, 1968), 55 (further references will be given parenthetically in the text).

30. Houston A. Baker Jr., "Workings of the Spirit: Conjure and the Space of Black Women's Creativity," in *Zora Neale Hurston: Critical Perspectives Past and Present,* ed., Henry Louis Gates Jr. and Kwame Anthony Appiah (New York: Amistad Press, 1990), 280–307.

31. For the methodology of classical ethnography, see James Clifford, *The Predicament of Culture: Twentieth-Century Ethnography, Literature, and Art* (Cambridge, Mass.: Harvard University Press, 1988), 21–53.

32. Ibid., 29.

33. Michael Taussig, *Shamanism, Colonialism, and the Wild Man: A Study in Terror and Healing* (Chicago: University of Chicago Press, 1987), 10, 369.

34. George Marcus, "Past, Present, and Emergent Identities: Requirements for Ethnographies of Late Twentieth-Century Modernity World-Wide," in *Modernity and Identity,* ed. Scott Lash and Jonathan Friedman (Oxford: Blackwell, 1992), 309–30, esp. 313–14. Marcus provides a list of modernist anthropology exemplars, including Taussig, *Shamanism, Colonialism, and the Wild Man;* Michael Herzfeld, *Anthropology through the Looking Glass: Critical Ethnography in the Margins of Europe* (New York: Cambridge University Press, 1987); Bruno Latour, *Pasteurization of France* (Cambridge, Mass: Harvard University Press, 1989); Paul Rabinow, *French Modern: Norms and Forms of the Social Environment* (Cambridge: Massachusetts Institute of Technology Press, 1989); and Michael Fisher and Mehdi Abedi, *Debating Muslims: Cultural Dialogue in Postmodernity and Tradition* (Madison: University of Wisconsin Press, 1990).

35. For other readings that see Hurston as a precursor of what has been called the postmodern turn in anthropology, see Staub, *Voices of Persuasion,* 79–109; Jacobs, "From 'Spyglass' to 'Horizon'"; and Mikell, "Feminism and Black Culture." Staub and Jacobs limit their comments to *Mules and Men.*

36. Posnick, *Color and Culture,* 209–11.

37. Clifford, *Predicament of Culture,* 117–51. Lynda Hill notes this connection but gives it short shrift; for her, Hurston's use of "shock techniques," her "resistance to the dominant school of empiricism," and "the creative license she takes" bring her close to the French surrealist ethnographers. Hill, *Social Rituals,* 36–37. While I largely agree with Hill's argument, I do not think Hurston "resisted" empiricism but took it to its last consequences, and I see Hurston's surrealism in her fascination with the opacity of cultural practice and daily life.

38. Clifford, *Predicament of Culture,* 146, 148.

39. Maya Deren, *Divine Horsemen: The Living Gods of Haiti* (1953; reprint, Kingston, N.Y.: McPherson and Co., 1983).

40. Financed by the anthropologist Janet Belo, Hurston made a second set of films in April and May 1940 around Beaufort, South Carolina, but I have not been able to see them.

41. See René Crevel, "Negress in a Brothel," and Surrealist Group in Paris (A. Breton, R. Caillois, R. Char, R. Crevel, P. Eluard, J.-M. Monnerot, B. Péret, Y. Tanguy, A. Thirion, P. Unik, P. Yoyotte), "Murderous Humanitarianism," in *Negro: Anthology Made by Nancy Cunard, 1931–33* ed. Nancy Cunard (New York: Negro Universities Press, 1969), 352–56; Jane Marcus, "Bonding and Bondage: Nancy Cunard and the Making of the *Negro* Anthology," in *Borders, Boundaries, and Frames: Essays in Cultural Criticism and Cultural Studies,* ed. May Henderson (New York: Routledge, 1995), 33–63.

42. Shari Benstock, *Women of the Left Bank, 1900–1940* (Austin: University of Texas Press, 1987), 392.

43. Posnick, *Color and Culture,* 212.

Chapter 8: Inner-City Surrealism

1. *In the Street* is available in VHS format from Cecile Starr, 35 Strong St., Burlington, VT 05401, USA (e-mail: Suzanne.Boyajian@verizon.net).

2. For biographical information on Helen Levitt, see Maria Morris Hambourg, "Helen Levitt: A Life in Parts," in *Helen Levitt,* ed. Sandra S. Phillips (San Francisco: San Francisco Museum of Modern Art, 1991), 45–63. On James Agee, see James Bergreen, *James Agee: A Life* (New York: Dutton, 1984). For the production of the film, an excellent commentary, and a thorough review of Levitt's film career, see Jan-Christopher Horak, "Seeing with One's Own Eyes: Helen Levitt's Films," *Yale Journal of Criticism* 8.2 (1995): 69–85.

3. Horak, "Seeing with One's Own Eyes," 75.

4. Hambourg, "Helen Levitt," 49; James Agee, *Agee on Film: Reviews and*

Comments (Boston: Beacon Press, 1958), 262–64 (subsequently cited parenthetically in the text as *AF*).

5. Siegfried Kracauer, *Theory of Film: The Redemption of Physical Reality* (New York: Oxford University Press, 1960), 202–3.

6. Jonas Mekas, *Movie Journal* (New York: Macmillan, 1972), 49.

7. Ken Kelman, "The Quintessential Documentary," in *The Essential Cinema,* ed. P. Adams Sitney (New York: New York University Press and Anthology Film Archives, 1975), 216–18.

8. Horak, "Seeing with One's Own Eyes," 74–77.

9. Manny Farber, "In the Street, 1952," in *Negative Space* (New York: Praeger, 1971), 45–46; Hambourg, "Helen Levitt," 48–49; Sandra S. Phillips, "Helen Levitt's New York," in *Helen Levitt,* ed. Sandra S. Phillips (San Francisco: San Francisco Museum of Modern Art, 1991), 29–31.

10. William Stott, *Documentary Expression and Thirties America* (1973; reprint, Chicago: University of Chicago Press, 1986), 128. On 1930s documentary aesthetics, see also Carl Fleischhauer and Beverly W. Brannan, eds., *Documenting America* (Berkeley: University of California Press, 1988); and Paula Rabinowitz, *They Must Be Represented* (New York: Verso, 1994), 35–104.

11. An example of this type of aestheticist disavowal is Hambourg's assertion that, much like T. S. Eliot's work, Levitt's art is not political; it attempts "to elucidate the collective and personal conditions that constitute existential truths." Hambourg, "Helen Levitt," 60.

12. Ibid., 47–48. Phillips, "Helen Levitt's New York," contextualizes her photographic work in relation to that of her contemporaries.

13. James Agee and Walker Evans, *Let Us Now Praise Famous Men* (Boston: Houghton Mifflin, 1969), xviii, xix, xxii (further references are given parenthetically in the text as *LUS*).

14. Stott, *Documentary Expression and Thirties America,* 53.

15. George W. Stocking Jr., "The Ethnographic Sensibility of the Twenties and the Duality of the Anthropological Tradition," in *Romantic Motives: Essays on Anthropological Sensibility,* ed. George W. Stocking Jr. (Madison: University of Wisconsin Press, 1989), 208–76.

16. James Agee, "Southeast of the Island: Travel Notes," in *Collected Short Prose of James Agee,* ed. Robert Fitzgerald (London: Calder and Boyards, 1972), 177–201. The essay was commissioned for a special issue of *Fortune* on New York City (July 1939) but eventually rejected. It appeared posthumously in *Esquire* (December 1968). This issue of *Fortune* may have been intended to accompany the celebration of the World's Fair in Flushing Meadows, on the outskirts of New York, and the publication that same year of two important documentary works on the city: Berenice Abbott with Elizabeth McCausland, *Changing New York* (New York: E. P. Dutton and Co., 1939); and *The WPA Guide to New York*

City: The Federal Writers' Project Guide to 1930s New York (New York: Random House, 1939).

17. James Agee, Introduction to *A Way of Seeing,* by Helen Levitt (1966; reprint, Durham, N.C.: Duke University Press, 1989), xiii. See also Agee's observations on graffiti in his essay on Brooklyn: "All over the city on streets and walks and walls the children, and the other true primitives of the race have established ancient, essential, and ephemeral forms of art, have set forth in chalk and crayon the names and images of their pride, love, preying, scorn, desire." Agee, "Southeast of the Island," 189.

18. Walter Benjamin, *Baudelaire: A Lyric Poet in the Era of High Capitalism,* trans. Harry Zohn (London: Verso, 1983), 14–16.

19. Walker Evans, *American Photographs* (New York: Museum of Modern Art, 1938). Evans's interest in this type of material never abated. In the mid-1950s he prepared a photo-essay on "street furniture"—hydrants, signposts, barber poles, lampposts, drinking fountains, and mailboxes—for publication in *Fortune.* And at the end of his life, he made a series of Polaroids that revisit much of the found and ephemeral material photographed in *American Photographs:* peeling posters, graffiti, and rubbish. See Judith Keller, *Walker Evans: The Getty Museum Collection* (Malibu, Calif.: The J. Paul Getty Museum, 1995).

20. Roger Cardinal, "Les Arts Marginaux et l'esthétique surréaliste," in *L'Autre et le Sacre: Surréalisme, Cinéma, Ethnologie,* ed. C. W. Thompson (Paris: L'Harmattan, 1995), 51–71.

21. Julien Levy, *Memoirs of an Art Gallery* (New York: G. P. Putnam's Sons, 1977), 29–30.

22. For some samples, see David Leddick, *Nude Men: Pioneers of the Male Nude, 1933–1955* (New York: Universe Books, 1997).

23. Brassaï, "Du mur des cavernes au mur d'usine," *Minotaure* 3–4 (1933): 8–9.

24. Cartier-Bresson showed his work at the Julien Levy Gallery in 1933 and 1935, this last time in a group show with Walker Evans and the Mexican surrealist Manuel Alvarez-Bravo, whose aesthetic is reminiscent of Cartier-Bresson's. Lévy, *Memoirs of an Art Gallery,* 296, 301. For this period of Cartier-Bresson's work and his film work in the United States, see Peter Galassi, *Henri Cartier-Bresson: The Early Works* (New York: Museum of Modern Art, 1987). According to Hambourg, Levitt first saw Cartier-Bresson's pictures at this show ("Helen Levitt," 48).

25. Helen Levitt, *In the Street: Chalk Drawings and Messages, New York City, 1938–1948* (Durham, N.C.: Duke University Press, 1987).

26. Roger Caillois, "The Myth of the Secret Treasures in Childhood," *VVV* 1 (June 1942): 5–7. The article is illustrated with a second photograph by Levitt. It shows two masked children, one climbing a tree, the other on the ground

leaning against the trunk, both inscrutable and slightly otherworldly. It is reproduced in Levitt, *Way of Seeing*, 9.

27. James Agee, "The American Roadside" and "Cockfighting," in *James Agee: Selected Journalism*, ed. Paul Ashdown (Chattanooga: University of Tennesee Press, 1985), 42–62, 19–29 (quotation is from "The American Roadside," 43).

28. James Agee, "Plans for Work: October 1937," in *Collected Short Prose of James Agee*, ed. Robert Fitzgerald (London: Calder and Boyards, 1972), 131–48.

29. Miles Orvell, *The Real Thing: Imitation and Authenticity in American Culture, 1880–1940* (Chapel Hill: University of North Carolina Press, 1989), 272.

30. Stott, *Documentary Expression and Thirties America*, 261–314; Orvell, *Real Thing*, 272–86; Peter Cosgrove, "Snapshots of the Absolute," *American Literature* 67.2 (1995): 329–57; Paula Rabinowitz, *They Must Be Represented: The Politics of Documentary* (London: Verso, 1994), 46; T. V. Reed, "'Unimagined Existence' and the Fiction of the Real: Postmodern Realism in *Let Us Now Praise Famous Men*," *Representations* 24 (1988): 156–76; Jean-Christopher Agnew, "History and Anthropology: Scenes from a Marriage," *Yale Journal of Criticism* 3.2 (1990): 29–50; Michael E. Staub, *Voices of Persuasion: Politics of Representation in 1930s America* (New York: Cambridge University Press, 1995), 32–53.

31. David Bordwell and Kristin Thompson call these documentaries "rhetorical formal systems." David Bordwell and Kristin Thompson, *Film Art: An Introduction* (New York: McGraw-Hill, 1990), 99–105. For Bill Nichols, they were "didactic," the voiceover working as a self-legitimating, unquestioned master-discourse. See Bill Nichols, "The Voice of Documentary," in *Movies and Methods*, vol. 2, ed. Bill Nichols (Berkeley: University of California Press), 259–73.

32. Eric Barnouw, *Documentary: A History of the Non-Fiction Film* (New York: Oxford University Press, 1993), 120. See also Stott, *Documentary Expression and Thirties America*, 212; and William Alexander, *Film on the Left: American Documentary Film from 1931 to 1942* (Princeton, N.J.: Princeton University Press, 1981).

33. Agee, Introduction, xi.

34. Ibid., xi, x.

35. Ibid., x–xi, xv, xii (these descriptions refer to plates 46, 3, and 74).

36. On surrealism in New York during this time, see, for example, Martica Sawin, *Surrealism in Exile and the Beginning of the New York School* (Cambridge: Massachusetts Institute of Technology Press, 1995); Michael Leja, *Reframing Abstract Expressionism* (New Haven, Conn.: Yale University Press, 1994); Dickran Tashjian, *A Boatload of Madmen: Surrealism and the American Avant-Garde, 1930–1950* (New York: Thames and Hudson, 1995). The literature on *View* is rather scarce. See Catrina Neiman, "*View* Magazine: A Transatlantic Pact," In View: *Parade of the Avant-Garde*, ed. Charles Henri Ford (New York: Thunder's Mouth Press, 1991), xi–xv; and passing comments in Martica Sawin, Dickran Tashjian,

and Peter Wollen, *Raiding the Icebox: Reflections on Twentieth-Century Culture* (Bloomington: Indiana University Press, 1993). For an insider's account, see John Bernard Myers, *Tracking the Marvelous: A Life in the New York Art World* (New York: Random House, 1983), 19–75.

37. Myers, *Tracking the Marvelous,* 23. The location of *View*'s office is quite expressive: 1 East Fifty-Third Street, across Fifth Avenue from the Museum of Modern Art and next to the glamorous Stork Club.

38. In its regard toward commercial design, MoMA was being faithful to Alfred Barr's original plan for the museum to present "the practical, commercial, and popular arts as well as the so-called fine arts." On these shows, see Mary Anne Staniszewski, *The Power of Display: A History of the Installations at the Museum of Modern Art* (Cambridge: Massachusetts Institute of Technology Press, 1998), 152–60.

39. Parker Tyler, "Americana Fantastica," *View* 2.4 (January 1942): 5.

40. Siegfried Reinhardt, "Pathos," *View* 4.4 (December 1944): 153; Siegfried Reinhardt, "Americana Fantastica," *View* 5.3 (October 1945): 6; Joe Massey, "They Cannot Stop Death," *View* 3.4 (December 1943): 123; Joe Massey, "Three Poems," *View* 4.2 (May 1944): 54; Paul Childs, "Brown Sugar," with illustrations by the author, *View* 4.1 (March 1944): 7–8, 26, 30–31; Childs Zapaulski (Paul Childs), "Durosa's Durosagram," *View* 4.2 (May 1944): 54; Leo Poch, "The Watermelons," *View* 4.3 (October 1944): 94; Joan Doleska, "Traffic Will Be Heavy," *View* 4.3 (October 1944): 95–96; Eduard Roditi, "William Harnett: American Nechromantic," *View* 5.4 (November 1945); "Visions of the Comte de Permission," *View* 5.5 (December 1945); "The Alienation of Language: Letters from a Corsican Boy to his English Sweetheart," *View* 5.5 (January 1946).

41. "Tropical Americana," *View* 5.2 (May 1945): 5, 9, 14 (Burkhardt's scrapbook is on pp. 15–19).

42. Eduard Roditi, "California Chronicle," *View* 1.3 (October 1940): 3; Troy Garrison, "City of the Psychopathic Angels," *View* 1.3 (October 1940): 4; Brion Gysin, "That Secret Look," *View* 1.7–8 (October–November 1941): 7. Additional examples are Forrest Anderson, "Boston–San Francisco," *View* 1.4–5 (December 1940–January 1941): 2, an account of a hallucinated transoceanic journey, and Leonora Carrington, "White Rabbits," *View* 1.9–10 (December 1941–January 1942): 12.

43. André Breton, *Nadja,* trans. Richard Howard (1928; reprint, New York: Grove Press, 1960), 32, 34.

44. Louis Aragon, *Paris Peasant,* trans. Simon Watson Taylor (1926; reprint, Boston: Exact Change, 1994), 134.

45. While postwar existentialism is frequently invoked in relation to the French interpretation of some American films as "noir," most critics and historians have neglected the genre's surrealist filiation. Yet, as James Naremore points out in his cultural history of film noir, "[W]hat needs to be emphasized is that French ex-

istentialism was intertwined with a residual surrealism, which was crucial for the reception of any art described as *noir.*" The name "film noir," he continues, derives from the *série noir,* a collection of hard-boiled fiction conceived and edited by Marcel Duhamel, a former surrealist active in the Breton group during the late 1920s and early 1930s. In addition, Hollywood thrillers were "admired and discussed in *L'Age du cinéma,* a surrealist publication of 1951, and in *Positif,* which maintained strong connections to surrealism throughout the 1950s and 1960s. They were also given their first important study in a book that was profoundly surrealist in its ideological aims: Raymond Borde and Etienne Chaumeton's *Panorama du film noir américain* (1955), which has been described as a 'benchmark' for all later work on the topic." James Naremore, *More Than Night: Film Noir and Its Contexts* (Berkeley: University of California Press, 1998), 17–18.

46. Parker Tyler, "Every Man His Own Private Detective," *View* 1.9–10 (December 1941–January 1942): 2, 6.

47. This widely accepted reading was first proposed by Allan Kaprow, "The Legacy of Jackson Pollock" (1958), in *Essays on the Blurring of Art and Life* (Berkeley: University of California Press, 1993), 8–26 (further references appear parenthetically in the text).

48. A thorough exploration of these issues was presented in the three-part exhibition *Micropolíticas,* Espai d'Art Contemporani de Castelló (Spain), January 31 to September 21, 2003. See Juan Vicente Aliaga, María del Corral, and José Miguel G. Cortés, *Micropolíticas: Arte y cotidianedad, 2001–1968* (Castellón: Espai d'Art Contemporani de Castelló, 2003).

Index

Dial, The (magazine), 20
Dietrich, Marlene, 81, 187
documentary film. See cinema and the left
Dodge Luhan, Mabel, 183
Doolittle, Hilda, 38, 90, 100, 180, 183
Dos Passos, John: and the cinema, 95–97, 111–13; and noise, 107–8; 129; and popular culture, 82–83, 111–15; and popular speech, 102–7; and technology, 113–14; theater of, 82–83
Dubois, W. E. B., 209–10, 234
Duchamp, Marcel, 58, 62–63, 129, 248
Durham, Jimmy, 174, 270
Durrell, Lawrence, 181

Edison, Thomas Alba, 23, 85, 127–28, 131, 158
Eisenstein, Sergei, 32, 86, 89, 90, 93, 94, 111, 259
Eliot, T. S.: and conservative modernism, 181, 189; influence on Agee, 242; influence on Dos Passos's USA, 105; and jazz, 136–40; and noise, 121–40
Ellerman, Winifred (Bryher), 90, 183
Ellington, Duke, 257
Ellison, Ralph, 138, 212
Eluard, Gala, 146
Eluard, Paul, 152
Epstein, Jean, 31
Ernst, Max, 146, 149, 155, 160, 248, 261
Evans, Walker, 86, 217, 238, 245–46, 250

Fairbanks, Douglas, 28, 34, 40–41
Fanon, Franz, 224–26
Farrell, Joseph T., 4, 8, 180
Faulkner, William, 81, 180
Federal Theater Project, 86, 95, 216
Federal Writers' Project, 212, 244
Firbank, Ronald, 186

Fitzgerald, Francis Scott, 81–82
Ford, Charles Henri: and Blues, 180, 182, 185–86, 193; and Parker Tyler, 179–81, 195; queer modern, 185, 194; and View, 241, 261–67; and The Young and Evil, 179–81, 195–206
Foucault, Michel, 122, 192
Frank, Waldo, 45, 95, 245
Freeman, Joseph, 89
Freud, Sigmund, 31, 128, 130–31, 243, 256
Frontier Films, 95, 253

Garbo, Greta, 157, 166, 187
Geertz, Clifford, 228
Genet, Jean, 192, 204
Giacommetti, Alberto, 146, 149, 150
Gide, André, 194, 196, 204
Girard, René, 189
Gold, Mike, 82–83, 85, 89
Greenberg, Clement, 4, 25, 70, 125, 196, 206
graffiti, 246–47
Griffith, D. W., 20, 34, 41, 85–86
Grosz, George, 85
Guattari, Félix, 6, 10, 78
Gunning, Tom, 23, 66, 167
Gysin, Brion, 265

H. D. See Doolittle, Hilda
Hall, Stuart, 111, 192
Hansen, Miriam, 3, 12, 21
Hare, David, 248
Harrison, Barbara, 183, 187, 205
Hartley, Marsden, 52, 183, 244
Haywood, "Big" Bill, 85, 102
Heartfield, John. See Herzfelde, Helmut
Hellman, Lillian, 95
Hemingway, Ernest, 81–82, 129
Henri, Robert, 56
Herbst, Josephine, 86